Zechariah

REFORMED EXPOSITORY COMMENTARY

A Series

Series Editors

Richard D. Phillips
Philip Graham Ryken

Testament Editors

Iain M. Duguid, Old Testament
Daniel M. Doriani, New Testament

Zechariah

RICHARD D. PHILLIPS

PUBLISHING
P.O. BOX 817 • PHILLIPSBURG • NEW JERSEY 08865-0817

Page design by Lakeside Design Plus

Printed in the United States of America

Library of Congress Cataloging-in-Publication Data

Phillips, Richard D. (Richard Davis), 1960–
    Zechariah / Richard D. Phillips.
        p. cm. — (Reformed expository commentary)
    Includes bibliographical references and index.
    ISBN-13: 978-1-59638-028-8 (cloth)
    ISBN-10: 1-59638-028-4 (cloth)
    1. Bible. O.T. Zechariah—Commentaries.   I. Title.
    BS1665.53.P45 2007
    224'.98077—dc22

                                                        2006101519

To

Sinclair B. Ferguson, Richard B. Gaffin, Jr., William S. Barker,
William Edgar, and my other teachers in divinity
and pastoral ministry at
Westminster Theological Seminary in Philadelphia
With thanks for their zeal for truth, reverence for God's Word,
and love for Christ

and to

The Lord Jesus Christ, "The Branch . . . who shall build
the temple of the LORD" (Zech. 6:12).

CONTENTS

Part 3: The Oracles of Zechariah

SERIES INTRODUCTION

In every generation there is a fresh need for the faithful exposition of God's Word in the church. At the same time, the church must constantly do the work of theology: reflecting on the teaching of Scripture, confessing its doctrines of the Christian faith, and applying them to contemporary culture. We believe that these two tasks—the expositional and the theological—are interdependent. Our doctrine must derive from the biblical text, and our understanding of any particular passage of Scripture must arise from the doctrine taught in Scripture as a whole.

We further believe that these interdependent tasks of biblical exposition and theological reflection are best undertaken in the church, and most specifically in the pulpits of the church. This is all the more true since the study of Scripture properly results in doxology and praxis—that is, in praise to God and practical application in the lives of believers. In pursuit of these ends, we are pleased to present the Reformed Expository Commentary as a fresh exposition of Scripture for our generation in the church. We hope and pray that pastors, teachers, Bible study leaders, and many others will find this series to be a faithful, inspiring, and useful resource for the study of God's infallible, inerrant Word.

The Reformed Expository Commentary has four fundamental commitments. First, these commentaries aim to be *biblical*, presenting a comprehensive exposition characterized by careful attention to the details of the text. They are not exegetical commentaries—commenting word by word or even verse by verse—but integrated expositions of whole passages of Scripture. Each commentary will thus present a sequential, systematic treatment of an entire book of the Bible, passage by passage. Second, these commentaries are unashamedly *doctrinal.* We are committed to the Westminster Confession of Faith and Catechisms as containing the system of doctrine taught in the Scriptures of the Old and New Testaments. Each volume will teach, promote, and defend the doctrines of the Reformed faith as they are found in the Bible. Third, these commentaries are *redemptive-historical* in their orientation. We believe in the unity of the Bible and its central message of salvation in Christ. We are thus committed to a Christ-centered view of the Old Testament, in which its characters, events, regulations, and institutions are properly understood as pointing us to Christ and his gospel, as well as giving us examples to follow in living by faith. Fourth, these commentaries are *practical,* applying the text of Scripture to contemporary challenges of life—both public and private—with appropriate illustrations.

The contributors to the Reformed Expository Commentary are all pastor-scholars. As pastor, each author will first present his expositions in the pulpit ministry of his church. This means that these commentaries are rooted in the teaching of Scripture to real people in the church. While aiming to be scholarly, these expositions are not academic. Our intent is to be faithful, clear, and helpful to Christians who possess various levels of biblical and theological training—as should be true in any effective pulpit ministry. Inevitably this means that some issues of academic interest will not be covered. Nevertheless, we aim to achieve a responsible level of scholarship, seeking to promote and model this for pastors and other teachers in the church. Significant exegetical and theological difficulties, along with such historical and cultural background as is relevant to the text, will be treated with care.

We strive for a high standard of enduring excellence. This begins with the selection of the authors, all of whom have proven to be outstanding communicators of God's Word. But this pursuit of excellence is also reflected in a disciplined editorial process. Each volume is edited by both a series editor and a testament editor. The testament editors, Iain Duguid for the Old Testament and Daniel Doriani for the New Testament, are accomplished pastors and respected scholars who have taught at the seminary level. Their job is to ensure that each volume is sufficiently conversant with up-to-date scholarship and is faithful and accurate in its exposition of the text. As series editors, we oversee each volume to ensure its overall quality—including excellence of writing, soundness of teaching, and usefulness in application. Working together as an editorial team, along with the publisher, we are devoted to ensuring that these are the best commentaries our gifted authors can provide, so that the church will be served with trustworthy and exemplary expositions of God's Word.

It is our goal and prayer that the Reformed Expository Commentary will serve the church by renewing confidence in the clarity and power of Scripture and by upholding the great doctrinal heritage of the Reformed faith. We hope that pastors who read these commentaries will be encouraged in their own expository preaching ministry, which we believe to be the best and most biblical pattern for teaching God's Word in the church. We hope that lay teachers will find these commentaries among the most useful resources they rely upon for understanding and presenting the text of the Bible. And we hope that the devotional quality of these studies of Scripture will instruct and inspire each Christian who reads them in joyful, obedient discipleship to Jesus Christ.

May the Lord bless all who read the Reformed Expository Commentary. We commit these volumes to the Lord Jesus Christ, praying that the Holy Spirit will use them for the instruction and edification of the church, with thanksgiving to God the Father for his unceasing faithfulness in building his church through the ministry of his Word.

Richard D. Phillips
Philip Graham Ryken
Series Editors

PREFACE

I was first motivated to study and teach Zechariah because of the strong connection between Israel's postexilic setting and the situation of Christian believers in a postmodern world. Both of us look back on a legacy that is both glorious and tragically disappointing. We have ample reasons to see the faithfulness and power of God, along with concerns regarding the worldliness and weakness of God's people. Many of us experience this individually. How do we think about our victories and failures? How do we approach God and face the future with confidence, trusting him while being realistic about ourselves? To the believers of Zechariah's day and ours, God calls out in grace: "Return to me, and I will return to you" (Zech. 1:3).

The people to whom God commissioned Zechariah as a prophet are not often considered heroes of the Bible. This book does not present the mightiness of a man like Moses, or the fidelity of a Joshua, or even the heart of a king like David. Zechariah recounts no famous battles in which God's people cast down their enemies and claimed his Promised Land. Instead, Zechariah presents a people whose record has been disgraced by sin and whose covenant with God lay broken—a reality amply illustrated by the ruins of Jerusalem to which they returned, with its broken-down temple. This is why Zechariah's message is so important to our time. Do people who have failed God—people surrounded not with the scenes of spiritual advance but rather besieged by spiritual collapse—have a book in the Bible for them? The whole Bible is for everyone, of course. But people who long to start over with God, and a generation that wonders if the flame of bygone years can be relit, find a message particularly suited to their needs in the book of Zechariah.

In truth, although this book claims few epic heroes, the believers of Zechariah's time were very much like earlier Bible champions. They resembled

Moses as he knelt before the burning bush, doubting his ability to serve as Israel's redeemer. Like Joshua as he stepped into Moses' shoes, they needed the encouragement of a divine commissioning. Like King David, it was their love for God that led them into their hardships. Their battles of faith were every bit as important as the conquests of earlier heroes. The shattered city they labored to rebuild was as beloved to God as Jerusalem had ever been. And the temple they rebuilt, though not outwardly as glorious as the original of Solomon's day, would serve just as truly to bring the people into God's presence for worship. The reality is that God always uses failures to do his work: it is his gracious delight to call, atone, restore, and equip weak and sinful people to bring glory to himself. This is true because the hero of Zechariah is none other than Jesus Christ, whose portraits fill this prophecy with a depth and vibrancy unsurpassed anywhere else in the Old Testament.

This is a message we all need to hear: by God's grace in Christ, the role he has assigned to us is no less significant than the greatest deeds ever performed by God's choicest saints. Like Zechariah's generation, God would lift up our heads with a fresh vision of his message of old: "Not by might, nor by power, but by my Spirit, says the LORD" (Zech. 4:6). May God bless all who read these studies with refreshment to hope in God's grace and with strength for the work he has given each of us to do.

These messages were first preached in the evening services of Tenth Presbyterian Church in Philadelphia from November 2000 to July 2001, and again as an evening series at First Presbyterian Church of Coral Springs/Margate, Florida, in 2005 and 2006. I thank these wonderful congregations, and am especially grateful to their sessions for the time they permit me for careful study and preparation. I am also appreciative of Philip Ryken and Iain Duguid, whose editorial labors have measurably improved the quality of this book. This commentary is dedicated to the staff and faculty of Westminster Theological Seminary in Philadelphia, with gratitude for my priceless years of study there and for the lifelong influence this great institution has exercised on my ministry.

Additionally, I give praise to God for the devoted ministry of my dear wife Sharon, not merely for her unflagging support, but also for the delight she brings into my life, and for the godly joys of our children: Hannah, Matthew, Jonathan, Ellie, and Lydia. Lastly, I give thanks to the Lord of hosts, whose grace in Christ is truly new every morning and new in every generation. To him be glory forever.

Zechariah

RETURN TO ME

PART 1

The Eight Night Visions

1

RETURN TO ME

Zechariah 1:1—6

The LORD was very angry with your fathers. Therefore say to them, "Thus declares the LORD of hosts: Return to me, says the LORD of hosts, and I will return to you, says the LORD of hosts."
(Zech. 1:2–3)

One of the great questions of life is "How do we start again?" It is a question every sinner faces at one time or another. Broken marriages face the question, as do broken friendships and broken dreams. It was a question pressing hard upon the people of Judah in the time of the postexilic prophet Zechariah, who was charged with speaking for God to a people trying to start over again. Theirs was a broken relationship with God, a broken covenant. Having returned from bondage in far-off Babylon, their generation was asking, "How do we start again?"

The opening passage of this book clues us into the approach this prophet takes. Beginning in verse 2 of chapter 1, Zechariah points the people to the Lord. Three times in two verses he confronts them with the name "the Lord Almighty." In order to deal with the past, and therefore with the present and the future, he says, the people would have to turn to God. That is always true.

The power to heal what is broken, to start again what is ended, and to raise up what is cast down is always and only found with the Lord. "How do we get right with God, and what will it mean to us if we do?" That is where Zechariah begins, and that was the issue facing those who had come back to the Lord to start over again.

Approaches to the Study of Zechariah

We should begin our study of Zechariah by specifying the approaches that will enable us to interpret this book of Scripture rightly. First, we will approach Zechariah *historically*. We should always be historical in our study of Scripture, since the books of the Bible were given by God through actual men in the context of real circumstances and settings. As a result, our study of Zechariah will increase our knowledge of Old Testament history. We will become familiar with important figures unknown to many Christians: Sheshbazzar, the prince of Judah; Zerubbabel, the son of Shealtiel of the house of David and ancestor to our Lord Jesus; the high priest Joshua, of the line of Zadok; as well as Zechariah and his prophetic colleague Haggai.

Second, we will consider this book *doctrinally*. While this and every book of Scripture comes to us out of a historical setting, it also is part of the whole Bible given by God for our instruction in salvation. The book of Zechariah has a great many truths to set before us, doctrines of our faith that were at a particular stage of development in the progress of God's redemptive work. We want to take stock of its teaching both in light of how it was then presented and how the various subjects would ultimately be rounded out in the completed canon of Scripture.

Third—and this is a strong emphasis in the book of Zechariah—we will approach this material *christologically*. We will trace the line of thought as it leads to Jesus Christ, the Messiah anticipated by the Old Testament, and the Savior who fulfills its promises and answers its questions. So frequent and dramatic are the pointers to Christ in Zechariah that the book might be dubbed *The Gospel according to Zechariah*. It is sometimes said that the gospel is in the Old Testament *concealed* and in the New Testament *revealed*. When we get to the book of Zechariah, Christ is barely concealed but often blatantly revealed to the eyes of those trained by the later revelations of the New Testament.

Fourth, we will approach this book from a *practical* perspective, applying its message to our own setting and lives so as to derive its full benefit. Though we are separated by time and circumstances from the prophet and his generation, the issues of faith and godliness have not ultimately changed. Everything God revealed in this book for individuals and for Israel as a whole finds a contemporary application for Christians and the church.

THE HISTORICAL SETTING OF ZECHARIAH

First, let us consider the historical setting from which this book of Scripture comes to us. A good place to start is in the year 586 BC, when the Babylonian conqueror Nebuchadnezzar seized and destroyed the Israelite capital, Jerusalem. This was an event long portended in the prophetic writings, most nearly by the prophet Jeremiah, whose title, "the weeping prophet," was earned from his participation in those horrible events. At the beginning of his prophecy, Jeremiah explained all that was going to take place, and why:

> The LORD said to me, "Out of the north disaster shall be let loose upon all the inhabitants of the land. For behold, I am calling all the tribes of the kingdoms of the north, declares the LORD, and they shall come, and every one shall set his throne at the entrance of the gates of Jerusalem, against all its walls all around and against all the cities of Judah. And I will declare my judgments against them, for all their evil in forsaking me. They have made offerings to other gods and worshiped the works of their own hands." (Jer. 1:14–16)

Despite warning after warning, from prophet after prophet, the day finally came when the Lord brought judgment upon his people for their sins, and especially the sin of idolatry to which they were so addicted. At the end, the situation was as described in Jeremiah's brokenhearted book of Lamentations: "How lonely sits the city that was full of people! . . . The LORD has afflicted her for the multitude of her transgressions; her children have gone away, captives before the foe" (Lam. 1:1, 5).

Jerusalem lay in ruins, empty, her walls torn down, and her buildings scorched with fire. Thus concluded a key stage in the history of God's people, one brilliantly begun in the exodus, gloriously advanced under King David, but brought to ruin by the sins of his hardhearted people. Despite their status as God's people, despite God's presence in their midst, despite the institutions of the theocracy, the temple and the royal palace, and despite the holy hill of Zion where Israel worshiped, even the Israelites were not spared the judgment for their sins. The fall of Jerusalem stands as a lasting testimony to the folly of presumption and the wages of sin.

The Israelites went into exile, to weep by the waters of Babylon while the Promised Land was inhabited by other people (Ps. 137:1). Yet God promised grace to his people in their sorrow. Through Jeremiah he said:

> For thus says the LORD: When seventy years are completed for Babylon, I will visit you, and I will fulfill to you my promise and bring you back to this place. For I know the plans I have for you, declares the LORD, plans for wholeness and not for evil, to give you a future and a hope. Then you will call upon me and come and pray to me, and I will hear you. You will seek me and find me. When you seek me with all your heart, I will be found by you. (Jer. 29:10–14)[1]

Other prophecies of hope came from the latter chapters of Isaiah, written about two hundred years beforehand. So specific were Isaiah's predictions that he even named the ruler who would restore the fortunes of Israel: "I will raise up Cyrus in my righteousness: I will make all his ways straight. He will rebuild my city and set my exiles free" (Isa. 45:13 NIV).

Liberal critics of Scripture use this prediction to claim a postexilic dating for the latter chapters of Isaiah, presupposing that actual foretelling is impossible. But God's expressed purpose was to give confidence to his people at a time when many would have wondered about his ability to save. When this specific prediction was fulfilled, it was a staggering proof of God's sovereignty. "I am God," he insisted, "and there is no other; I am God, and there is none like me, declaring the end from the beginning and from ancient times things not yet done, saying, 'My counsel shall stand, and I will accomplish all my purpose'" (Isa. 46:9–10).

Cyrus the Great was the Medo-Persian emperor who overthrew Babylon and gave the orders for the Israelites to return to their land (see Ezra 1:1–4). Accordingly, in 538 BC, forty-eight years after the fall of Jerusalem, Sheshbazzar received

---

1. This prophecy was fulfilled most clearly when the temple was rebuilt in 515 BC, seventy years after the exiled people arrived in Babylon. It was only then that the return was fully accomplished.

the temple articles from Cyrus and led the return of the first party to the ruins of Jerusalem. It was a moment of epochal significance and great drama.

Sheshbazzar, the son of Jehoiachin, the last legitimate king of Judah before and during the exile, would have been fairly aged by this time. We do not read a great deal about him in Scripture, except to learn that he succeeded in laying the foundation for a rebuilt temple on Mount Zion (Ezra 5:16).

The second chapter of Ezra, which along with Nehemiah is the main historical record of this period, tells us that the initial party returning to Jerusalem consisted of 42,360 Israelites. Although Cyrus had placed Sheshbazzar in command, it seems clear that from the start the acting leader was the younger and presumably more able Zerubbabel, the son of Sheshbazzar's older brother Shealtiel, along with Joshua the high priest. These two represented the kingly and priestly lines going back to David and Zadok his faithful priest.

One of this multitude was Zechariah, who must have been a young man or boy at the time of the return. He is named in verse 1 as son of Berechiah, and grandson of Iddo. In the record of Nehemiah 12, Zechariah is listed as the head of the house of Iddo, so many commentators reasonably suggest that Zechariah's father must have died young, leaving him as the principal heir of Iddo's house. His was a priestly family, something Zechariah held in common with both the prophets Jeremiah and Ezekiel.

The New Testament provides one additional piece of biographical information having to do with Zechariah's death. In Matthew 23, as Jesus was speaking his woes upon the Pharisees and upon Jerusalem, he recounted the people's record of killing the prophets. "On you," he cried, "may come all the righteous blood shed on earth, from the blood of innocent Abel to the blood of Zechariah the son of Barachiah, whom you murdered between the sanctuary and the altar" (v. 35). Liberal commentators consider this an error in the Bible, since 2 Chronicles 24:20–22 records a different Zechariah being slain in the temple courtyard, long before the time of our prophet. This assumes that there could not have been two different prophets of this name (and Zechariah is a fairly common name in Scripture) so that Jesus was therefore in error. Rather than presupposing Jesus' fallibility, we do better to accept his word and conclude that our Zechariah, the postexilic prophet, had his own life ended at the hands of the people in the very temple God used him so mightily to see to completion. As such he was the last of the prophets slain in the Old Testament, a line started outside the gates of the Garden with the murder of Abel by his brother Cain.

There would be sixteen years between Israel's initial return with the laying of the temple's foundation in 536 BC and the beginning of Zechariah's ministry. His prophecy, we are told, begins "in the eighth month, in the second year of Darius" (1:1)—that is, in the year 520 BC. Darius was a general who assumed the Persian throne after a plot resulted in the apparent suicide of Cambyses, the son and successor of Cyrus, who had been away effecting his conquest of Egypt. By this time a dispirited restoration community in Jerusalem had become bogged down both spiritually and materially. One commentator explains:

> If the returned exiles expected the dawn of Yahweh's universal reign, with Jews and Gentiles flocking to Jerusalem, their hopes soon faded. Jews did not leave the population centers of [Babylonia] in vast numbers, and interference from the longtime inhabitants of the land frustrated the building efforts, bringing the work on the temple to a halt.[2]

Two months before Zechariah's first vision from God, the prophet Haggai had broken the silence and called the people into action: "Go up to the hills," he cried, "and bring wood and build the house, that I may take pleasure in it and that I may be glorified, says the LORD" (Hag. 1:8). While Haggai focused the people on building the temple for the Lord, God came to Zechariah and focused him on rebuilding the people and their faith.

RETURN TO ME!

The opening lines of Zechariah highlight a doctrinal theme that will be important throughout the book: repentance. Zechariah explains the situation: "The LORD was very angry with your fathers. Therefore say to them, Thus declares the LORD of hosts: Return to me, says the LORD of hosts, and I will return to you, says the LORD of hosts" (Zech. 1:2–3). We are reminded here of the Lord Jesus' teaching as he started his gospel ministry five hundred years after the prophet: "Repent," Jesus cried, "for the kingdom of heaven is at hand" (Matt. 4:17).

2. Thomas E. McComiskey, *The Minor Prophets: An Exegetical and Expository Commentary*, 3 vols. (Grand Rapids: Baker, 1998), 3:1004.

There are at least four points to be made about repentance from this passage. First is *the need for repentance*. This need is established by the fact that God judges all sin. The problem with the Israelites' forefathers was that they doubted God's judgment and therefore denied the need for their own repentance. Since they were God's chosen people, and since they possessed such divinely ordained institutions as the temple, they thought God would never punish them. This is why they ignored and often persecuted the prophets God sent to them. The fall of Jerusalem and the Babylonian captivity were God's telling response to their hardness of heart in refusing to repent. Zechariah's generation asked, "How do we start again, when our relationship with God is damaged by sin?" This is a question many people ask today. The answer is that we begin with repentance.

Zechariah pressed the need for repentance upon his own generation by recalling their nation's recent history. He warned, "Do not be like your fathers, to whom the former prophets cried out, 'Thus says the LORD of hosts, Return from your evil ways and from your evil deeds.' But they did not hear or pay attention to me, declares the LORD" (Zech. 1:4). Then he asked leading questions designed to make his point: "Your fathers, where are they? And the prophets, do they live forever?" (Zech. 1:5). The answer was obvious as they stood amidst the ruins of the once magnificent city. Their fathers had gone into slavery and exile, and even the prophets were gone. Finally, Zechariah drove home the reality of God's prophetic Word: "But my words and my statutes, which I commanded my servants the prophets, did they not overtake your fathers?" (Zech. 1:6).

Though these events were in the past, the Word of the Lord had prevailed and come forward into the present. As Isaiah had said, "All flesh is grass. . . . The grass withers, the flower fades, but the word of our God will stand forever" (Isa. 40:6–8). The one thing that could never fail was God's Word, and Zechariah was bringing it forward into this new generation. Zechariah's name means "the Lord remembers"; on the one hand God remembered his people, but on the other he remembered his words and decrees, which must always be reckoned with, then as now.

Verse 1 says, "The word of the LORD came to the prophet Zechariah." If any one message characterized the prophetic mission—any one "word of the LORD"—it was this call to repentance. Although the prophets of old were gone, God had raised up a new prophet to perform the same task and bring the same message. The forefathers had realized this in exile, once it was too late, repenting and saying, "As the Lord of hosts purposed to deal with us for our ways and deeds, so has he dealt with us" (Zech. 1:6). A clear expression of repentant prayer among at least some of the exiles is found in Daniel 9, where that prophet-in-exile expounded upon these very words. His and others' willingness to repent left this later generation of their children without excuse if they did not follow suit.

If the first lesson is the need for repentance, the second is *a definition of repentance*. Repentance is both turning from sin and turning to God. God had said to the earlier generations, "Return from your evil ways and from your evil deeds—" (Zech. 1:4), and that is no less a requirement now. Repentance is turning away from sin, both from the way of sin and the works of sin. Repentance is about both our actions and our attitude. We tend to think we have repented if we just curb our behavior a small bit, but repentance includes our hearts and desires, as Zechariah explained, "Return from your evil ways and your evil deeds." Along with turning from sin, we are called to turn to God. Zechariah 1:3 puts this directly: "Return to me, says the Lord of hosts, and I will return to you, says the Lord of hosts."

These two are inseparable—turning from sin and turning to God. On the one hand we cannot turn to God except by turning from the sin he abhors; on the other hand until we come back to God, we simply lack the strength to overcome the sin that holds us in bondage. Only his light can cast out our darkness.

Zechariah's words are especially striking in light of the particular audience to whom he was speaking. These were the people who had returned to the land. The majority of their fellow countrymen had remained comfortably ensconced in Babylonia, where the Jews had grown prosperous. Yet as Haggai's prophecy made clear, the hearts of the returnees were not fully devoted to the Lord. They had walked back down the long road to God's city, yet they had stopped short of God himself. Partly due to opposition from nearby enemies and partly due to their own indifference, the restoration community had lost interest in rebuilding God's temple. T. V. Moore describes the situation before Zechariah:

> He had witnessed the growth of that selfish greed for their own individual interests, and their neglect of the interests of religion, that was so mournful

a characteristic of this period. . . . Now, as the temple was to them the grand symbol of revealed religion, indifference to it was an undoubted symptom of backsliding and spiritual declension.[3]

"Return to me!" says the Lord, and that is a command we too must note. It is not enough for us merely to call ourselves Christians and to go to the places where the Lord is worshiped and served. We must actually worship and serve him from the heart. "Return to me," God said to this people who had come so far to the city but had grown cold in their hearts toward him. "Return to me, and I will return to you." That is always the rule of spiritual life and blessing.

This leads to the third point about repentance: *God graciously receives all who turn to him.* "I will return to you," he promised. What a blessing those words must have been to these children of idolaters, sons of an adulterous generation whom God might well have repudiated altogether. Yet this is the grace that always characterizes the heart of our Savior God. Even before the exile he had given every chance for the people to repent, inviting their return to him in faith: "Return, faithless Israel, declares the LORD. I will not look on you in anger, for I am merciful, declares the LORD; I will not be angry forever. Only acknowledge your guilt, that you rebelled against the LORD your God" (Jer. 3:12–13).

This is our great incentive for repentance, that however great our sin and backsliding, God is ready to receive those who come to him in repentance and faith. This is the gospel according to Zechariah, the good news of great joy that God will gladly receive those who turn to him in repentance and faith.

Jesus taught this in the parable of the prodigal son. The prodigal had taken his share of the father's wealth, which he then squandered in sinful living, only to find himself in desperate straits. Despondent, but having come to his senses, he determined to go back to his father, begging for mercy. But Jesus said:

While he was still a long way off, his father saw him and felt compassion, and ran and embraced him and kissed him. And the son said to him, "Father, I have sinned against heaven and before you. I am no longer worthy to be called

3. T. V. Moore, *Haggai, Zechariah, & Malachi* (Edinburgh: Banner of Truth, 1979), 118–19.

your son." But the father said to his servants, "Bring quickly the best robe, and put it on him, and put a ring on his hand, and shoes on his feet. And bring the fattened calf and kill it, and let us eat and celebrate. For this my son was dead, and is alive again; he was lost, and is found." And they began to celebrate. (Luke 15:20–24)

Such is our God; why would anyone refuse his loving heart?

This leaves a fourth and final point about repentance: *it is only through the blood of Jesus Christ that God forgives those who repent.* We noted that our approach to Zechariah will be christological, and here is where the opening verses point to Christ. God's call to repentance was directly linked to the rebuilding of the temple. There is a reason for that, for it was at the temple that the blood sacrifices were offered that dealt with the problem of sin. God is a holy God; he must always judge sin. Therefore God could not accept these sinners unless atonement was made. In Zechariah's day this required the blood of lambs at the very temple they were to rebuild, but ultimately it required the death of Jesus Christ on the cross. Jesus is the true Lamb of God, and his was the blood shed to take away our sin. Theologian J. I. Packer explains: "Between us sinners and the thunderclouds of divine wrath stands the cross of the Lord Jesus. If we are Christ's through faith, then we are justified through His cross, and the wrath will never touch us, neither here nor hereafter. Jesus 'delivers us from the wrath to come' (1 Thess. 1:10)."[4]

When we repent, therefore, we must come through faith in Jesus Christ and in his blood, which turns God's righteous anger into joyful acceptance and love. Because Jesus was slain upon the cross for us, God robes us in his righteousness and is glad to receive us with arms open wide in bounteous grace as we return in penitent faith.

An Urgent Appeal

Our approach to Zechariah will be historical, doctrinal, christological, and also practical. Therefore, we must apply these words to our own situation: "Return to me, says the LORD of hosts, and I will return to you" (Zech. 1:3).

---

4. J. I. Packer, *Knowing God* (Downers Grove, IL: InterVarsity, 1978), 141.

The earlier generation of Israelites thought God would not judge them for their sin; the ruins of their city bore eloquent testimony to their folly. Our generation is also piling up ruins out of folly, even within the church. "Do not be deceived," Paul wrote: "God is not mocked, for whatever one sows, that will he also reap. For the one who sows to his own flesh will from the flesh reap corruption, but the one who sows to the Spirit will from the Spirit reap eternal life" (Gal. 6:7–8).

If you are a Christian, but backslidden into sin and spiritual decline, remember the history lesson Zechariah placed before his generation. Your sin will not bring blessing but ruin, however sweet its deceptive song in your ears. If you persist in sin you will at the least bring upon yourself God's chastisement, and at the worst you will prove that you have really not believed at all, ultimately to reap the destruction you are now sowing with the seeds of sin. In fact, this invitation from God speaks grace to every Christian, every day—backslidden or not! In the ups and downs of our spiritual lives, how wonderful to see God's open arms encouraging continual repentance and trust!

If you are not a Christian, these words are especially for you. If God hates sin enough to punish even his own people, what do you think will happen to you? If God allowed his chosen people Israel—the elect nation of his own love and purpose—to fall to the sword, to be dragged off in chains, and the city and its temple reduced to ruin—what, then, will be your fate if you continue to rebel, you who have no such claim upon his affection? The lesson is clear: You must repent at once, turn from your sin and to this God of grace who offers everyone salvation through the blood of the Savior Jesus Christ. If you will repent and turn to him in faith, your sins will be forgiven on the spot and you will enter into everlasting life.

"Return to me," says our God, "and I will return to you." "Come to me," he offers, "return!" Those who do will find God ready to forgive through Jesus Christ, ready to restore, and ready to bless from out of the depths of his abounding grace. No matter who you have been or what you have gone through, by turning to God you will be able truly to start again, because God will return to you.

2

HORSEMEN OF THE LORD

Zechariah 1:7–17

*I saw in the night, and behold, a man riding on a red horse! He
was standing among the myrtle trees in the glen, and behind him
were red, sorrel, and white horses. Then I said, "What are these,
my lord?" The angel who talked with me said to me, "I will show
you what they are." (Zech. 1:8–9)*

In Charles Dickens's familiar story, "A Christmas Carol," Ebenezer
Scrooge is visited by the ghosts of Christmas Past, Christmas
Present, and Christmas Future. These visions leave Scrooge a
changed man; no longer the champion of humbug, he becomes a paragon
of charity and joy.

The book of Zechariah tells us about a night even Dickens never dreamed
of, in which the prophet received not three but eight visions, and not fan-
tasy ghost-visits but actual revelations from the God of heaven. One after
another they came, all in one restless night, and the record of these visitations makes up the first six chapters of this book. Like Scrooge, that night
of visions changed Zechariah forever. He became a prophet, and a messenger of good news to the people.

Zechariah's First Vision

Given this subject matter, a word about visions may be helpful. Usually we think of prophets receiving words from the Lord, but it was not uncommon for them to receive visions as well. From early in the history of Israel we read of "seers" who stood just as important in the prophetic tradition as did "hearers" (2 Kings 17:13). Indeed, there are few prophets who do not report visions from the Lord, and all the major prophets—Isaiah, Jeremiah, Ezekiel, and Daniel—offer heavy doses of visionary revelation. Burke Long says, "The prophet not only is a messenger of Yahweh, delivering a word which he has received, but he also reports what he has seen, what has been uncovered for him, in extraordinary states of consciousness."[1]

Typically, a prophet was confronted with some extraordinary vision—either a stationary object or a dramatic scene that would unfold. Normally, the vision required some interpretation, usually by an angelic guide. Sometimes there was dialogue within the vision; on occasion a question and answer sequence took place between the angel and the prophet. Zechariah's first vision was one of these. Long classified it as a "dramatic word-vision," that is, a dramatic action in the heavenly realms with its own dialogue that provides the meaning.[2]

Visions are closely associated with apocalyptic literature. Apocalyptic is a genre associated with striking (and sometimes bizarre) imagery, and an extreme dualism between good and evil. Most famous is the book of Revelation, also known as the Apocalypse. Apocalyptic visions present a heavenly perspective of earthly events and reveal the sovereignty of God to an oppressed people. The contrast between the prophetic word and the apocalyptic vision may be generalized in these terms: whereas the prophetic word calls a sinful people to repentance, apocalyptic visions call a downtrodden people to hope and belief. God sent his prophetic Word to afflict the comfortable, but he gave visions of hope to comfort the afflicted. Zechariah's visions are similar to those of the book of Revelation, which were given to display Christ's victory to the weak and persecuted early church.

1. Burke O. Long, "Reports of Visions among the Prophets," *JBL* 95/3 (1976), 353.
2. Ibid., 359.

On the night of the twenty-fourth day of the eleventh month, Zechariah had his first vision: "I saw in the night, and behold, a man riding on a red horse! He was standing among the myrtle trees in the glen, and behind him were red, sorrel, and white horses" (Zech. 1:8).

Four features make up this vision: the man on the horse, the myrtle trees, the ravine, and the horses behind the first rider. The image of horsemen is familiar to the reader of the Old Testament. A mounted host was frequently used to display the angelic legions of God's heavenly army (see Deut. 33:2; 2 Kings 6:17; Ps. 68:17). Furthermore, horsemen are associated with royal wealth and power. Solomon's glory was displayed by his fourteen hundred chariots and twelve thousand horsemen (1 Kings 10:26).

What about the myrtle trees? Myrtles are evergreen shrubs that grow well in Israel. Isaiah uses them to represent God's salvation restoration. Isaiah 55:13 says, "Instead of the thorn shall come up the cypress; instead of the brier shall come up the myrtle." Apparently, myrtle was one of the types of branches used to make booths for the feast of tabernacles (Neh. 8:15). Some scholars therefore see them as representative of the covenant community, so that they represent the assembly of God's people into which the angelic figures have come. Others see the dark trees as merely providing a shadowy backdrop to lend a sense of foreboding to the vision. That they are in a ravine adds to the ominous mood. At least one scholar, Meredith Kline, sees this gully as representative of hostile spiritual and worldly powers.[3]

The colors of the other horses do not seem to convey a specific meaning. They are red, sorrel (a chestnut reddish brown), and white. There may be some intention to create the impression of flames, in keeping with the frequent biblical image of divine horses of fire. Or perhaps the different colors reflect military organization within the angelic ranks, the way modern regiments boast their distinctive colors. But the Hebrew text merely gives a general description: behind the rider on the red horse are horses red, sorrel, and white.

Seeing all these things, Zechariah indicated his need for help in understanding. "What are these, my lord?" he asked. "I will show you what they are," said the angel (Zech. 1:9).

3. Meredith G. Kline, "The Rider of the Red Horse," *Kerux* 5.2 (1990): 2–3.

THE REPORT OF THE HORSEMEN

The vision's meaning is found in the drama that unfolds with three actions, each of which have something to teach us. The first is *the report of the horsemen*: "So the man who was standing among the myrtle trees answered, 'These are they whom the LORD has sent to patrol the earth.' And they answered the angel of the LORD who was standing among the myrtle trees, and said, 'We have patrolled the earth, and behold, all the earth remains at rest'" (Zech. 1:10–11).

This scene is particularly delightful to me. As a young army officer, I had the privilege of commanding a reconnaissance unit not much different from the one pictured in this vision. There are two types of mounted units: heavy and light. Today, a heavy unit is composed of tanks. Its job is to concentrate combat power to smash enemy forces. These are not fundamentally different from the chariot units of Zechariah's day, a type of mounted unit we will see in a later vision. The other kind of mounted unit is the light cavalry, which appears here. Today these are more lightly armored units, whose mission is to spread out over the battlefield—particularly behind enemy lines—to provide commanders with accurate information about the enemy.

In this way, these riders present a graphic image of the *omniscience* and the *omnipresence* of God. God's angelic reconnaissance troop "patrols the earth" (Zech. 1:10). They go here and there, in all directions, without hindrance, representing his exhaustive knowledge of all things in all places. They remind Zechariah and the fledgling community at Jerusalem that God has knowledge of all things upon the earth and his presence is felt everywhere.

But more than omniscience, these riders portray the *omnipotence* of the Lord. Even a brief survey of military history will reveal that a commander whose cavalry operates freely throughout the land has a distinct advantage. This was a hallmark of such famous generals as Napoleon, Robert E. Lee, and Erwin Rommel: they took control of the theater of operations, with knowledge of everything that took place, because of the superiority of their mounted troops.

The combined effect of this omniscience, omnipresence, and omnipotence is an absolute sovereignty. Far more than any earthly conqueror ever dreamed, God possesses sovereignty on the earth. Jonathan Edwards says: "It is the will of God to manifest his sovereignty. And his sovereignty, like his other attributes, is manifested in the exercise of it. He glorifies his power in the exercise of his power. He glorifies his mercy in the exercise of his mercy. So he glorifies his sovereignty in the exercise of his sovereignty."[4]

These horsemen represent the exercise and the revelation of God's sovereignty. This directly challenges a common view of God. Many people suppose that God is only distantly concerned with the affairs of earth. Here, the will of man holds sway; the earth's scepter rests in the hands of earthly princes, captains of industry, and leaders of fashion. In Zechariah's day it was the Persian emperor who dominated the scene. But what God showed Zechariah he also shows to us. Kings may be powerful, but God is all-powerful. God's forces control the field from the east to the west. His sovereignty is manifested in his control of the affairs of men. God's horsemen range throughout the earth as a display of his unhindered reign.

This is not a popular teaching today—it never is—but the Bible forcefully asserts it. Psalm 47:8 says, "God reigns over the nations; God sits on his holy throne." This is a great comfort to God's people in affliction. God is present in our families, in our homes, in our workplaces, in the city, in the nation, and among the nations. He sees all things so that we are never far from his gaze. He knows what is happening to all his children and is present with us everywhere, even though we may not be able to see this. And where he is he is sovereign, a truth that brings hope to tearful eyes and strength to trembling hands.

Whenever we see angels in the Scripture we should remember what this vision reveals: God's omnipresence, omniscience, and sovereign omnipotence, all combining to empower God's loving care. Hebrews 1:14 says, "Are [angels] not all ministering spirits sent out to serve for the sake of those who are to inherit salvation?" Angels manifest God's tender concern for the church. John Calvin writes:

> The whole Scripture is full of evidences, which prove that angels are guardians to serve the godly, and watch over them; for the Lord, for whose service they are ever ready, thus employs them; and in this we also see the singular love of God towards us; for he employs his angels especially for this purpose, that he might show that our salvation is greatly valued by him.[5]

---

4. Jonathan Edwards, *The Works of Jonathan Edwards*, 2 vols. (Peabody, MA: Hendrickson, 1998), 2:850.
5. John Calvin, *The Minor Prophets*, 5 vols. (Edinburgh: Banner of Truth, 1986), 5:38.

Scripture does not reveal the ministry of angels so that we will worship them, or so that we will pray to them—both of these are expressly forbidden in God's Word (see Rev. 19:10). Rather, we are shown God's mighty angels to strengthen our trust in him. Angels embody his loving care and heavenly might. What a comfort it must have been to Zechariah to see God's angels! Likewise, God wants us to know that even when we seem to be alone, God is with us and his angels are watching over us.

The date that Zechariah gives for this vision is significant. The year was 520 BC. Two years earlier a time of tumult had begun in the Persian Empire. Cambyses, the son and heir of Cyrus the Great, had been overthrown by a rebellion after which he took his own life. One of his officers, Darius, gathered up the imperial forces and overthrew the usurper, establishing himself as king. It was two years before this infighting ended, a time that must have kindled hopes for independence in Jerusalem. Many may have pointed to God's promises of a restored nation and may have seen his hand in these events, expecting a fragmenting of power that would enable their return to political freedom. But that is not what happened. By 520—the year of this vision—all was calm. Darius held his grip on power firmly and Persia remained unassailable in her rule over the Ancient Near East.

This would have been a discouragement to this restoration community, dreaming as they did of a return to prior glory. They had returned from exile to reclaim the heritage of their past, focusing their hope on the temple they intended to rebuild on Mount Zion. That they lost interest in this project shows how ethereal the promises were becoming to them. In this context, the report of the horsemen could hardly have been encouraging: "We have patrolled the earth, and behold, all the earth remains at rest" (Zech. 1:11). This was not good news if what you were hoping for was a disruption of a foreign power and an opportunity to break the bonds of subjugation.

We see, therefore, the importance of God's sovereignty. This truth is central to the message Zechariah was commissioned to proclaim. We see this emphasis in the opening verses of the book, which read: "Thus declares the LORD of hosts: Return to me, says the LORD of hosts, and I will return to you, says the LORD of hosts" (Zech. 1:3). Since the Hebrew language does not have exclamation points, it uses repetition for emphasis instead: "LORD of hosts . . . LORD of hosts . . . LORD of hosts." This expression (Hebrew, *Yahweh Sabaoth*) is often translated as "LORD Almighty." This vision shows us the meaning of this expression. It presents the hosts of heaven, and Yahweh is their Lord. Their prowess and power depict the Lord's sovereign omnipotence to the eyes of our faith.

Zechariah spoke to this community that had sacrificed so much to come to Jerusalem, receiving, it seemed, so little in return. Their hopes had been so strong but were now so weak. A generation after the return they were still under the dominion of Persian kings. They were still vassals, dependent on the rule of greater powers, so they lost interest in rebuilding God's temple. It was to these people that the prophet spoke of the Lord Almighty, the sovereign ruler whose horsemen range throughout the earth. As Meredith Kline writes, "That personal presence of the Lord of Glory in the midst of the covenant community on earth was the all-important reality."[6]

THE ANGEL'S ANGUISHED PLEA

The second scene in this drama occurs in 1:12, where we hear *the angel's anguished plea*: "Then the angel of the LORD said, 'O LORD of hosts, how long will you have no mercy on Jerusalem and the cities of Judah, against which you have been angry these seventy years?' " Even the angel of the Lord—the rider on the red horse who received this report—was bewildered by a world at peace in its rebellion against God. Why, the angel inquired, did God allow Israel's oppressors to enjoy their spoils at leisure, while he withheld mercy from Israel?

This angel shows us much about the Bible's view of prayer. At first it may seem that he is irreverently chastising God. But God does not object: "The LORD answered gracious and comforting words to the angel" (Zech. 1:13). It is not inconsistent for faith to cry out to God. It will not anger him if you cry your tears on his breast. God invites his people to unburden their cares to him, for his affections are tender in the intimate concern he bears for all his children.

Notice, too, that the angel composes his prayer with promises from God. He knew that God promised only seventy years of subjugation, and that the time was soon to be over. What a model this is for our prayers. If we are going to pray with power, we will have to know the Scriptures. We will have to

6. Kline, "Rider," 4.

know what God has promised and then pray that he will do what he has promised to do. When our faith is weak and we are tempted, we should pray for God to send his Holy Spirit, because he has promised to do that. When we feel distant from God we remember James 4:8, which virtually quotes Zechariah 1:2: "Draw near to God, and he will draw near to you." When we face death, we pray the promise of a life to come and a resurrection body, drawing strength from God's promise.

What a comfort to learn that the angels pray for God's people. And what a further comfort it is to know that God invites us to cry out to him like this angel, reminding him of all that he has promised to do. Having prayed, we then must wait upon the Lord. Philippians 4:6–7 says: "Do not be anxious about anything, but in everything by prayer and supplication with thanksgiving let your requests be made known to God. And the peace of God, which surpasses all understanding, will guard your hearts and your minds in Christ Jesus."

GOD'S COMFORTING REPLY

The action in this vision began with the report of the horsemen, followed by the anguished plea of the angel. It concludes with *the comforting reply* that comes from the Lord:

> So the angel who talked with me said to me, "Cry out, Thus says the LORD of hosts: I am exceedingly jealous for Jerusalem and for Zion. And I am exceedingly angry with the nations that are at ease; for while I was angry but a little, they furthered the disaster. Therefore, thus says the LORD, I have returned to Jerusalem with mercy; my house shall be built in it, declares the LORD of hosts, and the measuring line shall be stretched out over Jerusalem. Cry out again, Thus says the LORD of hosts: My cities shall again overflow with prosperity, and the LORD will again comfort Zion and again choose Jerusalem." (Zech. 1:14–17)

God replied with a message of comfort to the angel's prayer for his grace. First he says, "I am exceedingly jealous for Jerusalem and for Zion" (Zech. 1:14). This highlights the Lord's zeal for his people and his anger toward the nations who dwelt secure. It is true that God had allowed Babylon and the other nations to oppress the Jews, as a judgment on their idolatry. But the nations had gloated. They had been cruel in their conquest and subjugation, so God's wrath had now arisen against the ungodly.

What does this tell you in your own struggle, when you look upon the unbelieving world and everyone seems happy? People indulge in sin, they mock your piety, and sometimes God's people are even cruelly persecuted by those who flaunt their wickedness. How are we to think about this? "I am jealous for my people," says the Lord, "but angry with those that feel secure." We are to realize what the writer of Psalm 73 said in his frustration about the happiness of the wicked. "It was oppressive to me," he said, "till I entered the sanctuary of God; then I understood their final destiny" (Ps. 73:16–17 NIV). Sin does not win out in the end.

This passage points out the folly of seeking peace and happiness apart from a saving relationship with God. Calvin was right when he said:

> Though men may think themselves happy, and flatter themselves and exult in their condition, they are yet in a most miserable state; for all happiness is ruinous which does not flow from the fountain of God's gratuitous love; in short, when God is not our Father, the more we abound in all kinds of blessings, the deeper we sink in all kinds of miseries.[7]

The giddy affluence of our time bears tragic testimony to this principle: without God there is no blessing. Indeed, no one in their right mind would say we in our materialistic Western society are really blessed today, despite all the godless happiness in which we revel.

But those who have God's favor are blessed, however little they may have, and whatever troubles surround them. God said to his own people: "I have returned to Jerusalem with mercy; my house shall be built in it" (Zech. 1:16). God spoke of growth and prosperity and building: "The measuring line shall be stretched out over Jerusalem" (Zech. 1:16). He speaks of abundance to come according to his design and as his own work, which therefore will be secure in him: "My cities shall again overflow with prosperity, and the LORD will again comfort Zion and again choose Jerusalem" (Zech. 1:17).

---

7. Calvin, *Minor Prophets*, 5:46.

GOD WITH US

This was God's message to Zechariah through this vision. The prophet saw the report of the horsemen, displaying God's sovereignty even though the enemy was at rest. Zechariah heard the prayer of the angel, beseeching God according to his promise, and then received the words of comfort from the Lord. The message of it all was: "The sovereign God is with you, in his power and glory and love, so do not fear."

This was virtually Zechariah's ordination ceremony as prophet of the Lord Almighty. "Proclaim this word," said the angel. This message was to shape his whole ministry. The vision was Zechariah's commissioning with a message of hope, good news of great joy: "I have returned to Jerusalem with mercy," said the Lord. "My house shall be built in it. . . . My cities shall again overflow with prosperity" (Zech. 1:16–17).

Zechariah's message conveyed that God was with his people, so that they should take heart. The Hebrew word for "God with us" is Immanuel, the very name given to Jesus Christ. The angel said to Joseph, "Behold, the virgin shall conceive and bear a son, and they shall call his name Immanuel" (Matt. 1:23). The case can be made strongly that the angel of the Lord in Zechariah 1 is the Lord Jesus in preincarnate form, since "the angel of the LORD" is how the second person of the Godhead typically is portrayed in the Old Testament. "Angel" means "messenger," and Jesus is the ultimate messenger who reveals God to men (see John 8:28–29; Heb. 1:2). He commands the mounted hosts of heaven (see Matt. 26:53). He intercedes for his people (see John 17; Heb. 7:25), which is what the angel of the Lord does here. This explains why God answered the angel's prayer with a promise of redemption: the angel who prayed was the very Redeemer whom God would send. Paul writes, "There is one God, and there is one mediator between God and men, the man Christ Jesus, who gave himself as a ransom for all" (1 Tim. 2:5–6). He is "the commander of the army of the LORD" Joshua encountered when he needed courage (Josh. 5:14), and the One Isaiah saw high and lifted up in the time of his discouragement (Isa. 6:1; see John 12:41). This is the One John saw in the opening vision of the book of Revelation, a vision closely related to these visions of Zechariah. These connections strongly suggest that the angel who came to Zechariah with this vision of salvation was the preincarnate Jesus himself.

What Jesus said to Zechariah, he also says to all who trust in him. As he said to his disciples before ascending into heaven: "Behold, I am with you always, to the end of the age" (Matt. 28:20). Jesus is Immanuel, God with us. "I will not leave you as orphans; I will come to you," he said to his disciples. "Because I live, you also will live" (John 14:18–19). Charles Spurgeon therefore exults:

> Behold a man riding upon a red horse. . . . This is to show his swiftness. He flies upon the wings of the wind to defend his people. . . . Riding on the horse is a symbol of his zeal. He comes with all his power and might, flying with all speed, so that none of his people should perish. He showeth himself strong on behalf of them that serve him, and is jealous for them with a fervent jealousy. . . . Rejoice, O ye people of God, that Jesus is in the midst of his saints with his sword girt upon his thigh.[8]

The Christian life is not unlike the experience of Zechariah's pilgrims squatting among the ruins of Jerusalem. We have great promises and a great hope of salvation—even of glory. Yet our present experience hardly matches our hope. So Christ appears, mounted on a red horse. It may not be that the color here refers to the blood he would shed, but Christians who read Zechariah in light of the completed Bible cannot help but entertain such thoughts. For Christ's intercession to God for us is red with his blood. His pierced hands and feet plead effectual prayers for his people in every storm of life. If God received his prayer in Zechariah's time—long before Jesus was born of the virgin, fulfilled the law, and shed his blood on the cross—how much more quickly will God show his love when summoned by the intercession of our crucified, resurrected, and ascended Savior.

Though we seem alone, God is with us, for Christ has offered up his plea. That is what Hebrews 13:5–6 tells us, the same message God gave to Zechariah long ago: "For he has said, 'I will never leave you nor forsake you.' So we can confidently say, 'The Lord is my helper; I will not fear; what can man do to me?'"

---

8. Charles Haddon Spurgeon, *Metropolitan Tabernacle Pulpit*, 63 vols. (Edinburgh: Banner of Truth, 1973), 10:781–83.

Can you say that? Can you say that God is with you, that the Lord is your helper? Can you say that Jesus Christ will not forsake you—in this life or the next? If you cannot, then you need to trust him now, for he is an all-sufficient Savior. His blood is all the redemption you will ever need. If you have trusted him, then believe the words God said to the prophet so long ago in answer to Christ: "I am jealous for you. I will come with mercy, to build, to bless you so that you overflow with prosperity."

3

I WILL RETURN TO YOU

Zechariah 1:16–21

Therefore, thus says the LORD, I have returned to Jerusalem with
mercy; my house shall be built in it, declares the LORD of hosts,
and the measuring line shall be stretched out over Jerusalem.
(Zech. 1:16)

*I*f you think you can't make it right, you're wrong." This message was plastered on a billboard placed by the local diocese of the Roman Catholic Church, accompanied by a picture of a wistful young woman. We might not agree with all of the Catholic theology behind that message, but the main point is one that all Christians heartily embrace: you can always come back to God.

This is the message of Zechariah's prophecy: "Return to me," says the Lord, "and I will return to you" (Zech. 1:3). This prophecy, which began the first chapter, also comes at the chapter's end as a promise of hope for Zechariah and his generation: "Thus says the LORD, I have returned to Jerusalem with mercy" (Zech. 1:16). Because God is so willing to return to us, we may always return to him. And if we think he can't make it right, we really are wrong.

WITH MERCY I WILL COME

Not only does this prophecy proclaim God's readiness to receive back every wayward sinner and every one of his fallen children, but it is a primer on how salvation works. The Lord speaks of five things he will do, and five things we can expect if we return to him. The first is *an offer of mercy.* Verse 16 states, "I have returned to Jerusalem with mercy."

In order for a sinner to draw near to the Lord, God must show mercy. God is holy and just, so apart from his mercy there is only wrath on the sinner. Before anything else takes place, before any other blessing can be applied, we must receive mercy from the Lord. This is the first promise God makes to the returning Israelites, and it speaks of his readiness to end their punishment. God had punished their fathers, but now he says, "I have returned with mercy." The effect of God's mercy is an end to his judgment on their sins.

The mercy of the Lord is the first thing a sinner must receive. As a pastor, I occasionally have someone come to me about a sin issue. There are two main categories of such people. Some admit what they are doing—perhaps it is an adulterous affair or cheating at work—but nonetheless are unwilling to give it up. They may profess belief in Jesus as Savior; they may acknowledge what they are doing as sin; and they may realize that God is displeased with what they are doing; but the key point is that they will not and do not want to turn away from their sin. Biblically, the message I give this kind of person is a warning that their eternal soul is in peril of hell. The apostle John explains, "No one who abides in him keeps on sinning; no one who keeps on sinning has either seen him or known him" (1 John 3:6). John is talking about a person who is hardened in his or her resolve to sin, and such an attitude is so incompatible with saving faith that no pastor has the right to assure such a person of peace with God.

This is one kind of sinner, but there is another: the person who has become embroiled in sin, who is perhaps deep in the grips of a certain lust or temptation, yet really wants to be free and deeply desires to return to God. Such people are like the pilgrims in Zechariah's day, who had returned to Jerusalem. God had judged their forefathers for the very hardhearted-ness I was just speaking about. Earlier generations of Israelites had prosti-tuted themselves to the world and its gods. The Lord brought them up short with the destruction of Jerusalem, tearing down the temple on Mount Zion and permitting a total defeat at the hands of their enemies. But this new

29

generation heard his words of comfort. They knew that salvation is of the Lord, and like many people a pastor will meet, they wanted to come back to him to be saved.

If the hardhearted sinner must be warned of the danger of God's wrath, what does this kind of sinner need to hear—the one who wants to make it right but fears that he can't? The answer is found in Zechariah 1:16: "I have returned to Jerusalem with mercy." The new life with God begins with his compassion, his free gift of forgiveness in Jesus Christ. The word for mercy (Hebrew, *racham*) speaks of God's attitude of grace. It is the feeling of a father for an injured child. Jeremiah used this word in Lamentations 3:22 as he looked through the disaster of Jerusalem's fall and into the future to this very grace: "The steadfast love of the LORD never ceases; his *mercies* never come to an end." This is the first step to a renewed relationship with God: we step by faith into his merciful arms to receive the embrace of his compassion.

The most important result of God's mercy is the forgiveness of our sins. Mercy and forgiveness are joined together, the latter being the expression of the former (see. Dan. 9:9). Calvin was right when he said of Zechariah 1:16: "It was necessary to give the people the hope of pardon and reconciliation, that they might look forward with confidence."[1] This is true for everyone who is returning to God from an exile in sin. Many people are sick of their sin. They are tired of the foul taste of iniquity, but it is so much a part of them, they are so deeply and habitually involved in it, that they simply don't know where to start. The place to start is with the mercy of God.

This means that before we do anything else, we must accept and rest upon the grace that God offers. This grace found its great expression in the gift of God's only Son to die in our place and bear sin's punishment: "For our sake [God] made him to be sin who knew no sin, so that in him we might become the righteousness of God" (2 Cor. 5:21). The first thing we must know, the place we must start, is the belief that in Christ, God has clothed us with his perfect righteousness and taken away the guilt of our sin. James Montgomery Boice explains how the gospel offers us salvation:

> It tells us that God loves us and has reached out to save us through the work of Jesus Christ. We could not reach God, because our sins separated us from

1. John Calvin, *The Minor Prophets*, 5 vols. (Edinburgh: Banner of Truth, 1986), 5:48.

him. But God removed our sins through Christ and so bridged the gap over these very troubled waters. Before, we were groaning after God but could not find him. Now we sing praises to the One who has found us.[2]

Do not try to build a relationship with God on the strength of your own repentance or your resolve to do better. Your inability and failure are what brought you to despair. The only rock on which you can build a sure foundation is the saving work of Jesus Christ, which flows from the merciful love of God the Father. Therefore, the first step in any return to God is with words like these from the Psalmist: "Let your steadfast love comfort me.... Let your mercy come to me, that I may live" (Ps. 119:76–77). As God said to Israel, he will surely say to you, "For a brief moment I deserted you, but with great compassion I will gather you" (Isa. 54:7).

God's Indwelling Spirit

Second, the Lord speaks of *his dwelling among his people*. Having spoken of his return to Jerusalem, God adds, "My house shall be built in it, declares the LORD of hosts" (Zech. 1:16). This meant that the people were going to rebuild the temple. Certainly, that would cheer them and give a sense of accomplishment, as well as a tie to the great days of the past. Of course, it would hardly be as impressive as the original version from Solomon's day; indeed, in Ezra we read that when the second temple was completed, the old men who had actually seen the original wept at the sight of the lowly building that was going up in its place (Ezra 3:12).

The true fulfillment of God's promise regarding the temple is the indwelling of God's Spirit among his people. When we come to God in faith, when we are received into his mercy, he comes to dwell within us by the power of his Holy Spirit. Paul states this directly: "Do you not know that you are God's temple and that God's Spirit dwells in you?" (1 Cor. 3:16).

This is the best possible news for those turning from sin to God. God not only shows you his mercy but he comes to dwell within you by his Spirit. Therefore, Christians gain exactly what we need: a new power from God for a new and holy life. The New Testament gives many descriptions of what

---

2. James Montgomery Boice, *Romans*, 4 vols. (Grand Rapids: Baker, 1991), 1:30–31.

this means. Philippians 2:13 says that God works within us "to will and to work for his good pleasure." The Spirit leads us (Rom. 8:14); he illuminates our minds with the knowledge of Christ (John 16:13–14); and he renews our inner nature (Titus 3:5). Perhaps the greatest assertion of God's work by the Spirit comes in 2 Corinthians 3:18: "We . . . are being transformed into [Christ's] image from one degree of glory to another. For this comes from the Lord who is the Spirit."

So can you return to God? Can you start over again? Can you walk in newness of life? Looking to your own power, the answer must be "No!" At best, we are merely managing the corruption of our hearts, and at worst we cry with Paul: "Wretched man that I am! Who will deliver me from this body of death?" (Rom. 7:24). But God says that he will come to dwell within us— he will set up his throne in our hearts—with his power and life to lead and change us. This is God's greatest gift—his own Spirit to dwell within. "I will build my house within you," he says, and therefore we can have power and peace as never before.

The vital importance of this is well taught by the very exile that forms the context for the book of Zechariah. One of the most alarming scenes in the Old Testament is recorded in Ezekiel 10 and 11, when God's glory departed from the original temple on Mount Zion. In a vision, the prophet saw the angels come in fiery chariots to remove the glory of the Lord. God enabled Ezekiel to see and record the shocking truth, as the presence of God rose up from the temple, God's glory went out to the walls, and then departed from the city.

Once the glory of the Lord had left, the temple was nothing more than a building, however great its outward splendor. The same is true for us. Jesus said, "Apart from me you can do nothing" (John 15:5). It was God's intention for Israel to learn this truth in Zechariah's day; so he took his presence out of the city and to Babylon, where he would empower and protect his people in exile. Thereafter Jerusalem was free to be destroyed, as it was. But now God tells Zechariah that he will return to Jerusalem with mercy. The people had returned to him and he would return to them. With him, they would see great things! Not only would their punishment end, but God says, "My house shall be built in it." Ezekiel had foreseen this return: "As the glory of the LORD entered the temple by the gate facing east, the Spirit lifted me up and brought me into the inner court; and behold, the glory of the LORD filled the temple" (43:4–5).

The same divine glory is present when the Holy Spirit comes to dwell in someone who looks to Christ in faith. Knowing the reality of God's return, like Zechariah and his fellow believers, we can say with the apostle Paul: "I can do all things through him who strengthens me" (Phil. 4:13).

TO BUILD AND TO BLESS

As we have contemplated what the New Testament says about God's indwelling Spirit, we can follow a discernible progression as God promises next to build and to bless. These are the third and the fourth things God does to restore his penitent people, beginning with his *promise to build*: "And the measuring line shall be stretched out over Jerusalem. Cry out again, Thus says the LORD of hosts: My cities shall again overflow with prosperity, and the LORD will again comfort Zion and again choose Jerusalem" (Zech. 1:16–17).

The image of the measuring line indicates a future filled with building and expansion. It is stretched out because architects will be planning, preparing for masons to cut and carpenters to break out their hammers. In a similar way, God has plans for each of his people. He has a pattern in mind for the building up of every Christian: the pattern set by Jesus Christ, the firstborn of the new human race. Romans 8:29 tells us that all God's people have been "predestined to be conformed to the image of his Son." We can each be certain, therefore, that God is laying out his measuring line over our character, our thought life, and our desires and affections: he has a Christ-conforming construction project in mind for us.

In this respect the Christian life is the same for each of us. But it is also true that God has special plans for each believer. He has installed individual gifts within each of us and had specific good works in mind when we were born and then spiritually born again in Christ. Paul says, "For we are his workmanship, created in Christ Jesus for good works, which God prepared beforehand, that we should walk in them" (Eph. 2:10). When we come to the Lord we can expect that he will shape our lives and ministry, sometimes in major and even radical ways, all the while fitting us for a place in his great masterwork that is the church.

Along with God's promise to build, believers who come to God can expect a fourth benefit: *the blessing of prosperity*. God states, "My cities shall again overflow with prosperity" (Zech. 1:17). Notice that the vision of building has expanded beyond the city to the surrounding towns, and there is an abundance of good things. Not only is the city expanded, but the whole land is made fruitful.

Likewise, God makes every believer's life prosperous with good things that will be a blessing to himself and to others. Although God does not intend for all Christians to abound in the wealth of the world—with money, power, or earthly fame—those who walk with God abound in the prosperity of a holy life. Believers are made rich in loyal friendships, useful service, healthy marriages, strong character, and they enjoy God's fatherly provision to meet all their needs.

God especially desires the spiritual prosperity of his people, and to this end he grants the comfort of assurance. The angel says: "And the LORD will again comfort Zion, and again choose Jerusalem" (Zech. 1:17). The comfort offered here is the knowledge of God's favor; God's people are comforted when they are assured of his love. That is why the idea of comfort is linked to God's choosing, or his sovereign election.

When God says he will again choose Jerusalem, the point is not that God's election is temporary and fleeting, dependent on our merits. That idea would hardly be a source of comfort! According to the Bible's doctrine of election, God "chose us in [Christ] before the creation of the world to be holy and blameless in his sight. In love he predestined us to be adopted as his sons through Jesus Christ, in accordance with his pleasure and will" (Eph. 1:4–5 NIV). God's eternal decree for our salvation is not subject to revision.

Therefore, the idea is not that his people were chosen, later discarded, and then rechosen, but rather that God will again manifest the benefits of their election, which had been hidden during the season of their chastisement. God assures the Jews that they were not forsaken after all, even though he sent a generation and more of his people into bondage. He was waiting for them on the other side with open arms, to choose them again, as it were. So, too, God hides his face from us when we drift into sin. Even God's elect children will not know the benefits of salvation if they wander into sin. Yet he is waiting, ready to embrace all his own as the father embraced the prodigal son in Jesus' parable (Luke 15:11–32), and to assure us of the unbreakable bond of love that holds all believers fast to him.

If we put verse 17 together, we see that when God undertakes a building project, it prospers with great abundance: "Thus says the LORD of hosts: My cities shall again overflow with prosperity, and the LORD will again comfort Zion and again choose Jerusalem." This shows that one does not lose out on life by becoming a Christian! Especially, those blessed with the comfort of spiritual assurance are rich indeed. What a precious promise this holds for Christians who have backslidden, and, accordingly, have seen their lives demolished the way Jerusalem was demolished by the Babylonians. The dominant word is "again," which appears four times in the Hebrew text of this verse. God is able to redo what has been undone. He says, "Proclaim *again*, My cities will *again* overflow, the Lord will *again* comfort Zion and *again* choose Jerusalem." It is hard to imagine a stronger invitation for those who have fallen away to come back to God's mercies and again receive his presence, to again be built up and be blessed again.

FOUR HORNS AND FOUR CRAFTSMEN

The fifth and final item in Zechariah's great call to return to God is one that suitably finishes God's offer of salvation. Let's review what God has promised so far: first, God offers mercy to receive sinners who repent; second, he promises to dwell among his people, living in our hearts by the Holy Spirit just as his temple restored his presence to Jerusalem; third, God says he will build us up in godliness; and, fourth, the blessing of prosperity will come to those who trust in him, bringing not only worldly provision but the priceless comfort of spiritual assurance. What more could we desire, except that he should assure us of his protection, his power preserving us from every foe. It is with this fifth blessing—*God's promise of protection*—that a second vision completes the message of chapter 1. Zechariah informs us, "And I lifted my eyes and saw, and behold, four horns! And I said to the angel who talked with me, 'What are these?' And he said to me, 'These are the horns that have scattered Judah, Israel, and Jerusalem'" (Zech. 1:18–19).

The visions of Zechariah often involve bizarre imagery that is difficult to understand. So it is with this second vision, yet the message is not far beneath the surface, which explains why the angel offers no interpretation.

The image of a horn is a symbol for earthly power. The idea apparently comes from domestic livestock, where the strongest animals are those with large horns. Thus, lifting up the horn became a symbol for pride and arrogant self-assertion. In the vision of Daniel 7, this kind of imagery represented nations rising up against God and his purposes (Dan. 7:15–28). Zechariah's second vision fits this pattern, and it makes sense that these horns also represent kings and other powers. It could be that they signify specific rulers, or that, as in Daniel's visions, the horns present a history of world empires. Probably, however, it is better to see them as representing all four directions of the map, from which opposition and oppression came to scatter the Jews.

We can see how this interpretation fits into the logic of chapter 1, because the Jews would remember their earlier defeats at the hands of such powers. This is something Christians have to worry about as well. "Yes," you reason, "God may show me mercy when I come back to him, and he may indwell me by his Spirit, and he may build me up and bless me—but all that can come crashing down if I am overcome by my great enemies—the world, the flesh, and the devil—as I have been before!" This was the point made to Zechariah by this vision: As the angel said, "These are the horns that have scattered Judah, Israel, and Jerusalem" (Zech. 1:19).

What is God's remedy to the threats and dangers that come against his people? The answer follows: "Then the LORD showed me four craftsmen. And I said, 'What are these coming to do?' He said, 'These are the horns that scattered Judah, so that no one raised his head. And these have come to terrify them, to cast down the horns of the nations who lifted up their horns against the land of Judah to scatter it'" (Zech. 1:20–21).

Despite the odd imagery, the meaning is evident. Yes, there are these horns, these powers that defeated Judah before and that terrify Israel now. But God has his own remedy: the four craftsmen whose hammers can terrify the horns and grind them into powder.

All through this chapter the dominant theme is the sovereign power of God. Nine times God is called by the name "Lord of Hosts." The horsemen in the first vision portray the meaning of this name perfectly: he is the Lord of the mounted hosts of heaven. This second vision offers another expression of his might, namely, that God has the answer to every kind of threat that may arise against his people.

The word "craftsmen" speaks of all sorts of artisans: carpenters and stonemasons and metalworkers. The emphasis is not on their particular skills, but their destructive power to tear down. I am reminded here of the child's game of paper, scissors, rock. Yes, God says, you are like paper, and these scissors may cut you up at any time. But here I have this rock in my hand, and it is a hammer that shatters your enemy so that he troubles you no more. This is the point God makes to Zechariah and to us: he is able to overthrow every enemy who threatens our salvation.

This has been true throughout history. God has always provided what is needed to protect and preserve his church. When there were great heresies, he lifted up valiant teachers of truth. When there was oppression, he made the blood of the martyrs the seed of future converts. The same is true for us individually. The craftsmen of this vision remind us of what God said through Jeremiah: "Is not my word like fire, declares the LORD, and like a hammer that breaks the rock in pieces?" (Jer. 23:29). God's Word, the Bible, is our ever-sufficient weapon in battle, both corporately for the church and individually for every Christian, capable of knocking down every upraised horn. Paul writes: "For the weapons of our warfare are not of the flesh but have divine power to destroy strongholds. We destroy arguments and every lofty opinion raised against the knowledge of God, and take every thought captive to obey Christ" (2 Cor. 10:4–5). This same Word—this hammer—that is so useful for building us up spiritually is equally useful in battle with every spiritual foe.

GOD CAN MAKE IT RIGHT!

The billboard mentioned at the beginning of this chapter said, "If you think you can't make it right, you're wrong." This invitation calls wayward sinners to come back to God, though the church that paid for the ad might say you are called back to the church and the priests and the sacraments. It is, in fact, important to understand this rightly. On the one hand, *you* cannot make it right when you fall into sin. For that matter, neither can the church by itself make it right, nor can the priests and the sacraments by themselves do you any good. None of these earthly powers and institutions and people really can make right what our sin has made wrong. But there is One who can make it right. Indeed, we might improve the billboard by having it say, "*You* may not be able to make things right, but *the God of grace* can." He abounds with power to save, through faith in the Savior Jesus Christ.

Some might object that what we see in this passage from Zechariah is not about us, that this is just a program for a long-distant city, a long time ago. In reply, we might turn to the eighth chapter of Romans, where Paul applies Zechariah's five salvation principles to the Christian, and even does so in precisely the same sequence.

Where does Romans 8 begin but with *the mercy of God* that was promised in Zechariah: "There is therefore now no condemnation for those who are in Christ Jesus" (Rom. 8:1). The reason for this freedom from sin's condemnation is the mercy of God through the cross, which takes away our sin. Paul proceeds to a lengthy discussion of *God's indwelling Spirit,* summed up in Romans 8:9, "You, however, are not in the flesh but in the Spirit, if in fact the Spirit of God dwells in you." What, then, about *building*? Romans 8:28 says, "We know that for those who love God all things work together for good, for those who are called according to his purpose." What about *the blessing of prosperity*? Romans 8:32 says, "He who did not spare his own Son but gave him up for us all, how will he not also with him graciously give us all things?" Like Zechariah, Paul considers the assurance of salvation to be the greatest prosperity of all. He asks, "Who is to condemn? Christ Jesus is the one who died—more than that, who was raised—who is at the right hand of God, who indeed is interceding for us" (Rom. 8:34). Finally, lest we should fear for the security of all these abundant blessings, Paul ends with words that virtually translate the message of *God's promised protection* found in Zechariah's second vision:

> Who shall separate us from the love of Christ? Shall tribulation, or distress, or persecution, or famine, or nakedness, or danger, or sword? As it is written, "For your sake we are being killed all the day long; we are regarded as sheep to be slaughtered." No, in all these things we are more than conquerors through him who loved us. For I am sure that neither death nor life, nor angels nor rulers, nor things present nor things to come, nor powers, nor height nor depth, nor anything else in all creation, will be able to separate us from the love of God in Christ Jesus our Lord. (Rom. 8:35–39)

This is the same salvation God set before the eyes of the prophet Zechariah, and the salvation our Bibles present to us today. It is an offer to every repenting sinner of mercy from God, and it leads to a perfectly secure salvation filled to the brim with every spiritual blessing.

Will you come to God through Christ, who died for you? Will you come back to him if you have strayed and are burdened down with sins? If you will come, God says to you, "I will return with mercy, I will build my house in you, I will construct, and I will bless. And I will protect all that is mine so that you fear no more. What you cannot make right I will," he says with boundless grace. That doesn't mean you won't have struggles—you will. But if you hold fast to God through faith in Christ, you will possess a salvation that begins with no condemnation because of his mercy and concludes with no separation because of God's eternal, all-conquering love.

4

THE CITY WITHOUT WALLS

Zechariah 2:1–5

Behold, the angel who talked with me came forward, and another
angel came forward to meet him and said to him, "Run, say to
that young man, 'Jerusalem shall be inhabited as villages without
walls, because of the multitude of people and livestock in it. And I
will be to her a wall of fire all around, declares the LORD, and I
will be the glory in her midst.' " (Zech. 2:3–5)

*T*he book of Zechariah is focused mainly on the city of Jerusalem.
The prophet was one of those who returned to Jerusalem in 538
BC to restore the city after its desolation some fifty years earlier at
the hands of Nebuchadnezzar of Babylon. They had not come to reestablish
the nation of Israel or the Davidic monarchy, but rather to restore what had
for four hundred years been at the center of Jewish life: the city of Jerusalem.

Jerusalem's significance goes back far into Old Testament times. Since
David's establishment of the city as Israel's capital and home to the ark of the
covenant in the tenth century BC, and especially after the construction of
Solomon's temple on Mount Zion, the city was the spiritual center of God's
people. God dwelt at Jerusalem, and there the people came to worship. But

as the record of prophets such as Isaiah and Jeremiah shows, a false sense of security arose over time. The people came to believe that no matter how great their sins were, Jerusalem—as God's city—would never fall. The events of 586 BC changed all that. God allowed Jerusalem's walls to be breached, the giant stones of the temple toppling as the city and its people fell to the sword.

This experience might have led to a decline in the spiritual importance of the city. One scholar writes, "The events of history had thoroughly demonstrated the falseness of any belief in [Jerusalem's] invulnerability, and the prophets had already explained the inadequacy of such a belief. . . . If anything new was to come out of that devastating experience, presumably it ought to have been a theology and practice that de-emphasized Jerusalem, since it had been the site of their greatest failure."[1] But the prophets labored hard to keep the people from losing interest in the city of God. Isaiah, for instance, spoke to the generation that would return with words like these: "Awake, awake, put on your strength, O Zion; put on your beautiful garments, O Jerusalem, the holy city" (Isa. 52:1).

From the perspective of the New Testament, we see why the theme of the holy city was so important, because it pointed to something greater to come: the New Testament church and the eternal city of God that is in heaven. Thus Abraham is a model of faith because "he was looking forward to the city with foundations, whose designer and builder is God" (Heb. 11:10). Hebrews 12:22 tells the early Christians, "You have come to Mount Zion and to the city of the living God" (Heb. 12:22). The city of Jerusalem was not an end in itself, but it was an important means that God wanted restored and a model for God's future work in the church.

GOD'S PERSPECTIVE ON THE CHURCH

God spoke to Zechariah about the city of Jerusalem in the third vision given to the prophet in 520 BC. The first vision is recorded in 1:7–17, in which God promises to return to Jerusalem to build and to bless. The second occurs in 1:18–21 and is an assurance of God's ability to overcome those who threaten to attack and scatter his people. The first is a vision of blessing; the second is one of security.

1. Donald E. Gowan, *Eschatology in the Old Testament* (Edinburgh: T&T Clark, 1986), 8.

The third vision picks up on a statement made in the first vision about God's plans to build up the city: "The measuring line shall be stretched out over Jerusalem" (1:16). In chapter 2 we meet the man with the measuring line: "And I lifted my eyes and saw, and behold, a man with a measuring line in his hand! Then I said, 'Where are you going?' And he said to me, 'To measure Jerusalem, to see what is its width and what is its length'" (Zech. 2:1–2).

There are a variety of opinions regarding the identity of this man with the measuring line. Most commentators see him as one of the many angelic messengers who populate Zechariah's visions. The point of the measuring line is that Jerusalem, so desolate and ruined in Zechariah's time, would be built up so as to be inhabited.

There is another view, however, that makes good sense in the context of this third vision. Elizabeth Achtemeier sees this figure with the measuring line as a visionary symbol of human expectations for the city, a measurement of the width and length of Jerusalem according to human reckoning. She writes: "This man has believed the prophet's message that Jerusalem will be rebuilt, but he expects the new Jerusalem to be no different from the old, and he would therefore conform its measurements to those it had before its fall."[2]

This view makes sense because of what happens next: "And behold, the angel who talked with me came forward, and another angel came forward to meet him and said to him, 'Run, say to that young man, "Jerusalem shall be inhabited as villages without walls, because of the multitude of people and livestock in it"'" (Zech. 2:3–4). Here the human perspective is corrected by God's perspective on the city. With great urgency, the angel is sent to stop the man measuring for the wall he assumed would be built.

This presents a point that should be well taken by us today. From what source are we to get our perspective on the church and on ourselves as Christians? What should provide our vision and aspirations and expectations regarding ourselves as God's people? There really are only two choices: we will gain our perspective either from man or from God.

If we are to take our view of the church from man, we might listen to the measurements of the world—perhaps the sociological surveys that are so common today. They tell us how many of us are getting divorced, what beliefs

2. Elizabeth Achtemeier, *Nahum—Malachi* (Atlanta: John Knox, 1986), 116.

42

are popular, and so on. At best these tell us only what *is* but not what *ought* to be. Looking at these surveys we often feel the way Zechariah did as he surveyed the toppled ruins of a once-glorious Jerusalem. The situation seems worse all the time, with little hope for improvement. Indeed, whenever we view the church through human yardsticks, as the man with the measuring line was doing to Jerusalem in Zechariah's vision, we end up limiting God by our meager, worldly appraisal of what can be achieved.

Zechariah's vision reminds us that we need our measuring line to be corrected and controlled by God's measurements. It is to him that we must turn for a vision of the church, both in terms of what it ought to be and what it will be. Specifically, it is from the Bible that we learn what the church really is, what its expectations should be, and what God intends to do in and through the church. The church is "the shoot I have planted," God says, "the work of my hands, for the display of my splendor" (Isa. 60:21 NIV). The church is the beloved bride of Christ (Rev. 21:9), the body of Christ (1 Cor. 12:12), the flock over which God is shepherd, precious to him and purchased with Christ's blood (Acts 20:28), in which God intends to display his manifold wisdom to the heavenly realms (Eph. 3:10).

What is true of the church is also true of us as individuals. Our expectations for ourselves, derived from the world, are far lower than those of God. We want to be comfortable, happy, secure. But God intends for us to bear and reflect his own glory forever, and that is why he refines our character and faith in trials and tribulations.

GOD'S VISION FOR THE CHURCH

If this prophecy tells us that the human perspective must be overruled by God's perspective, it also gives God's vision for his city. We learn this from the angel who gave instructions to the angel who served as interpreter for Zechariah: "Run, say to that young man, 'Jerusalem shall be inhabited as villages without walls, because of the multitude of people and livestock in it'" (Zech. 2:4).

This is a great description of the church: "a city without walls." The most immediate meaning has to do with the sheer abundance of people and provisions God intends for this city. He does not envision a modest enterprise, easily encompassed by walls. Literally, the angel says the city will be "as an unwalled village" because of the expanse of her people and beasts. The idea is that of an ever-growing urban sprawl, the way our cities today keep growing outward.

Some commentators argue that this prophecy has never found a literal, earthly fulfillment and therefore must point to some future time, perhaps in national Israel or in a millennial age after Christ's return. I would respond by pointing out that the basic idea was fulfilled in the years following Zechariah, for the rebuilt Jerusalem did indeed lead to a reestablished nation, one that grew and prospered as Zechariah could barely have hoped. But this vision of expansion is ultimately fulfilled in the church.

Think of the age of the apostles. Jesus sent them first to preach in Jerusalem, but he directed them to go outward from there, to be his witnesses "in all Judea and Samaria, and to the end of the earth" (Acts 1:8). This is exactly what happened; the book of Acts records the expansion of the gospel out from the Jews to the God-fearing Gentiles, and then to the Samaritans, and finally to the pagan Gentiles and across the ancient world to Rome itself. This is the very thing the angel showed Zechariah—an ever-spreading city of God—and today that city has expanded to every continent on the earth.

This vision forcefully confronts us if we are pessimistic about the success of the gospel. It is easy for us to think of the church as beleaguered, to see ourselves as a weak and besieged city, and therefore to become inward-focused and even pessimistic. But God tells us, as he told Zechariah, that his city will be vast because of the multitudes brought in. We are engaged in the gospel labor, in a giant divine enterprise that is designed, as God said to Abraham, to bring blessing to all the peoples of the earth (Gen. 12:3). That must have been a staggering thought to Zechariah, part of the small and weak remnant that had returned to reestablish the broken city. Like us, the prophet needed God to lift his eyes above his present struggles to see God's own vision for his own city. Elizabeth Achtemeier writes: "So few seem to take the word to heart, and the body of Christ appears so weak over against the powers and propaganda of the world. But here is another picture: God's redeemed crowding the streets of the new Jerusalem, bursting out beyond the city limits and covering the surrounding hills as the sand covers the seashore."[3]

3. Ibid., 117.

The most obvious meaning of this description is numerical expansion, but surely this idea of a city without walls speaks to the character of the church as well. We are a city, yes—we have a certain society with our own culture, our own way of speaking and acting. We should not be troubled by that. Yet ours is a city without walls, that is, without needless barriers, open to all who will come, inviting to those who would inquire. The church is to be the farthest thing from a secret or closed society; instead, we are a city without walls, freely sharing our secrets and inviting all to come in.

Isn't this what we find in the age of the apostles? Israel had been a city *with* walls. This is what things like the food restrictions and circumcision and prohibitions on table fellowship were all about. As we read Acts and the Epistles we find all of these temporary regulations abolished as the church spread outward into the world, openly inviting all who would come. In the greatest contrast to walled Judaism, Paul writes, "Here there is not Greek and Jew, circumcised and uncircumcised, barbarian, Scythian, slave, free; but Christ is all, and in all" (Col. 3:11).

This is the way it must be today as well. All must feel free to come, be welcomed, and feel loved. Yes, they must hear God's message of Jesus Christ as the only Savior from sin, but there must be no barrier save that of their own unbelief, and that must be powerfully confronted with both God's Word and God's grace as they are found in the church.

GOD'S PRESENCE IN HIS CITY

This vision begs a question that would have been obvious in Zechariah's time. If the city had no walls, what would protect it from the hostile forces outside? The answer is stunning in its simplicity and power. God says, "I will be to her a wall of fire all around" (Zech. 2:5).

Jerusalem had had a great wall before, but that did not keep her from destruction. Walls alone never provide real protection. That is not just true spiritually, but militarily as well. As Genghis Khan is said to have remarked, it is not the stoutness of the walls but the spirit of the defenders that determines the strength of a city. This reality was not lost on Zechariah. Achtemeier writes of this vision, "Lying at the young man's feet are the stones and rubble of the old walls that furnished no protection. Zechariah projects that picture into a lesson for the future: The only sure defense for Israel

45

is God himself, who will be like a wall of fire round about his people."[4] We are intended to recall the pillar of fire that guided Israel through the exodus; so shall God always be for his church, even surrounding us with his almighty presence.

This is why it is the greatest folly for Christians to rely on worldly sources of protection and strength. The Old Testament made this point over and over. Whenever Israel's king sought worldly power instead of God's favor, he was invariably defeated. But when the people humbled themselves before God in prayer, the Lord himself came to their defense. God always says to his people what he said to that faithful king, Jehoshaphat: "Stand firm, hold your position, and see the salvation of the LORD. . . . Do not be afraid and do not be dismayed. . . . The LORD will be with you" (2 Chron. 20:17).

Think of all the walls we Christians tend to erect around our lives, none of which offers the kind of security only God can give: money, position, romantic relationships, or political leverage. Taking the last example, we are surely allowed to participate in the political process. But instead of bombarding Washington with postcards, we would do better to live out our faith boldly before the world while we seek God's help in fervent prayer. God alone is the protector of his church, and he is an all-sufficient defender. The whole of church history bears this out, for as Jesus told Peter, the gates of hell will not prevail against his church (Matt. 16:18).

But, some will reply, the world may persecute the church. Yes, and God will preserve his church in persecution. Consider the suffering church in the Sudan. One of the war-torn villages there is Chali, which was also one of the first missionary stations in that country, from which the Uduk tribe was thoroughly converted to Christianity. In 1996 Chali was attacked by forces of the Islamic national government. The church was blown apart, Bibles were gleefully torn up, and the pages used to roll cigarettes. Most of the men were killed, some by crucifixion, while the women were taken and abused. All of this was because of their faith in Christ. This may lead some to question God's ability to protect his own. But the Uduks themselves do not question this about God. When rebels recaptured Chali in 2000, the Christians returned, and the first thing they did was rebuild their church.

---

4. Ibid.

There they gather daily to pray and worship God. Of God's sufficiency for them, their pastor, Simon Mamud, remarked, "We have nothing, but we have everything."[5]

God is able to protect and prosper his church in the face of the sword. What about the pen? Can God preserve the church from the assaults of intellectuals and sophisticated unbelief? One man who thought God could not was the French atheist Voltaire, whose writings were so popular during the Enlightenment. He wrote that in fifty years from his time no one would remember Christianity. "In twenty years," he said, "Christianity will be no more. My single hand shall destroy the edifice it took twelve apostles to rear." But twenty years passed and Christianity remained. Voltaire, however, died, and in death even he remembered Christianity. The doctor who attended him records that his last words were these: "I am abandoned by God and man! I will give you half of what I am worth if you will give me six months' life. Then I shall go to hell; and you will go with me. O Christ! O Jesus Christ!" Fifty years after Voltaire's famous boast, the house from which he had assaulted God's church with his pen was the headquarters of the Geneva Bible Society, from which the church was mass-producing and disseminating Bibles.[6]

What God promises for his church he also promises for each of his people. That is why Psalm 121 is such a comfort to every believer. It says in its closing verses: "The LORD will keep you from all evil; he will keep your life. The LORD will keep your going out and your coming in from this time forth and forevermore" (Ps. 121:7–8).

God's presence first means protection, but Zechariah 2:5 goes on to say much more: "I will be to her a wall of fire all around, declares the LORD, and I will be the glory in her midst." Surely Zechariah would think of the return of God's Spirit, his glory, to the temple the people were to be rebuilding in Jerusalem. What a motivation this is for God's people, that God will come to be the glory within his church! We think forward to that final consummation shown to the apostle John at the end of the book of Revelation:

> And he carried me away in the Spirit to a great, high mountain, and showed me the holy city Jerusalem coming down out of heaven from God, having

---

5. "We Have Nothing but We Have Everything," *WORLD* 15.24 (June 17, 2000): 46–48.
6. Cited from James M. Boice, *Psalms*, 3 vols. (Grand Rapids: Baker, 1994), 1:101.

the glory of God, its radiance like a most rare jewel, like a jasper, clear as crystal. . . . And the city has no need of sun or moon to shine on it, for the glory of God gives it light, and its lamp is the Lamb. (Rev. 21:10–11, 23)

Given all that is still to come, how tragic it is when the church exults in mere earthly riches. Like the man in Zechariah's vision, many today have adopted a worldly way of measuring the church. I have heard these measurements aptly referred to as "the ABC's of church success": attendance, buildings, and cash. Is it not true that the first question usually asked a church is, "How many people attend? How many members do you have?" What we ought to ask has to do with what this vision tells us. "Is God present in your church? Is he your glory? Is he the source of your power and your protection, is his Word proclaimed and adored, is God himself your glory and your strength?" That is how the Bible assesses the church, and it is the way we should think as well. Thomas V. Moore puts this especially well:

We learn here the true glory of the Church. It is not in any external pomp or power, of any kind; not in frowning battlements, either of temporal or spiritual pretensions; not in rites and ceremonies, however moss-grown and venerable; not in splendid cathedrals and gorgeous vestments, and the swell of music, and the glitter of eloquence, but in the indwelling glory of the invisible God.[7]

This applies as much to us as individuals as to the church. Jeremiah advises, "Let not the wise man boast in his wisdom, let not the mighty man boast in his might, let not the rich man boast in his riches, but let him who boasts boast in this, that he understands and knows me, that I am the LORD" (Jer. 9:23–24).

GOD'S INVITATION

We have sought *God's perspective* on the church; we have seen *God's vision* for the church; and we have been shown *God's presence* in the church as our protection and glory. In conclusion, we now turn to *God's invitation* to join the church, which is the prophet's own application of this text.

7. T. V. Moore, *Haggai, Zechariah and Malachi* (Edinburgh: Banner of Truth, 1979), 141.

48

We see it in verses 6 and 7: "Up! Up! Flee from the land of the north, declares the Lord. For I have spread you abroad as the four winds of the heavens, declares the Lord. Up! Escape to Zion, you who dwell with the daughter of Babylon."

In our next study we are going to look at these verses that form part of the conclusion to chapter 2, but as an application of our passage their meaning is clear. After all the wonderful things God has said about his church, this city that neither has nor needs any walls, he now invites everyone to come for salvation. By this, he does not merely mean that you should seek an affiliation with some particular church, although perhaps you should, but that you should come to him and therefore to his city. There, you should join in the everlasting communion of all the redeemed through faith in the Savior God has sent.

If you are not a Christian, if you have not come to God in faith, God invites you to come out of the world and into his city. Yes, he acknowledges, this world and all it stands for seem so strong according to man's measuring line, its glory so glittering, its rewards so sweet. As Paul writes in 1 Corinthians, however, "this world in its present form is passing away" (7:31 NIV), but the city of God will last forever. Indeed, in the day of God's judgment all that is exalted will be cast down; all wickedness, all that is opposed to him, will be judged. God calls you to come, having sent his Son Jesus to die on the cross that your sins might be forgiven and to rise again from the dead as the cornerstone of God's new city. Jesus Christ invites you into that city of refuge, where he is Shepherd and Savior and King.

The invitation of Zechariah 2:6–7 is especially addressed to those Israelites still living in Babylon, who had comfortably settled down in exile and may have forgotten their true citizenship. How great a danger this poses to worldly believers today! If you are a Christian, then you must love God's church, the city in which you hold eternal citizenship. You must make God alone your glory, the joy of the Lord your strength. You must offer all that you are and have to him, and to his great redemptive work through the gospel of Jesus Christ. This is what will last forever, long after every earthly fortress has fallen, and so we offer ourselves to God for the building of his city.

Through faith in Christ we have membership now in the city that is to come, the true church of God. Though now we see that city only by faith, the day will come when it will fill our sight and we will live there forever. Of it we are told:

The throne of God and of the Lamb will be in it, and his servants will worship him. They will see his face, and his name will be on their foreheads. And night will be no more. They will need no light of lamp or sun, for the Lord God will be their light, and they will reign forever and ever. . . . Blessed are those who wash their robes, so that they may have the right to the tree of life and that they may enter the city by the gates. (Rev. 22:3–5, 14)

5

THE TWO CITIES

Zechariah 2:6–13

"Sing and rejoice, O daughter of Zion, for behold, I come and I will dwell in your midst," declares the LORD. "And many nations shall join themselves to the LORD in that day, and shall be my people. And I will dwell in your midst, and you shall know that the LORD of hosts has sent me to you." (Zech. 2:10–11)

One of the great literary works in the history of the church is Saint Augustine's *City of God*. In it Augustine described the world and history according to two great cities, the City of Man and the City of God. He wrote: "Two societies have issued from two kinds of love. Worldly society has flowered from a selfish love which dared to despise even God, whereas the communion of saints is rooted in a love of God, even to contempt of self. . . . The one lifts up its head in its own boasting; the other says to God: 'Thou art my glory, thou liftest up my head' (Ps. 3:3)."[1] There are many different human societies, just as there are many languages, cultures, ways of dress, and so forth. Nonetheless, Augustine observed: "There exist

---

1. Augustine, *City of God*, trans. Walsh, Zema, Monahan, Honan (New York: Doubleday, 1958), XIV.28.

no more than the two kinds of society, which according to our Scriptures, we have rightly called the two cities. One city is that of men who live according to the flesh. The other is of men who live according to the spirit."[2]

Augustine's analysis is thoroughly biblical. The Bible presents two cities, or kingdoms, in conflict: one destined for condemnation and eternal destruction and the other destined for glory and eternal life. This is the background for Zechariah's visionary message, as it speaks of Babylon and Jerusalem. The prophet writes: "Up! Up! Flee from the land of the north, declares the LORD.... Up! Escape to Zion, you who dwell with the daughter of Babylon" (Zech. 2:6–7).

These two cities—Jerusalem and Babylon—symbolize the spiritual realms of which Saint Augustine wrote. One stands for the city of God's favor and the other for the city of God's wrath. All through the Bible, Jerusalem stands for the City of God and Babylon for the city of the world. The book of Revelation, most notably, uses Babylon as a symbol for the sinful world order that is opposed to God and that is destroyed by him in the final judgment (see Rev. 14–18).

JUDGMENT ON THE CITY OF MAN

God's visions to Zechariah continue with a command for God's people to flee from the land of the north—that is, from the region of Babylon where they had been living. God had exiled the Israelites there as a punishment for sin, but now he planned to restore them to their home. Therefore, the people should leave the comfort they had achieved in Babylon to embrace the challenges of rebuilding God's city. Zechariah 2:6–9 tells why: a great, coming judgment upon Babylon and the nations. There are two great cities, the City of God and the City of Man, and the latter will be judged and destroyed. Therefore God's messenger says: "Up! Up! Flee from the land of the north, declares the LORD. For I have spread you abroad as the four winds of the heavens, declares the LORD. Up! Escape to Zion, you who dwell with the daughter of Babylon" (Zech. 2:6–7).

The opening words in Hebrew are classified as an interrogative exclamation: "Hoy! Hoy!" This is the kind of thing you say to gain attention, much

---

2. Ibid., XIV.1.

like our expression "Hey!" It is followed by a command for the people to flee the lands of the north where God had earlier sent them. God was going to judge Babylon by striking it, and the people must leave before that happens. Two grounds are given for this judgment. First, God will judge Babylon in order to gain glory for himself, and, second, God will act to vindicate and defend his own people.

God is going to judge Babylon, first, for the sake of his own glory. This idea is expressed in Zechariah 2:8, a verse that contains one of the more difficult translation problems in the book of Zechariah. The English Standard Version puts it, "For thus said the LORD of hosts, after his glory sent me to the nations who plundered you." The contested phrase is "after his glory sent me." The New International Version renders it, "after he has honored me." Literally, the text merely says "after glory" (Hebrew, 'ahar kabod).

This phrase is taken a number of ways by the commentators. Some see the "glory" as referring to the rebuilt temple. Others see this term as referring to God himself. This seems to be the view of the English Standard Version, which refers to God by saying "his glory." The sense is that God is "the glorious One." Meredith Kline argues for this, pointing out that in the previous passage God had referred to himself as "the glory in her midst" (Zech. 2:5). The idea, in this case, would be that God in his glory would accompany the angel in making war on the Babylonians.[3] Another explanation is that kabod, the Hebrew word for "glory," also means "heaviness," so that the meaning is "with great heaviness or urgency he has sent me." But the best explanation is that presented by H. C. Leupold and Thomas McComiskey, that "after" should be rendered "in pursuit of." This reading of the passage fits the context quite well: "In pursuit of glory he has sent me against the nations."

This idea is consistent with the teaching of Scripture elsewhere, that God strikes his enemies in pursuit of, or for the sake of, his own glory. God's judgment on Pharaoh is an example. God said to him, while afflicting Egypt with terrible plagues: "For this purpose I have raised you up, to show you my power, so that my name may be proclaimed in all the earth" (Ex. 9:16). This is the very explanation given by the angel in this vision: "Then you will

---

3. Meredith G. Kline, *Glory in Our Midst: A Biblical-Theological Reading of Zechariah's Night Visions* (Overland Park, KS: Two Age Press, 2001), 79–80.

know that the LORD of hosts has sent me" (Zech. 2:9). God earlier glorified his power in the overthrow of mighty Egypt, and now he glorifies his holiness in his just judgment of Babylon and the other nations who plundered the Jews.

The second reason for God's judgment is his love for his people. God's angel would visit the Babylonians with wrath because "he who touches you [the Jews] touches the apple of his [God's] eye" (Zech. 2:8). We remember that God had sent the Jews into captivity in Babylon and elsewhere; he allowed the destruction of Jerusalem at Nebuchadnezzar's hands as a judgment for their sins. But that does not mean that he would tolerate those who brutalized Jerusalem and its citizens. Far from it! Instead, God himself will seek vengeance for all the vindictive harm done to his people.

Judgment is often presented in Scripture as a reversal of fortune for the wicked. So it is here. The charge against Babylon and the nations is that they had plundered. In judging them, therefore, God says, "Behold, I will shake my hand over them, and they shall become plunder for those who served them" (Zech. 2:9). This is the same kind of judgment about which we read in the book of Revelation, when God's final judgment comes upon the wicked of the earth. There the angels praise him for his justice: "For they have shed the blood of saints and prophets, and you have given them blood to drink. It is what they deserve!" (Rev. 16:6). God's judgment in Zechariah's day meant a great reversal of fortune on those who harmed his people, and it will mean the same in the return of Jesus Christ.

It is wonderful to read that God himself will vindicate his people, and even more to see them referred to as "the apple of his eye." The Israelites had been placed in exile because of their sin, they had been cast out of God's holy city and spread among the nations, and yet all the while God remembered them. He cherished them, he kept his eye upon them, and all that time they were "the apple of his eye."

This phrase appears elsewhere in the Old Testament, always as an expression of God's tender and fervent affection for his covenant people. "The LORD's portion is his people, Jacob his allotted heritage," Moses wrote. Speaking of Jacob, he said, "he encircled him, he cared for him, he kept him as the apple of his eye" (Deut. 32:9–10). What a statement of God's faithful grace that even in exile for sin Israel remained that to him! God allowed the nations to place their hands on his beloved people, yet all the while God readied himself for the day of vengeance and deliverance. The angel explains why to Zechariah: "For whoever touches you touches the apple of his eye" (Zech. 2:8). David Baron applies this to us:

> In this tender love and faithfulness of Jehovah to His unworthy Israel, you may see a picture of His unchangeable love and faithfulness to you also; for if you have learned to put your trust under the shadow of His wings, and in Christ have been brought into covenant relationship with Him, then you are loved of Him with the same love with which He loves His only-begotten Son, and are as dear and indispensable to Him as the dearest member of your body can be to you. You may therefore apply this figure also to yourself individually, and pray with David, "Keep me as the apple of Thine eye; Hide me under the shadow of Thy wings" (Ps. 17:8).[4]

How will this judgment of the wicked happen? The angel explains, "Behold, I will shake my hand over them" (Zech. 2:9). The manner in which the judgment comes will prove it to be the Lord's work. H. C. Leupold elaborates:

> The Angel of the Lord will not need to toil at subduing His foes. It will be only a matter of waving His hand. He merely indicates by a gesture what He wills, and it is done. Such is His omnipotence. As a result, those who had been the victors now become a spoil to those who had served them as Israel had. If the status of nations is radically altered with such ease, surely that is "glory."[5]

SALVATION FOR THE CITY OF GOD

We are considering the character and fate of these two different cities, the one of which is set apart for judgment. The vision then turns our eyes to Jerusalem and tells us of a great salvation for the City of God. The downcast Jerusalem of Zechariah's time will shout and rejoice over their spiritual blessings, the most important of which is the renewed presence of the Lord in their midst. This is the angel's exhortation to the people in light of God's coming: "Sing and rejoice, O daughter of Zion, for behold, I come and I will dwell in your midst, declares the LORD" (Zech. 2:10).

4. David Baron, *The Visions and Prophecies of Zechariah* (Grand Rapids: Kregel, 1972), 75.
5. H. C. Leupold, *Exposition of Zechariah* (Grand Rapids: Baker, 1981), 59–60.

Always, the chief and greatest blessing is not the gift of God but God himself. God's promised return was surely intended to revive efforts to rebuild God's temple, which would again represent God in the midst of his people.

But the scope of blessing would reach beyond the people of Israel. The angel continued, "And many nations shall join themselves to the LORD in that day, and shall be my people" (Zech. 2:11). Here we see the prophetic vision racing forward, beyond the horizon of Zechariah's time, to that day when the city without walls would expand outward into the earth, as the nations are drawn by the gospel to God and his salvation.

Verse 12 wonderfully adds that then "the LORD will inherit Judah as his portion in the holy land, and will again choose Jerusalem." This is when God will reap what he looked for all along in his dealings with the Jews. It was always his intention to receive as his own portion not just one tribe out of the sea of nations, but the nations themselves, in voluntary submission before his throne. "Many nations shall join themselves to the LORD in that day, and shall be my people" (Zech. 2:11), the angel said, and this is when God's portion will be realized. This is when Jerusalem will become all she was originally intended to be: the home of believers from all nations, all those washed and made clean in the blood of the Lamb and beloved of God. Because of this gathering of nations, the angels will sing of this forever in heaven, giving glory to God: "For you alone are holy. All nations will come and worship you" (Rev. 15:4). The Lord receives the firstfruits of this as Christian churches draw people from all tribes and tongues and nations to worship him even now. Paul said that Jesus has torn down the divisions of the world by his cross, "that he might create in himself one new man" (Eph. 2:15). How it glorifies God today when men and women with little else in common join as one people in the church to worship and serve the Lord through Jesus Christ!

CHRIST THE LORD

It is impossible to continue studying with these verses and to take seriously the specific statements they contain without pointing out that at the center of this vision is the Lord Jesus Christ.

As we follow the flow of this second chapter of Zechariah, it seems evident that the speaker of these oracles is the angel of the Lord we met in the first vision (1:11). Chapter 2 opens with a vision of a man with a measuring line. The interpreter angel is summoned by another angel and told to intervene. That other angel who begins speaking is surely the angel of the Lord who earlier appeared as the rider on the red horse and the chief of the hosts of heaven. He begins speaking in Zechariah 2:4, and it makes the most sense to understand that he is still speaking in these verses which run to the end of the chapter. After all, whom else would God send to wreak his vengeance but the commander of his mounted host of war?

In our study of the first vision I stated my opinion that this angel of the Lord is the preincarnate Christ, the second person of the Godhead before he took on human flesh and was given the name Jesus. These verses in chapter 2 support this interpretation in a most compelling manner.

Notice, for instance, the way the activity and speech of the angel and that of the Lord become essentially one in this vision. "I will shake my hand over them," says the angel, "and they shall become plunder for those who served them. Then you will know that the LORD of hosts has sent me" (Zech. 2:9). This deification of the angel of the Lord becomes even stronger when speaking of the return of the Lord to his people: "Sing and rejoice, O daughter of Zion, for behold, I come and I will dwell in your midst, declares the LORD. . . . I will dwell in your midst, and you shall know that the LORD of hosts has sent me to you" (Zech. 2:10–11). Here, the one who will come to dwell amidst the people is "the LORD," yet he is also the one whom "the LORD of hosts has sent." The same situation pertains to the ingathering of the nations: "And many nations shall join themselves to the LORD in that day, and shall be my people" (Zech. 2:11). The speaker is the one who is sent by "the LORD of hosts," that is, the angel of the Lord who speaks in Zechariah's vision. The people who are joined to the Lord will be his people.

Here we have an example of how the Old Testament cannot be reckoned with apart from the Trinity. We have two participants who are both referred to and exercise the rights of "the LORD"—One who sends and One who is sent. This strongly argues the identity of the angel as the preincarnate Jesus Christ. The data of this passage virtually demand two figures capable of the name "LORD of hosts." According to the New Testament, Jesus Christ is this only One who is sent by God and is also God himself. He is Jehovah Jesus, Christ "the Lord."

Moreover, this vision previews the redemptive program Christ would accomplish on the Father's behalf. He says, "I come and I will dwell in your midst" (Zech. 2:10). This is precisely what happened in the incarnation of Jesus Christ: "The Word became flesh," John tells us, "and dwelt among us" (John 1:14). And it was this same angelic legion we saw mounted in Zechariah 1, surely, who broke into the night sky above the shepherds in Bethlehem's fields to acclaim the birth of their Lord and ours (Luke 2:13–14). It was in the birth of the Christ-child, an event more splendid by far than the building of the temple, that God came to dwell among his people.

The promise of Zechariah 2:11 is also fulfilled in the coming of Christ. It is the fruit of his work that "many nations shall join themselves to the LORD in that day, and shall be my people." Indeed, it is only in Christ and his church that any semblance can be given to the fulfillment of this promise. It was at Pentecost, after Christ's death and resurrection, that the nations spoke as one through the Holy Spirit's ministry. It was through the apostles' missionary journeys that the Gentiles were made heirs of the promise and members of God's saving covenant. And it is in the still-ongoing missionary work of the church that many nations are joined with the Lord to become Christ's people.

The angel continued with a promise that God would be made known through his salvation: "I will dwell in your midst, and you shall know that the LORD of hosts has sent me to you" (Zech. 2:11). This is what Christ's saving work does, even as he said in John 5:36, "For the works that the Father has given me to accomplish, the very works that I am doing, bear witness about me that the Father has sent me."

The vision culminates with the idea of nations joining with the Lord and becoming his own people: "The LORD will inherit Judah as his portion in the holy land, and will again choose Jerusalem" (Zech. 2:12). The reader of the New Testament can hardly help but think as well of the vision of the Christian church as portrayed in the book of Hebrews: "You have come to Mount Zion and to the city of the living God, the heavenly Jerusalem, and to innumerable angels in festal gathering, and to the assembly of the firstborn who are enrolled in heaven, and to God, the judge of all, and to the spirits of the righteous made perfect, and to Jesus, the mediator of a new covenant" (Heb. 12:22–24). If Zechariah marveled at the vision presented by this divine angel-Savior, how much more must we marvel to see its more wonderful fulfillment in the coming of the One who was called Immanuel—"God with us"—even Jesus Christ (Matt. 1:23).

THREE COMMANDS FOR THE PEOPLE OF GOD

The magnitude of these promises must have been staggering to Zechariah's mind, standing amidst the ruins of earthly Jerusalem. The point of this oracle, however, was not merely inspirational but also motivational, and we miss the point if we do not consider the three sets of imperatives included—three commands for the prophet's generation and for our own.

The first command appears at the vision's beginning: "Up! Up! Flee from the land of the north, declares the LORD. . . . Up! Escape to Zion, you who dwell with the daughter of Babylon" (Zech. 2:6–7). The people of God must flee the worldly city, Babylon, since they cannot dwell there without risking participation in its judgment.

John Bunyan's *Pilgrim's Progress* presents this reality in classic form. "Christian" had been reading his Bible, and there he learned of a great judgment to come upon the City of Destruction, where he lived. He was searching for a way of escape when he encountered a man named "Evangelist." Hearing of Christian's fear of judgment, Evangelist inquired as to why he had not yet departed: "If this is your condition, why are you standing still?" Christian replied, "Because I do not know where to go." Then Evangelist gave him a scripture verse, "Flee from the wrath to come" (Matt. 3:7). Evangelist showed Christian the way to the Celestial City, the city of safety and salvation, and Christian began running. His wife and children cried for him to return, so he "put his fingers in his ears and ran crying, 'Life! Life! Eternal life!' " (cf. Luke 14:26).[6] We, too, must flee the City of Man, the City of Destruction. We must reject its standards and repudiate its ways, embracing those of the City of God to which we are fleeing for salvation. Martyn Lloyd-Jones explains: "It should not be our ambition to be as much like everybody else as we can, though we happen to be Christian, but rather . . . our ambition should be to be like Christ, the more like Him the better, and the more like Him we become, the more we shall be unlike everybody who is not a Christian."[7]

The second and more positive command is addressed to those already in God's city: "Sing and rejoice, O Daughter of Zion!" (Zech. 2:10). It was for

6. John Bunyan, *Pilgrim's Progress* (Nashville: Thomas Nelson, 1999), 11.
7. D. Martyn Lloyd-Jones, *Expositions on the Sermon on the Mount*, 2 vols. (Grand Rapids: Eerdmans, 1959), 1:37.

the sake of this second command that the great promises of blessing were given—and surely they were great enough to inspire such rejoicing! God's people, the recipients of so great a salvation, are to be characterized by a correspondingly great joy before the world.

One of the world's chief lies is that if you flee from sin you will lose out and be unhappy. But fleeing the pleasures of sin will not make you unhappy. Quite the opposite: life in God's City is more pleasant than all the carnal joys we leave behind. Believers have the joy of knowing the true and living God. Ours is the joy of redemption: the awareness that we are cherished with a love that is stronger than death. Ours is the joy of being used by God for things that really matter and endure forever. This is the joy spoken of by the prophet Zephaniah, in language similar to that in our text:

> Sing aloud, O daughter of Zion; shout, O Israel! Rejoice and exult with all your heart, O daughter of Jerusalem! The LORD has taken away the judgments against you; he has cleared away your enemies. The King of Israel, the LORD, is in your midst; you shall never again fear evil. On that day it shall be said to Jerusalem: "Fear not, O Zion; let not your hands grow weak. The LORD your God is in your midst, a mighty one who will save." (Zeph. 3:14–17)

Christians will face problems, but there is no problem for which Jesus Christ is not the answer. We will endure trials, but Christ is the balm upon all our wounds. We will know tears, but Christ is the Savior who dries our eyes and answers death with the promise of life. Therefore the apostle Paul could write from his prison cell: "Rejoice in the Lord always; again I will say, Rejoice" (Phil. 4:4).

This chapter of visions concludes with one last command, and it is addressed to the entire creation. It comes in one word in Hebrew: "Hush!" This presents something of a contrast, for verse 10 tells us to shout out in joy, greeting the Lord with the sound of triumph. Yes, but ours is not the boisterous, raucous happiness of the world. Rather, ours is that joy that is compatible with a quiet and gentle spirit, with reverence in worship before a holy throne. "Be silent, all flesh, before the LORD," the angel commands, "for he has roused himself from his holy dwelling" (Zech. 2:13).

Surely this speaks to the character of true worship. The Lord is the focus of what we are doing and we are attentive to him. We are still before the Lord because his activity is what matters and not ours; his Word is what we need to hear and understand, not ours; his presence calms our fears and stills the torrents of our souls as no human therapy ever could. "Be silent before the Lord," says the angel just as Jesus spoke to the tossing waves of the stormy sea: "Peace! Be still."

Zechariah's generation, like ours, was required to choose between two cities and two loves. For them, it must be Babylon or Jerusalem; it could not be both. This is a choice we also must make. "Flee from the wrath to come!" the vision tells us. Let us flee the city of this world and all that it loves. Let us instead come to the City of God, rejoicing with songs in our hearts. And there, in the temple that was built not by hands but by the death and resurrection of Jesus Christ, let us be still before the Lord, worshiping him in the quietness of gladness and peace. Through Jesus Christ, God "has roused himself from his holy dwelling" (Zech. 2:13) to live among us and make us his people forever.

6

THE SINNER'S NEW CLOTHES

Zechariah 3:1–5

Now Joshua was standing before the angel, clothed with filthy garments. And the angel said to those who were standing before him, "Remove the filthy garments from him." And to him he said, "Behold, I have taken your iniquity away from you, and I will clothe you with pure vestments." (Zech. 3:3–4)

There is a great problem that stands in the way of every utopian dream. It corrupts our every program, condemns all our plans, and confounds all our promises. The problem is sin. Sin is the infection that contaminates mankind and corrodes our every vision and destroys our every hope. Sin is also the guilt that mars our splendor, like graffiti on a newly painted wall, or like a new garment that is dragged through an open sewer.

The problem of sin affects not only man's program, but also God's. God, too, has a program. He has plans, he has made promises, and if he is going to fulfill them he is going to have to deal with our sin. This is what we find in the situation of the Jews who had returned to Jerusalem in Zechariah's time. God had providentially placed a friendly ruler on the Persian throne and brought them back to the holy city. In the visions the prophet has received so far, God has spoken of rebuilding, of returning in his glory, and of gathering the nations. It would be the achievement of all that Israel was ever meant to be. But, as we turn to this fourth vision, we find that God has to contend with the great problem of Israel's sin. Even God cannot ignore or brush aside sin, but must find a solution if these visions are to come true.

SATAN, THE ACCUSER

The problem of Israel's sin is symbolized in this vision by a man named Joshua, who was high priest at that time. Joshua is on trial in a most sobering courtroom setting: "Then he showed me Joshua the high priest standing before the angel of the LORD, and Satan standing at his right hand to accuse him" (Zech. 3:1).

Many commentators place this scene either in God's heavenly court or in the unfinished temple on Mount Zion, although the text does not specify. Joshua is "standing before" the angel of the Lord, a phrase often used for one in the performance of priestly duties. That same phrase, however, is also used to describe a judicial proceeding where a man is on trial. It makes sense that Joshua was going about his priestly work when he was suddenly confronted by this accusation of the devil. What began as a ministry ended up as a trial.

Since Joshua is the high priest, we therefore think of him representing the priesthood that had fallen into disrepute in the time of the exile. But since the high priestly office was representative not merely of the other priests but of the people as a whole, it is clear that Joshua also stands there on behalf of the entire nation. The accusation against him is another way of pointing out the unworthiness of the entire people God has promised to save so wonderfully in the preceding visions. Howard Vos puts it succinctly: "The high priest is standing before Jehovah on behalf of the people, and if he is rebuked and cast away, the significance is that the people of Israel would be cast away."[1]

This scene represented a matter that would have been on the minds of the people in Jerusalem. Their nation had fallen in sin. They had been defiled by their sojourn in Babylon and were disgraced in failure through the exile.

---

1. Howard F. Vos, *Zechariah*, unpublished manuscript, p. 17.

What a heavy weight of accumulated guilt they collectively must have borne! They would have been thinking of their sin, corporate and individual, so Joshua's fate would be of intimate concern to them all.

This vision first shows *a picture of Satan as our accuser.* Joshua stood before the angel, with Satan "standing at his right hand to accuse him" (Zech. 3:1). The Hebrew word *Satan* means adversary, and this name makes all too clear the purpose of the devil with regard to both God and man.

Scripture says many things about the devil. He is the deceiver (Gen. 3:4), the tempter (Matt. 4:3), a roaring and devouring lion (1 Peter 5:8), a persecutor of God's people (Rev. 2:10), and a murderer (John 8:44). But one of his most insidious roles is as the accuser of God's people. Here Satan stands beside God's chosen people, the very ones he himself labored to lead into temptation, now acting shocked as he points to the stains of their sins. I should add one description to his resume: Satan is a great actor, and here is one of his best parts, the outraged prosecutor in the courts of God's law.

Accusation is a potent weapon. It deters us in our spiritual work, and surely that is one of Satan's chief goals. It discourages us, as it discouraged Joshua here, with the idea that God will reject our service because of our sin. Mainly, of course, Satan seeks to cut the cords of our faith. "You are no saint," he tells us. "Others may be worthy of God, but surely you are not. Why don't you admit it and quit trying to be so pious? Why don't you just enjoy the pleasures of sin while you can, despairing of salvation?" Satan knows it is our faith that gives us strength and salvation, so just as Delilah put her scissors to Samson's hair, the devil targets his accusations against our faith. Martin Luther, who knew well what it was to be afflicted by the devil, wrote: "That is the way of the devil: he greatly inflates one's sin and magnifies it and makes God's judgments horrible, even as Rev. 12:10 tells us that the old dragon accuses the saints day and night before our God."[2]

The vision continues, "Now Joshua was standing before the angel, clothed with filthy garments" (Zech. 3:3). Imagine how great Joshua's sense of guilt and shame must have been. We know a little about him. He was the rightful high priest of the line of Zadok, of the house of Aaron. He was one of the key leaders of the party that came to reestablish Jerusalem and rebuild the temple. It was he who placed the altar to renew

2. Martin Luther, *Luther's Works*, vol. 20 (St. Louis: Concordia, 1973), 205.

the burnt offerings (Ezra 2:2; 3:2). Therefore Joshua was a man of high standing, so he must have borne this sense of unworthiness very heavily. Every true minister knows what this is like, to draw near to the pulpit only too well aware—no doubt with Satan's help—of his unfitness for so high an office and calling.

Satan seems to have had plenty of evidence to support his accusation. Satan may be a liar, but when it comes to accusing us he has plenty of truth on his side. This is what makes it so pitiful that many scholars seek to imagine what sin it might be that Joshua had committed—perhaps something he had done back in Persia that had been found out, the way our candidates for office fall prey to scandal when they are exposed to scrutiny. But there is no reason to search for some scandalous sin that had just been made public. Surely there were any number of sins Joshua was guilty of, just as is true of us all.

Joshua says nothing in his own defense, his mouth is stopped, nor does the angel of the Lord seek to deny the charges leveled against him. Spurgeon rightly says,

> Truly, dear friend, if Satan wants to accuse us, any page of our history, any hour of any day will furnish him material for his charges. Yesterday you were impatient, the day before you were proud, another day you were slothful, on another angry. Oh, what a den of unclean birds the human heart is! . . . If the old accuser wants reasons for accusation he may indeed find as many as he wills, and continue to accuse as long as ever he pleases, for we are altogether as an unclean thing.[3]

"The Lord Rebuke You!"

Joshua may have had nothing to say, but there was another who had words for the occasion, namely, the angel of the Lord. I have argued in prior chapters that this is none other than the second person of the Deity, the Son of God in preincarnate form. This passage is yet another that designates this angel as "the LORD." As the angel of the Lord speaks, we read: "And *the LORD* said to Satan" (Zech. 3:2). It may be true that we sinners have nothing to say

---

3. Charles Haddon Spurgeon, *Metropolitan Tabernacle Pulpit*, 63 vols. (Carlisle, PA: Banner of Truth, 1973), 11:67.

65

to Satan's accusations, but this angel of the Lord, whom we know as Jesus Christ, can reply on our behalf. And he said to Satan: "The LORD rebuke you, O Satan!" (Zech. 3:2).

What a comfort to see Jesus Christ taking up our defense. He is the One who stands up to Satan's accusations and turns them back upon him—who, as was prophesied, crushes the devil's head and feeds him dust to eat in frustration (Gen. 3:14–15). "The LORD rebuke you," he says, not because we are innocent, but for two reasons that are given here, the first of which is this: "The LORD who has chosen Jerusalem rebuke you!"

Christ rebukes Satan, first, on the basis of God's election. Satan's accusation maligned God's integrity for associating with sinners like this man Joshua. The angel replies with God's election because Israel's standing with God—his promised affection toward them—had never been grounded on their own worth. God would restore and bless his people simply because he had chosen to do so, out of his own sovereign purpose and grace. This is what God had always emphasized to Israel, as Moses explained: "It was not because you were more in number than any other people that the LORD set his love on you and chose you, for you were the fewest of all peoples, but it is because the LORD loves you and is keeping the oath that he swore to your fathers" (Deut. 7:7–8). David Baron comments, "If Israel's position as the Lord's peculiar people depended on their own faithfulness, then there would have been an end of them long ago; but Israel's hope and safety rest on the immutable character and faithfulness of the Everlasting, Unchangeable God, and that makes all the difference."[4]

It had never been because of their righteousness that God accepted his people, but because of his own love and grace. What a great comfort this is to us. Ephesians 1:4–6 says to Christians, "In love he predestined us for adoption through Jesus Christ, according to the purpose of his will, to the praise of his glorious grace." Christ rebukes Satan's accusations against believers on these very grounds: "He chose you because he loved you; and he loved you because he chose you."[5]

---

4. David Baron, *The Visions and Prophecies of Zechariah* (Grand Rapids: Kregel, 1972), 92.
5. Ibid., 93.

This shows us what a difference the doctrines of grace, like election, make in the life of a believing sinner. Instead of our own mouths being shut in guilt, it is Satan's accusing lips that are stopped. Surely Spurgeon was not wrong to point out that when God wants to shut the mouths of devils he preaches to them the doctrines we call Calvinism. He adds: "If God hath chosen his people, then it is of no use for Satan to attempt their overthrow. Christ does not here meet Satan with any 'ifs' and 'buts'. . . . But he meets him with the high mysterious truth which was settled before the world was, he throws as it were this chain into his teeth, and bids him champ that till he breaks his teeth. 'God hath chosen Jerusalem; let that be rebuke enough.' "[6]

We may use this same doctrine to rebuke our own doubts and fears and trepidation about salvation. If God has chosen us—and if we have turned to Jesus Christ in faith it is only because he has chosen us—then that alone is sufficient reply.

There was a second reason for this reproof from the angel of the Lord: "Is not this a brand plucked from the fire?" (Zech. 3:2). What a wonderful and practical description of the church and of every Christian delivered from condemnation. Whenever we see someone in low or mean or wicked conditions, we should think of this: God has saved us as burning sticks snatched from the fire.

God had brought his people back from the bondage in Babylon, out of the fire of his judgment on their sin. What was his intent in that redemption, but that he would go on to save them to the full! If God has shown mercy to Joshua, then surely he means to save him. Thomas McComiskey comments, "If he had wished to let them perish for their sin, the Lord would have left them in Babylon; but by snatching them from the flames of exile, he revealed that his grace was greater than their guilt."[7] How frustrating this must have been to Satan, despite his success in leading Israel into sin. And how comforting this must have been for Israel! The apostle Paul now offers the same comfort to believers in Christ: "He who began a good work in you will bring it to completion at the day of Jesus Christ" (Phil. 1:6). Thereby the devil is effectively rebuked.

6. Spurgeon, 11:67.

7. Thomas E. McComiskey, *The Minor Prophets: An Exegetical and Expository Commentary*, 3 vols. (Grand Rapids: Baker, 1998), 3:1070.

A Picture of Sin Removed

On what grounds can God accept a sinner like Joshua and those he represents? The first answer is that they are chosen and already snatched from the fire. But this still leaves an enormous question that must yet be resolved, namely, *how* God will accept a sinner such as he. After all, as the book of Exodus makes so clear, priests had to be spotlessly clean to enter God's presence; only men in clean and holy garments could ever serve as priests (see Ex. 28–29). So how can God receive this priest in soiled clothes? Zechariah's vision answers with *a picture of sin removed.*

Israel's problem was succinctly summarized in the plight of their high priest: "Now Joshua was dressed in filthy clothes as he stood before the angel" (Zech. 3:3 NIV). Some of the commentators see the dirt as blackened soot from the fire out of which he has come or his ritual contamination from the years spent in Babylon. But the Hebrew word here *(tsoim)* rules out so modest a view, depicting instead the worst sort of physical pollution and sheer filth. It is *sin* that Joshua bears. Joshua is not merely tarnished here and there, but is a veritable sewer of pollution. It is the same idea Isaiah had when he wrote, "All of us have become like one who is unclean, and all our righteous acts are like filthy rags; we all shrivel up like a leaf, and like the wind our sins sweep us away" (Isa. 64:6 NIV). This is how Joshua represents God's people, and this is how each of us actually is in our sins as we stand before the Lord.

How wonderful, then, to read what happens next. The angel of the Lord turned to the other angels in attendance. He commands them, "'Take off his filthy clothes.' Then he said to Joshua, 'See, I have taken away your sin, and I will put rich garments on you'" (Zech. 3:4 NIV). There can hardly be more precious words or a more precious sight than what we are presented with here. Christ takes away Joshua's sin, and this is a picture of our own redemption in Christ.

This vision does not provide a complete theology of redemption—it does not, for instance, depict the shedding of sacrificial blood. But its stunning portrayal of forgiveness and cleansing must have raised marveling questions in Zechariah's day. The answer to those questions can be none other than Jesus Christ. The high priest was the one who offered sacrifices for the sins of God's people. Jesus is the true high priest to whom Joshua in his office merely pointed. Hebrews 9:11–12 explains: "When Christ appeared as a high priest of the good things that have come . . . he entered once for all into the holy places, not by means of the blood of goats and calves but by means of his own blood, thus securing an eternal redemption." A fascinating detail is that in Hebrew, Jesus' name is *Joshua*. He is the Joshua who was to come, who cleansed this earlier Joshua through his own future coming to die as an atonement for sin.

This angel of the Lord could declare, "Behold, I have taken your iniquity away from you" (Zech. 3:4), because in his coming as incarnate Savior he had contracted to do that very thing, taking his people's sin upon himself at the cross. The New Testament explains what happened when Christ finally came and took up the cross: "For our sake [God] made him to be sin who knew no sin, so that in him we might become the righteousness of God" (2 Cor. 5:21). Jesus took our filthy rags and put them on himself, receiving in our place the punishment those sins deserve. Christ says to all who believe, "Behold, I have taken your iniquity away from you." As Paul explains, "He forgave us all our sins . . . he took it away, nailing it to the cross" (Col. 2:13–14 NIV). This is Christ's reply to Satan's accusations. And when our consciences receive Christ's testimony in faith, Satan has nothing left to say against us.

A black spot on the wall of a castle in Germany bears eloquent testimony to this truth. Wartburg Castle is where Martin Luther was taken for refuge after his heroic stand at the Council of Worms. Luther was immensely productive during this period, but he also felt himself suffering at the hands of the devil. He wrote to his friend Philipp Melanchthon on May 24, 1521, about a spiritual depression he had experienced, one in which he dreamed that Satan appeared with a long scroll on which his many sins were written with care, each of them read out one-by-one. All the while Satan mocked his pathetic desire to serve God, assuring him that after all he would end up in hell. Luther writhed in spiritual agony until, at last, he jumped up and cried: "It is all true, Satan, and many more sins which I have committed in my life which are known to God only; but write this at the bottom of your list, 'The blood of Jesus Christ, God's Son, cleanseth us from all sin.'" Then grasping an inkwell from his table, Luther threw it at the devil who thus fled, leaving the black spot on the wall that bears testimony to his deliverance still.[8]

8. Cited from Baron, *Zechariah*, 93–94.

69

This is how we should reply to our fears, to our sense of guilt, and to the accusations of the devil: with the blood of Christ that says to us, "Behold, I have taken your iniquity away from you."

RIGHTEOUSNESS FROM THE LORD

The Bible teaches that it is not enough for us to have our sins forgiven: we also need a righteousness in which to stand before God. Jesus spoke of this in his parable of the wedding feast. When the king came in to greet his guests, "He saw there a man who had no wedding garment" (Matt. 22:11). He had the man tied up and cast outside into the darkness, where "there will be weeping and gnashing of teeth" (Matt. 22:13). John Owen explains the significance of these garments:

> It is not enough to say that we are not guilty. We must also be perfectly righteous. The law must be fulfilled by perfect obedience if we would enter into eternal life. And this is found only in Jesus (Rom. 5:10). His death reconciled us to God. Now we are saved by his life. The perfect actual obedience that Christ rendered on earth is that righteousness by which we are saved. His righteousness is imputed to me so that I am counted as having perfectly obeyed the law myself.[9]

Theologians make the distinction between a righteousness that is *imputed* and one that is *infused*. Many people argue today that distinctions like this are needless and divisive, but they are in fact indispensable. *Infused* righteousness describes a righteousness that is *in* us, so that, however prompted by God's grace, we are justified because we *are* righteous. This is what the Roman Catholic Church teaches, although it is increasingly accepted in many Protestant circles. But notice that this is not the kind of righteousness the angel of the Lord provided to Joshua the high priest.

The angel of the Lord did not *infuse* righteousness—or anything else—into Joshua. He did not give him grace over a certain period of time in which he could clean up his own act. Instead, the Scripture depicts an *imputed* righteousness, a glorious garment that is the gift of God, bestowed by

9. John Owen, *Communion with God* (Edinburgh: Banner of Truth, 1991), 94–95.

abounding grace apart from merit and prior to any moral improvement in the individual. What the angel bestowed was not a righteousness achieved by Joshua but the righteousness of another—what Reformed theologians call an *alien righteousness*—the righteousness of Jesus Christ in all his glorious perfection.

The doctrine of imputed righteousness, as necessary to the Bible's teaching of justification, is not isolated to Zechariah. Isaiah sang of this imputed righteousness with great joy as he contemplated God's gift: "I will greatly rejoice in the LORD; my soul shall exult in my God, for he has clothed me with the garments of salvation; he has covered me with the robe of righteousness" (Isa. 61:10). The apostle Paul explained this in the New Testament, writing: "To the one who does not work but trusts him who justifies the ungodly, his faith is counted as righteousness . . . God counts righteousness apart from works" (Rom. 4:5–6).

When we put these two together—sin removed and righteousness received—we see the benefits that every sinner receives through faith in Jesus Christ. Donald Grey Barnhouse taught this by placing a Bible in his right hand. "This is your sin," he said,

> weighing you down in condemnation. In my other hand we see Christ, who has no such burden of sin. At the cross, He took your sin; by faith all of it is transferred to His account, to be put away in His death. Similarly, we may say this, as I place the Bible in my left hand. Here is the righteousness Christ has, of which you have none. When you trust in Him, God imputes His righteousness to you, clothing you in His own perfect and glorious dress. There is nothing more you could need or want than that. Make sure, therefore, that you are not relying in whole or in part upon any righteousness except that which alone satisfies the demands of God, the perfect righteousness of Christ that He freely gives to all who believe.[10]

HOLY TO THE LORD

What joy this is to behold, the removal of our sin and the gift of perfect righteousness. Amazingly, Zechariah interrupts the vision, spontaneously

10. Donald Grey Barnhouse, *Expositions of Bible Doctrines Taking the Epistle to the Romans as a Point of Departure*, 10 vols. (Grand Rapids: Eerdmans, 1959), 5:88–89.

crying out as he sees the clean garments being placed over Joshua's shoulders. There was one more thing needed: "And I said, 'Let them put a clean turban on his head.' So they put a clean turban on his head and clothed him with garments. And the angel of the LORD was standing by" (Zech. 3:5).

Many commentators puzzle over the significance of this, seeing it as simply the final touch on the glorious outfit. But Exodus 28 tells us of the headpiece worn by the high priest, with the significant feature that a plate was affixed to it. On the plate were these words: "Holy to the LORD." God said, "It shall regularly be on his forehead, that they may be accepted before the LORD" (v. 38). The piece of clothing Zechariah was longing to see put on, therefore, was that which proclaimed the priest (and thus the people) holy and accepted. Without this holy headpiece, Joshua could not hope to offer sacrifices for Zechariah and the other people in the presence of the Lord.

This vision has shown us Satan as our accuser, though rebuked by the grace-wielding angel of the Lord. Secondly, we saw a picture of sin removed, and, thirdly, of righteousness bestowed. The vision comes to completion with this priestly headdress, which symbolizes both our assurance of acceptance and our calling to practical godliness.

These two—assurance and practical godliness—always go together. If you have been forgiven, you are also called to lead a new life. Having been saved from our sin we must therefore walk in righteousness. Jesus taught this to the woman caught in sin, who in so many ways resembles the high priest Joshua of this vision. Just as Joshua was accused by Satan, she had been accused by the Pharisees, whom Jesus rebuked and sent away. After pointing out that her accusers were no longer present to condemn her, Jesus added, "Neither do I condemn you; go, and from now on sin no more" (John 8:11). Having been forgiven, we are to do the same. As Paul commented, "What shall we say then? Are we to continue in sin that grace may abound? By no means! How can we who died to sin still live in it?" (Rom. 6:1–2).

There is no greater comfort, and no stronger incentive to flee the pleasures of sin, than to know ourselves forgiven and safe in God's boundless grace in Christ. "Holy to the LORD," God affixes to his redeemed, both to comfort us with assurance and to charge us to live, as Paul says, in a manner "worthy of the gospel of Christ" (Phil. 1:27).

A GREAT SAVIOR

Perhaps Satan tried to bring down Joshua again. He might have waited for another chance when Joshua's spirits were low, when he had given in to sin, or when trials made him question God's love. Satan does that to us; he lies in wait like a lion in the grass. But surely Joshua knew what to do from this time forward. After this great encounter with his Savior, Satan's arrows would be wasted on Joshua.

The same should be true for us. We can be sure that Satan will find us when we are weak, when we are alone, when we are downcast after failure or proud because of success. He will come to accuse us and say, "You are a very great sinner." It will be true, although he will fail to point out any evidences of God's grace in our lives. "You are a great sinner!" he will say, pointing his finger in shrill outrage.

What will you reply? Will you deny it? Will you defend yourself with empty claims to a righteousness of your own? Or will you turn to the gospel proclaimed by Zechariah, to the Savior sent from God to redeem his people from their sin? "You are a great sinner!" Satan will cry. And, through faith in Christ, you have the privilege to reply: "Yes, I am a great sinner. But Jesus Christ is a greater Savior. I direct you to the cross, where his precious blood was shed for me, and to his perfect life, which is credited to my account before God. And I thank you for reminding me that henceforth I should live for him who has loved me so. For he has placed his name on me, and I am emblazoned in Christ, 'Holy to the LORD.'"

7

A SERVANT, A BRANCH, A STONE

Zechariah 3:6—10

> *Hear now, O Joshua the high priest, you and your friends who sit before you, for they are men who are a sign: behold, I will bring my servant the Branch. For behold, on the stone that I have set before Joshua, on a single stone with seven eyes, I will engrave its inscription, declares the LORD of hosts, and I will remove the iniquity of this land in a single day. (Zech. 3:8–9)*

One of the most important theological distinctions is that between justification and sanctification. It is essential the two not be confused or conflated. Justification is "an act of God's free grace, whereby he pardons all our sins and accepts us as righteous in his sight."[1] This is how the Christian life begins. Sanctification is "the work of God's free grace, whereby we are renewed in the whole man after the image of God, and are enabled more and more to die unto sin, and live unto righteousness."[2] This is how the Christian life proceeds.

---

1. Westminster Shorter Catechism, A. 33.
2. Ibid., A. 35.

It is important that we not confuse or combine justification and sanctification. In justification our faith is passive, receiving and resting on the finished work of Christ to reconcile us to God. We are justified by faith, apart from any works of our own. Paul writes, "To the one who does not work but trusts him who justifies the ungodly, his faith is counted as righteousness" (Rom. 4:5). It is vital that our Christian lives be founded not on our own works to any degree, but only on the saving work of Jesus Christ. J. C. Ryle comments on the harmful tendency of so many Christians to rest their acceptance with God at least in part on the improvement of their souls or on changes that have been made in their lives—that is, on their sanctification. He notes,

> They seem to imbibe the idea that their justification is, in some degree, affected by something within themselves. They do not clearly see that Christ's work, not their own work—either in whole or in part, either directly or indirectly— is the only ground of our acceptance with God: that justification is a thing entirely without us, for which nothing whatever is needful on our part but simple faith, and that the weakest believer is as fully and completely justified as the strongest.[3]

As damaging as it is to fail to distinguish between justification and sanctification, it is no less dangerous to think that one can be had without the other. Therefore, it is necessary that we realize that the new birth that gives us faith always produces both justification and sanctification. R. C. Sproul points out the necessary connection between the two: "If regeneration is real it will always and ever yield faith. If faith is genuine it will always and ever yield justification. If our justification is authentic, it will always and ever yield sanctification. There can be no true justification without real sanctification."[4]

CONDITIONS TO KEEP

Few portions of Scripture so helpfully distinguish and connect the matters of justification and sanctification as the third chapter of Zechariah,

3. J. C. Ryle, *Holiness* (Ross-shire, UK: Evangelical Press, 1979), 113.
4. R. C. Sproul, *The Mystery of the Holy Spirit* (Wheaton, IL: Tyndale, 1990), 123.

which deals with Joshua, the high priest of Israel during the restoration of Jerusalem. We first see him standing in sin-stained clothing before the Lord, with the devil at his side to accuse. Joshua's experience wonderfully illustrates Christ's work both in removing his sin and in clothing him with an imputed righteousness. "Behold," the angel of the Lord says to him, "I have taken your iniquity away from you, and I will clothe you with pure vestments" (Zech. 3:4).

This is a wonderful picture of how justification is accomplished. All this time, Joshua does nothing. He is the recipient of salvation, as Christ (acting here as the angel of the Lord) accomplishes his justification. Yet as the scene continues to unfold, we immediately proceed to sanctification. We hear this charge given to Joshua: "Thus says the LORD of hosts: If you will walk in my ways and keep my charge, then you shall rule my house and have charge of my courts, and I will give you the right of access among those who are standing here" (v. 7). This is consistent with all that the Bible says about salvation. Joshua is saved by grace, and then given commandments he must keep. He is justified, and is immediately called to begin the life of walking in God's ways that is sanctification.

Joshua's call to sanctification is expressed in terms of two obligations: to "walk in my ways and keep my charge" (Zech. 3:7). The first refers to personal godliness. Walking in God's ways means living after his fashion, according to his character as seen in his Word. The second deals with official faithfulness in ministry; the actual word for "charge" (Hebrew, *mishmor*) has to do specifically with ritual duties and the guarding of proper religion. If Joshua and the priests will do this, God promises them the reward of blessing.

God's demand for obedience is hardly a novelty in the Bible. It is the imperative David gave to Solomon as he passed to him the kingship: "Keep the charge of the LORD your God, walking in his ways and keeping his statutes, his commandments, his rules, and his testimonies, as it is written in the Law of Moses, that you may prosper in all that you do and wherever you turn" (1 Kings 2:3). In the New Testament we think of Paul's charge to his young protege, Timothy: "Keep a close watch on yourself and on the teaching," Paul told him, and again these correspond to both personal and official fidelity. "Persist in this, for by so doing you will save both yourself and your hearers" (1 Tim. 4:16).

We should first apply these conditions to those engaged in ministry. God is the source of every real spiritual blessing and, as Paul says, "God is not mocked" (Gal. 6:7). Therefore, ministers, like Joshua, must be faithful both on a personal and a professional level to expect God's continued endorsement. Calvin lucidly comments: "In short, pastors divinely appointed are so to rule over the Church as not to exercise their own power, but to govern the Church according to what God has prescribed, and in such a manner that God himself may always rule through the instrumentality of men."[5]

Our great cities are cluttered with magnificent church buildings that were erected by thriving believers in former years. Now they are largely empty because of the faithlessness of later generations. Written on them in letters of spiritual decay and civic irrelevance is the condition given to Joshua the high priest: "*If* you will walk in my ways and keep my charge." A poignant example is found at the corner of 22nd and Walnut Streets in downtown Philadelphia. Long ago a lovely Episcopal church stood there, but now something apparently more useful has replaced it: a gas station with a snack shop. The only memory of the former ministry is a hazy mural of the church painted on the adjacent building—thus the church is left only as a shadow upon a wall, and a warning to every church to heed this charge.

All of this applies not merely to ordained ministers but to anyone who would minister in God's name—and that should include all Christians. If we are to bear fruit in the church, if we are to be useful to Christ, if we are to be what the New Testament says we are—a kingdom of priests—then we must submit to the condition of walking in God's ways and keeping his Word. Like Joshua, we must measure our success not in terms of popularity or financial prosperity, not by numbers or excitement or power, but by our faithfulness on a personal and corporate level to the ways of God as revealed in his Word.

Two rewards are associated with obedience to these conditions. The first one has to do with Joshua remaining in his position of authority: "Then you shall rule my house and have charge of my courts." This probably implies that the temple would be rebuilt under Joshua's rule. The second privilege is even greater, namely, access to the heavenly courts of God: "I will give you the right of access among those who are standing here" (Zech. 3:7). "Those

5. John Calvin, *The Minor Prophets*, 5 vols. (Edinburgh: Banner of Truth, 1986), 5:93.

who are standing here" seems to indicate the angels who were attending this scene. Where angels go, Joshua could walk in prayer and in favor with God, if he kept the conditions laid down here.

Zechariah 3:7 concludes God's gracious dealings to restore Joshua and the Israelite priesthood. The entire portrait of Zechariah 3 grants a summary outline of the salvation God offers, in which justification and sanctification are distinct but always together. "Behold, I have taken your iniquity away from you, and I will clothe you with pure vestments" (Zech. 3:4)—this depicts the doctrine of justification. "If you walk in my ways and keep my charge, then you shall rule my house and have charge of my courts, and I will give you the right of access among those who are standing here" (Zech. 3:7)—that depicts the doctrine of sanctification. Justification is immediate, whereas sanctification is a lifelong process by which we are changed by God and progressively led into a life of obedience. Justifying faith is passive, as Joshua stood still while the angel took away his sins and cleansed him, whereas sanctifying faith is active in striving against sin and contending for holiness.

Signs of One to Come

Joshua not only teaches us principles of salvation, but he and his fellow priests also present a prophecy of the Savior to come. The vision continues: "Hear now, O Joshua the high priest, you and your friends who sit before you, for they are men who are a sign" (Zech. 3:8). Joshua and his fellow priests were *types*; that is, they were signs of something yet to come from God. Indeed, the word used specifies them as signs of wonder (Hebrew, *mophet*); what they signify is something marvelous to behold. This is certainly true of Joshua's experience in this vision. He is marvelously cleansed of sin and wonderfully called to obedience: this signifies the work of the One who is to come.

This statement is followed by a great promise of what God is going to do in answer to Joshua's need of grace: "Behold, I will bring my servant the Branch" (Zech. 3:8). Verse 9 adds a reference to "the stone that I have set before Joshua." These are all Old Testament descriptions of the Messiah: the Servant, the Branch, the Stone. Indeed, the use of these terms downloads whole strands of promises well-known in Zechariah's day. They were phrases that dominated the messianic expectation as set forth especially in the books of Isaiah, Jeremiah, and Ezekiel, books that all prophesied specifically about Zechariah's situation and generation.

Let us first consider the promise to send "God's servant." The Servant of the Lord is a figure who dominates the latter half of Isaiah's prophecy, the portion that speaks most directly of a promised salvation. The Servant is the One who will finally establish God's righteousness upon the earth. Isaiah introduces him: "Behold my servant, whom I uphold, my chosen, in whom my soul delights; I have put my Spirit upon him; he will bring forth justice to the nations" (Isa. 42:1). Ezekiel picks up this same language, linking the Servant to the Davidic line of kingship: "I will set up over them one shepherd, my servant David, and he shall feed them" (Ezek. 34:23).

The New Testament applies all of this to the Lord Jesus Christ. At Jesus' baptism the heavens opened and the voice of God was heard with words that deliberately echoed Isaiah 42: "This is my beloved Son, with whom I am well pleased" (Matt. 3:17). Matthew frequently quotes from Isaiah's Servant Songs in explaining Jesus' ministry (see especially Matt. 12:17). Jesus showed his servant character when he stooped to wash the disciples' feet in John 13. "The Son of Man," he said, "came not to be served, but to serve, and to give his life as a ransom for many" (Matt. 20:28). These passages from the Gospels make explicit what is already indicated in the Old Testament prophecies: Jesus Christ is the saving Servant.

What a wonderful promise this is to Joshua, that God would send this Servant into the world: a servant to God in establishing his rule and a servant to man in dying for our sins. Isaiah 53:5, which Matthew 8:17 explicitly applies to Jesus, tells us that the Servant "was wounded for our transgressions; he was crushed for our iniquities; upon him was the chastisement that brought us peace, and with his stripes we are healed."

This Servant is also called "the Branch," another messianic title prominent in Isaiah. Isaiah 11 explains that when the line of David will seem totally cut off, out of it will grow the Branch, the King of humble origins whose reign will spread in glory and accomplish all of God's will, even that final state of consummation dreamed of by all the prophets:

> There shall come forth a shoot from the stump of Jesse, and a branch from his roots shall bear fruit. And the Spirit of the LORD shall rest upon him. . . . Righteousness shall be the belt of his waist, and faithfulness the belt of his loins. The wolf shall dwell with the lamb, and the leopard shall lie down with the young goat, and the calf and the lion and the fattened calf together; and a little child shall lead them. . . . They shall not hurt or destroy in all my holy mountain; for the earth shall be full of the knowledge of the LORD as the waters cover the sea. (Isa. 11:1–9)

The Branch will arise from obscurity, but he will achieve the fullness of salvation and restoration to the glory of God. Jeremiah speaks of the Branch similarly, also linking him with the establishment of God's righteousness: "Behold, the days are coming, declares the LORD, when I will raise up for David a righteous Branch, and he shall reign as king and deal wisely, and shall execute justice and righteousness in the land. In his days Judah will be saved, and Israel will dwell securely. And this is the name by which he will be called: 'The LORD is our righteousness'" (Jer. 23:5–6).

Joshua's experience in Zechariah 3 is symbolic of this as well, since his salvation anticipates God sending this Branch, who will reign on the throne of David. What is said about the Branch clearly applies to the life and ministry of Jesus. Like the Branch of Isaiah, Jesus had a lowly beginning—born in a manger, in poverty and in weakness—and he appeared to have a contemptible end—his death on a cross as a criminal—yet he arose to the right hand of God where he reigns forever in glory. Out of the stump man cut off, God raised up the Branch in power. Jesus' career is aptly summarized in a hymn by Timothy Dudley-Smith:

> Within a crib my Savior lay,
> a wooden manger filled with hay . . .
> Upon a cross my Savior died,
> to ransom sinners, crucified . . .
> A victor's crown my Savior won,
> his work of love and mercy done,
> The Father's high ascended Son:
> all glory be to Jesus![6]

6. Words: Timothy Dudley-Smith. Words © 1968 Hope Publishing Co., Carol Stream, IL 60188. All rights reserved. Used by permission.

A Stone with Seven Eyes

The Lord promised to send his Servant, the Branch, and also a Stone. The prophecy continues: "For behold, on the stone that I have set before Joshua, on a single stone with seven eyes, I will engrave its inscription, declares the Lord of hosts" (Zech. 3:9).

This is a difficult verse to interpret with precision. Various commentators take the stone to symbolize any number of objects: a gem adorning the high priest's breastplate, a memorial stone marking out territorial ownership, a jewel for a crown, a stone put in the temple in place of the missing ark of the covenant, or a foundation stone for the new temple. The text says this stone was set *before* Joshua, which seems to indicate a large stone, thus ruling out a jewel for his breastplate or for a crown. Furthermore, it must have a logical relationship to the statement that is attached: "and I will remove the iniquity of this land in a single day."

This makes it most likely that the stone is related to the rebuilding of the temple, one of the major themes in Zechariah. The fact that this subject comes up again in the next chapter lends credence to this view. We remember, too, that Joshua and the priests are symbolic of what is to come; surely he points to the priestly character of the Messiah. This is the second way Joshua serves as a sign: in his priestly office. This recommends the idea of this stone as a cornerstone for the rebuilt temple. As Isaiah foretold, "See, I lay a stone in Zion, a tested stone, a precious cornerstone for a sure foundation; the one who trusts will never be dismayed" (Isa. 28:16 NIV).

This stone has seven eyes on it. Again, there are a variety of views about this. The seven eyes probably speak of either God's watching care for the church or else of the Holy Spirit resting upon the One whom God will send. T. V. Moore takes the former view, writing, "Seven being the number of perfection, the seven eyes represent the all-seeing eye of Jehovah, and show the sleepless regard which he bestows upon his Church."[7] A parallel passage in the book of Revelation seems, however, to support the latter view. There the Lamb on the throne is said to have "seven eyes, which are the seven spirits of God sent out into all the earth" (Rev. 5:6). Seven is the symbolic number of completeness or perfection, so that it is generally agreed that the phrase

7. T. V. Moore, *Haggai, Zechariah and Malachi* (Edinburgh: Banner of Truth, 1979), 149.

"the seven spirits of God" refers to the one perfect and all-seeing Holy Spirit. This indicates to many that the seven eyes in Zechariah's vision speak of the Holy Spirit coming upon the Messiah, providing him divine power and insight, which is exactly what happened in the life of our Lord Jesus at the time of his baptism (Matt. 3:16).

The Lord also says that he will engrave an inscription on the stone (Zech. 3:9). This probably indicates that God will beautify this stone the way an engraver does. Here we see Christ's divine character, for what is more lovely than godliness, so eminently revealed in the person of Jesus? Paul says, therefore, that we see "the light of the knowledge of the glory of God in the face of Christ" (2 Cor. 4:6). What could be more beautiful! Surely, Christians are not wrong to see this promise of engraving fulfilled especially at the cross, when the marks of thorns and nails and a spear-thrust were etched in Jesus' flesh. David Baron writes, "Beautiful were the gifts and graces which Christ received as a man; but beautiful beyond all beauty must be those glorious scars with which He allowed His whole body to be riven, that throughout the whole frame His love might be engraven."[8]

Moreover, we should note that the Branch and the Stone speak respectively of the two offices that are joined in Jesus Christ. As we have seen, the Branch referred to the Davidic kingship that would be restored. The Stone was the foundation for the temple that would be rebuilt. Both of these offices—the kingly and the priestly—are united in the Servant whom God promised to send. This union of offices was forbidden in the Old Testament, but is promised to be realized in the ministry of the Messiah. This important prophecy is validated in the New Testament, which tells us that the messianic king will also perform the functions of the priesthood.

The book of Hebrews fully develops the priesthood of Jesus Christ, of which Joshua the high priest is a symbol. First, Jesus fulfilled the priestly calling by offering himself as the perfect and final sacrifice. Hebrews 7:27 (NIV) explains, "He sacrificed for their sins once for all when he offered himself." Jesus is also the one who offers that sacrifice; he is the priest who enters into God's presence to present his own blood to atone for our sins: "He entered once for all into the holy places, not by means of the blood of goats and calves but by means of his own blood, thus securing an eternal redemption" (Heb.

---

8. David Baron, *The Visions and Prophecies of Zechariah* (Grand Rapids: Kregel, 1972), 117–18.

9:12). In that way, Jesus completed and fulfilled the priestly calling symbolized by Joshua the high priest and exercised in the temple Joshua was to rebuild. With what a sense of fulfillment would faithful priests like Joshua read the great statement in Hebrews, which speaks of the consummation of their own labors: "When Christ had offered for all time a single sacrifice for sins, he sat down at the right hand of God" (Heb. 10:12).

GOD'S PROMISED BLESSING

This glorious chapter, which began with the dreadful portrait of Joshua and Israel in their sin, ends with two great promises. The Lord prophesies to Joshua two wonderful blessings that result from God sending his Servant, who is the royal Branch and the priestly Stone: "I will remove the iniquity of this land in a single day. In that day, declares the LORD of hosts, every one of you will invite his neighbor to come under his vine and under his fig tree" (Zech. 3:9–10).

From Zechariah's perspective, these were both yet to come; they were things God would do in the future. We view this from a different point in history and find that at least one of these promises has already been perfectly fulfilled: "I will remove the iniquity of this land in a single day" (Zech. 3:9). Just as the day of atonement was the single day each year under the old covenant when Israel's sins were atoned for, this statement ultimately points forward to the day Christians remember as Good Friday. It was the worst and darkest of all days, in that it saw the unjust murder of God's Servant-Son on the cruel cross. But God made it the best of all days for those who trust in him, for on that cross Jesus took away our sins once and for all. On that single day, the promised Stone laid the foundation for the eternal temple by making the perfect and all-sufficient sacrifice of his own blood, which he himself offered to God as the perfect and acceptable high priest. That sacrifice laid the foundation on which every believer's hope of salvation securely rests: the Son of God has taken away our sin.

The second promise speaks of security and blessing as a result of Christ's ongoing rule, symbolized by neighbors sitting at peace beneath the vine and the fig tree (Zech. 3:10). As Isaiah foretold, "The wolf shall dwell with the lamb, and the leopard shall lie down with the young goat" (Isa. 11:6). This promise still awaits its final fulfillment, when the return of Christ in glory brings all things to consummation. We hear the echo of Zechariah's Old Testament prophecy in the New Testament promise: "Christ, having been offered once to bear the sins of many, will appear a second time, not to deal with sin but to save those who are eagerly waiting for him" (Heb. 9:28).

What is yet to come on a cosmic scale is already a personal reality for all who join themselves to Christ by faith. Having peace *with* God through the forgiveness of our sins, we now enjoy the peace *of* God and every spiritual blessing in Christ as he lives within us by his Spirit (see Rom. 5:1; Phil. 4:7; Eph. 1:3). Even in a spiritually barren world, we have the privilege of inviting our neighbors to join us beneath the vine and fig tree of God's saving blessings through faith in Jesus Christ.

Understanding this relieves our anxiety over the Bible's requirement that believers live in obedience to God. Yes, there are conditions we must fulfill if we are to have our sins removed and if we are to dwell in the blessing that God offers. We must trust Christ as Savior for justification and obey Christ as Lord for sanctification. Those are both blessedly true. But at the heart of this chapter is not God's commands, but rather his promises to us. Before the imperative comes the indicative. Every command and requirement in this chapter is preceded by either an act of God's grace or a promise of future salvation. The angel did not challenge Joshua somehow to remove his own filthy clothes, but declared instead, "Behold, I have taken your iniquity away from you, and I will clothe you with pure vestments" (Zech. 3:4). Only then was obedience made the condition of further blessing: "If you will walk in my ways and keep my charge, then you shall rule my house and have charge of my courts" (Zech. 3:7). Then, lest Joshua and his priestly colleagues should believe that their obedience was the cause of their blessing, God reminds them that they are but a sign of the One who will come: "Behold, I will bring my servant the Branch" (Zech. 3:8).

It turns out that, far from being in conflict, there is the most blessed complementarity between God's saving acts and our obedient response. The apostle John stated it in his memorable words, "We love because he first loved us" (1 John 4:19). So it is in all of salvation. We live in holiness because God first cleansed us. We serve God because God in Christ first served us. We obey—and through the obedience of faith enter into the fullness of salvation's blessings—because God has come to us as Lord and made us his own at the priceless cost of Christ's precious blood.

God's plan for salvation was not to redeem Joshua and then sit back and see what he and his fellow Israelites would do. Instead, the vision directs us to the greater Joshua who would come, Jesus Christ. This is the lesson of this marvelous vision: not that salvation depends on our faithfulness, but that God sent his own Son, Jesus Christ, to be the servant who would come as the royal branch and the priestly stone, through whom forgiveness and blessing come to us who believe, so that we will truly be God's people.

8

THE GOLDEN LAMPSTAND

Zechariah 4:1–6

*Then the angel who talked with me answered and said to me,
"Do you not know what these are?" I said, "No, my lord." Then he
said to me, "This is the word of the Lord to Zerubbabel: Not by
might, nor by power, but by my Spirit, says the Lord of hosts.*
(Zech. 4:5–6)

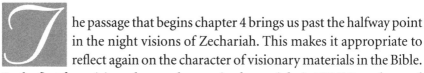he passage that begins chapter 4 brings us past the halfway point
in the night visions of Zechariah. This makes it appropriate to
reflect again on the character of visionary materials in the Bible.
In the first four visions the prophet received one night in 520 BC we detected
a general pattern. In each case, the prophet is shown a vision which an angel
interprets. The prophet interacts as appropriate, and in this process the
meaning is made clear.

The first four visions have brought a message of God's promise to protect,
bless, forgive, and receive into his service. The visions were calculated to comfort
the anxieties of Zechariah's generation, people who must surely have wondered
if God's favor would be upon them as of old, and who would have been especially anxious over the record of sin that had brought God's judgment in the past.

Now, at the halfway point of these eight visions, the text seems to mark a transition into a new set of visions: "The angel who talked with me came again and woke me, like a man who is awakened out of his sleep" (Zech. 4:1). This seems to indicate some intermission between this and the prior visions. Either Zechariah was so entranced by the events of chapter 3 that he had to be distracted away from them, or, as most commentators see it, he had lapsed into a lowered state of consciousness from which he had to be roused for the visions yet to come. One thing is clear: he was not awakened from actual sleep, because he is said to have been roused "*like* a man who is awakened out of his sleep." What was true for Zechariah is true of us generally: unless God's Spirit awakens us from spiritual lethargy, we lack the ability to receive his Word.

THE VISION OF THE LAMPSTAND

When Zechariah was wakened to the necessary prophetic state, he was faced with an arresting, but beautiful vision: "And he said to me, 'What do you see?' I said, 'I see, and behold, a lampstand all of gold, with a bowl on the top of it, and seven lamps on it, with seven lips on each of the lamps that are on the top of it. And there are two olive trees by it, one on the right of the bowl and the other on its left' " (Zech. 4:2–3).

The first item Zechariah mentions is the lampstand. Most of the older commentators understand this as the golden lampstand described in Exodus 25:31–40, which goes by the Hebrew word used here, the *menorah*. This lampstand stood within the original temple and is famously depicted on Titus's Arch in Rome. This beautiful object consisted of a golden base and shaft, from which protruded six stems—three on either side—so that the whole presented the appearance of a tree of light that held seven lamps.

If this is the case, there were some features added to this visionary lampstand that would have been unfamiliar to Zechariah. The first was a bowl above the lampstand, from which came seven channels or pipes, apparently to provide a steady supply of oil to the lamps. The Hebrew text suggests that there were actually forty-nine channels, seven for each of the seven lamps.[1]

---

1. The Hebrew text says "seven and seven channels," which should be taken distributively. See Thomas E. McComiskey, *The Minor Prophets: An Exegetical and Expository Commentary*, 3 vols. (Grand Rapids: Baker, 1998), 3:1082.

Additionally, there were two olive trees, one on each side of the lampstand, which are described more fully later in this chapter.

In an influential study published in 1970, Robert North challenged this picture of what Zechariah saw. Drawing especially on archeological findings, he argued that this vision presents not a seven-stemmed lampstand, but a kind of lampstand with a single basin on top, with seven smaller lamps affixed upon the rim of the basin, and with each of the seven lamps having seven wicks. According to this view, the construction formed a beautiful and elaborate golden candelabra.[2]

Almost the whole of current scholarship has accepted North's argument, largely because of archeological evidence that supports his view. We should be careful about assigning too much weight to the findings of archeology, which here (as is often the case) relies on a very few samples. But North also makes textual points to strengthen his case. He points out that verse 2 employs the word *mutseqet*, rendered as "lips" by the English Standard Version and as "channels" by the New International Version, and which the older view sees as "pipes" for oil to pass from the basin to the lamps, whereas verse 12 uses *tsanterot*, which very clearly means "pipes." *Mutseqet* (Zech. 4:2) comes from the verb "to pour," and more naturally would be translated as "spout" or "place where oil flows." It would seem from this that the seven lamps each had seven indentations where a wick would fit in, so that in this way each of the seven lamps shone forth with seven lights.[3]

What is certain is that Zechariah, in his heightened state of spirituality, was confronted by a brilliant and stunning scene centered around a marvelous lampstand of gold. If we put ourselves in his place, we can imagine the impression it made, which is more important than an agreement on its details. Out of the darkness of the night, Zechariah beheld a blazing lampstand. Its image conveyed majesty, beauty, priceless value, all in the form of light shining into darkness.

To explain the themes suggested by this lampstand, we need only turn to other places in the Bible where this symbol occurs. Because of the prominence of light as a symbol, we have a wealth of options. But three main options stand

2. Robert North, "Zechariah's Seven-Spout Lampstand" *Biblica* 51 (1970): 183–201.
3. Ibid., 195.

out as those we should consider with respect to Zechariah's golden lampstand: it signifies God's temple, God's saving presence, and God's people.

Those who understand the lampstand to represent the seven-stemmed menorah of the holy place naturally associate Zechariah's vision with the temple. Zechariah was a priest, so he would have been quite familiar with the temple's lampstand. Part of the temple service, morning and night, was to enter the holy place to trim its wicks and replenish its oil (Ex. 30:7–8). Indeed, however we visualize Zechariah's visionary lampstand, the context of chapter 4 demands that we connect this vision to the temple, for verses 7–9 tell us that its main purpose is to encourage the efforts to rebuild the temple.

Another likely idea represented by this lampstand is God's own presence, bringing blessing and grace. "For you are my lamp, O LORD," David sang, "and my God lightens my darkness" (2 Sam. 22:29). The book of Revelation shows that in the heavenly city to come, God's light will shine forever: "The city has no need of sun or moon to shine on it, for the glory of God gives it light, and its lamp is the Lamb" (21:23). Isaiah associates the coming of light into darkness with the Immanuel ("God with us") who was to come (Isa. 9:2), and this is associated with Zechariah's lampstand by the previous vision that focused on the coming Messiah. Jesus, who is Immanuel, said of himself: "I am the light of the world. Whoever follows me will not walk in darkness, but will have the light of life" (John 8:12). Meredith Kline sees an explicit link between Zechariah's vision and Jesus' reference to himself as the light: "Christ, the true anointed Servant, the true Israel, is the true menorah-light, the perfect likeness of [God]. And as the true menorah, Christ carries out the menorah mission of witnessing to the living God, who has 'given him for a witness to the peoples' " (Isa. 55:4).[4]

Third, the lampstand may easily be thought of as representing the people of God. Thomas V. Moore explains, "This candlestick represented the Theocracy, the Church of God, an image of great beauty, showing her mission to be a light-bearer in a dark world. The material, gold, indicated the purity, preciousness and indestructibleness of all that pertained to her."[5]

4. Meredith G. Kline, *Glory in Our Midst: A Biblical-Theological Reading of Zechariah's Night Visions* (Overland Park, KS: Two Ages Press, 2001), 143.

5. T. V. Moore, *Haggai, Zechariah, & Malachi* (Edinburgh: Banner of Truth, 1979), 153.

This idea is expressed very plainly by God's promise to make Israel "a light for the nations" (Isa. 42:6), and by Jesus in Matthew 5:14, where he pictures Christians as lamps on a stand, saying, "You are the light of the world."

A GREAT SPIRITUAL PRINCIPLE

Given the familiarity of the lampstand as a symbol, Zechariah's puzzled response may seem odd. He gasped to the angel, "What are these, my lord?" (Zech. 4:4). It is perhaps significant that he speaks of the plural "these," indicating the variety of elements in the vision. In any case, we are struck by Zechariah's confusion, and the angel suggests that he ought to understand: "Do you not know what these are?" the angel answered. "No, my lord," the prophet replied (v. 5). The angel gives him an answer, and in this John Calvin sees evidence of God's willingness to make clear his Word in answer to our prayer. "The Lord will supply us also with understanding," he writes, "when we confess that his mysteries are hid from us, and when conscious of our want of knowledge, we flee to him, and implore him not to speak in vain to us, but to grant to us the knowledge of his truth."[6]

This exchange reminds us that visions often present unusual and even confusing sights. This vision showed not merely the symbolic lampstand, but also the spiritual realities associated with it that are normally unseen by us. Zechariah's question is one we also need to ask: "What is it?" Is it God's temple, or God's presence, or God's people, or something else? It is noteworthy that the angel did not settle this matter. Visions are picture-books, not puzzle books; the angel leaves the picture unsolved, instead pressing forth the spiritual application. In other words, its message lay not in the physical realm but in the spiritual realm. He explained: "This is the word of the LORD to Zerubbabel: Not by might, nor by power, but by my Spirit, says the LORD of hosts" (Zech. 4:6).

Here is the principle animating this vision, and to make it the angel directs our attention away from the lights to the flow of oil that fuels the lamps. Oil is one of the clearest symbols in all the Bible, consistently pointing to the Spirit of God. Just as the flow of oil keeps the lights shining, so the Holy Spirit empowers and animates every spiritual work. The message of the

6. John Calvin, *The Minor Prophets*, 5 vols. (Edinburgh: Banner of Truth, 1986), 5:109.

Spirit's presence is directed to Zerubbabel, the prince and political leader of the restoration community. Our next study will examine God's message to him in detail, but this brief statement gives it in sum. We may consider verse 6 as a motto to guide and inspire Zerubbabel and his fellow builders: "Not by might, nor by power, but by my Spirit, says the LORD of hosts."

The words "might" and "power" (Hebrew, *hayil* and *koah*) are practically the same. The first is often associated with the might of numbers, as in a warhost or great workforce, while the second speaks more directly of physical strength. The point, however, is in the contrast: it is not by might, not by power, but by God's Spirit. This is a motto given to Zerubbabel and thereby to the whole community to guide all their labors and spiritual life. H. C. Leupold explains, "If success is to be gained in the achievements of the people of God it will not be secured by what man can do but by the Spirit's work."[7]

ZERUBBABEL AND THE TEMPLE PROJECT

One of the things clearly symbolized by the lampstand is the temple, and this chapter especially emphasizes the project to rebuild the temple on Mount Zion (v. 9). Obviously, then, the direct application of the vision is to encourage Zerubbabel to press on with renewed vigor, despite his lack of numbers and strength. In this respect this vision is a promise of success in rebuilding the temple. For this work, verse 6 provides both a principle and a promise: "Not by might, nor by power, but by my Spirit, says the LORD of hosts."

There was indeed little might or strength to Zerubbabel's situation, and this probably explains the near-abandonment of the work on the temple. The restoration community had arrived some eighteen years earlier to a wrecked city, in the midst of suspicious and hostile neighbors. It was hard enough just to make a living, much less to restore a building that had once been a wonder of the world. Haggai's prophecy, which so closely parallels Zechariah, makes it clear that the people had become preoccupied with making a living and finding comforts for themselves. "My house," he said, "lies in ruins, while each of you busies himself with his own house" (Hag. 1:9). Leupold says of Zerubbabel's predicament: "He was the man before

---

7. C. H. Leupold, *An Exposition of Zechariah* (Grand Rapids: Baker, 1971 reprint), 87.

whom all manner of obstacles piled up, both in the administration of the civil affairs of the nation and in the directing of the work of constructing the Temple. . . . Affairs in Israel were in such a tangle and difficulties so numerous as to seem to threaten the very future of the nation."[8]

Morale must have been low. Many of the people, experiencing such hardship, would have doubted God's power or his commitment to help them. The pressure on Zerubbabel would have been great, as the failure to build the temple presented a growing scandal and symbol of spiritual failure. Losing hope or interest, many fell into sin and decided to make the best of things by assimilating with the Gentile people around them (see Haggai's rebukes). These feelings and temptations are also familiar to Christians, so the principle of Zechariah 4:6 gives inspiration to us as well.

The book of Ezra tells us of a specific event that may be in view here. The Gentile people around Jerusalem were predictably hostile to the city's restoration, partly because of the Jews' unwillingness to associate with them. Ezra 5 reports a letter written by a local Persian governor named Tattenai that probably coincides closely with this vision in Zechariah 4. Tattenai sent his officials to Jerusalem challenging their authorization to build the temple. Unsatisfied, they sent an appeal to King Darius in Babylon, accusing the Jews of sedition and asking him to find out if they had ever been authorized to rebuild the city.

This presented Zerubbabel with a serious threat. Cyrus, who had authorized the return and rebuilding, was long dead. Darius, the current ruler, was not even his direct successor, having come to power after a recent civil war. What would happen if Darius would listen to his governor, as he might be expected to do? The Jews were in no position to argue their case and, as historians have generally agreed, Darius was even then campaigning in this corner of his empire, thus quite available to suppress the work at Jerusalem. Neither might nor power would possibly avail for Zerubbabel; he would have to rely upon the Lord.

Ezra 6 tells us what happened. Darius reacted to his governor's complaint by ordering a search of the royal archives to see if a record could be found. A scroll of Cyrus's earlier order was unearthed, and as a result Darius gave his support not to Tattenai, his own governor, but to Zerubbabel

8. Ibid., 86–87.

and the Jews. "Let the temple be rebuilt," he ordered. Tattenai was forbidden to interfere with the rebuilding and, moreover, Darius ordered that he immediately provide the necessary money and materials—even the animals needed to restore the temple sacrifices—upon pain of death (Ezra 6:1–12). Not by might, nor by power, but surely by the Spirit of God who was working through all these events—and, no doubt, in response to fervent prayer—Zerubbabel's position was completely reversed. Ezra 6 concludes with this record:

> According to the word sent by Darius the king, Tattenai, the governor of the province Beyond the River, Shethar-bozenai, and their associates did with all diligence what Darius the king had ordered. And the elders of the Jews built and prospered through the prophesying of Haggai the prophet and Zechariah the son of Iddo. They finished their building by decree of the God of Israel and by decree of Cyrus and Darius and Artaxerxes king of Persia; and this house was finished on the third day of the month of Adar, in the sixth year of the reign of Darius the king (Ezra 6:13–15).

The lessons in all of this are clear. First, God is able to overcome all obstacles; by his Spirit he is able to overrule kings and direct the affairs of men so that his people have all they need. Second, this being the case, we are exhorted to prayerful obedience even in times of trouble, knowing that God is able to "supply every need of yours according to his riches in glory in Christ Jesus" (Phil. 4:19).

CHRIST'S SPIRIT-ANOINTED MINISTRY

The golden lampstand is also a symbol for God's saving presence. In this respect, Zechariah's vision is a promise of the coming of God, especially as fulfilled in the ministry of Jesus Christ. The apostle John writes, "The true light, which enlightens everyone, was coming into the world" (John 1:9). This, then, is the principle for Christ's Spirit-anointed ministry: "Not by might, nor by power, but by my Spirit, says the LORD of hosts" (Zech. 4:6).

The truth of this saying is eminently displayed in the life of Jesus. He never trusted worldly power, but sought the pleasure of his Father in heaven. As the lampstand depended on the flowing oil, Jesus likewise performed his works

93

in the power of the Holy Spirit. In the synagogue of Nazareth he inaugurated his ministry with this very emphasis: "The Spirit of the Lord is upon me, because he has anointed me to proclaim good news to the poor" (Luke 4:18).

When Jesus was baptized at the Jordan and received the sign of God's favor, he was equipped neither with high worldly office, nor riches, nor a legion of soldiers, but with "the Spirit of God descending like a dove and coming to rest on him" (Matt. 3:16). Jesus then went out into the desert to join battle with the devil, overcoming three great temptations. In this, too, he was "led up by the Spirit" (Matt. 4:1). This principle holds true all through Jesus' life and ministry. His was a spiritual rather than a worldly ministry, and because of that he was crucified as a criminal, horrifically murdered by people who wielded worldly might and power. But in the contest between those two powers—that of God's Spirit and that of the world—Jesus' resurrection displays the victory. Paul explains that Jesus "was declared to be the Son of God in power according to the Spirit of holiness by his resurrection from the dead" (Rom. 1:4). "Not by might, nor by power, but by my Spirit, says the LORD of hosts." This is the principle of God's saving presence in the world, and the means by which Jesus conquered sin and death for us. By this same rule he reigns even now in heaven as Lord of all.

A MOTTO FOR THE CHURCH

The vision of the golden lampstand also represents the people of God, which in the Old Testament was Israel and in the New Testament is the church. The vision, in this case, promises the spiritual empowering of God's people for their work of shining forth God's light. Both for Zerubbabel and the Israelites and for us today this is to be the motto for service to God: "Not by might, nor by power, but by my Spirit, says the LORD of hosts."

Jesus concluded the ministry of his first coming not with the cross, or even with his resurrection or ascension into heaven, but with his outpouring of the Spirit on the church at Pentecost. It was by sending the Spirit to God's people on earth that Jesus empowered his disciples to carry on with his own work. Meredith Kline explains:

> The Son is anointed with the Spirit and he is the anointer with the Spirit. . . . Messiah commands the [church] to fulfill its mission as a light to the Gentiles,

the mission which he models. . . . that is, Christ promulgates the Great Commission. And in order to empower the menorah-church for that mission, which is accomplished not by human might but by God's Spirit, Messiah, the anointed with the Spirit, becomes the anointer with the Spirit. . . . He complements the charge of the Great Commission with the charism of Pentecost.[9]

What is it that protects the church and enables her to persevere and prevail in a hostile world? The answer is God's sufficiency by means of his Spirit. This is why the book of Zechariah was so popular in the time of the Protestant Reformation. Many of the Reformers literally fled for their lives, some barely escaping persecution and death. They were frequently faced with militant opposition—with mighty emperors and powerful kings determined to snuff them out—while those seeking to restore the true church seemed so very poor and weak. Calvin therefore writes, feeling the force of this truth from his own precarious experience and that of many of his friends:

> When therefore we now see things in a despairing condition, let this vision come to our minds—that God is sufficiently able by his own power to help us, when there is no aid from any other . . . so that experience will at length show that we have been preserved in a wonderful manner by his hand alone . . . Whenever, then, earthly aids fail us, let us learn to recumb on God alone, for it is not by a host or by might that God raises up his Church, and preserves it in its proper state; but this he does by his Spirit, that is, by his own intrinsic and wonderful power, which he does not blend with human aids; and his object is to draw us away from the world, and to hold us wholly dependent on himself.[10]

This message is greatly needed today, when many churches have decided that if they are going to survive and grow it will be by the adoption of "might and power." This takes many forms: the redefinition of worship as entertainment; the packaging of religious goods and services which we may "sell" to the consumer market; and the avoidance of truths that might cause offense to unbelievers. Surely we should seek to be useful to the world in appropriate ways, and we want to remove any unnecessary offense, such as that created by

---

9. Kline, *Glory in Our Midst*, 142.
10. Calvin, *Minor Prophets*, 5:111–12.

our own sin. But this principle should ever guide our actions in the church: "Not by might, not by power, but by my Spirit, says the LORD of hosts."

If we rely on God's Spirit, this will be seen in our bold proclamation of the gospel, which Paul describes as "the power of God for salvation to everyone who believes" (Rom. 1:16). Paul asserted this principle to the Corinthians, writing of his own unwillingness to employ the faddish methods of the day: "I decided to know nothing among you except Jesus Christ and him crucified. And I was with you in weakness and in fear and much trembling, and my speech and my message were not in plausible words of wisdom, but in demonstration of the Spirit and of power, that your faith might not rest in the wisdom of men but in the power of God" (1 Cor. 2:2–5). Paul was talking about a plain and straightforward witness, unadorned by the eloquence of Greek rhetoric or formal debate, so that it would be by God's Spirit through God's Word that hearts were touched, minds were persuaded, and converts were won. Later, he said the same thing in different words: "We have renounced disgraceful, underhanded ways. We refuse to practice cunning or to tamper with God's word, but by the open statement of the truth we would commend ourselves to everyone's conscience in the sight of God" (2 Cor. 4:2). So should it be for us in the church.

This principle applies to our lives as individual Christians. Without the Spirit's work we cannot even come to faith. What about Christian growth and sanctification? What is the power that enables us to turn from sin and live holy lives? Paul answers: "If you live according to the flesh you will die, but if by the Spirit you put to death the deeds of the body, you will live" (Rom. 8:13). Sanctification is not achieved by our own might or power, but by God's Spirit through our believing use of the ordinary means of grace: God's Word, the sacraments, and prayer. The Spirit is Christ's gift, not a power we can "plug into" at our will or whip up by the right spiritual technology. Instead, where there are faith in Christ and humble reliance on God's power, where God is glorified instead of man, where God's Word is faithfully taught, and where believers join in fervent prayer, there Jesus sends the Spirit as God's loving provision. Jesus explained, "If you then, who are evil, know how to give good gifts to your children, how much more will the heavenly Father give the Holy Spirit to those who ask him!" (Luke 11:13).

What about our effectiveness in Christian service and witness? Is it by might? Is it by power? Should Christians aim to achieve positions of power or wealth or prestige in order to make an impression for Jesus? This is the way many of us are tempted to think. But it is not by might, not by power or riches or glamour or popularity that we really serve Christ well. It is by the Spirit of God working in and through us as we trust and obey God's Word.

Like the Stars Forever

This leads us back to the vision of the lampstand, blazing as it was before the wondering eyes of the prophet. We have seen that this vision points to the temple building—the symbol of God's presence on earth—to the Messiah Jesus Christ, and to the church. That means that each and every believer is included in this vision, being joined to Christ through faith and having entered into the spiritual body of his church. Every Christian is a lamp on a stand, precious to God, called as a humble light-bearer before the darkness of the world. Jesus says to each of us, "You are the light of the world. . . . Let your light shine before others, so that they may see your good works and give glory to your Father who is in heaven" (Matt. 5:14, 16).

These words express the central purpose of our lives, that God would be glorified through us. The vision tells us how this will happen. The power for the lamps comes from the oil God provides, his own Holy Spirit. The flame is our testimony before the world, in words and in deeds. We are the lamps that shine in his power: we fulfill our function not by might, not by power, but by the Spirit God will surely give us as we believe, obey, and pray.

The question, then, is this: whose light do we want to shine? Whose glory do we wish to extol? If it is our own, then it will have to be by might and by power—by wealth, by worldly influence, by fame and popularity. These can seem very impressive to our eyes, but they are lights that burn dimly at best and briefly. But if we will offer up ourselves, our lives, as wicks for that eternal flame—not by might but by God's own Spirit—then ours will be a light that blazes beautifully now and brilliantly forever. As the angel said to the prophet Daniel in another vision, "Those who are wise shall shine like the brightness of the sky above; and those who turn many to righteousness, like the stars forever and ever" (Dan. 12:3).

9

The Day of Small Things

Zechariah 4:6—10

Then the word of the LORD came to me, saying, "The hands of
Zerubbabel have laid the foundation of this house; his hands shall
also complete it. Then you will know that the LORD of hosts has sent
me to you. For whoever has despised the day of small things shall
rejoice, and shall see the plumb line in the hand of Zerubbabel."
(Zech. 4:8–10)

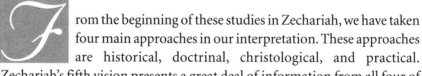 rom the beginning of these studies in Zechariah, we have taken four main approaches in our interpretation. These approaches are historical, doctrinal, christological, and practical. Zechariah's fifth vision presents a great deal of information from all four of these perspectives. Historically, we see God's prophetic message that motivated the Jews to complete the second temple in 516 BC. As we read elsewhere in Scripture, "The elders of the Jews built and prospered through the prophesying of Haggai the prophet and Zechariah the son of Iddo. They finished their building by decree of the God of Israel" (Ezra 6:14). Christologically, both the temple and Zerubbabel the Davidic prince point to Jesus Christ and the temple-building work he came to do.

This passage is also extremely practical in its message, and we will consider the angel's message to Zerubbabel from this standpoint. Finally, there are a number of doctrinal headings touched upon in this fifth vision, including the doctrines of the Holy Spirit and of Christian sanctification. But first we should consider what this passage tells us about God's grace and its availability to all who turn to him in faith.

Grace Renewed

If we put ourselves in the shoes of Zechariah and all the other Israelites who had come back with him to Jerusalem, we can view the message of this vision from a fertile perspective. What were the questions and fears of that generation? Surely they wondered if they were cut off from God's grace because of their own sins and even more because of the sins of their fathers. Jerusalem was in ruins. The rubble bore stark testimony to God's judgment on sin, for when the Israelites turned from the Lord and refused to hear his prophets' call to repentance, God's wrath fell upon them. David had established the city around 1000 BC and after four hundred years of steady descent into depravity and idolatry, it was destroyed at God's command in 586 BC. God's destruction of his own holy city is a stark testimony to the danger of presumption and sin. The people were taken to Babylon as captives, and even the sacred artifacts of the destroyed temple were taken to be strewn in the treasure rooms of the Babylonian gods.

These settlers had returned by faith in the words God had given the prophets—encouragements regarding hope for a new future. God told Isaiah, "Comfort, comfort my people. . . . Speak tenderly to Jerusalem, and cry to her that her warfare is ended, that her iniquity is pardoned" (Isa. 40:1–2). Or again, "The ransomed of the Lord shall return and come to Zion with singing; everlasting joy shall be upon their heads; they shall obtain gladness and joy, and sorrow and sighing shall flee away" (Isa. 51:11). But as grand as such promises were, they had not exactly been experienced by this restoration band. It would not at all be surprising for them to doubt God's favor, to question the extent of their restoration and the validity of their claim upon God's grace.

This situation is similar to Christian experience. We, too, come to God out of a Babylonian captivity to sin. We come in answer to God's call, with great promises ringing in our ears. Yet we live in what has been called "the gap between promise and reality."[1] The Bible tells us that in Christ we are royal children, on whom the Lord of heaven has lavished his love and affection. Yet, as Paul says, all this is "hidden with Christ in God" (Col. 3:3). Our royal sonship is largely unseen in this life, unrecognized even by us except through the eyes of faith. We are told of fellowship with God and his great family, yet our experience is often one of loneliness. We are promised vast riches, kept securely for us by God, yet our reality is so often one of poverty. We are told about a vast power made available to us in Christ, yet we feel so weak and ill-equipped to face the demands of life.

In short, we feel the way Zechariah and his people must have felt, expecting the fulfillment of great and surpassing promises, while we experience a life that is far from glorious. This is where Zechariah's visions come in. They set before the eyes of faith manifestations of what is real but unseen, what is spiritually true even though unapparent in our outward circumstances.

These visions told the prophet and his first hearers that God had not changed. He was still the God of grace, the God whose favor extends to all who come to him in faith, as they had done by returning to Jerusalem to rebuild. "Return to me," he told them, "and I will return to you" (Zech. 1:3). This is our hope as well; these visions of grace and forgiveness and renewed power from on high show that blessing is accessible to us if only we will turn to the Lord in faith. This is the source of our hope and confidence: while circumstances change, God's character never does. J. I. Packer explains:

> Nothing can alter the character of God. In the course of a human life, tastes and outlook and temper may change radically: a kind, equable man may turn bitter and crotchety; a man of good-will may grow cynical and callous. But nothing of this sort happens to the Creator. He never becomes less truthful, or merciful, or just, or good, than He used to be. The character of God is today, and always will be, exactly what it was in Bible times.[2]

This means, for instance, that God is holy, just as he was before and just as he always will be. Sin will always lead to judgment, and rebellion will always bring his displeasure. But it also means that God is loving and gracious now

---

1. See Iain M. Duguid, *Living in the Gap Between Promise and Reality* (Phillipsburg, NJ: P&R, 1999).
2. J. I. Packer, *Knowing God* (Downers Grove, IL: InterVarsity, 1978), 69.

as he is shown to be in the Bible. So repentance and faith will always lead to forgiveness and restoration; those who return to the Lord will always find that he eagerly returns to them. God's grace is new in every circumstance because it is founded not on the circumstances themselves, but on the changeless character of God. This is what Jeremiah saw as his source for hope in the immediate aftermath of the horror of Jerusalem's fall: "The steadfast love of the LORD never ceases; his mercies never come to an end; they are new every morning; great is your faithfulness" (Lam. 3:22–23).

It is this great love and mercy from the Lord that generates everything we read in this fourth chapter of Zechariah. The vision of the lampstand told the Israelites that the temple would be rebuilt, that God's presence and power would dwell among them, and that their generation would know and have the light of God again. The motto of Zechariah 4:6—"Not by might, nor by power, but by my Spirit, says the LORD of hosts"—assured them that they would not have to rely on their own power or strength, but that God's Spirit would propel and sustain them far beyond what their own power could do.

WHO ARE YOU, O MOUNTAIN?

All of this explains why Zechariah 4:6 has been so beloved to God's people. Verses 7 to 10 go on to apply its message, spurring Zerubbabel and the Jews on to renewed effort. Theology is always immensely practical, and this message of God's mighty help makes at least three applications. First, it shows us that *although there are obstacles, God is sufficient to overcome them.* This was the point of the angel's exclamation: "Who are you, O great mountain? Before Zerubbabel you shall become a plain" (Zech. 4:7).

Zerubbabel apparently was inhibited by the enormity of the task at hand and the weakness of his own position. This passage speaks of a mountain of obstacles, although in Old Testament usage we should think specifically of world powers arrayed against God's people. God spoke of Babylon this way in Jeremiah 51:25: "Behold, I am against you, O destroying mountain, declares the LORD, which destroys the whole earth." It was on mountains that temples were erected, and where spiritual forces were thus represented; it was these, personified in the political enemies of the Jews, that verse 7 especially describes as being cast down. Yes, these obstacles—these powers—are far too great for Zerubbabel to overcome or stand against, but God says to his servant that the mountain will be made level ground before him.

We, too, face many great obstacles in our struggle with sin, the world, and the devil. Some of us will have actual enemies or persecutors—perhaps a boss or a neighbor or a government power—and God does not promise us immediate success against every worldly threat. But what this mountain pointed to—the spiritual powers that oppress us through sin and temptation and spiritual attack—will ultimately be cast down before the one who trusts the Lord. Indeed, the verse expresses itself in such a way that God will cast the mountain down before the feet of Zerubbabel, giving testimony to his servant of his almighty power.

We should apply this statement to Christian ministry, both individually and corporately in the church. We will always encounter opposition in ministry; worldly and spiritual powers are intent on thwarting the advance of God's kingdom. However, God tells us to press on in the face of such obstacles. Notice that Zerubbabel is to leave the leveling of the mountain to God, while he gets on with the work God has given him. Likewise, God will make level paths for the ministry he wants us to do.

In 1970 Jack Miller suddenly resigned from both his job as a seminary professor and as pastor of a small church. The reason was frustration over his sense of failure in both arenas. Despite all his labors, he did not think he was making an impact in people's lives. He was angry not only at himself but at his students and congregation, all of whom together had seemed to conspire to block his ambition to succeed as a servant of God. In the days of depression after his resignation, Miller tells of being confronted by the words of John 7:38, where Jesus promises: "Whoever believes in me, as the Scripture has said, Out of his heart will flow rivers of living water." Realizing that he had been relying on works—on power and on might—he began instead to trust in the grace of God. He stopped trying to manipulate success but trusted God's Spirit to remove obstacles and empower his ministry. Describing the change this made, Miller writes, "I had taken hold of this promise, and now in my weakness I was inviting others to do the same. I was saying that the normal Christian life was one filled with grace, obtained by weak people as they relied on the promises of God."[3]

---

3. C. John Miller, *A Faith Worth Sharing* (Phillipsburg, NJ: Presbyterian & Reformed, 1999), 95.

"Who are you, O great mountain?" This is what God declares in our hearing, as we though weak nonetheless step forward in faith in obedience to his Word. Verse 7 continues, "And he shall bring forward the top stone amid shouts of 'Grace, grace to it!' " On the one hand, this declares the principle of every spiritual achievement—the working of God's grace—while on the other hand it seeks God's favor for Zerubbabel's work done in obedience to him.

This is the principle the apostle Paul found in his weakness, when he had prayed to God for spiritual help: "My grace is sufficient for you, for my power is made perfect in weakness" (2 Cor. 12:9). To this, Paul replied, "I will boast all the more gladly of my weaknesses, so that the power of Christ may rest upon me. . . . For when I am weak, then I am strong" (2 Cor. 12:9–10). Yes, every Christian will be faced with obstacles and opposition, but God's power is greater still.

A second practical lesson flows from this, namely, that *God's power for us spurs us on to action* and not to inaction. Zerubbabel is told that the mountain will fall before his feet, making a level path, and he therefore is to bring forth the capstone. The Hebrew term in verse 7 refers to the "topstone" or "headstone" (*even haroshah*). It likely signifies the stone at the top of the building that marks its completion. Zerubbabel is thus told that he will see this success, amidst cries of grace unto God. Therefore the angel says, "The hands of Zerubbabel have laid the foundation of this house; his hands shall also complete it" (Zech. 4:9).

This is a principle by which we are to live as Christians. We are shown the end from the beginning, and this emboldens us to action. Zerubbabel was shown a vision of the ceremony that would mark the temple's completion, as would in fact take place four years later, in 516 BC. Therefore, he knew that he did not lay the foundation in vain, for his present work would bear fruit. In the same way, nothing done by faith is ever wasted. It is God's power that ensures success and motivates the effort, but God's people have to do the work nonetheless. Notice that it will be Zerubbabel's hands that will lay the stone. This is the way it is in every spiritual endeavor. God gives us strength through faith and then calls for us to use it. Paul applies this principle to our spiritual lives, saying, "Continue to work out your salvation with fear and trembling, for it is God who works in you to will and to act according to his good purpose" (Phil. 2:12–13 NIV).

Third, the angel concludes by describing God's aim in all of this: "Then you will know that the LORD of hosts has sent me to you" (Zech. 4:9). *God's aim in our work is the increased knowledge of him.* The Christian life is about the increasing knowledge of God, and of his grace, and of the truthfulness of his Word.

An old Christian once showed a Bible with verse after verse marked with the initials "TNT." When asked what those initials meant, the longtime believer was able to say, "It means 'tried and true.' I write that when I have tried it and found out that it is true, and now my Bible is full of those marks."

This is what God wants to do in our lives. Jesus prayed to the Father, "And this is eternal life, that they know you the only true God, and Jesus Christ whom you have sent" (John 17:3). This is how we measure progress in the faith, by our knowledge of God: of his character, his faithfulness, his presence and his grace in our lives. This knowledge comes through experiences like the one before Zerubbabel and the other Jews, as we trust God in the face of threats and obstacles and know his salvation as he works it out in our lives. This is how Peter concluded his second and last epistle: "But grow in the grace and knowledge of our Lord and Savior Jesus Christ. To him be the glory both now and to the day of eternity. Amen" (2 Peter 3:18).

THE DAY OF SMALL THINGS

The angel comments on Zerubbabel's situation with a wonderful statement of wisdom for the life of faith: "For whoever has despised the day of small things shall rejoice" (Zech. 4:10). This is an exhortation to us to begin the work God has set before us, whether it is a needed change of lifestyle, a call to a certain ministry, or a commitment to study and grow in God's Word.

"Where does a person like me begin such a daunting endeavor?" we are prone to ask. The answer is that we begin by beginning: by trusting in the Lord, by doing what is there before us to do, by not despising the day of small things. This is what Zerubbabel modeled when he first laid the temple's new foundation—a small beginning that led to bigger and better things. Surely this exhortation was given as a spur to motivate the Jews in their work on the temple. Small beginnings, we are reminded, lead to great endings when they are done through faith in God. This is true when we are battling sin. It is true for churches when God sets before us a spiritual challenge or ministry opportunity. The day of small things requires faith to believe that what we dare to begin will be carried through in the power of God. Paul wrote, "I can do all things through him who strengthens me" (Phil. 4:13). That is the kind of faith that begins even in small things, expecting God to do something great.

We can apply this statement directly to the matter of spiritual growth and sanctification. Where does the godly life begin? It begins where we are, with small steps of obedience as a tangible expression of our faith. Paul wrote: "Do not be deceived: God is not mocked, for whatever one sows, that will he also reap. For the one who sows to his own flesh will from the flesh reap corruption, but the one who sows to the Spirit will from the Spirit reap eternal life" (Gal. 6:7–8). This means that each of our actions—even our thoughts—have real significance, however small. It has been said, "Sow a thought and reap an action; sow an action and reap a habit; sow a habit and reap a lifestyle; sow a lifestyle and reap a character; sow a character and reap a destiny." Who, then, will despise the day of small things, which have much larger things growing within?

This is also true when it comes to the matter of discerning our calling in life. Many Christians struggle to know what God would have them to do and therefore seek specific direction. Some of us will obtain a dramatic sense of calling, even very early in life, and will follow that course from then on. But, for most, a calling is found by means of the principle of verse 10—that is, by not despising the day of small things.

This means that if we have a gift or ability, we should start putting it to use for God's service. If we can teach, we should help lead a Bible study. If we excel at hospitality, we should use our homes to minister—perhaps to host a small group or to help others in need. If God has gifted us for encouragement, then we should start looking for people who need a reminder of God's grace and caring love; they are all around us. "But I don't know where to begin!" someone may object. But God says, "Who will despise the day of small things?"

There are, of course, people who do despise the day of small things. This statement suggests that there were people jeering Zerubbabel's ambitions for God's temple, mocking his feeble efforts, and despising his day of small things. We may find this to be true as well. Perhaps we decide to devote ourselves more seriously to the Lord by making real lifestyle changes. But people will say, "Who appointed you a saint?" The answer is that Jesus Christ did, and he calls us to follow him, starting with small things. Or we may decide God has called us to a change of direction in answer to some ministry calling. We can expect people to ask why we think we are so important, what makes us so serious and ambitious. Let them despise the day of small things, so long as we are trusting in the Lord.

This is what Hudson Taylor experienced when he began to dream great things for serving God as a missionary to China in the mid-nineteenth century. Among the many obstacles were the difficulty of learning the Mandarin language, his lack of money, and the fact that he recently had fallen in love with a woman. Believing that God had called him, however, Taylor pressed on with his plans. One minister asked him how he expected to get to so distant a place with no money. Taylor replied that he did not know. "It seemed to be probable," he writes, "that I should need to do as the Twelve and seventy had done in Judea, go without purse or scrip, relying on Him who had sent me to supply all my need." Unable to find a suitable missionary society to support him, Taylor concluded, "So God and God alone is my hope, and I need no other." Warned by an experienced missionary that with his light-colored hair and blue eyes he would be rejected by the Chinese, Taylor entrusted this problem to the Lord as well.[4]

The record of history shows that Hudson Taylor did go to China and founded the China Inland Mission, a great missionary society that succeeded in reaching millions of people with the gospel of Jesus Christ. One of Taylor's mottos is in line with our text: "A little thing is a little thing," he said, "but faithfulness in a little thing is a big thing!" This reflects our Lord Jesus' own teaching. In his parable of the talents, the master said to the servant who had done his best with what he had, "Well done, good and faithful servant! You have been faithful with a few things; I will put you in charge of many things. Come and share your master's happiness" (Matt. 25:21 NIV). What matters the most, therefore, is not the scale or the scope or the subject of the endeavor, but the faith that is willing to begin and to respond to our Lord with trusting obedience.

We should not be surprised to learn that this principle, like the principle of Zechariah 4:6, is found at work in the life of Jesus. As we saw in our

---

4. Cited from Marshall Broomhall, *The Man Who Believed God* (Chicago: Moody Press, 1929), 41–52.

studies of chapter 3, Jesus comes as a small branch, a shoot growing up from the stump of the house of Jesse. He was born in a manger, in impoverished obscurity. He grew up in a backwater town as a simple laborer. But out of these small things, not by might nor by power but by God's Spirit, came forth our Savior and Redeemer and King of kings. Jesus' own life and ministry prove that small things done by God's will produce great results through his power.

Seeing that this is true of Jesus, we should expect the same for ourselves. Surely this is the angel's point as he continues: "For whoever has despised the day of small things shall rejoice, and shall see the plumb line in the hand of Zerubbabel" (Zech. 4:10). The plumb line is a weighted cord used to ensure the building of straight walls. The point is that when others see Zerubbabel going about the work in faith, they will rejoice and take heart themselves because of his "straight" example. This reminds us that in this passage Zerubbabel does not stand for us, first of all, but for Jesus Christ, the builder of God's true temple. Likewise, when we see Jesus building by the spiritual principles in Zechariah 4, we are emboldened to take up tools for ourselves. Seeing the plumb line in the hand of such a builder tells us that we shall at length see great things that are only dimly visible now. John Calvin writes, "For though the Lord begins with little things, and as it were in weakness, yet the plummet will at length be seen in the hand of the Architect for the purpose of completing the work."[5]

If this encourages our faith through its picture of Christ, the Davidic prince at work, the passage concludes with a reminder of God's presence through his Holy Spirit: "These seven are the eyes of the LORD, which range through the whole earth." Some commentators link this to the seven lights of the lampstand, although that seems unlikely since the passage has now moved on to the stone laid by Zerubbabel. Back in chapter 3, we read of a stone on which there were seven eyes (Zech. 3:9). In commenting on that passage, I argued that this spoke of the Holy Spirit indwelling and empowering the Messiah to come, the foundation stone of the temple. Now we are reminded that this same Holy Spirit represents the omniscience of God as he gazes upon all his people in all their endeavors for him. Verse 10 thus

---

5. John Calvin, *The Minor Prophets*, 5 vols. (Edinburgh: Banner of Truth, 1986), 5:120.

encourages us that since Christ has taken up his work we can be sure of success, and not the least because of God's watching care and pleasure.

FAITH MOVING MOUNTAINS

What great encouragement this passage has for us! Like the Jews of old, we find that the unchanging God will surely respond with grace for those who trust in him. We are not left to our weakness, nor are we abandoned to search out some might of our own devising or left to resort to worldly methods in order to do the work God has given us to do. We, too, are able to rely on God's Spirit to provide what we need, on God's strength to overcome obstacles on our behalf, and on God's Messiah who leads us.

Who, then, will despise the day of small things? On the contrary, "Men will rejoice when they see the plumb line in the hand of Zerubbabel" (Zech. 4:10 NIV). How wonderful it is for us, too, to see Christians who undertake great things by faith, in the power of Christ who builds his church through our labors!

None of this will be seen apart from faith. It was faith that this vision was given to inspire—faith that what we dare to begin for God will not be done in vain. It is by faith that we, too, stand before mountains and watch them fall. On this we have the word of our Lord Jesus himself, who said to his disciples, "For truly, I say to you, if you have faith like a grain of mustard seed, you will say to this mountain, 'Move from here to there,' and it will move, and nothing will be impossible for you" (Matt. 17:20).

10

THE TWO OLIVE TREES

Zechariah 4:11–14

He said to me, "Do you not know what these are?" I said, "No, my lord." Then he said, "These are the two anointed ones who stand by the Lord of the whole earth." (Zech. 4:13–14)

iblical writers frequently employ a literary strategy called *chiasm*. A chiastic structure, named for the Greek letter chi (x), associates ideas through symmetric parallelism. For instance, if there are four verses organized as a chiasm, the progression would be a, b, b', a', the letters showing the linked pairs. Most important, however, is the idea of climactic centrality. A chiastic structure builds its ideas toward the center and then back out. The pair in the center is of greatest significance to the message, and the structure communicates this to readers who are familiar with it.

The eight night visions in Zechariah seem to be organized in a loosely chiastic pattern. The first vision, for instance, features horsemen who have gathered from the four corners of the earth. The eighth and last vision features four chariots. The link between other pairs is not as obvious, but it is quite clear that there is a climactic link between the fourth and fifth visions—

the central passages found in Zechariah 3 and 4. These two visions form the heart of the visionary sequence, dealing with the two key leaders in Jerusalem: Joshua the high priest and Zerubbabel the governor, and through them the religious and political institutions of the city. These two visions answer vital questions about the restoration of the priesthood and the royal house. They also mark a transition from hope to action. The first four visions told the Jews that God was willing to extend his grace in response to their renewed faith. The second set of four visions challenged them to build and serve in response. This is consistent with the Christian life; we receive salvation as a gift, but then are charged to live and serve to the glory of God.

THE TWO OLIVE TREES

Another reason to think of the fourth and fifth visions as a linked pair is the way they are brought together as a summary in Zechariah 4. This chapter began with the vision of the lampstand, followed by a message for Zerubbabel to build the temple. But now, before we move on, the prophet stops the angel with a question that takes us back to the vision. He realizes that there is an element that has not yet been explained, namely, the two olive trees on either side of the lampstand. These olive trees supplied the oil for the seven lamps, signifying the Spirit's sufficiency for God's work.

Now Zechariah turns back to the vision, asking, "What are these two olive trees on the right and the left of the lampstand?" (Zech. 4:11). Receiving no answer, the prophet becomes a bit more specific: "What are these two branches of the olive trees, which are beside the two golden pipes from which the golden oil is poured out?" (Zech. 4:12). As happened before, the angel responds as if the prophet should understand: "Do you not know what these are?" (Zech. 4:13). Zechariah says, "No, my lord." "Then he said, 'These are the two anointed ones who stand by the Lord of the whole earth'" (Zech. 4:14).

This is hardly a straightforward explanation, yet there is little dispute regarding the meaning of this passage. Zechariah sees two olive trees, and on each of the trees is a branch sprout, or even a cluster of fruit, beneath which are pipes or channels. These sprouts pour golden oil—that is, olive oil, which we have seen symbolizes the Holy Spirit—into the channels which deliver the oil to fuel the lights on the lampstand. Zechariah asks about the trees, but when he fails to receive an answer he specifies the sprouts. "These are the two anointed ones who stand by the Lord of the whole earth" (Zech. 4:14), the angel replies.

Some writers see the sprouts as the two great prophets of the day, Haggai and Zechariah. Others think of them as the two dispensations of law and gospel. But there is no basis for either of these views except a predisposition to discover them. What makes the most sense in the context of this passage, and what is the view of the great majority of commentators, is that these two branches are the two subjects of these visions, namely, Joshua the priest and Zerubbabel the prince.

The language used by the angel makes this certain. The English Standard Version (ESV) says, "These are the two anointed ones." The original Hebrew reads, "These are the two sons of oil," which we might almost translate as "oily ones." The ESV interprets this rightly, that these two are the ones who were anointed for office. When we look through the Old Testament, we find three types of people anointed for their office: prophets, priests, and kings. Of the three, two were established, regular offices ordained by God as the permanent institutions of the theocracy: the priesthood and the kingship. The high priests and the kings were anointed to show that in their office they were mediators of God's Spirit. It was through their godly performance of office that God's blessing came to the people. Joshua and Zerubbabel are branches of the olive trees; in their activities they were extensions and applications of these two mediatorial offices.

This completes the vision. The priesthood and the kingship, as ordained by God, mediated God's Spirit just as the oil flowed through the channels into the lampstand. The oil is the Spirit, who fuels the flames, makes bright the light, and empowers every spiritual work.

TWO ANOINTED OFFICES

On the basis of this symbolism, we should take some time to reflect on these two offices. The priests served to represent sinful people before the holy God, to offer sacrifices to atone for their sins, and to intercede in prayer in order to attain God's favor. The kings ruled on God's behalf, governing his people and establishing his righteousness upon the earth.

When we think of the priesthood, we should specifically think of the high priest, since Joshua held that office. Every year on the day of atonement, the high priest entered into the Lord's presence to make atonement for the sins of the people. First he offered a sacrifice for his own sins, and then he cleansed himself. After that he entered the inner sanctum—the holy of holies where God himself dwelt—bearing the blood of a sacrifice for the sins of the nation. There he saw the ark of the covenant, with its cherubim and their upswept wings, the footstool of the throne of God and the chariot seat of the Lord. Inside the ark were the tablets of the Ten Commandments, resting before the eyes of the Lord while the high priest, representing the sinful people, stood before him. The people had broken those commandments, and the high priest came in to offer the blood of a substitute in their place. He poured the blood upon the mercy seat, the tray that covered the ark, so that instead of seeing the broken law God now saw the blood of the sacrifice. Thus his anger was propitiated through an atonement made for the people's sins.

By removing the barrier of sin, the high priest opened up the channel of blessing, the outpoured Holy Spirit. This is what happened when Solomon inaugurated the first temple. After the ark was brought in and the sacrifices were offered, "a cloud filled the house of the LORD . . . for the glory of the LORD filled the house of the LORD" (1 Kings 8:10–11). It was through the priests' work of offering sacrifices and making intercession that God's Spirit came to the people.

The other anointed office represented in this vision is that of the king. The king was also anointed as a mediator. The people were to obey the king, and the king was to obey God. According to the law that Moses established:

> When he sits on the throne of his kingdom, he shall write for himself in a book a copy of this law, approved by the Levitical priests. And it shall be with him, and he shall read in it all the days of his life, that he may learn to fear the LORD his God by keeping all the words of this law and these statutes, and doing them. (Deut. 17:18–19)

The king was to be the model believer, therefore—the principal covenant-keeper and a student of God's Word, of which he had made a personal copy by his own hand, reverent in worship and careful in obedience. In this manner he secured God's favor not merely for himself, but also for the whole of the people.

The model king was David, whose name meant "beloved," and who was called the "man after God's own heart" (1 Sam. 13:14): "With upright heart he shepherded them and guided them with his skillful hand" (Ps. 78:72). Through David, God's favor was upon the people. God said, "I have found David, my servant; with my holy oil I have anointed him, so that my hand shall be established with him; my arm also shall strengthen him. The enemy shall not outwit him; the wicked shall not humble him. I will crush his foes before him and strike down those who hate him. My faithfulness and my steadfast love shall be with him, and in my name shall his horn be exalted" (Ps. 89:20–24). It was no small thing, therefore, for Zerubbabel to represent the Davidic throne.

Some scholars believe that the book of Zechariah records a transfer of focus from the kingship to the priesthood, especially since Zechariah 6:11 shows a crown being placed on the head of the high priest. Prior to the exile, the kings were in the foreground, which is why the main history of that period is called the Book of Kings. After the exile, however, there were no kings. Jeconiah, also known as Jehoiachin, was the last legitimate king. He died in exile. Zerubbabel was heir to the throne, but never actually reigned as king. He served instead as governor under the Persian emperor, though he did exercise royal rule in Jerusalem. After Zerubbabel, the kingly line faded into obscurity. This fulfilled the curse God imposed on wicked Jeconiah: "Write this man down as childless, a man who shall not succeed in his days, for none of his offspring shall succeed in sitting on the throne of David and ruling again in Judah" (Jer. 22:30).

If Zerubbabel was Jeconiah's grandson, we can see why some would think that the royal line was cut off. But this becomes a real problem when we realize that Jeconiah also appears in Matthew's genealogy of Jesus Christ, as does Zerubbabel. If no heir of Zerubbabel could be enthroned, Christ's kingship would seem to be in question.

The answer to the problem seems to be found in the differences between Matthew's and Luke's genealogies, discrepancies that focus, it turns out, on the parentage of Zerubbabel (and of Shealtiel, who is sometimes listed as his father). Apparent discrepancies occur in the Old Testament as well as the New Testament genealogies. In several places, Zerubbabel is called the "son of Shealtiel" (Ezra 3:2, 8; 5:2; Neh. 12:1; Hag. 1:1, 12, 14; 2:2, 23). But in 1 Chronicles 3:19 we find that he was in fact

Shealtiel's nephew. Similarly, Shealtiel is often listed as Jeconiah's son, but Luke's genealogy lists him as the son of a man named Neri.

What seems to have happened is that with the collapse of the royal house in the conquest and exile, family relationships became understandably complicated. We know from the Scriptures that the great majority of the Jews were killed. Those who were left were led into captivity, no doubt with many families torn apart. Numerous adoptions must have taken place, either formally or informally. Many younger men would have taken over for elders in their extended family, and were afterwards referred to as their "sons" regardless of actual blood relationships.

Admittedly, the Gospel genealogies are difficult. However, J. Gresham Machen is right when he argues that Matthew's genealogy, being the more Jewish, records the line of legal descent. Matthew answers the question, "Who is the legal heir to the throne?" In that genealogy, Shealtiel was the next living relative in line for the throne after Jeconiah, though not of his direct descent. From him the royal line passed on to Zerubbabel his nephew, and on through the generations to Joseph, who married Mary and gave the royal right to his adopted son, Jesus. Under this way of thinking, Luke's gospel records the actual bloodlines, answering the question, "Who is born of whom?" Here we find that Shealtiel and Zerubbabel were not of Jeconiah's cursed line, but came from a different branch of David's family. Their bloodline passed to Joseph, so that he was biologically of the house of David and also the legal heir.[1] Incidentally, we know from Romans 1:3 that Mary also was a descendant of David.

The point of all this is that there is no reason to think that Zechariah's prophecy shows the kingship set aside, even though it is historically true that the priests would come to the fore in the generations to come. Far from putting aside the king's house, this vision greatly encourages Zerubbabel in his royal office. The same is true of the message of Haggai: " 'I will make you like my signet ring,' " the prophet said to Zerubbabel, " 'for I have chosen you,' declares the LORD Almighty" (Hag. 2:23 NIV). Zerubbabel was the present occupant of the royal office, and through his offspring the true messianic king would come in due time.

---

1. See Machen's outstanding discussion in *The Virgin Birth of Christ* (New York: Harper & Bros., 1930), 202–9.

THE TWOFOLD MINISTRY: PRIEST AND KING

In our study of Zechariah 4, we have noted the vision of the golden lampstand as a pattern for spiritual blessing. There are two olive trees, one representing the priesthood and the other the kingship, both mediating the Spirit into the lampstand so that it burns and glows, casting warmth and light into the darkness. When we remember that the two branches from which the Spirit-oil flows represent Israel's fallen and failed leaders—Joshua with his dirty clothes and Zerubbabel with his unfinished temple—we see how God's grace is the key motive power for the hopes of his people. One writer states: "The pattern is always the same. The Lord plucks sinners from the fire, cleanses and forgives them, and, by the power of His Holy Spirit, enables them to be His shining light in a sin-darkened world."[2]

Earlier, when we studied the lampstand, we considered its likely symbolism in terms of three main options: the temple, the presence of God in the ministry of Jesus Christ, or the people of God as his servants in the world. As we saw then, there is no pressing need to choose between these interpretations since they are organically connected. Both Jesus and the church are symbolized by the temple, and there is the closest possible connection between Christ and his people. We should now return to these three symbols and see what the olive trees say about each one.

If the lampstand represents the temple—which at some level it must, given the message of this chapter—how is it that the two offices of priest and king serve as the means of its blessing? The answer to this is not difficult. The temple is where the sacrifices were offered for the covering of sin, and this was the job of the priests. Therefore, if the temple was to shine its light, to make its proclamation about God and salvation, it would be through the restored order of priests. This is why the vision of Joshua's cleansing in chapter 3 is so important. It is only as the priestly work was accepted by God that the Holy Spirit could return to the temple.

The importance of the royal, or political, leadership is evident from this whole chapter. Like Solomon before him, Zerubbabel was to build the temple.

2. Fred Hartman, *Zechariah: Israel's Messenger of the Messiah's Triumph* (Bellmawr, NJ: Friends of Israel, 1994), 54.

This meant he had to gather the resources, organize the labor force, and provide protection against potential enemies. Indeed, in this vision we see just how the priesthood and the kingship interrelated in Old Testament Israel. The kings reigned on God's behalf, implementing the laws and defending the nation, while the priests did the spiritual work of bringing the people into fellowship with God. It is through the joint work of these two offices that the Holy Spirit came to the temple and thus to the nation.

When we turn to the ministry of Jesus Christ, these two offices come to their fullest realization. As the lampstand represents the presence of God in Christ, so the two olive trees signify the union of these two offices in his one ministry. In verse 14 the angel describes Joshua and Zerubbabel as "sons of oil," signifying their anointed offices. Jesus Christ is the true "Son of Oil." This is what the term "Messiah" or "Christ" literally means—Anointed One. He is the Anointed One who truly mediates the Holy Spirit, through whom come blessing and power for salvation.

This connection provides us with a key insight, namely, that the designed effect of Jesus' ministry was the sending of the Holy Spirit. Historically, this was the culmination of his first coming: he was born, lived, died for us, rose from death, and ascended into heaven. But his work was not accomplished until Pentecost, when the Spirit came upon the church. As Paul summarized, "Christ redeemed us . . . so that we might receive the promised Spirit through faith" (Gal. 3:13–14).

The Christian life is life in the Holy Spirit. This is what Paul was talking about when he said, "It is no longer I who live, but Christ who lives in me" (Gal. 2:20). This means it is not enough for us simply to know Bible truths; we must have power to lead the life spoken of in the Bible. We tend to think in terms of our forgiveness, as if that were an end in itself, when in fact it is a means to this end: that God would fill us with his Spirit for doing his will. John 3:34 says the Father gave Christ the Spirit without limit. The reason for this is that "from his fullness we have all received, grace upon grace" (John 1:16). Christ was filled with the Spirit, so that he might fill us in turn, even as this vision of the olive trees so vividly depicts. God's grace flows by his Spirit because of the twofold ministry of Jesus Christ, our priest and our king.

When we think about Jesus' ministry as high priest, we remember that the priest mediated between man and God. The priest represented sinners before God by offering sacrifices for sin. God must judge us for our sin: this is the great barrier between us and God's salvation, and the great obstacle to the outpouring of his Spirit. Jesus as high priest removes the barrier. Hebrews 9 tells us the whole Old Testament sacrificial system pointed forward to his great and true sacrifice. How effective, how sufficient, was the blood of Christ, "who through the eternal Spirit offered himself without blemish to God, [to] purify our conscience from dead works to serve the living God" (Heb. 9:14). The apostle Peter writes, "Christ died for sins once for all, the righteous for the unrighteous, to bring you to God. He was put to death in the body but made alive by the Spirit" (1 Pet. 3:18 NIV).

As our living high priest, Jesus brings us to God and puts our sins away. Furthermore, as our living priest Christ continually intercedes for us. His wounds plead effectual prayers, reminding the Father of his covenant of grace and securing for us the riches of God's Spirit. How essential is this priestly ministry! Were it not for this mediatorial work, Christ as prophet could speak only judgment, and Christ as king could only rule with a rod of iron.

But because Christ has come as priest, he reigns as king for our salvation, and through this office he also sends God's Holy Spirit. His first coming meant the coming of God's kingdom, as through the Spirit he pushed back the reign of death and of sin and Satan. This is no less true now, as Jesus reigns in heaven, having declared, "All authority in heaven and on earth has been given to me" (Matt. 28:18). It is through Jesus Christ that what was said of Zerubbabel fully comes to fruition. After Zerubbabel, the kingship dwindled until it was a stump that was cut off. But Jesus is the Shoot or Branch that grows from the stump and becomes the whole tree.

What does a king do? The answer is that he rules, and Jesus rules in us by God's Spirit. As Josiah sent his officials to tear down the Asherah poles and break apart the Baals, so Christ the King sends his Spirit to root out our idols. A king conquers, and through his Spirit Christ conquers our hearts, bringing us to faith. A king arms and equips and empowers his servants, and Christ does all these things for us through the Holy Spirit. John Calvin writes, "From him abundantly flow the heavenly riches of which we are in such need. The believers stand unconquered through the strength of their king, and his spiritual riches abound in them."[3]

3. John Calvin, *Institutes of the Christian Religion*, ed. John T. McNeill (Philadelphia: Westminster, 1960), II.xv.5.

The great design of Christ's ministry is to send the Spirit, and this happens through the channel of our faith, just as the olive trees in Zechariah's vision sent their oil through the pipes into the golden lampstand. Christ's role is to reconcile us to God as priest, and to rule and conquer as king. Our role is to receive these vast blessings through faith, as is well depicted by these empty pipes that connect into the olive trees, and receive from Christ the life-giving benefits of his saving work. In this way we are, as Paul says, "the fullness of him who fills all in all" (Eph. 1:23).

THE OLIVE TREES AND THE CHRISTIAN LIFE

This leads us finally to apply the vision to ourselves, God's people—that is, to our own sanctification and witness in the world. Revelation 1:5–6 says that Christ "loves us and has freed us from our sins by his blood and made us a kingdom, priests to his God and Father." We have been made a kingdom and priests. Peter also refers to us as God's temple: "a holy priesthood, to offer spiritual sacrifices acceptable to God through Jesus Christ" (1 Peter 2:5). Peter adds, in words strongly reminiscent of Zechariah's vision: "You are a chosen race, a royal priesthood, a holy nation, a people for his own possession, that you may proclaim the excellencies of him who called you out of darkness into his marvelous light" (1 Peter 2:9).

How do Christians exercise priesthood and kingship? First, we do this in our fight against sin. Augustus Toplady rightly spoke of the double nature of sin in his great hymn "Rock of Ages": "Be of sin the double cure, cleanse me from its guilt and power." For this double cure we draw upon Christ's twofold work. We draw upon his priestly work to cleanse us from sin's guilt. And we draw upon Christ's kingly office for deliverance from sin's power. Through faith in the Priest-King Jesus Christ, believers are to live as justified saints—those cleansed and armed for holy battle through the Spirit-empowered ministry of Christ.

The same can be said about our witness. Like Israel's priests, we hold before the world the gospel of Christ's saving blood. God has given us the priestly ministry of reconciliation: "Therefore, we are ambassadors for Christ, God making his appeal through us. We implore you on behalf of Christ, be reconciled to God" (2 Cor. 5:20). Our message to the world is the cross, where Christ's blood was shed to reconcile sinners to God. Our witness requires that we also participate in Christ's royal office. As we pray, so we do: "Your kingdom come, your will be done, on earth as it is in heaven." We serve as Christ's royal officials in this world, extending his reign through works of righteousness and mercy and truth. Like a light on a lamp, Jesus said, "let your light shine before others, so that they may see your good works and give glory to your Father who is in heaven" (Matt. 5:16).

This is how Christians live in this world: having been reconciled by a priest and called into the service of a king, we are agents of Christ's twofold ministry in the power of the Spirit he sends. John Calvin rightly concludes:

> Thus it is that we patiently pass through this life with its misery, hunger, cold, contempt, reproaches, and other troubles—content with this one thing: that our King will never leave us destitute, but will provide for our needs until, our warfare ended, we are called to triumph. Such is the nature of his rule, that he shares with us all that he has received from the Father. Now he arms and equips us with his power, adorns us with his beauty and magnificence, enriches us with his wealth. These benefits, then, give us the most fruitful occasion to glory, and also provide us with confidence to struggle fearlessly against the devil, sin, and death.[4]

May Jesus Christ, our high priest and king, send each of us his Spirit in abundance, to bring us to God and rule within us as we look to him in faith.

4. Calvin, *Institutes*, II.xv.4.

11

THE FLYING SCROLL

Zechariah 5:1–11

He said to me, "What do you see?" I answered, "I see a flying
scroll. Its length is twenty cubits, and its width ten cubits." Then
he said to me, "This is the curse that goes out over the face of the
whole land. For everyone who steals shall be cleaned out accord-
ing to what is on one side, and everyone who swears falsely shall
be cleaned out according to what is on the other side."
(Zech. 5:2–3)

n his novel *The Plague*, Albert Camus tells the story of a group
of people afflicted with bubonic plague and then quarantined so as to bar escape. The characters are all faced with the
unavoidable reality of suffering and death, and in this context they must
come to grips with meaning and reality, all in accordance with Camus's
existential philosophy. Camus wrote *The Plague* in occupied France during World War II, with Nazi soldiers in uncontested control of his own
quarantined existence, a setting that surely shaped his thoughts about
the inevitability of evil and death.

Camus's grim portrait of this world is to some degree in agreement with the biblical picture. The Bible, too, sees a sinister reign of evil, and a disease within our race that leads to death. The visions in Zechariah 5:1–11 deal with this reality. But while Camus's world without God was one of grim resolve absent of hope, the prophet's was one of sober resolve full of hope, because of a God who is greater than evil.

Zechariah 5 presents two visions, the sixth and seventh, which are so closely connected that we should consider them as a single unit. Whereas Camus pictured evil that could not be escaped, the visions of Zechariah 5 argue that where God dwells, the plague of sin must be removed. They make three points regarding sin: *sin discovered, sin judged,* and *sin removed.*

THE FLYING SCROLL: SIN DISCOVERED

As often has been the case in these night visions of Zechariah, the imagery here is bizarre but the meaning is nonetheless fairly clear. Chapter 5 begins with the prophet telling us what he saw in this new vision:

> Again I lifted my eyes and saw, and behold, a flying scroll! And he said to me, "What do you see?" I answered, "I see a flying scroll. Its length is twenty cubits, and its width ten cubits." Then he said to me, "This is the curse that goes out over the face of the whole land. For everyone who steals shall be cleaned out according to what is on one side, and everyone who swears falsely shall be cleaned out according to what is on the other side." (Zech. 5:1–3)

To understand the symbolism in these visions, we need to look elsewhere in Scripture. In the prophetic literature, and especially in the prophets around the time of the exile, scrolls appear as messages from God to the leaders or people. The Lord told Jeremiah to prepare a scroll for wicked king Jehoiakim, warning him of impending disaster because of his sin (Jer. 36:1–3). Similarly, one of Ezekiel's opening visions also included a scroll with "words of lamentation and mourning and woe" (Ezek. 2:9–10). With those precedents, the appearance of a scroll likely caused Zechariah's heart to skip a beat. As a prophet representing a generation returning from exile in judgment, a symbol of God's chastisement must have been most alarming.

121

The key information about this scroll appears in verse 3, which makes two references to the Ten Commandments. On one side is the eighth commandment, against stealing, and on the other is the ninth commandment, against giving false testimony. These particular sins—theft and false swearing—are specifically emphasized as prevailing problems in Zechariah's time, especially since he later exhorts: "These are the things that you shall do: Speak the truth to one another; render in your gates judgments that are true and make for peace; do not devise evil in your hearts against one another, and love no false oath, for all these things I hate, declares the LORD" (8:16–17).

Meredith Kline points out that the description in verse 3 of "one side" and the "other side" may allude to the two tablets of the Ten Commandments. Moreover, the specific charges speak to a violation of the first great commandment—to love God—and the second great commandment—to love our neighbors. To "swear falsely by my name" dishonors God and stealing harms our neighbors.[1] We should note as well that these are both mercantile sins. Then, as now, the way God's people conduct their business shows the character of their worship. Kline explains, "They repudiate Yahweh, King of Glory, prostituting themselves to the love of the glory of the world, to the worship of Mammon. . . . [These sins] would change the holy community into something indistinguishable from the world. They would turn Jerusalem into Babylon. Therefore, the King of Zion sends the curse scroll over the whole face of the land to excise them."[2]

The flying scroll of the law shows that *sin will be discovered.* It goes throughout the land, seeking out those who have sinned. They may hide in their houses, but the scroll will enter the house and find them. Sin will be discovered, says this vision, and this is a shocking thought. Few people today really believe this, perhaps because the vast majority of our sins seem to go undetected. Even if found out, they are likely to be tolerated by other people and society. However, even if they are not tolerated, we do not truly expect to be punished for most things the Bible calls sin. We live a sin-tolerant existence.

But this experience poorly prepares us for the situation when it comes to God, for he says that every sin will be found out. None will go undetected.

---

1. Meredith Kline, *The Glory in Our Midst: A Biblical-Theological Reading of Zechariah's Night Visions* (Overland Park, KS: Two Age Press, 2001), 178.
2. Ibid., 181.

Like today's heat-seeking missiles, this vision shows the scroll of the law honing in on every transgressor and transgression. In the last words of Ecclesiastes, Solomon warns, "For God will bring every deed into judgment, with every secret thing, whether good or evil" (Eccl. 12:14). Arthur Pink observes:

> How solemn is this fact: nothing can be concealed from God! . . . Though He be invisible to us, we are not so to Him. Neither the darkness of night, the closest curtains, nor the deepest dungeon can hide any sinner from the eyes of Omniscience. The trees of the garden were not able to conceal our first parents. No human eye beheld Cain murder his brother, but his Maker witnessed his crime. Sarah might laugh derisively in the seclusion of her tent, yet was it heard by Jehovah. Achan stole a wedge of gold and carefully hid it in the earth, but God brought it to light. David was at much pains to cover up his wickedness, but ere long the all-seeing God sent one of His servants to say to him, "Thou art the man!" And to writer and reader is also said, "Be sure *your* sin will find you out" (Num. 32:23).[3]

Sinners are rightly uneasy to feel God's eyes upon them. It is like being in a room with a portrait of some old and grim warrior on the wall behind us; wherever we go its eyes seem to follow us. People always want to leave such a room, and likewise sinners are uneasy about God's omniscience.

The other detail we are told is the scroll's dimensions: "Its length is twenty cubits, and its width ten cubits" (Zech. 5:2)—that is, thirty feet long and fifteen feet wide. This is more like a billboard than a scroll; obviously it was designed to be noticed and read. Those also happen to be the dimensions of the holy place within the temple, the room just outside of the veil covering the holy of holies, God's inner sanctum in Israel. The holy place was where the priests served the Lord. Surely this detail is significant. The holy place is where God communicated with man regularly; there he gave revelation of himself through the lampstand and the table of showbread.

This sin-seeking scroll, bearing God's law and reflecting the dimensions of the holy place, reminds us that what determines sin is God's revelation. We are not the ones who create moral reality, try though we might. We cannot revise moral truth by deciding for ourselves what is right and wrong. This scroll goes forth with God's law, not with man's opinion; its

---

3. Arthur W. Pink, *The Attributes of God* (Grand Rapids: Baker, 1975), 17–18.

dimensions are not those of the latest poll but of God's holy character. Our moral judgment is fatally flawed, like a distorted mirror in a carnival. What is straight our hearts show as crooked, and what is crooked as straight. So God gives us his law as a mirror in which to see ourselves truly—to know sin and ourselves as sinners the way that God does.

This message is of great importance to our age of moral relativism. What was wrong yesterday is tolerated today and will be approved tomorrow. We have thrown out the word "sin" for "dysfunction" and left its definition to be decided by sociologists and psychologists and legislators. As our theories and tastes change so do our moral codes. But this vision declares that God determines what is right and wrong. His standards are based not on our studies or trends or claims to progress, still less on our abilities, but on his holy character as revealed in his law. He has fixed the dimensions of sin and righteousness; he has revealed these to us, and they are as unchanging and unchangeable as he is.

If you want to know what is right or wrong, the place to start is the Ten Commandments, which this scroll displays in large letters: revelation from God that is clear and unambiguous and utterly binding. What you see condemned in God's law may not seem so bad to you. Everybody else might do it. The government might allow it. The gatekeepers of popular culture might applaud it. But it is by his law that God identifies sin, and every sin will surely be discovered.

THE SCROLL'S CURSE: SIN JUDGED

The vision of the scroll proclaims that sin will be discovered, and the angel's words tell the tale of *sin judged*: "I will send it out, declares the LORD of hosts, and it shall enter the house of the thief, and the house of him who swears falsely by my name. And it shall remain in his house and consume it, both timber and stones" (Zech. 5:4).

What happens when God's law discovers sin? The answer is that God's curse is sent forth. God said in giving his law, "See, I am setting before you today a blessing and a curse: the blessing, if you obey . . . and the curse, if you do not obey the commandments of the LORD your God" (Deut. 11:26–28). Sin receives God's curse. The scroll reveals God's active hostility toward sin and the sinner. It is like the angel of death who visited Egypt in its last and greatest plague, entering every house and taking the life of every firstborn. This was God's active judgment, visiting wrath on those found in sin. "It shall enter the house of the thief, and the house of him who swears falsely by my name. And it shall remain in his house and consume it, both timber and stones" (Zech. 5:4). Elizabeth Achtemeier rightly comments:

> We have so sentimentalized the deity that we do not believe he would curse any one or any lifestyle. But the prophets know better. God demands obedience to his commandments and he will settle for nothing less. Presented with less, he does indeed eat away at the structures of a disobedient life, like a leprous mold (Lev. 14:34–35), or an unseen moth or a penetrating dry rot (Hos. 5:12); and our illnesses and anxieties, our distorted relationships and broken homes, our servitudes and murderous societies are symptomatic of his unseen but judging presence.[4]

Sin is cursed because God is holy. God hates sin, and he cannot ignore sin without compromising his holiness. We may try to hide in houses, or to defend ourselves with public opinion or intellectual defiance, but surely Charles Feinberg is right to say of this vision: "God himself will bring forth the curse, and it will accomplish its devastating work. The sinners cannot shut themselves up in their houses to guard against the curse; it will enter despite their efforts. The destruction will be complete, leaving no trace of the house . . . and the consumption of the house includes those who reside there."[5]

THE WOMAN IN THE BASKET: SIN REMOVED

Verses 5–11 move on to show the seventh vision, which clearly forms one message with the one before it. Having been discovered and judged, sin is then pictured as a woman in a basket, there to be removed from the land:

> Then the angel who talked with me came forward and said to me, "Lift your eyes and see what this is that is going out." And I said, "What is it?" He said, "This is the basket that is going out." And he said, "This is their iniquity in

---

4. Elizabeth Achtemeier, *Nahum-Malachi* (Atlanta: John Knox, 1986), 128.
5. Charles Feinberg, *The Minor Prophets* (Chicago: Moody Press, 1990), 294.

all the land." And behold, the leaden cover was lifted, and there was a woman sitting in the basket! And he said, "This is Wickedness." And he thrust her back into the basket, and thrust down the leaden weight on its opening. (Zech. 5:5–8)

Zechariah is shown a bushel container, probably something like a barrel. The angel says that inside is "the iniquity of the people throughout the land." When the lid is raised a woman is seen, and lest she should escape, the cover is slammed back down.

The point of this vision is not that all our problems can be blamed on women. It does show us, however, that there is a face on evil. Sin is not just something happening "out there." Sin is done by sinners: by people we pass in the street, by people we go to work with and live with and sit beside in church. Sin is done by us: by me and by you. The sins of God's people placed in this basket were not just abstract societal woes. They were not the product of bad environments or poor education or poverty. They were the works of the people themselves. Every Israelite hearing of this vision should have seen his own face on the woman in the basket. When you read these verses you should see, "Then the cover of lead was raised, and there in the basket sat someone who looked like me!"

This vision makes a point that people don't like to hear today. We often hear that God hates the sin but loves the sinner. There is truth in this because it reminds us that while sin is certain of judgment, sinners can escape judgment through faith in Christ. But there is a danger in saying that God hates sin but not sinners: unless and until you repent, God's wrath burns not just against your sin, but also against you. Hell is not populated with sin, but with sinners. This vision shows sin taken away—not in the abstract, but as it is personalized. It tells us that there will be faces of real people in hell.

Zechariah 5:9–11 completes the vision:

Then I lifted my eyes and saw, and behold, two women coming forward! The wind was in their wings. They had wings like the wings of a stork, and they lifted up the basket between earth and heaven. Then I said to the angel who talked with me, "Where are they taking the basket?" He said to me, "To the land of Shinar, to build a house for it. And when this is prepared, they will set the basket down there on its base."

The stork was a bird common to the Ancient Near East, known for its strong wings and long migrations. Two women with such wings lift the basket of iniquity and, aided by God's breath, the wind, they remove it from the land of God's people, taking it to Babylon. The Hebrew text actually names the place as Shinar, the location of the tower of Babel in Genesis 11, site of the world's first organized rebellion against God. H. C. Leupold explains, "Shinar represents the world, generally speaking, as contrasted with the church. It follows the principles of wickedness; it shall acquire more and more of wickedness."[6]

Revelation 17 picks up on this imagery, showing a woman "arrayed in purple and scarlet, and adorned with gold and jewels and pearls, holding in her hand a golden cup full of abominations and the impurities of her sexual immorality. And on her forehead was written a name of mystery: 'Babylon the great, mother of prostitutes and of earth's abominations' " (vv. 4–5). Babylon is where sin was taken and set up in a house, far away from God's realm. Revelation goes on to show the sinful world's judgment: "Fallen! Fallen is Babylon the Great! She has become a home for demons and a haunt for every evil spirit. . . . She will be consumed by fire, for mighty is the Lord God who judges her. . . . The smoke from her goes up for ever and ever" (Rev. 18:2, 8; 19:3 NIV).

This completes the message of Zechariah 5, which shows sin discovered because of God's omniscience, sin judged because of God's holiness, and sin removed by God's almighty power.

SIN TAKEN AWAY

However impressive this vision may be, it does not seem to have happened so far. Sin is not found out, judged, and removed, but instead seems to prosper quite well in this world. This is not, however, completely true. The whole record of history shows that the wicked are ultimately cast down and the proud are humbled. Albert Camus, living under Nazi rule, may have found that hard to see, but the record of that very war bears it out. The reason is stated by the psalmist: "The face of the LORD is against those who do evil, to cut off the memory of them from the earth" (Ps. 34:16). Still, it is true that

6. H. C. Leupold, *An Exposition of Zechariah* (Grand Rapids: Baker, 1971), 108.

God has yet to put an end to all sin. Wickedness has not yet been placed in a basket and removed, nor was it eradicated from Jerusalem in Zechariah's day.

How, then, are we to understand this vision's fulfillment? First, it informs us about God's principles. God's kingdom is incompatible with sin. Chapter 4 promised the completion of God's temple in Jerusalem, and now chapter 5 informs us that sin must therefore be dealt with. In this respect, this vision pictures the purification of God's people. "Be holy, for I am holy," God says, both to Old Testament Israel (Lev. 11:45) and to New Testament followers of Christ (1 Peter 1:16). God will not dwell with sin; one or the other must depart. If we are to be God's people, then we, like him, must be radically committed to the removal of sin and the pursuit of holiness.

Second, this vision tells us how things will be in the end. The removal of sin from God's world is the uniform prediction of the Scriptures. Revelation 21:27 tells us of the heavenly city: "Nothing unclean will ever enter it, nor anyone who does what is detestable or false, but only those who are written in the Lamb's book of life." God's city, in the end, will be clear not only from sinners and sin, but even from the principle of sin, which God will remove utterly, like the woman in the basket. This means that we must all, in the end, face God and deal with our sins. If we have not dealt with sin before the day of judgment, we will be cast away from him into hell for eternal condemnation. This is what this vision of the woman in the basket ultimately prefigures: sinners cast away from heaven and into hell, desperately seeking to escape like the woman from the basket, only to have it shut tight.

How then can our sin be removed before the day of judgment? The Bible's answer is through faith in Jesus Christ. Paul writes, "He forgave us all our sins, having canceled the written code, with its regulations, that was against us and that stood opposed to us; he took it away, nailing it to the cross" (Col. 2:13–14 NIV). The scroll of God's law that so threatens us was caught in its flight by Jesus Christ, the one man who never violated its letter or spirit, so that he alone is free of its condemnation. Jesus fulfilled the law, and as he was nailed to the cross so was the law, no longer to condemn those who belong to him through faith and whose sins are paid by his blood.

Zechariah's vision-scroll bears a curse for sinners, but Christ has taken and exhausted that curse for us. Galatians 3:13 says, "Christ redeemed us from the curse of the law by becoming a curse for us." If we are joined to Christ through faith, he has taken our sin away, bearing it in our place on the cross, so that we will be forgiven instead of cursed: "As far as the east is from the west, so far does he remove our transgressions from us" (Ps. 103:12).

TWO DIFFERENT VISIONS

This pair of visions communicates a grim message, featuring curses and judgment. It is the kind of thing Camus depicted in *The Plague* as the inescapable lot of those consigned to a world of pestilence and death. All sin will be discovered, then judged, then removed with the sinner who is cast into darkness. Since all of us are sinners, this paints a pretty dismal picture, like the one Camus could not shake as he watched Hitler's soldiers govern by cruel and uncontested force.

But there is something especially remarkable about Camus's book. He wrote *The Plague* from a village in France named Le Chambon, a Huguenot community of Reformed Christians who lived and still live in France. The Christians of Le Chambon did not share Camus's resignation about sin's reign and the ultimacy of death. In the midst of their quiet rural existence, while Camus was dipping his dreary pen in their midst, these Christians were risking their lives to rescue Jewish refugees from the Nazis. After the war, it was learned that the Huguenots of Le Chambon had received, sheltered, and helped with the escape of thousands of Jewish refugees. The Nazis sought the Jews to send them east to Auschwitz and other now-infamous destinations. But the Christians of Le Chambon did not bow before what seemed inevitable. They acted on the principle that evil is destined to be cast out, and that even now those who serve the kingdom of God by faith may see sin's overthrow, both in their own lives and in their sphere of influence.

The Christians of Le Chambon saved the lives of more Jews than their own population, at the imminent risk of detection and the most severe Nazi reprisals. All the while that Camus was writing about the absurdity of life, and about accepting the human disease and just trying to find some semblance of personal meaning, he was literally surrounded by the exact opposite: evidence of light over darkness, and by victory achieved through faith in Jesus Christ. It is inconceivable that Camus would not have been intimately acquainted with the efforts of Le Chambon's Christians, yet he somehow failed to realize that sin does not have the last word when it comes to the saving work of God through Jesus Christ.

This leads to an all-important question. Where do you stand with respect to God and your sin? Are your sins still upon you, so that you resent the thought of God staring at you? Be sure that God is there and your sins will be discovered. If they are not taken from you by the cross of Christ, you will be judged by God's curse. You will be cast from God's presence into the realm of darkness forever. God's holiness stands against you and if you die in your sins you will be lost. Jesus said, "If you do not believe that I am the one I claim to be, you will indeed die in your sins" (John 8:24 NIV).

But there is no reason for that to happen to you. The Bible says: "While we were still weak, at the right time Christ died for the ungodly. . . . God shows his love for us in that while we were still sinners, Christ died for us" (Rom. 5:6, 8). Jesus himself said, "Truly, truly, I say to you, whoever hears my word and believes him who sent me has eternal life. He does not come into judgment" (John 5:24).

Your sins will not be hid from God, and they will not escape judgment. But if you will confess them, if you will discover them and judge yourself a sinner, turning to Christ in faith, then your sin will be removed and placed on his cross. Then you will be brought to God, to know his love and to live now as a beloved member of his family, and later to enter the city where sin dwells no more, forever. There we will be completely clean and holy! Wonderful the thought: we will be free from sin.

12

THE FOUR CHARIOTS

Zechariah 6:1—8

*Again I lifted my eyes and saw, and behold, four chariots came
out from between two mountains. And the mountains were
mountains of bronze. The first chariot had red horses, the second black horses, the third white horses, and the fourth chariot
dappled horses—all of them strong. Then I answered and said to
the angel who talked with me, "What are these, my lord?"*
(Zech. 6:1–4)

The prophet Elisha experienced a stunning deliverance. Elisha
was using his prophetic powers to thwart the king of Aram's
military plans against Israel. So the king directed his horsemen
and chariots against this single man, cornering him and his servant in the
town of Dothan. "When the servant of the man of God rose early in the
morning and went out, behold, an army with horses and chariots was all
around the city. And the servant said, 'Alas, my master! What shall we do?'
He said, 'Do not be afraid, for those who are with us are more than those
who are with them' " (2 Kings 6:15–16).

We can imagine how bewildered the servant was at this calm reply. Surely, he would have rubbed the sleep from his eyes and stuck his head out to look once more. Again, he saw nothing but the threatening hosts of Aram. Therefore, the prophet prayed: " 'O Lord, please open his eyes that he may see.' So the Lord opened the eyes of the young man, and he saw, and behold, the mountain was full of horses and chariots of fire all around Elisha" (2 Kings 6:17).

God intervened by blinding the horsemen of Aram, so that Elisha was able to lead them into captivity. It was a great deliverance that still speaks to God's people about his power to help and save.

This account from earlier days must have been well known to the Jews of Zechariah's day. Because of it, a vision featuring the chariots of God would have brought great encouragement for God's weak and weary people. This is how the vision of Zechariah 6 begins: "Again I lifted my eyes and saw, and behold, four chariots came out from between two mountains" (v. 1).

Zechariah 6 brings us to the last of the visions the prophet received on that sleep-disturbed night in 520 BC. From here we can look back on all eight of these visions and better understand their organization. The first and last visions contain divine horsemen and speak of Jerusalem's relation to the nations. The first tells of a world at peace, in which Israel's oppressors rest secure. This last vision shows God disturbing that ungodly peace with his judgment on those nations. In between these two visions, God deals with the Jewish people and their internal problems. The result of the whole series of visions is a message of encouragement, along with an exhortation to build the temple and spiritually renew the nation.

The Four Chariots

Zechariah 6:1–8 centers on a vision of four chariots going forth between two bronze mountains: "Again I lifted my eyes and saw, and behold, four chariots came out from between two mountains" (Zech. 6:1). As we have seen in earlier visions, while these figures are difficult to identify precisely, their spiritual message is not hard to grasp.

First, we consider the meaning of these two bronze mountains. Bronze was a valuable alloy in those days, more valuable then than now, signifying might. Bronze added strength to a weapon or shield. Jeremiah was called a bronze wall to symbolize his impregnability against attack (Jer.

1:18). Here we have two mountains which seem to astonish Zechariah because they are whole mountains of bronze. John Calvin understands them as the hidden counsel of God, which cannot be broken. Others see them as the spiritual wall of protection God has placed around his people. Some commentators see the mountains as Mount Moriah and the Mount of Olives in Jerusalem, and others as guardian pillars of God's heavenly temple. Since the mountains in Zechariah's vision serve as a gate for the heavenly chariots, the last suggestion makes the most sense. First Kings 7:13–22 tells us that Solomon's temple had two bronze pillars astride its doors; this vision seems to expand them exponentially to depict the gate of the Lord's heavenly abode.

Coming out from between these mountains are four chariots drawn by horses. We are reminded of the first vision, with its four horsemen who came from the corners of the earth to give their report. We observed then that those light cavalry signified God's omniscience and sovereign omnipresence. By contrast, the chariots were the heavy cavalry, the shock troops not unlike our modern-day tank units. Chariots went forth not to scout but to crush the power of an enemy.

These chariots were drawn by horses of different colors: "The first chariot had red horses, the second black horses, the third white horses, and the fourth chariot dappled horses—all of them strong." Just as in chapter 1, the prophet inquires, "What are these, my lord?" (vv. 2–4). In the first vision, we concluded that no clear meaning could be assigned to the colors, but here the colors are slightly different and may be more significant. In particular, the book of Revelation offers a compelling parallel.

Revelation 6 tells of the opening of the seals in heaven. As each of the first four seals is opened, a horseman of a certain color appears. First, the rider on the white horse "came out conquering, and to conquer" (Rev. 6:2). The rider of the red horse then came with a sword to shed blood in war, while the rider of the black horse spoke of grief and death. The final horse was a pale one, its rider going forth to bring pestilence of every kind (Rev. 6:3–8). These roughly correspond to the chariots of Zechariah's vision, although the order is different and the final horse here is dappled or multicolored. Whether or not there is an intentional correspondence between the two passages, Revelation tells us what associations these colors have in similar apocalyptic materials.

The Providence of God

What, then, are these chariots? Like the horsemen of chapter 1, they are surely part of God's angelic host. Their going forth signifies God's initiative in the world—what theologians call his *providence*. The horsemen of chapter 1 showed God's omniscience and sovereign control of the theater of the world. Now these chariots, offensive shock-troops, go forth from God's throne as agents to achieve his will. Psalm 68:17 says, "The chariots of God are twice ten thousand, thousands upon thousands." So armed, God is able to ensure that all his foes are subdued and that his will is done in every corner of the globe.

Today people speak of being lucky, but other generations thanked God for his providential care. Christians believe that God is actively involved in the affairs of people and nations, and furthermore that his will overrules the will of men. R. L. Dabney writes: "We believe the Scriptures to teach, not only that God originated the whole universe, but that He bears a perpetual, active relation to it; and that these works of providence are 'His most holy, wise, and powerful preserving and governing all His creatures and their actions.'"[1]

The term "providence" is naturally related to God's *providing* for his own people. It speaks of God's involvement not merely with the great affairs of state but with individual lives and problems. Paul Helm explains:

> An important part of our faith as Christians is that God cares for us, and that the detail and direction of our lives are under the purposeful control of God. We draw comfort from the fact that nothing is too small to escape the attention of God, nor too minute for him to bother about. We draw inspiration from the fact that God has the power to make difficulties disappear.[2]

God's providence extends to the details of our lives. Jesus taught that we should be anxious for nothing because not even a sparrow falls to the ground without the Father's consent. "Fear not," he said, "you are of more value than many sparrows" (Matt. 10:31).

What is true of our small lives is also true of the great events of the world. Paul writes that "for those who love God all things work together for good"

---

1. Robert Lewis Dabney, *Systematic Theology* (Edinburgh: Banner of Truth, 1985), 276.
2. Paul Helm, *The Providence of God* (Downers Grove, IL: InterVarsity, 1994), 18.

(Rom. 8:28). This is true only because God is working in all things for the good of his people. This is why God could make prophecies and ensure that they would come true. Prophecies rely on more than foresight; they require God's providential working to bring all things together according to his will.

Zechariah looked upon this vision of the chariots and asked, "What are these, my lord?" The answer adds emphasis to our view of God's providence. As he has done before, the interpreter angel defines one symbol by the use of another. He says, "These are going out to the four winds of heaven, after presenting themselves before the LORD of all the earth" (Zech. 6:5).

Winds are another divine agency. Isaiah 11:15 speaks of God sweeping his hand like a scorching wind across Babylonia. Ezekiel's first vision began with the sight of a windstorm coming down out of the north, and with it the glory of God (1:4). It is not, therefore, a gentle summer breeze that the angel identifies with these chariots, but a gale-force wind that sweeps human barriers aside. The psalmist says: "He makes the clouds his chariot; he rides on the wings of the wind; he makes his messengers winds, his ministers a flaming fire" (Ps. 104:3–4). Angels, chariots, mighty winds, and flames of fire—all are used in the Bible to show God's invincible but invisible agencies for doing his sovereign will.

The horses of Zechariah's vision go forth "after presenting themselves before the LORD of all the earth" (Zech. 6:5). What a picture of God's sovereignty! He is enthroned, the Lord of all the world, and these mighty chariots stand before him, ready to go forth with the speed and power of the wind to do his bidding, straining at their harnesses, and chomping at the bit to be let loose: they are "impatient to go and patrol the earth" (Zech. 6:7). And as this vision shows, God is willing to send them. His sovereignty is not merely hypothetical but actual, for these chariots do go forth at his command.

GOD'S JUDGMENT ON THE NATIONS

The rest of the vision gives specifics about the procession of these chariots: " 'The chariot with the black horses goes toward the north country, the white ones go after them, and the dappled ones go toward the south country.' When the strong horses came out, they were impatient to go and patrol the earth. And he said, 'Go, patrol the earth.' So they patrolled the earth" (Zech. 6:6–7).

First, we are shown the chariot with black horses, signifying grief and death, heading toward the north country—that is, to Mesopotamia and Babylonia. This is the direction from which the greatest grief had come upon God's people. The Assyrians from the north had conquered the northern kingdom. Later, Babylon came to destroy Jerusalem. Zechariah and his countrymen had returned from captivity there to rebuild the city, but the looming hand of their present northern rulers, the Persian Empire, overshadowed their work. Imagine the emotions of Zechariah as the vision shows the black horses headed north, bringing death to the enemies of God.

According to the New International Version, the chariot with white horses then went to the west. This follows a scholarly tradition that in fact changes the Hebrew text to fit its own expectation. It seems logical that the four chariots should go to the four directions, but this is not what the text states. For one thing, the first chariot, the one with red horses, is not mentioned at all. What the Hebrew text clearly says (as accurately rendered by the English Standard Version) is that the chariot with white horses, signifying conquest, follows the one with black horses into the lands of the north: "The chariot with the black horses goes toward the north country, the white ones go after them" (Zech. 6:6). Finally, the chariot with the dappled horses goes to the south—that is, to Egypt, the other great threat to the people of God.

These maneuvers show God's judgment on those who opposed and oppressed his people. C. F. Keil explains:

> Two chariots go into the north country, which is one representative of the heathen world-power: first of all the black horses, to carry famine thither, as one of the great plagues of God with which the ungodly are punished. . . . Then follow the white horses, indicating that the judgment will lead to complete victory over the power of the world. Into the south country, i.e., to Egypt, the other representative of the heathen world-power, goes the chariot with the speckled horses, to carry the manifold judgment of death by sword, famine, and pestilence.[3]

This vision thus shows that God will defend his people, judging those who oppress them and rising up with power to overthrow those who oppose

---

3. C. F. Keil and F. Delitzsch, *Commentary on the Old Testament*, 10 vols., *The Minor Prophets* (Peabody, MA: Hendrickson, 1996), 10:552.

him. This is not merely a narrow or specific prophecy regarding Babylon and Egypt, but rather this vision shows what we may regard as a fixed principle, that God punishes those who afflict his people and judges the enemies of his church.

The vision concludes with the angel calling to Zechariah; literally, he is shouting to the prophet, perhaps because of the din: "Behold, those who go toward the north country have set my Spirit at rest in the north country" (Zech. 6:8). God's Spirit was disturbed by the afflictions of his people there. Until the black chariot had visited grief and death and the white horses had come to conquer God's enemies, his own Spirit must be uneasy. But seeing these chariots go forth, God speaks of his Spirit now at rest in that place, his anger there having ceased with the knowledge of the vengeance they will deliver.

GOD'S PEOPLE AND THE WORLD

Zechariah's eighth vision provides a message of God's providential rule carried out by divine charioteers, with his judgment going forth upon those who had abused his people. Surely this vision, which completes the eight night visions of Zechariah, was intended to make an impression on the prophet and his generation by making them aware of certain spiritual realities.

The first of these realities has to do with the relationship between God's people and the world. Remember the situation of this remnant community in the ruined city of Jerusalem. They were small in numbers, weak in every measurable way—militarily, economically, politically—and of absolutely no significance on the world stage of that day. Meanwhile, we turn our eyes to the north and see the great city-states of Mesopotamia, now organized under the imperial hand of Persia. The comparison is laughable! God's people are so small, weak, and insignificant; the powers of the north so great, mighty, and important. If we look to the south and see great Egypt with its pyramids and sprawling cities along the Nile, the same can be said.

Is this not a perfect picture of the church within the world? Christians are not that numerous, and when it comes to the things that make for worldly power we are woefully empty-handed. In many places today, Christians are a tiny minority. They meet in barns in outlying districts, in secret houses, fleeing a hostile authority. The state has might, money, and media. Compared to these things the church is weak, and vulnerable.

But God bids his people to see a sight perceived only with the eyes of faith. Here is what only Elisha could see, until God opened the eyes of his servant: The chariots of God! They are around our enemies. They encircle our foes as God's protecting agents. Here is the situation of the church in the world: yes, the church is weak and the world is strong, but God is mighty over all and he is not distant from our affairs. Psalm 121 says: "He will not let your foot be moved; he who keeps you will not slumber. . . . The LORD will keep you from all evil; he will keep your life. The LORD will keep your going out and your coming in from this time forth and forevermore" (Ps. 121:3, 7–8).

In this there is a message to the world—to Babylon and Egypt and all their modern-day representatives: they will be punished for what they do to the church. As the Lord said in chapter 2: "He who touches you touches the apple of his eye" (Zech. 2:8). God takes note when mocking unbelievers afflict the man or woman who trusts the Lord; his Spirit will not rest until they are judged by him.

This is something the world finds hard to believe. Zechariah's vision would have brought no fear to the mighty of the north, confident in their might. But they were wrong. T. V. Moore reflects on the circumstances in which this vision was given, when God's people were so weak and the world so strong:

> Could the haughty nobles of Babylon, in the gorgeousness of its magnificence, and the pride of its power, have heard the threatening of this obscure Jew, amidst the ruins of Jerusalem, with what derision and contempt would they have treated this threat! The anathema that was so feebly uttered against the mightiest and richest city of the world, to the eye of sense seemed like the ravings of lunacy. Yet that feeble whisper was the uttered voice of Jehovah, and the elements of ruin in their remotest lurking-place heard the summons, and began to come forth . . . until the glory of these high palaces was dimmed, and the magnificence of these gardens and temples was covered, and now the winds whistle through the reeds of the Euphrates, where Babylon then sat in her pride; and loneliness, desolation and death are stationed—there the sentinel witnesses of the truth that His word returns not to him void, that His spirit is quieted in the land of the north.[4]

4. T. V. Moore, *Haggai, Zechariah, & Malachi* (Edinburgh: Banner of Truth, 1979), 171–72.

Christians are not the judge of our unbelieving neighbors, but it is helpful for us to know that God will judge them on our behalf: God will vindicate us, turning our shame into glory, our turmoil into peace, and our loss into reward. This enables us to love those who hate us, confidently leaving judgment to the Lord. Paul says, therefore, "Beloved, never avenge yourselves, but leave it to the wrath of God, for it is written, 'Vengeance is mine, I will repay, says the Lord.' To the contrary, 'if your enemy is hungry, feed him; if he is thirsty, give him something to drink; for by so doing you will heap burning coals on his head.' Do not be overcome by evil, but overcome evil with good" (Rom. 12:19–21).

Therefore, Christians and churches must not fear the world. We must not be intimidated by its scoffing. We must not shrink back from being different. We must not cower before its use of power. Instead, like Elisha, we are called to see God's chariots of fire; like Zechariah, let us learn from this vision that God's agents move throughout the earth to secretly but mightily support his people, breaking the bow that is aimed against us. As God encouraged King Asa, "For the eyes of the LORD run to and fro throughout the whole earth, to give strong support to those whose heart is blameless toward him" (2 Chron. 16:9). Instead of fearing the world we must fear God, who rules these fierce chariots. Instead of eyeing public opinion, we must keep his Word. We must not allow our churches to become secularized—to look more and more like the world with its fleshly appetites, its pride, and its ideas of success. We must not adopt the world's ideas, ambitions, or lifestyle. We do not have to, even though we suffer, because God is almighty to preserve us. Christians must not fear the world, but God.

Moreover, this vision reinforces a principle for the church's spiritual battles. An earlier vision gave this motto: " 'Not by might, nor by power, but by my Spirit,' says the Lord" (Zech. 4:6). How strongly that is reinforced in this final vision! If God's chariots go forth to strike down the worldly powers of this world, then surely our task is not to seek that same kind of worldly power. The safety of Jerusalem was not to be found in swords and horses and chariots of their own, but in the chariots that ride forth from these mountains of bronze. This is no less true today. Our security as the church of Jesus Christ—our prosperity and success—comes not by winning elections, passing laws in capital cities, seizing control of the media, or our success in raising funds. Instead, the church advances by God's grace with the power of truth and the compelling authority of holiness. As Paul summed it up: "Though we live in the world, we do not wage war as the world does. The weapons we fight with are not the weapons of the world. On the contrary, they have divine power to demolish strongholds. We demolish arguments and every pretension that sets itself up against the knowledge of God, and we take captive every thought to make it obedient to Christ" (2 Cor. 10:3–5 NIV).

GOD'S PEOPLE AND HISTORY

The second category in which we should consider this vision is God's people and history. What did this vision say to Zechariah and to the Jews about the future, and hence about the meaning of their own lives? On the basis of this vision, what ought they to make their ambition in life, what are the things that were going to count, and were going to last forever?

Surely the prophet, bleary-eyed after such a night of visions, would have walked outside his dwelling to look at the place where the temple once stood and had started to rise again. With his natural vision there was nothing but a poor foundation, a building begun but left unfinished, perhaps with construction materials scattered around. It looked like the kind of thing that would never amount to much. But then he would have remembered the visions he had received that night, by revelation from God. What that heap signified was the eternal temple, not one with bronze pillars but mountains of brass, from which came forth the chariots of God to do his will on the earth. Surely, the prophet must have gone on to say to others, "Don't you see, that is where all this is going. God's plan is going forth. It will not fail. It will move forward one generation to the next until history reaches its divinely ordained culmination." As Paul later wrote in Ephesians, God is working out his mysterious purpose in history until "the fullness of time, to unite all things in [Christ], things in heaven and things on earth" (Eph. 1:10).

In the darkness of that night, Zechariah must have resolved, "I will not give in to the world. I will not surrender to its vision, in which Babylon is great and Jerusalem is small. I will offer myself and my labors to that kingdom God is working out in my own time in ways both small and large, but which someday will fill the earth. I will commit myself to that plan of history over which he is Lord. I will rejoice now even in sorrow and trouble, so that on that great day to come I may have my share in the city without walls, there to see with my own eyes the glory of God who dwells within."

God's visions to Zechariah were intended to shape his view of life and history, and they should do the same for us. The wicked may prosper for a while, but they will be cast down. The towers of men will all fall down, "for the present form of this world is passing away" (1 Cor. 7:31). This is what history shows: first Babylon and Egypt, then Greece, then Rome, and some-day it will be modern empires that will fall, especially as they turn against God and his church.

Surely, then, we, like the faithful of all generations, ought to fix our eyes and our hearts not on the splendor of this age, but on the city to come, the Jerusalem of God, "the city that has foundations, whose designer and builder is God" (Heb. 11:10). Let us labor for a heavenly reward, seeking our trea-sure there. Let us commit ourselves—our time, our talents, and our resources—to the service of Christ and to the city he is building, with the plumb line even now in his hand. Let us look around at the world in which we live, not fearing because of God's presence to save, but seeing his chari-ots of fire and living for him through faith in Jesus Christ.

13

THE PRIEST ENTHRONED

Zechariah 6:9–15

*It is he who shall build the temple of the LORD and shall bear
royal honor, and shall sit and rule on his throne. And there shall
be a priest on his throne, and the counsel of peace shall be
between them both. (Zech. 6:13)*

e have arrived at a point of transition in our studies of Zechariah, a transition signaled by the prophet's statement, "And the word of the LORD came to me" (Zech. 6:9). In previous passages, the phrase "I lifted my eyes and saw" served as his transition clause. This signals us that the visions are over and now we are dealing with more conventional verbal revelation from God.

The first six chapters consisted of visions the prophet received on a single night. Now comes revelation that serves as an appendix to those visions; the symbolic act that takes place here is a fitting conclusion to the visions the prophet had received.

A CROWN FOR JOSHUA

This episode was triggered by the arrival of a contingent from Babylonia. At this time the great majority of Jews had not come back to their ancestral home but remained in the lands to which they had been exiled, where many of them were living comfortably. The delegation came with an offering, probably for the rebuilding of the temple. Their names were Heldai, Tobijah, and Jedaiah, and they were enjoying hospitality in the house of Josiah son of Zephaniah (Zech. 6:9–10). Zechariah is told to go to them, take an offering, and use it to fashion a crown: "Take from them silver and gold, and make a crown, and set it on the head of Joshua, the son of Jehozadak, the high priest" (Zech. 6:11).

It is unclear what kind of crown this was, partly because the word "crown" is plural in the Hebrew text, although the attached verb is singular. The most logical explanation is that Zechariah was to make a crown which involved a weave of silver and gold strands, and which therefore was thought of as multiple. There may be a connection with the vision of Revelation 19:12, where the mounted Lord is seen with "many diadems" upon his head. The idea in both cases is probably the same: a multilayered crown, in Zechariah's case one made of silver and gold.

So far this is a straightforward and encouraging command. The exiles had come with resources to further the work, and God memorializes their gift with a symbol of sovereignty and success. We would expect the crown to go to the royal prince, Zerubbabel, but instead Zechariah is directed to Joshua the high priest.

This is so unexpected that liberal scholars often replace Zerubbabel for Joshua. But there is no textual evidence to support a change. Furthermore, there are problems with the idea of Zerubbabel receiving the crown. This would have been taken as an act of rebellion against the Persian throne. The meaning would have been that Zerubbabel now was king, and not merely the imperial governor. But Joshua had no claim to royal office. To place the crown upon his head was not a political gesture, but a symbolic action—a prophetic act.

There are five reasons to see this as prophetic symbolism rather than a political statement. First, the kings of Israel had to be of David's line. Joshua was not, and thus was ineligible to serve as king. Second, verse 12 associates this crown with the one "whose name is the Branch"—a well-established designation for the Messiah—and Joshua was not the Messiah. Third, this crown is not given to Joshua to wear and keep, but is placed on his head and then taken to the temple as a memorial. Fourth, the vision in chapter 3 first introduced Joshua and his associates as "men who are a sign" of things to come, and he surely continues in that capacity here.

The fifth and final reason this must be symbolic is that Joshua was the high priest, an office that provided visual symbolism. The high priest was a mediator, representing man to God and God to man. His resplendent attire represented the people in righteousness before God and God in holy glory before the people. The high priest was the symbolic God-man, visually portraying the true Mediator to come. It makes sense, therefore, that this coronation ceremony serves a similar function; it visually depicts the Messiah in his office and work.

THE PRIEST ENTHRONED

A royal crown is placed on the head of the high priest. Verse 13 continues: "[He] shall bear royal honor, and shall sit and rule on his throne." This was not possible under Israel's current constitution as a nation, and thus it pointed to a new era, a new constitution. The old covenant maintained a strict separation of power between priest and king. No king could perform priestly duties. In fact, one king who dared to transgress this rule was afflicted with leprosy on the spot (2 Chron. 26:16–20). But now a union of offices is symbolically depicted. Zechariah predicts a new kind of priest: a royal priest seated in majesty and power, and therefore a new administration for God's people.

To grasp the significance of this episode, we must recall the central role of the kings in Israel's history. We know the moral importance of a leader in our own time, but this was particularly vital for Israel. The kings not only set the moral and spiritual tone but actually represented the people before God.

The main history of the period leading up to the exile, tellingly named The Book of Kings, gives us a feel for the tension when one king died and was to be replaced by another. In the ninth century BC, Asa was a godly king who brought blessing (although he became arrogant later in life). When he died his son Jehoshaphat assumed the throne, an even more godly king who, no doubt, relieved the fears of many people. But Jehoshaphat's great mistake was to marry a daughter of the apostate northern king, so that his son and successor was brought up by a daughter of Ahab and Jezebel. The Bible says of this man, Jehoram, who succeeded Jehoshaphat to the throne: "He did what was evil in the sight of the LORD" (2 Kings 8:18). This was an unmitigated disaster, a time when much that had been gained was subsequently lost.

This shows how important the king was. Zechariah's action speaks of the Messiah as a king who is also a priest. What an unqualified blessing! Instead of serving his dynastic dreams through war and the accumulation of wealth, the aims of this sovereign are first and foremost spiritual. The priest's primary purpose was to bring the people to God, and this priest would minister with royal authority, a king whose aims are the holiest aims of God.

A true priest-king is the perfect leader. A priest has compassion on his flock; he serves and ministers to their needs. His rule is based not on the sword he wields against them but on the sacrifice he offers for them. This is a king who dies for his subjects, as Jesus said of himself: "The good shepherd lays down his life for the sheep" (John 10:11). Alexander Maclaren writes, "His rule is wielded in gentleness. . . . His scepter is not the warrior's mace, nor the jeweled rod of gold, but the reed—emblem of the lowliness of His heart, and of authority guided by love."[1]

It is obvious to the Christian that the symbolism in Zechariah prefigures the ministry of the Lord Jesus Christ. The book of Hebrews informs us that Jesus ushers in a new kind of priesthood, one symbolized by the mysterious figure of Melchizedek from Genesis 14, who was simultaneously priest and king. Melchizedek's name meant "King of Righteousness," and as ruler of Jerusalem he was "King of Peace" (*Salem* being the word for "peace"). Hebrews 7 makes the point that this union of offices, king and high priest, has been effected in the ministry of Jesus Christ. As priest Jesus offered the sacrifice to satisfy God's judgment on our sin, and having been raised from death and ascended into heaven, he presented that sacrifice at the very throne of God. God thereupon enthroned him as our king, a priest even now upon his throne on high, reigning forever with everlasting life. Hebrews 8 then opens with words that could practically have been written as a commentary on our passage in Zechariah: "We have such a high priest, one who is seated

1. Alexander Maclaren, *Expositions of Holy Scripture*, 11 vols. (Grand Rapids: Eerdmans, 1959), 4:318.

at the right hand of the throne of the Majesty in heaven, a minister in the holy places, in the true tent that the Lord set up, not man" (Heb. 8:1–2).

This is what the coronation of Joshua the high priest proclaimed amidst the ruins of long-ago Jerusalem. A sovereign would rule the people for God, but as a priest his ministry from that throne would be a spiritual work of bringing the people into God's blessing. Indeed, the order presented here is not insignificant. It is not a king who joins a priestly order, but a priest who ascends the royal throne. This is also how Paul describes the order of Jesus' ministry: "He humbled himself by becoming obedient to the point of death, even death on a cross. Therefore God has highly exalted him and bestowed on him the name that is above every name" (Phil. 2:8–9). This is how the throng of worshipers in heaven even now understands the glorious reign of Christ. The apostle John looked, and on a throne in heaven he saw a Lamb who had been slain. He tells us: "And they sang a new song, saying, 'Worthy are you to take the scroll and to open its seals, for you were slain, and by your blood you ransomed people for God from every tribe and language and people and nation' " (Rev. 5:9). The Lamb symbolizes the priestly office; indeed, it is the sacrifice for whose blood the priests existed. And it is as the Savior who died for us that Christ receives acclamation as our enthroned king.

All this is foretold by Zechariah: "There shall be a priest on his throne, and the counsel of peace shall be between them both" (Zech. 6:13). Scholars debate which two are brought together in harmony, but most agree that it is these two offices of king and priest. It is not merely that Christ unifies these offices harmoniously, but that from this union he works peace, the *shalom* of God, for those who enter his reign. Thus are fulfilled the words of Isaiah 9:6, "His name shall be called Wonderful Counselor, Mighty God, Everlasting Father, Prince of Peace."

Just as we saw in the vision of the two olive trees in chapter 4, it is from the harmony of his work as priest and king—as minister and sovereign, as servant and Lord—that Christ sends God's Spirit to God's people, resulting in peace. T. V. Moore writes:

> This is done by Christ in the exercise of these two offices, by one of which he purchases redemption, and by the other applies it; by the one expiates sin, and by the other extirpates it; and thus reconciling man and God, causes peace

on earth, and good will to man. We have, then, in these words a full description of the atoning work of the Messiah, and the application of that work in the development of the Church.[2]

THE TRUE TEMPLE'S BUILDER

This episode not only depicts the dual office of the Messiah, but also speaks about his person and work. Zechariah was instructed to say to Joshua: "Thus says the LORD of hosts, 'Behold, the man whose name is the Branch: for he shall branch out from his place, and he shall build the temple of the LORD. It is he who shall build the temple of the LORD'" (Zech. 6:12–13).

Back in chapter 3 we examined the designation "the Branch," which speaks of the Messiah's humble origins and weakness in the world. Here in chapter 6 there is a play on words: he is *the Branch*, and he will *branch out* (Zech. 6:12). The point is that he will go forward and succeed in his work, despite his apparent obscurity. This was true of Jesus Christ, symbolized here by Joshua. He did not appear in open glory and power, yet both of these attended his progress. Likewise, his church began as a little shoot from Israel, and by God's power it has branched throughout the earth. So also it is in our hearts. Christ is planted by the Holy Spirit in our affections and our thoughts, a little Branch amidst the jungle of our worldly lusts. But he grows, branching forth until someday he will have filled us with all his glorious fullness.

This is *how* the Messiah works, but we also find here *what* his work is: "He shall build the temple of the LORD" (Zech. 6:13). This is a striking statement. After all, the point of the visions was to motivate the people in rebuilding the temple in Jerusalem, despite obstacles and problems. In chapter 4 we saw the prophecy that Zerubbabel, their civil leader, would oversee the completion of that project. In obvious contrast to him and to the temple rising brick by brick in Jerusalem, this One to come, this Branch, will build another, different temple: the true temple of the Lord. To make this point, the Lord tells Zechariah to point to Joshua in his symbolic function and say, "Behold, the man.... It is he who shall build the temple of the LORD" (Zech. 6:12–13). This is a future temple to be built by the Messiah in days ahead. Zechariah's contemporary Haggai also prophesied about this temple, saying, "The treasures

2. T. V. Moore, *Haggai, Zechariah, & Malachi* (Edinburgh: Banner of Truth, 1979), 179.

of all nations shall come in, and I will fill this house with glory, says the LORD of hosts" (Hag. 2:7). A new and greater temple will be built, different from the temple in Jerusalem. Just as this new temple will unite the offices of king and priest—having been built by a priest-king who there will reign—so also the temple will be not merely for the Jews but also for the ingathering of the nations as they come to worship God.

This brings us back to the three men who came from Babylon with their silver and gold. Their arrival pointed to greater things to come and prompted this symbolic gesture: "The crown shall be in the temple of the LORD as a reminder to Helem, Tobijah, Jedaiah, and Hen the son of Zephaniah. And those who are far off shall come and help to build the temple of the LORD" (Zech. 6:14–15). The point of this memorial—the placing of this crown in the temple the Jews were building—was to signify a greater temple, into which not just some Israelites from Babylon but people from all the nations would stream. The crown would be a memorial to the zeal of these exiles who brought their riches, and to the man who received them into his home with godly hospitality. But it would also memorialize the promise that just as Josiah son of Zephaniah received these visitors into his home, so also the people of God would bring in the nations and make the true spiritual house in which God's glory would shine.

This passage is significant in that it specifies Christ's ultimate work as the builder of God's true temple. This was the highest achievement to which any king could aspire. David asked for permission to build God's house, but was told that the honor would go to his son, a man not of war but of peace. Solomon built the first temple, thus achieving his highest glory. But God's promise to David involved another, greater Son, who would build the true temple of the Lord. The promise of 2 Samuel 7:13–14 includes words that could not possibly apply to Solomon or any one else except the One who was both David's offspring and God's own divine Son: "He shall build a house for my name, and I will establish the throne of his kingdom forever. I will be to him a father, and he shall be to me a son."

Christ's work is to build the temple where God dwells among his people in glory. Jesus began this building in his incarnation, when God came to dwell in human flesh: "The Word became flesh and dwelt among us, and we have seen his glory, glory as of the only Son from the Father" (John 1:14).

Jesus also spoke of his death and resurrection as the rebuilding of God's temple: "Destroy this temple, and in three days I will raise it up" (John 2:19). As Alexander Maclaren explains:

> Christ is Himself the true Temple of God. Whatsoever that [it] shadowed Christ is or gives. In Him dwelt all the fullness of the Godhead. "The glory which once dwelt between the cherubim, 'tabernacled among us' in His flesh. As the place of sacrifice, as the place where men meet God, as the seat of revelation of the divine will, the true tabernacle which the Lord hath pitched is the Manhood of our Lord.[3]

The New Testament also speaks of the church as the temple Christ proceeds to build. In building the church, he made himself the cornerstone on which its dimensions are based. Now we "like living stones are being built up as a spiritual house, to be a holy priesthood, to offer spiritual sacrifices acceptable to God through Jesus Christ" (1 Peter 2:5). Paul says the same thing in Ephesians 2:19–22, writing to Gentiles who have been incorporated with Jews into the people of God: "In him you also are being built together into a dwelling place for God by the Spirit" (Eph. 2:22).

We are God's temple, in and through Christ. This is true of believers individually, as Christ makes God's Spirit to dwell in us. But it is especially true of us together as the church, where God is found and known and worshiped in this world. The building of this temple, God's true spiritual house, is the meaning and end of history. Though so little of its final glory can now be seen, by faith we should come to the gathering of God's people with awe, for God is there, and the work he invites us to share in the church is one that will shine in the heavens forever.

When all this happens, Zechariah is told, then "you shall know that the Lord of hosts has sent me to you. And this shall come to pass, if you will diligently obey the voice of the Lord your God" (Zech. 6:15). This does not mean that by disobedience the Jews could frustrate God's promised plans, but rather it speaks of their own participation in these blessings and their own fellowship with God in the true house he would build. The same assertion was made when the completion of the physical temple was promised:

---

3. Maclaren, *Expositions*, 4:319.

"Then you will know that the Lord of hosts has sent me to you" (Zech. 4:9). The point was that seeing God's promises come true is proof of God's Word. Now we find that the final manifestation of divine revelation will be given when God's spiritual house is completed and set forth in glory. Then, every knee shall bow "and every tongue confess that Jesus Christ is Lord, to the glory of God the Father" (Phil. 2:11).

Behold, the Man!

The visions of Zechariah show that God was concerned that the temple be rebuilt in Jerusalem. Now in the appendix to those visions, through the symbolic act that concludes this portion of the prophet's book, God makes a point his people should not fail to notice. Important as the temple was, it was not the source of Israel's hope. Far more important is the Priest-King who comes to build the true temple, not just one of stone but a spiritual house for God. God lifts Israel's eyes from the material to the spiritual, from the temple building to the temple builder, there to rest their hope. Acting on behalf of God, Zechariah placed a crown on the head of the high priest. Then, with a finger pointed at the One he symbolically represented, the prophet cried, "Behold, the man" (Zech. 6:12).

These are words that echo throughout the Bible, as the core of God's message for the salvation of sinners: "Behold, the man." First he was known simply as the offspring of the first woman, Eve. To Satan in the Garden, God had spoken of him: "I will put enmity between you and the woman, and between your offspring and her offspring; he shall bruise your head, and you shall bruise his heel" (Gen. 3:15). "Behold, the man," we hear, and the first thing we know about him is that he will be a man, the son of a human mother. Later God identifies him as the seed of Abraham, and thus a descendant of the man of faith. The generations passed, and in the day of Moses God said once more, "Behold, the man!" This time he is a prophet, one like Moses who would speak from God to the people. God said, "I will raise up for them a prophet like you from among their brothers. And I will put my words in his mouth, and he shall speak to them all that I command him" (Deut. 18:18). Later still, David is shown a king to sit on his throne forever (see 2 Sam. 7). These are the lines sketched in the pages of Scripture, on the fabric of God's redemptive history. "Behold, the man!" God says to our faith, adding colors and badges to the uniform of our Savior. In Isaiah 53, he is the priestly Servant: "He has borne our griefs and carried our sorrows . . . he was wounded for our transgressions; he was crushed for our iniquities . . . and with his stripes we are healed" (Isa. 53:4–5).

So varied are these images that some expected multiple Messiahs, unable to imagine these portraits ever coming together. But the visions in Zechariah achieve this, and with them we have reached the Old Testament's most complete portrait of the awaited Messiah. A crown is placed on the high priest's head, to go with the garments of righteousness he earlier received. "Behold, the man," says the Lord. This is the One who will sit enthroned, robed in majesty, to build the spiritual house that will be God's eternal temple.

How many Jews in Zechariah's day must have looked ahead to this Priest-King in faith—surely the prophet himself did. They wondered when he would appear and what he would look like; their hearts burned to see the day when this Messiah would be unveiled to the eyes of God's people. "Behold, the man!"

That day did come, at last, when the Priest-King was presented before the crowds of Jerusalem. Just as Zechariah had placed a crown of woven strands upon the head of Joshua, so a crown was placed on the brow of God's true Messiah. A purple robe was draped around his shoulders and a scepter was placed into his hand. And with words that echoed back to the earliest time of God's revelation, the cry was lifted to the assembled throng, "Behold, the man!" It was all just as Zechariah had prefigured, yet so very different.

Jesus Christ was crowned, not with woven silver and gold, but with a crown of woven thorns to signify the curse of God on sinful mankind. The purple robe was given not to honor but to mock him, whom they had beaten and abused until he was barely recognizable. John tells us: "So Jesus came out, wearing the crown of thorns and the purple robe. Pilate said to them, 'Behold the man!' When the chief priests and the officers saw him, they cried out, 'Crucify him, crucify him!'" (John 19:5–6).

I wonder what Zechariah would have thought, to have seen the horrible fulfillment of what God had promised through his own pen. But the writers of the New Testament tell us clearly what to make of it. Here is where God's true temple was built; here is where man can meet with God. Why? Because Christ's suffering death was suited to our need, that as sinners we might be forgiven by God, and that as rebels we might be restored to his love. It was our sins that placed the crown of thorns on Jesus' head, and that nailed his hands and feet to the cross. For this suffering sacrifice is the work of God's Priest, who ministers peace between holy God and guilty man, the Lamb who takes away our sin; this is the reign of God's King, who for love of us was willing to die. This is the temple God has built for us; if you will not come to him here, confessing that Christ died for you, then you may not come to God at all.

Therefore, when we compare the fulfillment to what the prophet prefigured, we are not disappointed, but held in rapt and reverent awe. The prophet wove a crown of silver and gold, but how much more precious is the crown of thorns! Oh, that we would see more beauty there than in all the silver and gold this world can offer! Zechariah spoke of royal honor bestowed upon the priest. But in Christ is a majesty far more sublime than any human mind could ever devise. The priest ascends a cross for his throne, upon which a placard was nailed to proclaim, "Jesus of Nazareth, the King of the Jews" (John 19:19). Thus he was enthroned, Priest and King. Here is the man, here is the answer long awaited, and God raised him up that all might look on him, believe, and be saved.

PART 2

The Delegation from Bethel

14

TRUE FASTING

Zechariah 7:1–14

Then the word of the LORD of hosts came to me: "Say to all the people of the land and the priests, When you fasted and mourned in the fifth month and in the seventh, for these seventy years, was it for me that you fasted? And when you eat and when you drink, do you not eat for yourselves and drink for yourselves?"
(Zech. 7:4–6)

hat is true spirituality? Or, to put it differently, What is true religion, and how do we distinguish it from false? What does it look like? In what does it consist?

The polls show that we are living in very religious times. Books on spiritual themes sell brilliantly; the Bible, especially, is a consistent best-seller. When asked, Americans by large majorities profess belief in God and in the afterlife; churches are filled with people, and often with money as well. Yet if we ask how powerfully the Bible and Christianity impact our society, the answer will have to be hardly at all. The problem is that people profess a faith that barely impacts their lives, a religion that ranks lower on their list of priorities than most items on their shopping list.

FALSE RELIGION REPROVED

This question of true versus false religion was prompted in Zechariah's time by a delegation which arrived in Jerusalem from Bethel, a town not far to the north. In earlier times, Bethel had been a seat of idolatry and rebellion against the Lord. But since the various judgments associated with the exile had come, the current inhabitants were looking once again to Jerusalem and the Lord. Verse 3 indicates that they realized there were prophets again in Jerusalem; this, along with rebuilding of the temple, foretold a return of God's favor and prompted their question about fasting: "Should I weep and abstain in the fifth month, as I have done for so many years?" (Zech. 7:3).

The Old Testament ordered only one fast, the day of atonement (Lev. 23:29), but after the fall of Jerusalem a number of other fasts had been established. Indeed, exilic Jewish religion was obsessively focused on fasting and mourning for the catastrophe that had befallen them. The psalmist records the words of their lament: "By the waters of Babylon, there we sat down and wept, when we remembered Zion" (Ps. 137:1).

The exilic Jews observed four major fasts associated with the events of Jerusalem's fall. On the ninth day of the fourth month, they mourned the breaching of the city's walls. On the eighteenth day of the fifth month, they fasted for the burning of the city and temple. On the third day of the seventh month, they remembered the murder of Gedaliah the governor. Finally, on the tenth day of the tenth month, they fasted to recall the day Nebuchadnezzar set up his siege around the city.

Two years had passed since Zechariah's visions exhorted the people to renew their efforts on the temple, and no doubt a great deal of progress had been made. In two more years the second temple would be finished, and everyone must have realized that the restoration of Jerusalem was going to be a success. This accounts for the question about the fast in the fifth month, which had specific reference to the destruction of the temple. "Now that a new temple is going to be finished, should we continue to mourn the old one?" The question called into doubt the whole calendar of fasting, along with the whole attitude of mourning that dominated the exilic period. The question seems to indicate an eagerness to put all this behind.

What a surprise it must have been when the delegation from Bethel received a stinging rebuke from the Lord. Zechariah says the word of the

Lord came to him. His reply was for the benefit of all the people, not just for the priests who had been asked about this issue. His rebuke condemned the false spirituality of the fasts in three ways. First, he asked, "When you fasted and mourned in the fifth month and in the seventh, for these seventy years, was it for me that you fasted? And when you eat and when you drink, do you not eat for yourselves and drink for yourselves?" (Zech. 7:5–6).

This makes the vital point that true spirituality must be directed toward God. In the Hebrew this comes across even more strongly: "Were you fasting for me, even for me?" asks the Lord. Their fasting was not for the Lord at all, but for themselves. They were fasting as an end in itself, as a religious exercise; at best their fasting was driven by self-pity for the sorrows they had endured.

This kind of self-centered spirituality abounds in our time. People think they could use a little religion. It will shore up their image, maybe even do them some good to go to church, read the Bible, engage in this ceremony or that good deed. But it has little to do with God himself! People ask me why they should attend church, and the first answer I give them is that God is worthy of their praise. He deserves and demands our worship! But often that is the farthest thing from the minds of people in our age of self-service, self-love, and self-worship. God condemned the fasting of these Jews because it was all about themselves: it was directed to their own emotional needs and spiritual experiences. Even worse was the idea that fasting was a way to manipulate God to regain their former blessings. Now that things were looking up again they wanted to stop fasting.

When God entered into covenant with his people, he bound himself to them. "I will be their God," he promised. This is what a saving relationship with God is all about, that we would receive not merely the gifts of God— his blessings of prosperity or peace or joy—but God himself as the greatest gift. God's gift of himself finds its highest expression in our Lord Jesus Christ, who "gave himself for us to redeem us" (Titus 2:14). God's gift is himself. Therefore his people are able to say with the psalmist, "Whom have I in heaven but you? And there is nothing on earth that I desire besides you. . . . God is the strength of my heart and my portion forever" (Ps. 73:25–26). Christians are to say, before all the riches of this world, "What I really want is God: he is my portion, and if I have him, I have all things."

What, then, does God want in return? What does love ever desire but love in return? God, who made us, and who owns us as the potter does the clay, nevertheless desires the willing gift of our hearts to him. "My son," he says in Proverbs 23:26, "give me your heart." Deuteronomy 32:9 tells us, "The LORD's portion is his people." Therefore, it is not petty religious observance that the Lord desires, it is not fasting or feasting that matters to him, but the giving of our hearts in whatever we are doing. "When you fasted and mourned," God asks, "was it for me, even for me?"

This means that any religious expression or act we may offer, whether it is coming to church, giving money, or doing good deeds, reading the Bible or praying—even fasting and mourning—means nothing to God unless it is done for his pleasure, his glory, his service, and his love. Unless our worship is offered in sincerity, God rejects it. "I hate, I despise your feasts, and I take no delight in your solemn assemblies" (Amos 5:21), he says. Despite all the elaborate show of these Jewish fasts, with all their loud laments and showy tears, God simply asks, "Was it for me, even me?"

This condemns all hypocritical religion, of course, but it also ennobles everything we do that is truly for God. Certainly it means that God is pleased if we worship out of a desire for him, to hear his Word and offer him the praise of our hearts. It means as well that the mother who toils in the weary labor of raising children, unnoticed and unlauded by the world, if she does it for God with gratitude and a desire for his pleasure, then this is accepted with God's highest commendation. The same is true for the man or woman who labors in obscurity, treating people with dignity and working above the call of duty simply unto the Lord. This is true for every Christian who abstains from sin, not just out of a desire for personal blessing but out of love for God. "Whatever you do," Paul wrote, "work heartily, as for the Lord and not for men" (Col. 3:23). Whenever and wherever God can say, "It was for me," this is the true religion he desires.

This is the first rebuke against these fasts. But a second problem is revealed by the delegation from Bethel's question: a shallowness in their thinking. Now that the temple was restored, they wanted to stop fasting. But, as God's response reveals, they were concerned with the consequences of past sin—the fall of the city, destruction of the temple, and exile of the people—and not with the sin itself. God wanted the people to mourn not just the disaster brought on by sin but the sin itself: "But they refused to pay attention and turned a stubborn shoulder and stopped their ears that they might not hear. They made their hearts diamond-hard lest they should hear the law and the words that the Lord of hosts had sent by his Spirit through the former prophets. Therefore great anger came from the Lord of hosts" (Zech. 7:11–12). The people of Jerusalem did not listen to God when he rebuked them, so God did not listen to their cries when disaster came: " 'As I called, and they would not hear, so they called, and I would not hear,' says the Lord of hosts, 'and I scattered them with a whirlwind among all the nations that they had not known. Thus the land they left was desolate, so that no one went to and fro, and the pleasant land was made desolate' " (Zech. 7:13). The fasts observed during the exile pointed to the various days on which calamity struck; on a certain day of a certain month they fasted because a certain thing took place then. But there was little fasting for the sins that grieved God's heart and caused his judgment. Now they wanted to stop fasting altogether, when the problems they ought to have been lamenting were still all too present.

This provides us a standard to evaluate our own spirituality. Is it sin or the consequences of sin we are concerned about? Are we happy if things seem to be going smoothly, even though sin is all too evident? If so, then our attitude is very different from God's. It is ever the case that "man looks on the outward appearance, but the Lord looks on the heart" (1 Sam. 16:7).

Zechariah adds to this a third response, reminding the people that if they were seeking true religion they need only have consulted God's Word. "Were not these the words that the Lord proclaimed by the former prophets?" he asks (Zech. 7:7). This is what we always find with false spirituality. People are looking for some new angle, seeking a new program or experience or high, when God's Word presents us with clear instruction as to our duty to him.

So what is true religion? What does real spirituality look like? First, it is a desire for God himself, for his pleasure and his glory; second, it is concerned with the inner realities of sin and righteousness and only then with consequences and external blessings; third, true spirituality is that which draws from God's Word, hearing and believing and doing according to what God has spoken in the Bible. As such, God's reply through Zechariah warns us against formalistic, self-centered, and man-invented worship. James Montgomery Boice explains: "God is not content with mere ceremonial acts.

On the contrary, he actually hates such acts if they are not preceded and accompanied by a genuine love for God and other people."[1]

This is a serious matter. There can hardly be anything more dangerous than a false spirituality that tells us we are doing well when actually God is not pleased. A religion like this is a menace to our souls because it deceives us as to our danger; it tells us we are headed for heaven when in fact we are bound for hell. Yet it is all too common. Martyn Lloyd-Jones wrote:

> We can worship religion, and we can be very religious without God. I mean by that, that we can be very punctilious in the observance of days and times and seasons. We can fast, we can deny ourselves things, and the whole time we are just centering upon ourselves and thinking about how we are going to improve ourselves and make ourselves better.... We may be highly religious, but there may be no place for God; or even if he does come in, he is simply there as someone who may be of help to us. We are at the centre of our religion; our religion really is a religion without God. And that is, I suppose, the last, and the ultimate, sin.[2]

A CALL TO TRUE RELIGION

This is the danger these Jews were in, and we see why they were reproved so strongly. But next comes an exhortation to true religion, based on the teachings of earlier prophets and featuring four precepts that reflect God's own spirituality: "And the word of the LORD came to Zechariah, saying, 'Thus says the LORD of hosts, Render true judgments, show kindness and mercy to one another, do not oppress the widow, the fatherless, the sojourner, or the poor, and let none of you devise evil against another in your heart' " (Zech. 7:8–10).

These verses contain a short catalogue of God's attributes, speaking of justice, mercy, and compassion. Psalm 98:9 says of God, "He will judge the world with righteousness, and the peoples with equity." The word for mercy is *hesed*, the great word for God's covenant love, which is also found in Psalm 23, where the believer says, "Surely goodness and mercy shall follow me all

---

1. James Montgomery Boice, *The Minor Prophets*, 2 vols. (Grand Rapids: Zondervan, 1986), 2:184.
2. D. Martyn Lloyd-Jones, *Sanctified through the Truth* (Wheaton, IL: Crossway, 1989), 85.

the days of my life" (Ps. 23:6). Lamentations 3:22 links God's love and compassion, saying, "The steadfast love of the LORD never ceases; his mercies never come to an end."

When the prophet speaks of true spirituality, he points to things that are found in God himself. True religion, therefore, is a matter of *godliness*. It is God's stated objective that we would become more like him. "Be holy," says the Lord, "because I am holy" (Lev. 11:44). This might be said of his other qualities as well: Be just as God is just, merciful and compassionate because that is what he is like. If we love God we will become more like him, for love always emulates its object.

God's goal ought to be our goal, so Christians ought to study the life and teachings of Christ. But first a word of caution is needed. It is a great mistake to think we can be justified by imitating Jesus, for unlike Jesus we are condemned by the guilt of our sin and require faith in his death for our forgiveness. Jesus is first the *object* of our faith and only then our *example* in faith. But it is also a great mistake, having been saved through faith in Christ, to forget that we are called to follow and emulate him through faith. Martin Luther was right when he said, "Surely we are named after Christ, not because he is absent from us, but because he dwells in us, that is, because we believe in him and are Christ one to another and do to our neighbors as Christ does to us."[3] Having been justified by the blood of Christ, Christians are called to justice; having been sheltered by Christ's mercy, we naturally feed and protect the weak; having been served by Christ's love, we offer love to the world.

Love always changes and shapes us. A teenager who idolizes a sports star will wear his jersey. The uniform of Christ is truth and love as taught in the Bible. Furthermore, when we love someone we are eager to give to him or her. Yet we ask, "What can I give to the God who needs nothing? How can I show love to God?" The answer is by giving and showing love to our neighbor. God does not need justice or mercy or compassion from us, but our neighbor does. Because we love God, we will protect the weak and undertake the cause of the poor, all in his name (see Zech. 7:9–10).

What we find with this delegation from Bethel is the exact opposite of love for God. Their thoughts were on themselves. Things were looking good

---

3. Martin Luther, "The Freedom of a Christian," from *Martin Luther's Basic Theological Writings* (Minneapolis: Fortress, 1989), 620.

again, so they wanted to feast instead of fast. But God wanted them to show concern for the true matters of religion. As James wrote: "Religion that is pure and undefiled before God and the Father is this: to visit orphans and widows in their affliction, and to keep oneself unstained from the world" (James 1:27). The same is true today. We may wear Christian symbols as jewelry and erect Christian symbols on our buildings, but any true Christian and church must walk in the world with truth and love if they wish to bear the true signs of Christ.

Had these priests from Bethel merely consulted their Bibles, they could have anticipated Zechariah's reply. Isaiah said, "Is not this the fast that I choose: to loose the bonds of wickedness, to undo the straps of the yoke, to let the oppressed go free, and to break every yoke?" (58:6). More famously, Micah said, "He has told you, O man, what is good; and what does the LORD require of you but to do justice, and to love kindness, and to walk humbly with your God?" (Mic. 6:8). These men came wanting new direction, but Zechariah pointed them to the prophets: "You have the answer, in God's Word." He simply repeated the message of these earlier prophets. True spirituality, therefore, comes from the Bible as it is studied, believed, and put to work in practical ways.

Zechariah 7:12 provides one of the strongest statements in the Old Testament on the inspiration of Scripture. The prophet is recalling the unbelief of the forefathers and speaks of "words that the LORD of hosts had sent by his Spirit through the former prophets." This tells us why true spirituality is based on the Bible: it is not just a book of good thoughts, but the Word of God that is communicated by the Holy Spirit. Through his Word, God's Spirit works in us. Since it is in the Bible that God speaks, and through the Bible that the Spirit works in us, true spirituality demands a faithful study of the Bible. Donald Grey Barnhouse wrote: "There is only one way to find righteousness and true holiness, and that is through the Word of God, and the applications of its principles to the life by the Holy Spirit. . . . It is through the sanctifying power of the Word of God that spiritual life is communicated to the believer."[4]

---

4. Donald Grey Barnhouse, *Expositions of Bible Doctrines Taking the Epistle to the Romans as a Point of Departure*, 10 vols. (Grand Rapids: Eerdmans, 1959), 3:346–47.

This is Zechariah's call to true spirituality: a life in imitation of God, a life of truth and love for others, and a life of faith in the Bible, applying its teaching in practical ways as God's Spirit works in us.

A WARNING AGAINST UNBELIEF

This leaves the third major point of our passage, which is the warning found in Zechariah 7:11–14. We have seen a reproof of false religion, an exhortation to true religion, and now we have a warning against unbelief and hardness of heart.

This warning has two parts, and the first comes through a recounting of the people's determined efforts to reject God that nonetheless failed to push God out of the picture. First, they "refused to pay attention" (Zech. 7:11). This was the first strategy in avoiding God: simply to ignore prophets like Isaiah and Jeremiah, like students in a poorly disciplined classroom. Next, they "turned a stubborn shoulder" (Zech. 7:11). The language here is from an agrarian setting: literally, they "pulled back a shoulder," like an ox refusing to bear the yoke, in response to God's commands to faith and obedience. Third, they "stopped their ears that they might not hear" (Zech. 7:11). Fourth, they "made their hearts diamond-hard lest they should hear the law and the words that the LORD of hosts had sent by his Spirit through the former prophets" (Zech. 7:12). Now that is determined opposition to the call of God! Yet it did not succeed. God did not go away, but responded with judgment for the unrepentant sins of the Jewish people.

This condemnation applies to anyone who is not yet a Christian. You don't want to be told what to do; you don't like the idea of God running your life. So you just pay no heed to him. You are aware, either from your conscience or from a Christian witness, that God makes demands of you, that he requires your worship, that he calls you to live for him and turn from selfish and sinful ways. But you pull away your shoulder, easily avoiding that kind of burden. If someone speaks to you about God, or you encounter a preacher on the radio, you stop your ears or turn the channel. And should any message get through, you quickly reinforce the ramparts of your heart, fighting to ensure that nothing will penetrate a weak point in the line.

It is possible to do all these things. It is possible to reject God and deny him all your life. But it is not possible to make him go away. For this reason, it simply is not possible to avoid the consequences of false religion and self-worship. Zechariah 7:12 tells the story as it was at the end for the preexilic Israelites, and as it will be at the end for everyone who will not turn to God in faith: "Therefore great anger came from the LORD of hosts." This is speaking of the wrath of God, which in the end will strike everyone who will not repent, just as Jerusalem's walls were broken and her buildings put to flame. "Why do I need to pay attention? Why do I need salvation?" you ask. The answer is here: God will not go away, and his wrath awaits those who reject him. As the calm of the sea is shattered by a sudden storm, so shall the wrath of God come upon all who will not listen while he calls.

Every Christian, having trusted Christ's saving work, is safe from God's wrath, but the principle still applies. If you are a believer, you must not refuse God's Word. You must not lift the shoulder to avoid what the Bible says about practical areas of your life. Christians may indeed harden their hearts against God's Word. It happens with regard to money, or free time, in romantic relationships and at work. But Zechariah's teaching shows that the most determined attempts to escape God's sovereign rule are futile. God has saved us to holiness, and he is a shepherd who will see his flock to that destination. If our hardhearted neglect of his commands requires him to use the staff and the rod, then he is willing to do just that, for "the Lord disciplines the one he loves, and chastises every son whom he receives" (Heb. 12:6).

This composes the first warning: the most determined rejection of God does not and will not succeed. The second warning comes in the last two verses of the chapter: " 'As I called, and they would not hear, so they called, and I would not hear,' says the LORD of hosts, 'and I scattered them with a whirlwind among all the nations that they had not known' " (Zech. 7:13–14).

The Old Testament Jews did not hear God when he called, and when the consequences arrived, he gave them the same in return. This is the most horrible judgment—to be without God when he is needed! And of course we do need him. In the same way, people today do not want God in their lives, and they are getting what they asked for. They want to be godless, and so they have no God in their lives, no Savior, and no Lord, then as the consequences of their sin are inevitably felt, even as Jerusalem felt the siege engines of Babylon. May God save us from similar unbelieving folly!

THE EVIL OF EVILS

The great Puritan Jeremiah Burroughs wrote a book called *The Evil of Evils*. It is with this thought that Zechariah 7 ends. What was the true evil, about which the people should mourn and fast? Was it the memory of a destroyed city? Was it their pilgrimage in exile? Was it their affliction at the hands of the Babylonians? These were the things these men had mourned in their fasting, and when they seemed to be removed they wanted to stop fasting. But none of these mere consequences is the true evil of evils, about which we should most grievously mourn. As Zechariah makes clear, the evil that stands behind and causes all our other evils is our own sin. This is what we should mourn and lament: not just the consequences, but the sin itself.

It was because of sin that God turned away from his people. It was for sin that the Almighty scattered Israel among the nations. It was sin that made desolate the pleasant land, as Zechariah 7:14 puts it, leaving it scarred and empty after war and desecration. This is the message: Let us hate sin. Sin destroys us, consumes our years, corrupts our hearts, and if not atoned for by the blood of Christ, it condemns our souls. Let us hate sin because of its consequences, yes; but even more, let us hate sin because it is evil, because it is hateful to God, because his wrath abides on sin, and because sin is opposed to the will of our loving Lord.

What is true fasting but a hatred of sin, a loathing of evil, and a mourning for the transgressions that stand between us and God? True fasting, then, is a resolve to oppose sin with all the strength God gives us. A choice example from church history is the collection of resolutions written by Jonathan Edwards as a teenage Christian:

> Resolved, never to do any manner of thing, whether in soul or body, less or more, but what tends to the glory of God. . . .

> Resolved, never to give over, nor in the least to slacken, my fight with my corruptions, however unsuccessful I may be.

> Resolved, never to do anything, which I should be afraid to do, if I expected it would not be above an hour before I should hear the last trump.[5]

---

5. Jonathan Edwards, *The Works of Jonathan Edwards*, 2 vols. (London: Westley, 1834), 1:xx–xxii.

It is the pursuit of the things Zechariah writes about—especially justice, mercy, and compassion, instead of a spirit of oppression and evil in our hearts (Zech. 7:9–10)—all in the power of the Holy Spirit through faith in Jesus Christ. This is true fasting in a world of sin.

True religion is also a love of God's answer to the problem of sin, even Jesus Christ, the Lamb of God who takes away our sin. True spirituality is a thirst for the Spirit of God to dwell within us through his Word for newness of life. This is what frees us completely from our sin: the blood of Christ to remove its guilt and the Spirit of God to overcome its power. True religion motivates us to strive against sin in the world, and to serve the cause of truth and justice and love so far as God should give us opportunity. May God grant to us such a spirit, such true religion, by his Word and through faith in Jesus Christ.

15

A Promise to Bless

Zechariah 8:1—17

Thus says the LORD: I have returned to Zion and will dwell in the midst of Jerusalem, and Jerusalem shall be called the faithful city, and the mountain of the LORD of hosts, the holy mountain.
(Zech. 8:3)

he seventh and eighth chapters of Zechariah are closely linked, together offering the Lord's answer to the question brought by the delegation from Bethel: "Now that the temple is going to be rebuilt, do we have to keep fasting?" The Lord responded first by pointing out what true religion is all about. The key to chapter 7 was God's query in verse 5: "Was it for me that you fasted?" God rebuked their ritualistic piety because it was neither motivated by a love for him nor directed to a concern for their fellow man. Chapter 7 confronted the Jews with their duty to think first about God and the well-being of others, which together are essential to true religion.

But someone may wonder, "Isn't that a bit one-sided and unbalanced in its negative terms?" Of course, we should be motivated by love for the Lord, a loathing of sin, and a sense of duty to others. But doesn't the Lord call us to receive blessings? The Bible often speaks of spiritual riches for those who come to God in faith. Where is this emphasis? The answer is found in Zechariah 8, which presents the rest of the picture. Chapter 7 contains God's reproof against Israel's false religion, while chapter 8 brings his positive incentive in terms of the blessings of true faith.

A PROMISE TO BLESS

When Zechariah reminded people of God's judgment in permitting the destruction of Jerusalem and the captivity of the surviving Israelites, they might well have wondered if God's affections had been transferred elsewhere. Quite to the contrary, chapter 8 begins with a statement of fervent love: "Thus says the LORD of hosts: I am jealous for Zion with great jealousy, and I am jealous for her with great wrath" (Zech. 8:2). This jealousy is a zealous ardor which God has for his people. It is because of this love that God returns with the promises that follow.

First comes a promise of God's return to the city: "I have returned to Zion and will dwell in the midst of Jerusalem, and Jerusalem shall be called the faithful city, and the mountain of the LORD of hosts, the holy mountain" (Zech. 8:3). This echoes the great promise given in 1:16, "I have returned to Jerusalem with mercy; my house shall be built in it, declares the LORD of hosts, and the measuring line shall be stretched out over Jerusalem." Then, the promise of God's return inspired the renewed effort on the temple; now that this work was moving along, God directs attention to further blessings: "Jerusalem shall be called the faithful city, and the mountain of the LORD of hosts, the holy mountain" (Zech. 8:3).

The point of this promise is that the restoration of Jerusalem will be a success. God promises that he will return to the temple mount and that it will again be called the holy mountain because he will be there. There could hardly be a stronger endorsement of the temple rebuilding. What was said in Psalm 46:5 could be said of Jerusalem once again: "God is in the midst of her; she shall not be moved; God will help her when morning dawns."

Here we see the cause-effect relationship of spiritual blessing. God had reproved the fathers of the Jews for a lack of truthfulness. Now we find that in returning to them, God will bestow the very thing he desires. As the New

International Version renders verse 3, "Jerusalem will be called the City of Truth." God's presence always means moral and spiritual renewal. John Calvin explains:

> God is never idle while he dwells in his people; for he cleanses away every kind of impurity, every kind of deceit, that where he dwells may ever be a holy place. Therefore the prophet not only promises here an external blessing to the Jews, but also shows that God performs what is far more excellent—that he cleanses the place where he intends to dwell, and the habitation which he chooses, and casts out every kind of filth.[1]

We might ask how God works renewal today. The answer is found in Jesus' prayer on the night of his arrest, "Sanctify them in the truth; your word is truth" (John 17:17). It is therefore in the preaching and believing of his Word that God is present. Perhaps the classic example comes from Calvin's Geneva. In the early sixteenth century, Geneva was infamous for its immorality. Nothing the governing council did made any impact, including their decision to join the Protestant Reformation. But, as is always true, a merely outward religious affiliation made no real impact on the situation.

Calvin arrived at Geneva in August 1536 and began preaching the Bible. After a difficult beginning, Calvin's ministry of God's Word began to transform the city. James Montgomery Boice describes the impact of Calvin's ministry:

> He had no money, no influence, and no weapon but the Word of God. But he preached from the Bible every day, and as he did, under the power of his preaching, the city began to change. As the Genevan people acquired knowledge of God's Word and allowed it to influence their behavior, their city became a model city from which the gospel spread to the rest of Europe, Great Britain and the New World. . . . There has probably never been a better example of extensive moral and social reform than the transformation of Geneva under John Calvin, and it was accomplished almost entirely by the preaching of God's Word."[2]

The renewal that Geneva experienced on a civic level also takes place in the lives of individuals, through the power of God's Word.

---

1. John Calvin, *The Minor Prophets*, 5 vols. (Edinburgh, Banner of Truth, 1986), 5:194.
2. James Montgomery Boice, *Romans*, 4 vols. (Grand Rapids: Baker, 1995), 4:1859.

A second promise of blessing speaks of prosperity and peace: "Thus says the LORD of hosts: Old men and old women shall again sit in the streets of Jerusalem, each with staff in hand because of great age. And the streets of the city shall be full of boys and girls playing in its streets" (Zech. 8:4–5). This blessing would not be possible without peace and prosperity. Undoubtedly, at this time Jerusalem was not a place where you brought children, nor where many elderly were found, so this provides another lovely picture of promised blessing. This, too, is a result of God's return: first there are truth and holiness; then follow peace and prosperity, where even the elderly and the young could rejoice.

The third promise foretells the city's repopulation with people from the east and west: "Behold, I will save my people from the east country and from the west country, and I will bring them to dwell in the midst of Jerusalem," says the Lord (Zech. 8:7–8). The city had been depopulated after the Lord abandoned it; with his return people come to serve him there again.

This pattern of blessing describes how the church is built up today. Many Christians measure success merely in terms of the final blessing—the ingathering of many people. But true and lasting blessing starts with God's presence in the church. This is why our first priority must always be to worship him rightly and teach his Word faithfully. The result is spiritual prosperity and peace, so that God's people grow in faith and enjoy loving community. When, and only when, these first two blessings are enjoyed will numerical growth be a true blessing; the Bible's plan of true church success starts with a focus on God, the enjoyment of spiritual prosperity, and then God's ingathering of people into his congregation.

So it was for Jerusalem of old. God's promises assured the success of the Jews' venture to restore God's city. They were building the temple, but would that be in vain? No, for God would come to dwell there. His coming would have the effect of purifying and transforming the city, producing peace and prosperity, and God would gather many from the east and the west to add numbers to their city. The Lord concludes all this with the great covenant promise of nothing less than the renewal of his relationship with the people: "They shall be my people," he says, "and I will be their God, in faithfulness and in righteousness" (Zech. 8:8). Calvin writes: "The whole hope of the people depended on this one thing, that God remembered the covenant which he had made with them."[3] The covenant had been broken, and the people in exile had good reason to think themselves cast off by God. But this great promise assures them of his renewed commitment, which made all the difference. In light of this, the question about fasting seems petty indeed. In view of God's amazing grace, the people ought not concern themselves with missing an occasional meal but should offer themselves gladly to the Lord.

WHEN FULFILLED?

These are very great promises, so the question naturally arises as to when and in what sense they are fulfilled. The promises showed that the restoration would be a success. The religion of the fathers would be reestablished and the city and nation would be greatly increased. Periods of great blessing were in fact achieved in years ahead. After Zechariah's time, Nehemiah would lead the effort to rebuild Jerusalem's walls, providing peace and prosperity. In the centuries leading to the birth of Christ, Jewish society would be revived in Jerusalem. Yet we have to admit that nothing quite like the picture of these verses was ever fully realized. Zechariah himself, far from growing old in a city of truth, was murdered on the temple mount that, far from retaining its holiness, was thus desecrated. How and when, therefore, are we to see these promises fulfilled?

Among those who take the Bible's promises seriously there are two main answers to this question. Dispensationalists, those who believe that Old Testament Israel does not find its fulfillment in the New Testament church, hold that these promises must be physically fulfilled in the future, either in a Jewish restoration yet to come or after Christ's return when, they believe, he will reign upon the earth for a literal thousand years. Covenant theologians, on the other hand, assert that Old Testament Israel finds its fulfillment in the New Testament church. Biblical support for this view abounds, such as Paul's reference to the church as "the Israel of God" (Gal. 6:16), and his teaching that Christians have been grafted into the olive tree of Israel (Rom. 11:17). According to covenant theology, Zechariah's promises have reference to Christ's church. They are fulfilled spiritually in the age of grace through those who have entered the church. The church is the true temple in which

3. Calvin, *Minor Prophets*, 5:200.

God keeps his promise to come and dwell by his Spirit; it is in the church that God brings spiritual prosperity and to the church that even now he is bringing the nations. The ultimate fulfillment of God's promises will take place in the return of Christ to gather all his people into God's eternal house.

The vision of future Jerusalem we saw in chapter 2 supports the view that these promises are fulfilled in the church. That vision showed Jerusalem as a city without walls, with God present as its glory, and with a wall of fire around it, into which, we are told, "many nations shall join themselves to the LORD in that day, and shall be my people" (2:11). It is difficult to envision all this in terms of the earthly city of Jerusalem, but it fits the New Testament depiction of the church very well, which is often described in the New Testament as the true and spiritual Jerusalem (see Gal. 4:25–26; Heb. 12:22).

The point is not that Zechariah's generation of Jews was involved in something merely symbolic. Far from it; they were involved in the very work that leads through the church to the eternal city in heaven. God states here his ultimate intention, toward which these Jews labored in redemptive history. There is a straight line from what Zechariah and his colleagues did by faith, to the continuance of Old Testament religion in the time of Christ, to Jesus' fulfillment of that dispensation and its obligations, and through him to the present age of the ingathering into his church, and undoubtedly to our glorious dwelling with God in heaven. Here all of us join in that same work until the end of days, when God's city will shine like the brightness of the heavens. In the crucial juncture of history that was Zechariah's time, God came to Jerusalem to renew his covenant, and through their faithful response to him these promises will yet come to pass in glorious fulfillment.

REASONS TO BELIEVE

Zechariah 8:1–5 provides great promises of blessing, but God's promises always call for faith in response. This is the point of verse 6, where God challenges the people of Jerusalem to believe these extravagant claims: "Thus says the LORD of hosts: If it is marvelous in the sight of the remnant of this people in those days, should it also be marvelous in my sight, declares the LORD of hosts?" In the midst of these promises to bless comes a challenge to trust in God by believing his Word.

It is hard for us to believe God's promises, because they involve far more than could naturally be achieved. Another example of this comes from Acts 12 when the apostle Peter was imprisoned and awaiting execution. His friends gathered for an all-night prayer meeting, pleading with the Lord to spare Peter's life. God sent his angel to deliver him, and the apostle then went to the very house where the people were praying. Here is where the story becomes humorous, because when Peter knocked on the door they didn't want to stop praying. If they had really believed God would answer their prayers, they would have been waiting for a knock! Finally, they sent a servant girl, Rhoda, to answer the door. Recognizing Peter, she ran back inside, leaving him standing outside. Upon hearing her report, the praying Christians rebuked her: "You're out of your mind," they said, and finally they decided it must be Peter's ghost. Tired of waiting outside, Peter knocked again. Acts 12:16 says that when they finally saw him "they were amazed." This shows how difficult it is for us really to believe what we profess about God.

This is the kind of unbelief God is challenging in Zechariah 8:6. He has made great promises, and he acknowledges that they may seem marvelous—that is to say, impossible—to the Jews, but only if they are thinking according to human standards. If they would only think about what God can do, instead of what man can do, then they would be eager to believe. Indeed, it seems that the Lord anticipated their temptation to unbelief, because the verses that follow provide a number of reasons to believe.

There are three reasons to highlight, beginning with the phrase that is repeated all through this chapter, like a steady drumbeat announcing each new promise of blessing: "Thus says the LORD of hosts." This title points to God's sovereign command of the legions of heaven. We might ask ourselves why this phrase occurs over and over: "Thus says the LORD of hosts . . . Thus says the LORD of hosts." Surely it is meant as an aid to our faith. It is as if the prophet is saying, "Before you hear this next promise—a promise you can hardly account as possible—let me remind you that it is the sovereign Lord, the Lord of hosts, who speaks."

God's Word is backed up by his sovereign might, a point made particularly clear by the prophet Jeremiah. He prayed, "Ah, Lord GOD! It is you who has made the heavens and the earth by your great power and by your outstretched arm! Nothing is too hard for you" (Jer. 32:17). God replied to Jeremiah, concurring with that assessment: "Behold, I am the LORD, the God of all flesh. Is anything too hard for me?" (Jer. 32:27). The answer is that nothing is too hard for God, but the problem is that we imagine what is possible according to men and not to God. Here is a reason to believe: God is not like us and nothing is too hard for him. He is the almighty Lord and what he promises, he brings to pass.

Once we understand this, God's promises become a great source of faith and hope. These promises supply a second reason to believe. The promise of a king inspires men to deeds of reckless ambition; how much more ought the promise of God to inspire the greatest boldness in his people. Jeremiah Burroughs writes:

> The saints of God have an interest in all the promises that ever were made to our forefathers, from the beginning of the world they are their inheritance, and go on from one generation to another. . . . Every time a godly man reads the Scriptures (remember this when you are reading the Scripture) and there meets with a promise, he ought to lay his hand upon it and say, This is part of my inheritance, it is mine, and I am to live upon it.[4]

Certainly this was the effect God's promises ought to have had on the people in Jerusalem, but to them he gave a third reason for confidence: "I will be their God, in faithfulness and in righteousness" (Zech. 8:8). God was renewing his covenant with the people. Normally this is simply rendered, "They will be my people and I will be their God." But here the Lord adds that he will be faithful and righteous to them. Surely this was meant as a reason to believe and trust. God is ever faithful; it is his very nature to be true to his Word. The same is true of his righteousness. God must ever be acquitted in his own court, and therefore we find our confidence in him. The psalmist says, "Forever, O LORD, your word is firmly fixed in the heavens. Your faithfulness endures to all generations; you have established the earth, and it stands fast" (Ps. 119:89–90). "Righteousness and justice are the foundation of your throne; steadfast love and faithfulness go before you" (Ps. 89:14). This is also the message of one of our great hymns:

4. Jeremiah Burroughs, *The Rare Jewel of Christian Contentment* (Edinburgh: Banner of Truth, 1964), 82–83.

Great is thy faithfulness, O God my Father;
there is no shadow of turning with thee;
Thou changest not, thy compassions, they fail not;
as thou hast been thou forever wilt be.[5]

These are great reasons for us to believe. God is sovereign and almighty, able to do all that he says. God has made great promises to us in his Word. And these promises are sealed by his own faithful nature and the necessity that he be found righteous in all that he does. Notice that all these reasons have to do with the character of God. Strong faith is found not by looking to ourselves but by looking to him, and finding there a God we can trust, whose promises ought to be precious to every believer.

A MOTIVE TO SERVE

There is a contrast between the reproofs of chapter 7 and the promises of chapter 8, but they both serve the same end. Chapter 7 defined true religion as justice, mercy, and compassion, and in 8:16–17 we find the same emphasis: "These are the things that you shall do: Speak the truth to one another; render in your gates judgments that are true and make for peace; do not devise evil in your hearts against one another, and love no false oath, for all these things I hate, declares the LORD." Once again, we find that true religion is found in godliness, with truth and love as the pattern for our lives.

In addition to this, however, the Lord calls for another aspect of true spirituality, namely, service for the advancement of his kingdom. In our day this means helping to build the church, and especially to support its evangelistic witness to the world. In those days it meant rebuilding the temple in Jerusalem. We find this in verses 9–11, which exhort God's people to carry through with that project. This reminds us that God's grace never calls for sloth. Far from becoming lazy because God has promised success, the Lord exhorts, "Let your hands be strong . . . that the temple might be built" (Zech. 8:9).

If we think back to the original question that prompted chapters 7 and 8, we see the point that is made in these verses. A delegation came from Bethel asking if they could stop fasting now that the temple was being built.

5. Thomas O. Chisholm, "Great Is Thy Faithfulness," 1923.

The Lord responded first by reproving their insincere externalism in religion. "When you fasted and mourned . . . was it for me?" God inquired (Zech. 7:5). True religion, he impressed upon them, is directed toward God from the heart. But now in chapter 8, after these great promises of blessing, he gives an incentive to go with that reproof. What is true religion? It is a desire to serve God out of confidence in his promise to bless. True religion is motivated by devotion to God, yes, but also out of a desire to realize his salvation.

Many Christians feel that their faith is shallow if they are motivated by a desire for rewards in heaven. Some lament, "If I didn't believe in heaven and hell, then I'm not sure I would want to serve God." But far from considering this a false motive, it is one the Bible itself commends. In 2 Corinthians 5:10, Paul reminds believers that their earthly deeds will be presented to Christ to receive what they are due. Knowing this, he observes, "We make it our aim to please him" (2 Cor. 5:9).

The Bible never condemns a desire for spiritual blessing. Turning to God for blessing simply takes him at his Word, acknowledging that he is the Lord Almighty, and that he and not the idols of the world is the source of salvation. This is saving faith. Psalm 34:8 says, "Oh, taste and see that the LORD is good! Blessed is the man who takes refuge in him!" This is a high, not a low, expression of a trusting relationship in God.

This motive is precisely what we find in Zechariah 8:9–11. First, the Lord recalls the time before the work on the temple began: "Before those days there was no wage for man or any wage for beast, neither was there any safety" (Zech. 8:9). As Zechariah's contemporary, the prophet Haggai revealed that the reason the people did not prosper in those days was that they were not interested in God's house, the temple. God was withholding his favor, and those days were thus characterized by economic depression, external danger, and internal strife. "Why?" Haggai asked them. The Lord answered, "Because of my house that lies in ruins, while each of you busies himself with his own house" (Hag. 1:9). This teaches the principle that disobedience brings God's displeasure. Knowing this should motivate us to faithful service.

Next, Zechariah reminded the people of God's intended blessings: "For there shall be a sowing of peace. The vine shall give its fruit, and the ground shall give its produce, and the heavens shall give their dew. . . . As you have been a byword of cursing among the nations, O house of Judah and house of Israel, so will I save you, and you shall be a blessing" (8:12–13). This is salvation by grace; everything we read here speaks of God's gracious initiative. But it is also through faith, for God clearly expects a believing and obedient response.

Therefore he says: "Fear not, but let your hands be strong" (Zech. 8:13). This is a call to faithful and bold service to the Lord, always based on the promises of God (see 1 Sam. 23:16–17). It is grace that produces faith; God's promises remove our fear and strengthen our resolve. Certainly we will have trials, but as Psalm 34:19 says, "Many are the afflictions of the righteous, but the LORD delivers him out of them all." Here is a great incentive for true and obedient faith, that is, for the true religion that pleases God. Echoing the exhortation of Zechariah 7, God says: "Speak the truth to one another; render in your gates judgments that are true and make for peace; do not devise evil in your hearts against one another, and love no false oath, for all these things I hate, declares the LORD" (Zech. 8:16–17). In this God calls sweetly, with the knowledge of his blessings, in prosperity and in want, to all who seek him and long to do his will.

SEEKERS OF BLESSING

All this talk of seeking blessings may worry some about a self-absorbed narcissism that merely wants to get and not to give. Our answer is that true religion involves a genuine relationship that both gives and receives. God gives himself to his people and receives our love in return; we give our hearts to God and receive from him eternal life: "They shall be my people," says the Lord, "and I will be their God, in faithfulness and in righteousness" (Zech. 8:8).

Christians are not opposed to love of self but rather to the worship of self, which in the end is self-destroying. We practice self-denial in this life, not because we long to be miserable, but because we are in training for another life to come. We embrace a struggle with the flesh, the world, and the devil, considering with Paul that "the sufferings of this present time are not worth comparing with the glory that is to be revealed to us" (Rom. 8:18). C. S. Lewis was right when he said the problem with most people today is not that they want too much but that they settle for too little. Mankind was made to enjoy

God's glory, and, when this concept is rightly understood, Christians are the greatest glory-seekers of all! We long for the weight of glory that awaits the redeemed in Christ, and if we do not belong in this world it is because our citizenship is in heaven (Phil. 3:20).

So are we Christians, and do we serve the Lord because we are seeking blessing? Absolutely! We seek the greatest blessing imaginable: the blessing of knowing God and walking in his way and finding his pleasure through Jesus Christ, his Son and our Savior. And we seek the blessing of dwelling in and building up God's city, the church, like the faithful builders of long-ago Jerusalem, glorifying in our knowledge that we serve a king whose name is above all names and whose kingdom shall have no end.

16

FROM FAST TO FEAST

Zechariah 8:18–23

*Thus says the LORD of hosts: The fast of the fourth month and the
fast of the fifth and the fast of the seventh and the fast of the tenth
shall be to the house of Judah seasons of joy and gladness and
cheerful feasts. Therefore love truth and peace. (Zech. 8:19)*

One of the most remarkable scenes in the Gospels is found in John
4, where Jesus converses at the well with a Samaritan woman. Their
interaction presents three points that correspond closely to the
concluding words of God's reply to the delegation from Bethel, in Zechariah
8:18–23. First, Jesus spoke to her about the spiritual transformation he came
to bring, offering her "a spring of water welling up to eternal life" (John
4:14). Second, Jesus referred to a new age inaugurated by his coming, in
which this transformation would be experienced. "I know that Messiah is
coming," she said, and Jesus replied, "I who speak to you am he" (John
4:25–26). The third point is made in the remarkable conclusion to John 4,
after the woman experienced this transformation and was born again.
Returning to her town, she spread the news about the man she had met. The
result was that a whole town of Samaritan Gentiles came to saving faith in

Christ. Their response to Jesus marks a beginning of the fulfillment of Zechariah's prophecy that the nations will come "to seek the LORD of hosts" through a Jewish Savior (Zech. 8:22–23). The Samaritans exclaimed of Jesus: "We know that this is indeed the Savior of the world" (John 4:42).

All through our studies of Zechariah, we have observed that this book of prophecy is strongly directed to the coming of Jesus Christ. As the prophet concludes the Lord's reply to the delegation from Bethel, he speaks of a revival in the spiritual life of God's people—fasts turned into feasts—in the age of grace to come, so that the church will fulfill its ultimate mission: bringing the multitudes of the nations to God to worship and be saved. In Zechariah 8:18–23, the prophet foresees a glorious salvation, one that is not only for the Jews, but also for the whole world.

FROM FAST TO FEAST

Back in Zechariah 7:3, we read the question asked by the delegation from Bethel: "Should I weep and abstain in the fifth month, as I have done for so many years?" The most direct answer to that question comes in verses 18 and 19 of chapter 8, but even then we would hardly call this a direct answer. Some people say you can never get a straight answer from politicians; whatever you ask, they reply with a scripted message. If anything, the situation is worse with prophets. Instead of a straight answer, the prophet unfolds an eschatological, theological panorama.

A prophet is not an administrator. He does not reply with a procedural solution, but with a grand vista of salvation. A prophet's job was to foretell and to "forthtell." He foretold a great hope for God's people; what God has planned in the distance, the prophet brings near to searching eyes. He also "forthtold" divine expectations for the covenant community, holding up God's commands for their present behavior. In this respect, the Old Testament prophets provide a useful model for preachers today, whose primary calling is not to give pronouncements on every matter of social concern, but to proclaim the gospel and provide biblical instruction in godliness. It is in this manner, both foretelling and forthtelling, that Zechariah replies to the question about fasting: "Thus says the LORD of hosts: The fast of the fourth month and the fast of the fifth and the fast of the seventh and the fast of the tenth shall be to the house of Judah seasons of joy and gladness and cheerful feasts. Therefore love truth and peace" (Zech. 8:19).

We should understand this proclamation as nothing less than an advance promise of the gospel, that God will cause fasts to give way to feasts. This is the character of the new covenant, with its transforming power articulated, for instance, in Jesus' great statements called the Beatitudes: "Blessed are the poor in spirit, for theirs is the kingdom of heaven. Blessed are those who mourn, for they shall be comforted. . . . Blessed are those who hunger and thirst for righteousness, for they shall be satisfied" (Matt. 5:3–6). This is what God promises to Jerusalem through the prophet. As one writer puts it, "God comes to change her despair for delight, her suffering for singing, her poverty for plenty, her ruin for restoration, her abandonment for his abiding presence."[1]

Zechariah is speaking of a time yet to come, which the New Testament identifies as the coming of Christ. Our Lord dealt with this matter directly, in these very same terms, early on in his ministry:

> Now John's disciples and the Pharisees were fasting. And people came and said to him, "Why do John's disciples and the disciples of the Pharisees fast, but your disciples do not fast?" And Jesus said to them, "Can the wedding guests fast while the bridegroom is with them? As long as they have the bridegroom with them, they cannot fast. The days will come when the bridegroom is taken away from them, and then they will fast in that day. (Mark 2:18–20)

John the Baptist represents the old covenant at its best, and his was a ministry of fasting—of repentance, mourning for sin, and longing for the Savior. The Bible commends fasting as a means of spiritual preparation for the blessings we anticipate from God. We are seeing a renewed emphasis on fasting today, but much of it reflects the attitude of the delegation from Bethel, which was rebuked for its external reliance on methods. Some people today likewise treat fasting as little more than a way to get what they want from God. True fasting is meant not for our own benefit but for God's, as an expression of a broken heart for sin or of mourning for the sorrow and suffering in this world. This is what dominated John the Baptist's ministry: mourning for sin and sin's misery out of devotion to God.

---

1. Elizabeth Achtemeier, *Nahum—Malachi* (Atlanta: John Knox, 1986), 141.

Jesus brings in the new covenant situation, one of feasting and not fasting, of comfort for those who mourn, and of gladness for those who were sad. There is still mourning in the new covenant era, but mourning's answer is ready at hand. There is sickness over sin, but there are deliverance and redemption and forgiveness as near as the gospel message. "Can the wedding guests mourn as long as the bridegroom is with them?" Jesus asked regarding himself (Matt. 9:15).

This movement from the old covenant to the new covenant situation is recapitulated in the Christian's experience of conversion. It is impossible to be saved without mourning for sin, without the kind of sorrow these fasts represented. Without the bad news of God's judgment on sin generally, and on our personal sins specifically, the good news of Christ simply makes no sense. This is why so many people today think so poorly of the cross and the idea of substitutionary atonement—they have no sense of their own sin, they do not fear judgment, and they deny the idea of God's wrath. So they have no mourning, no fasting of the soul.

For this very reason many today know nothing of the true feast that is entered into by saving faith. Let me put this directly: If you know nothing of the fear of God and his wrath, the loathing of yourself as a vile sinner, and if you feel no weight of burden for the guilt of your sins, then inevitably you will think Christianity is a light matter, something perhaps of interest but of no great significance compared to the weightier matters of life in this world. But if you have known a dread of your sin, a despair of any righteousness before God, and if you have cried in the manner of David in Psalm 32—"my bones wasted away through my groaning all day long. For day and night your hand was heavy upon me; my strength was dried up as by the heat of summer" (Ps. 32:3–4)—then you also know the sheer joy of the words that open that psalm: "Blessed is the one whose transgression is forgiven, whose sin is covered. Blessed is the man against whom the LORD counts no iniquity" (Ps. 32:1–2). J. C. Ryle notes: "A sense of sin, guilt and poverty of soul is the first stone laid by the Holy Ghost, when He builds a spiritual temple. He convinces of sin. . . . It is not when we began to feel *good*, but when we feel *bad*, that we take the first step towards heaven. . . . To realize our spiritual need, and feel true spiritual thirst, is the ABC in saving Christianity."[2]

2. J. C. Ryle, *Holiness: Its Nature, Hindrances, Difficulties, and Roots* (Durham, England: Evangelical Press, 1979), 257.

182

Every true Christian knows what it means to go from the fast of conviction of sin to the feast of salvation through faith in Christ.

RESURRECTION REJOICING

This feast is what Christ's resurrection proclaims. Jesus said that none can fast while he is with them, but then he added this: "The days will come when the bridegroom is taken away from them, and then they will fast in that day" (Mark 2:20). Scholars debate the meaning of this statement. Is Jesus referring to the centuries between his first coming and his second coming, so that in our present age we will mourn his absence? Or is he referring to the three days between his death on the cross and his resurrection from the grave? The answer must be the latter, that Jesus' death caused the greatest mourning—even heaven wept and the skies turned dark and the rocks cried out—but his resurrection by the power of God caused the sun to shine again. By his resurrection Jesus is not away from us, but having ascended to heaven, he is with us by the Holy Spirit, and we therefore rejoice. Christianity, in contrast to the fasts we read about here, is a religion of great joy and spiritual feasting in Christ.

This is why Easter is the most joyful of all Christian holidays. Easter proclaims that our greatest sorrows have been transformed into joy through the resurrection of Christ. What has become of our sin, which we so lament? It has been taken away by the cross, and in the light of the open tomb we receive new garments of righteousness. As Paul wrote, "[Jesus] was delivered up for our trespasses and raised for our justification" (Rom. 4:25). What about death—surely that is a great source of sorrow for man? But in the resurrection Christ purchased and provides, our tears are turned to laughter. It is not that we have no tears, but that they are transformed by the light of his open tomb. Therefore we read in Scripture, "Death is swallowed up in victory. O death, where is your victory? O death, where is your sting?" (1 Cor. 15:54–55). This is the power that is ours in Christ, because he died for us, but more, because he was raised for us for newness of life. The fasts are made into feasts, and our mourning receives its answer of joy.

This is exactly what we find in the Gospel accounts. Think of the women who came with such grief to the tomb of Jesus that first Easter morning. Instead of the sealed tomb they found an angel of God. He said to them, "Do not be afraid, for I know that you seek Jesus who was crucified. He is not here, for he has risen, as he said. Come, see the place where he lay. Then go quickly and tell his disciples that he has risen from the dead" (Matt. 28:5–7). What is it, then, that we immediately read about those women? "So they departed quickly from the tomb with fear and great joy" (v. 8). This is what Christianity is about: fasts transformed to feasts. We find the same thing with the disciples. Having been scattered in defeat, having lost all joy and hope with the death of Christ, they are later utterly transformed. These weak and frightened men show up preaching with the greatest boldness before the very same leaders who had Jesus crucified. What accounts for this, but the power of the risen Christ? The fast of defeat on Good Friday was transformed by Easter into the feast of Pentecost. It is the resurrection of Jesus that changed and changes everything.

This is still what Christianity is about: fasting turned to feasting. Notice how Zechariah puts it, not that the fasts will be simply removed, but they "shall be to the house of Judah seasons of joy and gladness and cheerful feasts" (Zech. 8:19). Instead of lamenting those days in the fourth, fifth, seventh, and tenth months—all of which referred to incidents from the conquest and fall of Jerusalem—the Jews will look back on them with gratitude. They will say, "It is good that the Lord afflicted us, for he was preserving us from sin for himself." Thomas McComiskey rightly says: "They will rejoice in their captivity. . . . They will see the captivities of the two kingdoms not as cruel strokes from an uncaring God, but as the discipline of a loving God, angered that his people should forfeit the treasures of his love for the worthlessness of pagan idols and unjust gain."[3] This is what we find in our Christian experience. Many believers end up praising God for a great affliction in their lives, because they see in it God's fatherly discipline drawing them back to himself. They are grateful for their trials that led them back to the Lord.

Christianity, therefore, is a religion characterized by joy. Yes, we have trials and sorrows, and we shed real tears. But there is an answer for our afflictions, and because of that answer, a spiritual joy transforms all our sadness. This is why the apostle could command, "Rejoice in the Lord always; again

3. Thomas E. McComiskey, *The Minor Prophets: An Exegetical and Expository Commentary*, 3 vols. (Grand Rapids: Baker, 1998), 3:1154.

I will say, Rejoice" (Phil. 4:4). A moribund Christianity is one that has lost sight of Easter; Christians whose habitual expression is a sour face have surely forgotten the promise and joy of the open tomb.

This does not mean there is no place for fasting in the Christian life. Christ having come with every spiritual blessing from God, ours is a religion of joy. This is why the sacrament by which we remember Christ's death is a feast— the Lord's Supper. Yet there is always a "not yet" to our spiritual condition today. Alongside our "Hallelujah!" there remains a "Maranatha!"—"Come, Lord Jesus!" We will all experience times of grief, remorse, anxiety, or need, for which fasting will be a healthy approach for our worship of God. But even our fasting is performed with the certainty that "joy and gladness and cheerful feasts" (Zech. 8:19) have been prepared for us by God.

True spiritual joy stokes the fires of a new zeal to live for God. "Therefore," says the prophet, "love truth and peace" (Zech. 8:19). In the same way that confidence of victory gives soldiers bravery in battle, the joy of salvation is the tonic God employs to strengthen our hearts and hands for his work. It is always, as Paul writes to Titus, "the grace of God that . . . teaches us to say 'No' to ungodliness and worldly passions, and to live self-controlled, upright and godly lives in this present age" (Titus 2:11–12 NIV).

THE NATIONS WILL COME

Zechariah first foretells the transformation of religion in the new covenant to come as God's response to the question about fasting. We might think of this as the inward effect of Christ's coming. But there is also an outward effect, namely, the accomplishment of God's saving purpose in the world through the church.

The last verses of chapter 8 make three points, beginning with a stirring prophecy of Christianity's effect on the world: "Peoples shall yet come, even the inhabitants of many cities. The inhabitants of one city shall go to another, saying, 'Let us go at once to entreat the favor of the LORD and to seek the LORD of hosts; I myself am going.' Many peoples and strong nations shall come to seek the LORD of hosts in Jerusalem and to entreat the favor of the LORD" (Zech. 8:20–22).

Zechariah prophesies a time when the nations will come to God because of his people. Furthermore, this will not be a military conquest or the result of legislation, but a spiritual movement as peoples from all the nations and tongues are drawn to God. This is something the prophets long had foreseen, as in Isaiah 2:2–3:

> It shall come to pass in the latter days that the mountain of the house of the LORD shall be established as the highest of the mountains, and shall be lifted up above the hills; and all the nations shall flow to it, and many peoples shall come, and say: "Come, let us go up to the mountain of the LORD, to the house of the God of Jacob, that he may teach us his ways and that we may walk in his paths." For out of Zion shall go the law, and the word of the LORD from Jerusalem.

When the prophets speak of "the last days," they mean the days of the Messiah, in both his first and his second coming, and this reference is to the present age of grace in which the gospel is drawing multitudes to his church. This was always God's purpose through Israel. All the way back in the book of Deuteronomy, we read that if Israel will keep God's law the nations will be drawn to the Lord: "Keep them and do them, for that will be your wisdom and your understanding in the sight of the peoples, who, when they hear all these statutes, will say, 'Surely this great nation is a wise and understanding people'" (Deut. 4:6). Prophets like Isaiah and Micah made it clear that this ingathering would be fulfilled in the age to come, that is, in the new covenant in Christ. This is precisely what we do find in the New Testament, as graphically demonstrated on the day of Pentecost, when men from all nations spoke as one when the Holy Spirit descended on that first Christian gathering. T. V. Moore describes this best:

> When this prediction was uttered nothing seemed more hopelessly improbable than its fulfillment. The Jews were a poor, despised, obscure tribe in the heart of Syria, whose existence was only known to the mighty world by their furnishing a trophy to the victorious arms of Babylon. Greece was just rising in the firmament of human history. . . . Rome was then in the rugged feebleness of her wolf-nursed infancy, and slowly continued to grow until she ruled the earth. . . . Five hundred years rolled away, and yet this prophecy remained unfulfilled, indeed seemed further from fulfillment than when it was uttered.
> But at length the time arrived, and there came to Jerusalem "men out of every nation under heaven—Parthians, Medes and Elamites, and the dwellers

in Mesopotamia, and in Judea and Cappadocia, in Pontus and Asia, Phrygia and Pamphylia, in Egypt, and in the parts of Libya about Cyrene, and strangers of Rome, Jews and proselytes, Cretes and Arabians" (Acts 2:9–11), all came up to Jerusalem to seek the face of Jehovah, and from the lips of a Jew they heard words that caused them to cry out, "Men and brethren what shall I do?" They scattered to their own homes again, and carried with them the strange words that had so deeply moved their souls, and being followed by these wonder-working men, there soon began to work a new life among the nations of the earth, and this life took hold in its origin and efficacy upon a *Jew*. . . . All rested their hopes for eternity upon a Jew; and soon received as divinely inspired the words and writings of men who were Jews.[4]

This is what Zechariah 8:23 shows: at a ratio of ten-to-one, men were grabbing hold of the coats of a Jew and coming to seek the Lord, which is precisely what happened in the apostolic age and continues to happen through the apostolic Scriptures as they are preached and taught and believed by people of every nation and tongue today: "Thus says the LORD of hosts: In those days ten men from the nations of every tongue shall take hold of the robe of a Jew, saying, 'Let us go with you, for we have heard that God is with you.'"

Second, these verses inform us that the mission of the church is to lead other people to God. It has been rightly said that the Christian church is the first and only organization which exists for the sake of nonmembers. Jesus said that the church exists as a light for the world: "Let your light shine before others, so that they may see your good works and give glory to your Father who is in heaven" (Matt. 5:16). Not all of us are called to be preachers, and few will be full-time missionaries, but all of us have this command laid upon us. Harry Ironside said, "It takes the whole Church to make His epistle, but each one of us is one little verse in that epistle."[5] If we are not having the kind of influence on the world around us as we see in these verses—together and individually—then we should prayerfully consider why and ask God for the grace to be more useful in his work of saving sinners through the gospel.

Third, these verses present a model for the church's evangelistic outreach. The people coming to God here are doing so voluntarily—even

4. T. V. Moore, *Haggai, Zechariah, & Malachi* (Edinburgh: Banner of Truth, 1979), 203–4.
5. Harry A. Ironside, *II Corinthians* (Neptune, NJ: Loizeaux, 1939), 70.

enthusiastically—because they have heard and seen something enormously attractive. "Let us go at once," they say, "to entreat the favor of the LORD and to seek the LORD of hosts; I myself am going" (Zech. 8:21). Verse 23 concludes, "In those days ten men from the nations of every tongue shall take hold of the robe of a Jew, saying, 'Let us go with you, for we have heard that God is with you.'"

This reminds us that evangelism is *personal*. The picture is of ten men coming to one of God's people to follow him in the way of the Lord. The statistics show that the majority of people who are saved today come to faith through the personal witness of a friend or family member. Even if they are converted through preaching in the church, the reason they came to the church in the first place was a Christian they knew there.

Furthermore, the people in this passage come because of what they have heard: "We have heard that God is with you." Evangelism, therefore, consists of a *message*. Paul challenges us, "How are they to call on him in whom they have not believed? And how are they to believe in him of whom they have never heard? And how are they to hear without someone preaching? And how are they to preach unless they are sent? As it is written, 'How beautiful are the feet of those who preach the good news!'" (Rom. 10:14–15). It is impossible for evangelism to take place without the proclamation of the gospel message, namely, the death and resurrection of God's Son for the reconciliation of sinners through faith in him.

Moreover, evangelism requires a *living witness*. Ironside writes, "Men will not read their Bibles, and we are called upon to live Christ so that as they read us they will see that there is reality in the gospel and the message we preach, because of the change that has come in our lives."[6] Therefore it is every Christian's duty to live so as to confirm the witness of Christ to the world, and especially in times of sorrow or struggle to show God's power to turn fasts into feasts.

What do people need to see in our churches and in our lives if we are to have the kind of magnetic pull that will make them want to come? It is not that we are fun-loving or impressive by worldly standards. Rather, they need to see the presence and power of God. They need acquaintance with

6. Ibid., 71.

realities higher than those of this world. They need models of a faith that enables us to live above the common level and to endure hardship and suffering. Their souls crave a noble theme that runs through our conduct and which has its origin in the divine. God has "put eternity into man's heart" (Eccl. 3:11), so it is as God dwells in us as the fire burned within the bush, that men and women will climb up the mountain to inquire of our God. Martyn Lloyd-Jones comments:

> The glory of the gospel is that when the Church is absolutely different from the world, she invariably attracts it. It is then that the world is made to listen to her message, though it may hate it at first. That is how revival comes. That must also be true of us as individuals. It should not be our ambition to be as much like everybody else as we can, though we happen to be Christian, but rather to be as different from everybody who is not a Christian as we can possibly be. Our ambition should be to be like Christ, the more like Him the better, and the more like Him we become, the more we shall be unlike everybody who is not a Christian.[7]

Lloyd-Jones concludes with words greatly neglected since his time: "What the Church needs to do is not to organize evangelistic campaigns to attract outside people, but to begin herself to live the Christian life. If she did that, men and women would be crowding into our buildings. They would say, 'What is the secret of this?' "[8]

How does Zechariah's prophecy foresee us succeeding in evangelism? First, evangelism is personal; second, evangelism consists of the gospel message that must be spoken and heard; and, third, that message must be seen in our own lives. The result will be God's revelation of himself through our witness to a world that has not known him. As the church has abandoned these principles, she has failed in the mission foretold in this passage; but as Christians have faithfully served God in this way, history has recorded the very thing we find here: ten men coming with each Christian, exclaiming with wonder: "Let us go with you, for we have heard that God is with you" (Zech. 8:23).

7. D. Martyn Lloyd-Jones, *Expositions on the Sermon on the Mount*, 2 vols. (Grand Rapids: Eerdmans, 1959), 1:37.
8. Ibid., 1:18.

A Man, A Jew

Zechariah speaks of people from all nations and tongues taking hold of one Jew by the hem of his robe. This depicts one person coming to God by the ministry and the credentials of another. We can hardly fail to notice what an apt picture this is of faith in Jesus Christ. Indeed, the Hebrew of this text literally speaks of "a man, a Jew," on whose coattails we are to grab.

God has provided one man to mediate between himself and sinful mankind. Paul explains, "For there is one God, and there is one mediator between God and men, the man Christ Jesus, who gave himself as a ransom for all" (1 Tim. 2:5–6). He is the One in whom Israel finds its fulfillment; Jesus is not just *a* Jew but *the* Jew through whom all may come to seek and find the Lord.

What does it mean to trust in Jesus, but to lay hold of his coat, that is, his righteousness, rejecting our own as filthy rags, and to seek his achievement in the place of our failure, finding shelter in his status as beloved son, to seek his merits for access into the love of the Father. It is in this sense that this prophecy is ultimately fulfilled: "In those days ten men"—which signifies a multitude—"from the nations of every tongue shall take hold of the robe of a Jew, saying, 'Let us go with you, for we have heard that God is with you'" (Zech. 8:23).

As the Samaritans learned during Jesus' visit, recorded in John 4, this one man, a Jew, is the Savior of the world, because he is the Holy One sent from God, the very Son of God sent to redeem us from our sins. This is why Jesus taught, "I am the way, and the truth, and the life. No one comes to the Father except through me" (John 14:6). If you will not lay hold of his hem, if you will not come to God through him, then according to the Bible you may not come at all. If you have not come to God through Christ, these words are for you. And if you will come, this description of a man holding to the coat of another will depict your salvation.

Understand that long ago, amidst the ruins of the once-destroyed, but now-reconstituted Jerusalem, a delegation came from nearby Bethel and asked a petty question about fasting. God answered them through the prophet. Would the project succeed? Would the temple rebuilding be a success? Would fasts give way to feasts? In answer to those questions God pointed to the individual Christian today, among others, as the proof of the hope that lies in him. Long ago—indeed, from before the creation of the world—he planned and foresaw the gift of his Son, to come and live with us, to die for us, and to rise again from the dead to redeem us from our sins. God foretold a glorious gospel success: "In those days ten men from the nations of every tongue shall take hold of the robe of a Jew, saying, 'Let us go with you, for we have heard that God is with you'" (Zech. 8:23). Happy indeed are all who hear and see and go with Jesus to see the face of God, for their fasts will be turned into feasts and they will praise him with great rejoicing forever.

PART 3

The Oracles of Zechariah

17

The Burden of the Lord

Zechariah 9:1–8

The burden of the word of the LORD is against the land of Hadrach and Damascus is its resting place. For the LORD has an eye on mankind and on all the tribes of Israel. (Zech. 9:1)

Many tall skyscrapers have an observation deck on their highest floor. Tourists can pay to take the long elevator ride to the top, and once there they marvel to see the landscape all around for astonishing distances. Things look different from such a height, and distances shrink to give us a whole new perspective. In many ways, the prophetic materials of the Old Testament provide that kind of view of the redemptive landscape. The prophet is taken up, and we go with him to gain a breathtaking view of distant events. From that height space shrinks and perspective changes. Episodes that are centuries or more apart may seem jammed together. For this reason it is not always easy to relate neatly what was seen from on high with what transpires here below. Sometimes prophecies are given in such a way that we can definitely see their fulfillment, while others are such that when we come down the elevator, things look quite different than they did from on high.

Zechariah 9 presents a prophecy of events that were distant to the prophet. It is labeled as a "burden" of the Lord, that is, a divine revelation usually associated with judgment and woe. (Some versions translate this as an "oracle" of the Lord.) Its subject is God's future wrath on the nations that opposed his people. Up to this point, Zechariah has focused on immediate issues, mainly the building of the temple and the restoration of the nation. But now a different lens is placed on his book. Now we will consider events centuries future, and especially the epochal coming of the Messiah, the true king of God's people. Charles Feinberg rightly says, "The last six chapters of this prophecy constitute an incomparable treasury of prophetic truth."[1]

A QUESTION OF AUTHORSHIP

At this point in our studies we encounter a question regarding authorship that has occupied learned minds for several hundred years. Today a large number of scholars, including practically all of liberal scholarship, consider the second half of Zechariah to have been written by a different author. In the commentaries, therefore, you will often find the first half referred to as I Zechariah, and the second half as II Zechariah. Some scholars also separate the last three chapters, the oracle about Israel, as having been written by yet another unknown author, designated III Zechariah.

Some conservative scholars are open to the possibility that Zechariah did not write these chapters, arguing that this does not challenge the authority or inspiration of the text. One reason for their openness is an apparent conflict with the New Testament. Matthew 27:9 cites Zechariah 11:12–13, but ascribes the passage to Jeremiah. This has long puzzled believers who are eager to affirm the accuracy of the New Testament. Indeed, one of the first to raise this issue was an Englishman named Joseph Mede in the early seventeenth century. His motive was not to attack but to defend the inerrancy of Scripture by resolving an apparent problem.

Today most of the liberal challenges to Zecharian authorship are based on other considerations. First, antisupernaturalists who deny the possibility of true prophecy respond to accurate predictions like the ones in this

---

1. Charles L. Feinberg, *God Remembers: A Study of Zechariah* (Portland, OR: Multnomah Press, 1979), 117.

passage by placing them later in history. Other critics point to major differences in style between the two halves of Zechariah, as well as to the significantly different tone of these chapters compared to the earlier ones.

What are we to make of this? First, does it make a difference if these chapters really should be found back in Jeremiah, or if they were inserted into Zechariah by a later writer? Might it be just as authentic, even though there was an error in the organization? Yes, it does matter. These chapters are presented to us as having come from the mouth of Zechariah, and if they really came from Jeremiah, about a hundred years earlier, or from someone else hundreds of years later, then the impression they make and the statements they convey are quite different. The meaning of a text is related to its historicity, and therefore we rely on God's providential care to preserve its reliable form. It is noteworthy that the way we have Zechariah today is the same as it was presented in the Greek translation used by our Lord Jesus and his apostles. This is the form in which this book entered the Jewish canon that now makes up our Old Testament. An error of this sort, therefore, can only loosen our confidence in the Bible God has preserved and given to us.

What, then, about the objections? First, and most significant, is the citation from Matthew 27:9. The key to understanding this is to realize that Matthew is actually citing two passages having to do with Judas's betrayal. He cites Zechariah 11:12–13, which mentions the thirty pieces of silver, but also alludes to Jeremiah 32:6–9, which adds the detail of the potter's field. Since Jeremiah is the more prominent of the two prophets, Matthew mentions only his name. The same phenomenon occurs in Mark 1:2–3, where both Isaiah and Malachi are quoted but only the more famous Isaiah is cited.

Under analysis, the other scholarly concerns similarly lose their force. It is argued that the tone of the second half differs strikingly from the first, but this does not prove a different author, especially since the genre and purpose of the chapters are different. It is apparent that these two halves of Zechariah were written at markedly different points in his life, the second half coming much later, so we are not surprised to find changes in his writing. In fact, we will find a great many similarities as well, though these are not often mentioned by the more radical critics.

Finally, there is the real objection: the striking accuracy of Zechariah's predictions. The assumption that true prophecy is impossible, since man cannot know the future, is directly challenged by the Bible, which shows men receiving revelation from God, who can and does know the future. Indeed, God gives these kinds of prophecies partly as a proof of himself—that is, as a challenge to these very scoffing skeptics. As he says in Isaiah 46:9–10, "For I am God, and there is no other; I am God, and there is none like me, declaring the end from the beginning and from ancient times things not yet done, saying, 'My counsel shall stand, and I will accomplish all my purpose.'"

Based on these considerations, the most reasonable approach is to receive the text as it is, a prophetic word from God through the prophet Zechariah.

JUDGMENT ON THE NATIONS

I mentioned that there are similarities that show a basic unity to Zechariah, and one of them occurs in the opening passage of the second half of the book. Back in chapter 1, in the first of the night visions, the mounted angel reported finding the world at peace. This was a cause for lament, because it meant that Jerusalem's oppressors remained safe and secure. However, God expressed his intention to shake things up. The next vision affirmed this, showing God coming to "cast down the horns of the nations who lifted up their horns against the land of Judah to scatter it" (1:21). That was how the first half of Zechariah began, and the second half begins by showing this very judgment unfolding. Zechariah 9:1–8 portrays God as a conqueror working his way methodically down from the north, overthrowing each of Israel's neighbors in turn.

The oracle begins this conquest in the north, saying, "The burden of the word of the LORD is against the land of Hadrach and Damascus is its resting place" (Zech. 9:1). There is great uncertainty regarding the identity of Hadrach, with much scholarly discussion. Some consider it to be the name of a particular king, and others link it to a smaller town near Damascus (Hatarikka). Both of these seem unlikely, mainly because it is described as "the *land* of Hadrach," which suggests a large territory and likely rules out a small city as well.

The best explanation is that the prophet refers to the Medo-Persian Empire. Chapter 1 spoke of God unsettling Israel's oppressors, and this was Israel's overlord, ruling the entire coast of Palestine down to Egypt. Under this view the name "Hadrach" is a combination of two terms meaning hard and soft (*chad* and *rak*), thus denoting Persia's divided character, being militarily and economically strong but famous for its moral weakness. This kind of code-word is occasionally used in Scripture, especially when designating a nation currently in power.[2]

This makes good sense of the text, namely, that God has an oracle of judgment against Persia, the very power then lording over his people. The judgment proceeds to work its way south along the invasion route toward one Persian possession after another, from Damascus to Hamath, then to Tyre along the Phoenician coast, and then down to the cities of Philistia— Ashkelon, Gaza, Ekron, and Ashdod.

The astonishing accuracy of these prophecies points to the invasion down this very route by the famous Macedonian conqueror, Alexander the Great. In the year 333 BC, Alexander won a great victory over the Persians at Issus. Instead of pursuing his enemy into the Persian interior, which would expose his line of supply to the powerful Persian navy in the Mediterranean Sea, Alexander brilliantly turned south to roll up the Persian cities along the coast. His strategy was to eliminate the enemy navy by removing its ports, marching through Phoenicia and Philistia down to Egypt, and only then returning north to deal with the Persian ground forces.

Alexander's route followed the precise line stated in our text. Most striking is the accuracy of this description of the fall of Tyre, a strong and wealthy city-state on the Mediterranean coast. Verse 2 speaks of their skill or wisdom, and the Tyrians were famous for their trading prowess and political maneuvering: "Tyre and Sidon . . . are very wise." Zechariah 9:3 says, "Tyre has built herself a rampart," and that was true. Originally built on the mainland, Tyre had been moved to an island half a mile offshore. There it was surrounded by a double wall 150 feet high and made more impregnable by its naval patrols. When Nebuchadnezzar besieged it in the early sixth century BC, the city successfully held out for thirteen years. This combination of skill and strength inevitably made Tyre vastly rich. She had "heaped up silver like dust," we read, "and fine gold like the mud of the streets" (Zech. 9:3). That is barely an exaggeration! As is so often true of well-positioned trading nations, Tyre gathered in wealth as easily as a doorway brings in dust.

But Zechariah's oracle nonetheless speaks of Tyre's destruction: "The Lord will take away her possessions and destroy her power on the sea, and

2. See Isa. 21:11; 29:1, 2, 7; and Jer. 25:26; 51:41.

she will be consumed by fire" (Zech. 9:4 NIV). Seeing this, all the nations nearby will tremble. This is precisely what happened when Alexander employed all his military genius to conquer Tyre, a victory that astonished and terrified his foes. Alexander built a massive causeway from the shore to the island, using stones, wood, and the rubble from the old city to create a land bridge a half-mile long. The city that had seemed impregnable fell to the young conqueror in just seven months, fulfilling this prophecy. Her wealth was taken and the city consumed by fire. Indeed, an older prophecy from Ezekiel 26:12–14 was fulfilled to the letter: "They will break down your walls and destroy your pleasant houses. Your stones and timber and soil they will cast into the midst of the waters. . . . I will make you a bare rock. You shall be a place for the spreading of nets. You shall never be rebuilt, for I am the LORD; I have spoken, declares the Lord GOD." Never has it been rebuilt, and Alexander's causeway remains to this day. It was, James M. Boice comments, "a monument to the truth of prophecy and the folly of human pride."[3]

Next lay the coastal cities of Philistia, which were terrified by Alexander's exploits. Zechariah 9:5 tells us, "Ashkelon shall see it, and be afraid; Gaza too, and shall writhe in anguish; Ekron also, because its hopes are confounded." One after another these cities fell to the Greeks. One of the ancient histories of Alexander, the *Anabasis of Alexander*, by Arrian, tells us what happened in Gaza after the invaders penetrated the walls, confirming this prophecy of her agony: "The Gazaeans held together and continued to resist, though their city was already in enemy hands; and all perished there, fighting each man at his post. Alexander sold their women and children into slavery, populated the city from the surrounding tribesmen and used it as a fortress town for the war."[4]

SALVATION FROM THE LORD

Zechariah's prophecy links God's judgment on the nations with salvation for Israel, consoling those who in the prophet's time were afflicted by these very cities. This has been a constant theme in this book, that however bleak

---

3. James M. Boice, *The Minor Prophets*, 2 vols. (Grand Rapids: Zondervan, 1986), 2:193.
4. Arrian, *Anabasis of Alexander* (Cambridge: Harvard University Press, 1976), 1:219.

the circumstances, God's people may look to him in faith and find a sure defense. In chapter 2, God said of Jerusalem, "I will be to her a wall of fire all around" (Zech. 2:5). Now in Zechariah 9:8, he says, "I will encamp at my house as a guard, so that none shall march to and fro; no oppressor shall again march over them, for now I see with my own eyes." Literally, God will encamp himself as a sentry around his people. One commentator writes: "It is Yahweh, the God of covenant love and loyalty, who posts himself as a guard by his people. What have they to fear? The city-states that appear in this section will fall before the might of conquerors, but God's people will be safe because Yahweh stands guard over them."[5]

Remarkably, this too unfolded in the time of Alexander, especially if we are to believe the record of events given by Josephus, the famous first-century AD Jewish historian. According to Josephus, Alexander became involved in affairs at Jerusalem during his siege of Tyre and Gaza. There had been a controversy over the expulsion of the Jewish high priest's brother because he had married a Gentile woman, and this man's father-in-law, the Persian governor of Samaria, cast his lot with Alexander and sought his aid against the faithful Jewish leaders. Alexander consequently approached Jerusalem with a powerful force.

Israel's high priest, a man named Jaddua, is reported to have acted as he should, for Josephus writes, "He therefore ordained that the people should make supplications, and should join with him in offering sacrifices to God, whom he besought to protect the nation, and to deliver them from the perils that were coming upon them."[6] This is the faith God's people are commended for all through Scripture.

Josephus tells us that God answered in a dream, telling Jaddua to adorn the city with wreaths and open the gates. The people were to appear wearing white garments, and the priests were to wear the blue and gold robes of their order, the high priest with the mitre and plate on his head, which read "Holy to the Lord."

Alexander observed this procession with astonishment, went forward alone, and upon reaching the high priest prostrated himself to the ground

---

5. Thomas E. McComiskey, *The Minor Prophets: An Exegetical and Expository Commentary*, 3 vols. (Grand Rapids: Baker, 1998), 3:1163.

6. Josephus, *Antiquities of the Jews*, XI.viii.3–5.

before him. Alexander's troops were horrified at this sight, and his general Parmenio inquired after his strange behavior. The great conqueror replied that he was worshiping not the priest but the God he served. "For it was he whom I saw in my sleep dressed as he is now, when I was at Dior in Macedonia. As I was considering with myself how I might become master of Asia, he urged me not to hesitate but to cross over confidently, for he himself would lead my army and give over to me the empire of the Persians."[7] According to Josephus, Alexander then accompanied the Jews to Jerusalem where he sacrificed to the Lord according to the high priest's instructions. Alexander then left, having first granted the Jews' request that they might continue to observe the law and serve the Lord in safety.

This is an uncorroborated account, and it is difficult to assess its historical accuracy. But it certainly is the kind of thing suggested by our passage, and easily within God's ability. What is certain is that as these mighty cities were conquered by Alexander, Jerusalem remained unharmed just as God had promised through Zechariah.

DOCTRINAL THEMES

As an introductory passage these verses present several themes that are important to Zechariah's overall message and to this second half of his book. First, we see a doctrine that is much emphasized all through Zechariah, namely, *the sovereignty of God.*

God's sovereignty is demonstrated in a number of ways, beginning with the accuracy of these prophecies. These verses were written at least 150 years before the events took place, yet they were fulfilled with astonishing accuracy. This is possible only because God is able to foretell the future, and he can foretell the future because he is in control of it.

Another way God's sovereignty is expressed is through this demonstration of his almighty power. Men may build the strongest of fortresses—and Tyre was as secure as a city can be—but no work of man can stave off God's hand. If God is able to control the destiny of armies and nations in this way, he is certainly up to the task of ruling our individual lives. Whatever he wills comes to pass unfailingly.

7. Ibid.

Notice that while history ascribes these feats to Alexander, God ascribes them to himself. "The Lord will strip her of her possessions and strike down her power on the sea" (Zech. 9:4). God's sovereignty does not rule out secondary causes, in this case the youthful genius of Alexander. But our passage shows that it is God's sovereign will that ultimately rules.

God's sovereignty is not merely hypothetical; our passage shows it extends beyond potential into action. The implication of this is seen in verse 1, although it is uncertain how these words should be rendered. Either "the eyes of men and all the tribes of Israel are on the LORD," as the New International Version puts it, or "The LORD has an eye on mankind and on all the tribes of Israel," as the English Standard Version translates it. In the first case this seems to mean that as God openly enters the scene, he is the One to whom men will have to pay attention. People ignored God then just as they do now, but since he is sovereign we must ultimately reckon with him. God is the One to whom we must give account and the One on whom we must rely.

It is equally true, however, that God's eyes are on us. "Now I see with my own eyes," says the Lord (Zech. 9:8). God never really had slumbered, but this language reinforces the idea of his active involvement. Therefore God is worthy of our praise and trust. He is sovereign, active, and almighty in his dealings with men.

God's sovereignty is the first thing we observe, but, second, this passage reveals the *certainty of judgment* upon the proud and wicked. The Bible says, "God opposes the proud but gives grace to the humble" (James 4:6; 1 Peter 5:5). Surely the case of Tyre eloquently makes this point. Isaiah had prophesied the city's doom in just those terms: "Who has purposed this against Tyre, the bestower of crowns, whose merchants were princes, whose traders were the honored of the earth? The LORD of hosts has purposed it, to defile the pompous pride of all glory, to dishonor all the honored of the earth" (Isa. 23:8–9).

Tyre's example reminds us of the prophecies of Babylon in the book of Revelation, representing the whole world order in rebellion against God: "Fallen, fallen is Babylon the great! . . . For her sins are heaped high as heaven, and God has remembered her iniquities. . . . She will be burned up with fire; for mighty is the Lord God who has judged her" (Rev. 18:2–8). Indeed, when we read in Revelation the description of Mystery Babylon, we see a strong tie to what the Old Testament says about Tyre: "Say to the prince of

Tyre, Thus says the Lord GOD: 'Because your heart is proud, and you have said, "I am a god, I sit in the seat of the gods, in the heart of the seas," yet you are but a man, and no god, though you make your heart like the heart of a god' " (Ezek. 28:2).

Tyre's example reminds Christians not to love the world or worldly things. As God says in Revelation 18:4, "Come out of her, my people, lest you take part in her sins, lest you share in her plagues." God will judge this evil world, and though it seems so comfortable now it will not escape justice. T. V. Moore observes of Tyre: "Never has every element of earthly prosperity seemed more completely under control than in her case. And yet they were all swept like chaff before the whirlwind of the wrath of God, when the time for the fulfillment of his threatenings had come."[8]

Materialism and proud humanism are not able to stand against the true God when he comes in judgment. Indeed, it is chilling to realize the strong parallels between what is said in verses 2 and 3 about Tyre and the situation of the West today. Like Tyre, we have come to rely upon our skill, especially when it comes to technological prowess, our wealth, and our military might. Trust in these has led us away from trust in God; these worldly idols have taught us to despise him and his law. Therefore, the example of Tyre instructs us that unless as a nation we repent, we can expect God to judge us in due time. Many scoff at the notion, but the God who raised up an Alexander is able to destroy our puny defenses.

What is true on the national and cosmic level is also true on the individual level. Ecclesiastes 12:14 reminds us, "God will bring every deed into judgment, with every secret thing, whether good or evil." There is no escape from the wrath of God, not by moving out to an island, not by erecting a high and mighty wall, and not by raising a façade of cultured unbelief. God raised up Alexander to destroy Tyre so that she seemed practically defenseless. At the end of days God will send the Lord Jesus Christ to reign forever as King and Judge.

Tyre's destruction shows the folly of pride, but when we move down to Philistia we see God's judgment on the idolaters there. This is what verse 7 is about: "I will take away its blood from its mouth, and its abominations from between its teeth." This shows God putting an end to false and

---

8. T. V. Moore, *Haggai, Zechariah, & Malachi* (Edinburgh: Banner of Truth, 1979), 225.

debauched worship. The Philistines practiced the grossest paganism, drinking animal blood and eating the flesh of banned animals. This shows that God will put an end to all idolatry, even bringing the remnant of their survivors into the company of God's people to worship truly.

This is what the second half of Zechariah 9:7 predicts: "[Philistia] too shall be a remnant for our God; it shall be like a clan in Judah, and Ekron shall be like the Jebusites." The Jebusites were the original inhabitants of Jerusalem, who were conquered by David and incorporated into the nation. God, therefore, is able to overthrow idolatry and establish true worship on the earth. Ultimately, this is fulfilled in the church. Never in the Old Testament do we read these things about the Philistines and Ekron; but in Acts 8 we see the evangelist Philip preaching the gospel in just those lands. As always, it is in Christ that the promises are finally made yes and amen.

Third, we see here that *God is the defender of his people*. This, of course, accompanies the idea of his judgment on the wicked. The coming of God always brings this double-edged sword: wrath upon the wicked and salvation for the godly. This is what the New Testament says about the second coming of Jesus Christ:

> God considers it just to repay with affliction those who afflict you, and to grant relief to you who are afflicted as well as to us, when the Lord Jesus is revealed from heaven with his mighty angels in flaming fire, inflicting vengeance on those who do not know God and on those who do not obey the gospel of our Lord Jesus. They will suffer the punishment of eternal destruction, away from the presence of the Lord and from the glory of his might, when he comes on that day to be glorified in his saints, and to be marveled at among all who have believed, because our testimony to you was believed. (2 Thess. 1:6–10)

The passage ends with God assuring us that he camps before the gate of his people (Zech. 9:8). The writer of Hebrews says the same: "For [God] has said, 'I will never leave you nor forsake you.' So we can confidently say, 'The Lord is my helper; I will not fear; what can man do to me?'" (Heb. 13:5–6). Psalm 121 adds, "The LORD is your keeper.... The LORD will keep you from all evil; he will keep your life" (vv. 5, 7).

What is true of our lives is also true of our souls. Paul affirms, "He who did not spare his own Son, but gave him up for us all, how will he not also with him graciously give us all things?" (Rom. 8:32). God was so ready and determined for our salvation that he sent his own Son to bear our sins on the cross. Therefore Paul can go on to ask, "Who shall separate us from the love of Christ? Shall tribulation, or distress, or persecution, or famine, or nakedness, or danger, or sword?" (Rom. 8:35). He answers, "For I am sure that neither death nor life, nor angels nor rulers, nor things present nor things to come, nor powers, nor height nor depth, nor anything else in all creation, will be able to separate us from the love of God in Christ Jesus our Lord" (Rom. 8:38–39).

So we have here two great truths set together. No city set against God can stand. No wall can keep him out; no sea can hold him back. Yet his own house stands secure, for there he stands guard before his people. Where, then, will you take your stand? Into whose safekeeping will you commit your soul? The psalmist was right when he said, "Blessed is the nation whose God is the LORD, the people whom he has chosen as his heritage!" (Ps. 33:12). Truly it was a wise man who wrote, "Blessed is he who trusts in the LORD" (Prov. 16:20).

18

BEHOLD, YOUR KING

Zechariah 9:9–17

Rejoice greatly, O daughter of Zion! Shout aloud, O daughter of Jerusalem! behold, your king is coming to you; righteous and having salvation is he, humble and mounted on a donkey, on a colt, the foal of a donkey. (Zech. 9:9)

hen we were studying the first half of Zechariah, I often pointed out how clearly this Old Testament book points forward to the person and work of our Lord Jesus Christ. When we turn to the second half, with its starker oracles of judgment and salvation, we find that this is only intensified. In fact, Zechariah is the Old Testament book most frequently quoted in the passion narratives of the four Gospels, beginning with the famous prophecy: "Behold, your king is coming to you; righteous and having salvation is he, humble and mounted on a donkey, on a colt, the foal of a donkey" (Zech. 9:9). Matthew 21:5 and John 12:15 specifically quote this verse, as it is fulfilled in the triumphal entry of Jesus into Jerusalem on Palm Sunday, immediately prior to his arrest and crucifixion.

THE RIGHTEOUS KING

Before we focus on Palm Sunday, we should see how this prophecy first spoke to its original recipients in the time of Zechariah. We saw in verses 1–8 a prophecy fulfilled in the conquests of Alexander the Great in 333 BC. The Bible ascribes those military conquests to the Lord himself, the Sovereign who stands above every human agency. Now we find that the military fulfillment points to a greater and spiritual fulfillment—to a spiritual conquest, and to a conquering hero very different from the kind represented by Alexander.

We remember that the Jews in Zechariah's time did not have a king. The last member of the royal family we hear of is Zerubbabel, who, although he was never crowned as king, nevertheless was governor in Jerusalem. When the first eight chapters of Zechariah were penned, Zerubbabel was very much an active participant, but now he seems to have departed from the scene. Now, in this kingless era, the Jews are told to look for the coming of the ruler God would send, one who fits and fulfills the messianic expectation of the Old Testament. Here is a king who is just and having salvation, who furthermore comes in meekness and affliction. David Baron writes:

> This prophecy was intended to introduce, in contrast to earthly warfare and kingly triumph, another Kingdom, of which the just King would be the Prince of Peace, who was meek and lowly in His Advent, who would speak peace to the heathen, and whose sway would yet extend to earth's utmost bounds. . . . If ever was a true picture of the Messiah-King and His Kingdom, it is this: and if ever Israel was to have a Messiah, or the world a Saviour, He must be such as is described in this prophecy—not merely in the letter, but in the spirit of it.[1]

The only person in all of history who fits this description is the Lord Jesus Christ. We have here a wonderful portrayal of his person, the Messiah who comes as king. First, Jesus is righteous. Many commentators think this simply states that his reign will be just, but this must also touch upon him as a person, that he himself is righteous. It is generally agreed that this passage

1. David Baron, *The Visions and Prophecies of Zechariah* (Grand Rapids: Kregel, 1918), 303–4.

draws from the description of the Servant of the Lord in Isaiah, which begins with these words: "Behold my servant, whom I uphold, my chosen, in whom my soul delights; I have put my Spirit upon him; he will bring forth justice to the nations" (Isa. 42:1). The One who establishes righteousness is the One who is pleasing in God's sight, the One who is himself righteous in all his ways. Jesus accomplished righteousness as the personal qualification for serving as God's righteous king.

This refers to what theologians call the *active obedience of Christ*. Jesus was born under the law, lived under the law all his life, and perfectly fulfilled the law—God's moral and spiritual requirements for man—to the smallest letter. "Do not think that I have come to abolish the Law or the Prophets," he said. "I have not come to abolish them but to fulfill them" (Matt. 5:17). Jesus achieved righteousness under God's law for our sakes. Paul writes, "None is righteous, no, not one . . . no one does good, not even one" (Rom. 3:10–12). Jesus is the sole exception to this rule, for he was born of the Holy Spirit as the true Son of God. He came to achieve a positive righteousness to bestow on all who look to him in faith.

It is for this reason that Zechariah says of him: "Your king is coming to you; righteous and having salvation is he" (9:9). Some regard this as saying merely that he will be saved and vindicated in his ordeal by God, which certainly is true. But the point of the verse is that he comes with all righteousness and salvation *to us* and *for us*. John Calvin says: "As he came for the sake of others, and has been for them endued with righteousness and salvation; then the righteousness and salvation of which mention is made here, belong to the whole body of the Church."[2]

Zechariah's oracle goes on to describe his coming with these words: "humble and mounted on a donkey, on a colt, the foal of a donkey." The donkey was a royal mount in Israel's earlier days. The judges, as well as David, rode a donkey, and Solomon, the king of peace, rode one in his coronation ceremony. This, therefore, was a sign of divine royalty, one characterized by humility and gentleness of spirit. Comparing this to the war horses ridden by worldly kings, Thomas McComiskey writes:

2. John Calvin, *A Commentary on the Twelve Minor Prophets*, 5 vols. (Edinburgh: Banner of Truth, 1986), 5:253.

The donkey stands out . . . as a deliberate rejection of this symbol of arrogant trust in human might, expressing subservience to the sovereignty of God. Jerusalem's king is of humble mien, yet victorious, and so it has always been that the church does not effectively spread the gospel by sword or by arrogance, but by mirroring the humble spirit of its king and savior.[3]

Such is the entrance of this messianic king, one who is righteous, with salvation, who comes not in worldly might but in weakness and in the folly of the cross. How well this fits the words of the apostle Paul, who wrote of Jesus in his saving work: "For you know the grace of our Lord Jesus Christ, that though he was rich, yet for your sake he became poor, so that you by his poverty might become rich" (2 Cor. 8:9). Jesus said of his own ministry: "The Son of Man came not to be served but to serve, and to give his life as a ransom for many" (Matt. 20:28).

Let us, then, meditate upon the contrast between the person of Christ and that of every earthly king. Whereas earthly kings rule for their own riches and glory, Christ rules for our salvation. Earthly kings reign over the people from above, in haughty power, but this king condescends to dwell among his own. Jonathan Edwards writes, "His condescension is great enough to become their friend, to become their companion, to unite their souls to Him in spiritual marriage. . . . Yea, it is great enough to abase Himself yet lower for them, even to expose Himself to shame and spitting; yea, to yield up Himself to an ignominious death for them."[4]

In Jesus' life and ministry we find one example of humble meekness after another. Arthur Pink writes:

Notice it in the men selected by Him to be His ambassadors: He chose not the wise, the learned, the great, the noble, but poor fishermen for the most part. Witness it in the company He kept: He sought not the rich and renowned, but was "the Friend of publicans and sinners." See it in the miracles He performed: again and again He enjoined the healed to go and tell no man what had been done for them. Behold it in the unobtrusiveness of His service: unlike the hypocrites who sounded a trumpet before them, He sought

3. Thomas E. McComiskey, *The Minor Prophets: An Exegetical and Expository Commentary*, 3 vols. (Grand Rapids: Baker, 1998), 3:1166.

4. Jonathan Edwards, *Altogether Lovely: Jonathan Edwards on the Glory and Excellency of Christ* (Morgan, PA: Soli Deo Gloria, 1997), 18–19.

not the limelight, shunned advertising, and disdained popularity. . . . When He, in fulfillment of prophecy, presented Himself to Israel as their King, He entered Jerusalem "lowly, and riding upon an ass."[5]

A king like this is worth shouting over, which is why the prophet enjoins the people: "Rejoice greatly, O daughter of Zion! . . . Behold, your king is coming to you; righteous and having salvation" (Zech. 9:9). On the day her king did come, when Jesus rode in on a donkey's back, this prophecy was fulfilled. Luke tells us, "The whole multitude of his disciples began to rejoice and praise God with a loud voice for all the mighty works that they had seen, saying, 'Blessed is the King who comes in the name of the Lord! Peace in heaven and glory in the highest!'" (Luke 19:37–38).

The King's Salvation

When we speak of the Savior, we often distinguish between his person and his work. Jesus is fit to be our Savior and Lord because of his person, as Zechariah 9:9 especially celebrates. But it is his work that actually achieves our salvation. While looking to him in loving faith, we trust and receive and rely upon his work for our deliverance. This is what the verses that follow pick up on, vividly portraying the salvation that he actually achieves for us and in us.

Zechariah 9:10 picks up on this symbolism of the humble king on a donkey and says of his work: "He shall speak peace to the nations; his rule shall be from sea to sea, and from the River to the ends of the earth." What follows in the rest of this chapter is a depiction of his reign and its progress, starting with the statement, "I will cut off the chariot from Ephraim and the war horse from Jerusalem; and the battle bow shall be cut off." This does not predict an end to all strife upon the earth, but rather that God's people will return to faithful dependence on the Lord. This is another point of continuity with the early chapters of Zechariah, which began with God saying, "Return to me, and I will return to you" (1:3).

The key to understanding this oracle is to know that from its earliest days God forbade Israel to employ the kinds of weapons used by other nations

5. Arthur W. Pink, *Comfort for Christians* (Grand Rapids: Baker, 1993), 75.

around them. Zechariah 9:10 speaks of chariots and war horses, and the mounted archers who rode on them. Deuteronomy 17:16 explicitly forbade Israel's kings from relying on these kinds of forces. Deuteronomy 20:1–4 explained why:

> When you go out to war against your enemies, and see horses and chariots and an army larger than your own, you shall not be afraid of them, for the LORD your God is with you, who brought you up out of the land of Egypt. . . . Do not fear or panic or be in dread of them, for the LORD your God is he who goes with you to fight for you against your enemies, to give you the victory.

The point of verse 10, therefore, is that the Lord will *take away worldly sources of strength from his people and lead them to trust in him.* Just as the messianic king comes not in worldly might, so also his reign is not to be established according to worldly principles. This is a reminder to anyone in the church who would foolishly seek worldly power to achieve spiritual ends. C. F. Keil comments, "Through the destruction of their military power . . . the covenant nation [will] be divested of its political and worldly character, and made into a spiritual nation or kingdom."[6] As one hymn puts it:

> For not with swords' loud clashing,
>   nor roll of stirring drums—
> With deeds of love and mercy
>   the heav'nly kingdom comes.

That is the first step in the King's reign, to restore the people to God through faith. Verse 11 tells of the second step, "As for you also . . . I will set your prisoners free from the waterless pit." Because of his covenant relationship to the people, God will *deliver them from their affliction.* The idea of a waterless pit seems to allude to the desolate conditions in which Zechariah's generation found themselves, but perhaps also to the pit into which Joseph was thrown by his angry brothers in Genesis 37. Like Joseph, the Jews were not quite perishing there, but they were languishing in vulnerable weakness.

---

6. C. F. Keil and F. Delitzsch, *Commentary on the Old Testament* (Peabody, MA: Hendrickson, 1996), 10:577.

Verses 13–15 indicate that this restoration will also involve the renewing of their fighting prowess, as they once more look to God in faith. The Lord sends those prisoners who hoped in him back to the fortress. He sees Judah and Ephraim, the two halves of Israel, working together as a bow and arrow; changing the metaphor, he says they will be like a hero's sword: "For I have bent Judah as my bow; I have made Ephraim its arrow. . . . I will stir up your sons . . . and wield you like a warrior's sword." Verse 14 offers imagery from days gone by, with the Lord appearing over them as a shield, while the trumpet sounds and lighting flashes, as God marches amongst his people for battle. "The Lord GOD will sound the trumpet and will march forth in the whirlwinds of the south," verse 14 says, recalling the days of the exodus when the glory cloud attended the people in triumph. Verse 15 shows them in their victory: "The LORD of hosts will protect them, and they shall devour, and tread down the sling stones."

The Hebrew text literally says they will *eat* the sling stones, a common weapon used by light troops in that day. This is paired with the idea that they "shall drink and roar as if drunk with wine" (Zech. 9:15). The picture is not that of some pagan battle debauchery. Rather, the people who began so weak and emaciated are now so strengthened by God's provision that they overwhelm the enemy. Finally, the description concludes, they shall "be full like a bowl, drenched like the corners of the altar" (Zech. 9:15). Those bowls were filled with blood, and likewise will Israel's warriors be covered with enemy blood.

There are clues here about the fulfillment of these prophecies. The earlier verses in chapter 9 spoke of Alexander the Great's victories over Persia, and though Jerusalem would be protected against Alexander, verse 13 says, "I will stir up your sons, O Zion, against your sons, O Greece." This shows Jews fighting the Greeks, something that happened during the reign of Antiochus IV Epiphanes, the Greek king who ruled Palestine from 175 to 163 BC.

After Alexander's sudden death in 323 BC, his empire fragmented into four pieces. One of his generals, Seleucus, gained control over the eastern territories that included the Middle East. Antiochus was one of his descendants, and thus ruled over the Jews. Concerned about the rising threat to his kingdom from Rome, which was just then attaining dominance in the ancient world, Antiochus labored to unite his realm around his pagan Greek culture. When the Jews resisted this, he responded brutally. He stopped the temple service and sacrifices, destroyed scrolls of the Scriptures, forbade circumcision, and even committed the ultimate insult of sacrificing a pig on a pagan altar in the temple. This seems to be the "abomination that makes desolate" Daniel prophesied (11:31; 12:11).

The Jews were in a completely vulnerable position militarily, having been placed under occupation. Indeed, their situation was very much that of Zechariah 9:10, with no regular army and only the Lord to turn to. But God raised up a leader, Judas Maccabeus, who led the Jews in a series of stunning victories that swept the Greeks from Jerusalem. The Maccabees secured a century of independence that lasted until the coming of the Romans in 63 BC.

The third phase of God's reign is portrayed in verses 16 and 17, which speak in wonderful terms of *God's care for his people,* resulting in the fullest blessing: "On that day the Lord their God will save them, as the flock of his people; for like the jewels of a crown they shall shine on his land. For how great is his goodness, and how great his beauty! Grain shall make the young men flourish, and new wine the young women."

God's salvation is comprehensive. God's people were defenseless sheep, but he was their shepherd, caring for them. As Psalm 23 puts it, "He makes me lie down in green pastures. He leads me beside still waters" (Ps. 23:2). He will make them beautiful and thriving, young men and women growing strong on his bountiful provision. Verse 16 describes the people as jewels in God's crown. The land is compared to the crown, and the people in the land to the jewels on the crown. God's people, therefore, are emblems of his sovereignty and his royal glory, reminding us that ultimately it is for the glory of his own name that the Lord saves his people.

Spiritual Fulfillment in Christ

Although we can see these promises partially fulfilled in the time of the Maccabees, there is much here that cannot be accounted for in that way. What we have spoken of here goes well beyond what Israel enjoyed in those days. Therefore, that local fulfillment must point to something greater, which is often how prophecies work in the Old Testament. We think of God's promise to David that a son of his would build God's house. Sure enough, David's son, Solomon, built God's temple, yet that near fulfillment anticipated the greater fulfillment yet to come, the house of God built by Jesus Christ, the greater Son of David. The same sort of thing is taking place here. Yes, these prophecies find a fulfillment in the victories later won on Judean battlefields, but ultimately they point to the victory over sin by the death and resurrection of Jesus Christ.

This can be seen in the way this passage centers on Christ's coming into Jerusalem. The core prophecy is that the messianic king would come as one righteous and having salvation, but also one who comes afflicted and humble on a donkey. In Jesus' day the Jews were expecting a military and political Messiah, a view that they might have justified as a literal reading of Zechariah's prophecy. But Jesus never presented his ministry that way and consistently opposed that idea of his reign. As he stated to Pontius Pilate, "My kingdom is not of this world" (John 18:36).

How is it, then, that a king who comes not on a war horse but on a donkey, not in power and pride but in weakness and affliction, can produce the kind of triumphs spoken of in Zechariah 9:11–15? How can we associate this meek figure with the bloody conquest spoken of here? The answer is that the enemy ultimately portrayed here is the enemy of sin, with its power and penalty of guilt. In the battle against the devil and sin, here is the great and mighty conqueror, of whom Isaiah spoke, saying, "Who is this who comes . . . in crimsoned garments . . . he who is splendid in his apparel, marching in the greatness of his strength? 'It is I, speaking in righteousness, mighty to save'" (Isa. 63:1).

This king comes in humility because he comes to save by means of a cross, yet that cross is the instrument of God's unconditional conquest of sin. It is a spiritual victory, yes, but a ruthless and violent act of war on the part of the Son of God against the spiritual powers of darkness in this world and their reign of sin and death. Verse 11 speaks of the prisoners set free "because of the blood of my covenant with you." This is the king who conquers sin by means of the cross, by means of his own blood to fulfill God's covenant of grace.

This is not the first prophecy of a king coming on a donkey, and the prior occasion also links his reign with the shedding of blood. In Genesis 49:10–11, the patriarch Jacob spoke in just these terms as he prophesied concerning the line of Judah, from which Jesus came: "The scepter shall not depart from Judah, nor the ruler's staff from between his feet, until tribute comes to him; and to him shall be the obedience of the peoples. Binding his foal to the vine and his donkey's colt to the choice vine, he has washed his garments in wine and his vesture in the blood of grapes."

This, then, is the king who triumphs through his own blood, whose victory is achieved through his atoning sacrifice. The salvation he gives corresponds to the progression we have seen in these verses. Verse 10 tells of God's people restored to him in faith, so they no longer trust in chariots and horses but in the Lord their God. In the same way, Christ converts sinners to faith in the Lord. Salvation begins in our lives when we are turned from the ways of the world to trust in the Lord. Because of the blood of his covenant, Christ sets the prisoners free: free from the pit of guilt, corruption, and separation from God into which we had been cast by our sin. We call this phase of salvation our *justification*, when we are forgiven and declared righteous in God's sight because of Jesus Christ, and subsequently are adopted as God's own into his family.

The next phase of this progression shows God's people returning to fighting strength. Christ has gathered his people, but they need to be strengthened; they are gathered in a fortress, fed with God's Word, and then sent onto the battlefield to push back the forces of sin in our lives and in the world. This takes place in verses 12–15 and refers to our *sanctification*, the present tense of salvation for all who have been saved, in which we are called to grow in holiness. This requires militant activity, like that which we see in our text, as we strive and fight against the flesh, the world, and the devil, through faith in Christ and by the power he gives. In spiritual terms, it is a bloody affair and Christ gives us the victory as he reigns through us.

All of this leads to the third phase of salvation, which is yet future to all of us who are presently living the Christian life. This phase is called *glorification*, and it is the culmination of Christ's saving work. Sanctification leads to glorification, for as we now are becoming more holy we are growing in glory, in Christ's likeness. Yet we all look forward to the day to come when the words of verses 16 and 17 will be so wonderfully fulfilled in us: "On that day the LORD their God will save them, as the flock of his people; for like the jewels of a crown they shall shine on his land. For how great is his goodness, and how great his beauty!" The apostle John speaks of this, inspiring us to battle today by the vision of what lies ahead, "We know that when he appears we will be like him, because we shall see him as he is. And everyone who thus hopes in him purifies himself as he is pure" (1 John 3:2–3).

THE REIGN OF PEACE

The whole of our salvation relies upon and is the fruit of the work of Jesus Christ, this king who rode so humbly into God's city long ago. His coming stands in the center of this chapter, just as his person and work stand in the center of our salvation hope.

Since salvation is all about him, let us conclude by focusing on Zechariah's words to describe his reign: "He shall speak peace to the nations; his rule shall be from sea to sea, and from the River to the ends of the earth" (Zech. 9:10). Peace is what Jesus brings; this is what the angels sang at his birth: "Peace on earth, goodwill towards men." Peace is what Jesus spoke about to his disciples, just before his death: "Peace I leave with you," he said. "My peace I give to you. Not as the world gives do I give to you. Let not your hearts be troubled, neither let them be afraid" (John 14:27). Peace is what Christianity achieves: peace *from* God through peace *with* God.

Zechariah speaks of Christ's peace going forth throughout the world, from sea to sea, and this is what happens when the gospel goes out into the hearts of men and women. There is no other true peace than that which Jesus gives. Only the peace of God can make peace upon this earth, for he alone calms the storms of our souls and gives us love for him and for others.

Because of Jesus, Christians may ride into trial or difficulty not on a war horse, not in a chariot of war, but meek and lowly on a donkey, relying on our Savior to give us total victory through faith in his name. Even amidst great anxieties he gives us "the peace of God, which surpasses all understanding" (Phil. 4:7). Benjamin B. Warfield writes:

> Jesus Christ is the Prince of Peace, because He takes away sin; and you and I are workers for peace when we preach His Gospel, which is the Gospel of peace just because it is the Gospel of deliverance from sin. Sin means war, and where sin is, there will war be. Righteousness means peace, and there can never be peace where righteousness has not first been realized.[7]

This is why the peace *of* God can come only when we have peace *with* God. Sin makes us enemies of God. It bars us from his peace and places us under his condemnation, and it leads us to war against God's will. Therefore

---

7. Benjamin B. Warfield, *Faith and Life* (Edinburgh: Banner of Truth, 1990), 30–31.

217

we must be brought into a right relationship with him, we must have peace with him, and our passage tells us it is through the blood of the covenant, the precious blood of Christ, that we can have peace with God.

If you have never come to God through faith in Christ, in his gift of forgiveness and righteousness from God, then you have no peace with God. Your sins stand between you and God; they testify still to your enmity to God and his wrath against you. Therefore, you must do what the prophet commands if you would be saved, if you would have peace: look to him, behold this king who comes, righteous and bearing salvation, coming forth in gentleness to be to you a Savior. The apostle Paul explains, "[he made] peace through his blood, shed on the cross" (Col. 1:20 NIV). Look to him, receive him in faith, and you will be saved.

19

THE GOOD SHEPHERD

Zechariah 10:1–5

The LORD of hosts cares for his flock, the house of Judah, and will make them like his majestic steed in battle. From him shall come the cornerstone, from him the tent peg, from him the battle bow, from him every ruler—all of them together. (Zech. 10:3–4)

One of the complaints preachers often hear is that their teaching is not practical enough. It is too focused on issues of doctrine and theology and other matters far above the realm of our daily living. "Stop being so high-in-the-sky," people cry, "and help me with the problems I have to face right now."

Reading the opening verses of Zechariah 10, I can't help wondering if the prophet is responding to that kind of complaint. In chapter 9, Zechariah looked wondrously into the future and spoke of a great day of deliverance, complete with typical prophetic symbolism. He spoke of the Lord appearing like lightning, and the people as jewels sparkling on God's crown. "That's all well and good, Zechariah," he might have been told, "but what about us? What about the difficulties dragging us down, not just in some dim future, but here and now?" Yet the prophet speaks not merely to distant people like us but to his own generation as well, with a message that is both practical and life-transforming. Here, as elsewhere, he directs their faith to the Savior God would send, news that is always the most relevant and valuable that a preacher has to give.

A CALL TO FAITH AND PRAYER

One of the things we know about Zechariah's generation, those faithful Jews who had returned to Jerusalem, is that they were beset with poor harvests. Years earlier, Haggai had begun this prophetic period by highlighting this issue: "You have sown much, and harvested little" (Hag. 1:6). The key to a successful harvest was not merely hard work, but rain, and rain was something the people could not produce. In order to enjoy a plentiful harvest, they required good rains in the autumn months, called the "former rains," which allowed the seeds to sprout and grow, and they also needed good rains in the spring months, called the "latter rains," which caused the corn and grain to swell on their stalks. The latter rain in springtime was especially important because of the drought that invariably occurred in the summer months that followed.

We therefore can see the situation. The people were daily checking the weather forecasts, all of them sweating out the lack of rain, lending their hope to the few clouds that appeared. In this urgent situation, Zechariah had been talking about a day to come when God would bless the people. He has the Messiah on his mind, the king who would come to save. But chapter 9 ends with words that would have been poignantly relevant to his own people, a promise of great harvests. He spoke of grain and new wine, a time of abundance and joy.

"That's what we're interested in, preacher," came the calls to the prophet. "Tell us how to get what we need, tell us how to bring the rains to help the harvest!" That is the kind of transition that may be involved between chapter 9 and the first verse of chapter 10.

Like any good minister, Zechariah did not just give the people what they wanted. As we see, he did apply his preaching to the present problem. But he did it in such a way as to call them to faith and repentance. Zechariah 10:1–2 is a call to true religion—a call to faith and prayer—as set against the false religion into which so many had fallen.

Verse 1 begins with Zechariah's direct answer to the problem of the rains. He said, "Ask rain from the LORD." The people were dependent on something they could not control. Without rain from heaven, their crops simply wouldn't grow, yet they could not make it rain. Therefore, they should turn to God in prayer, supplicating the One who *could* make it rain, the God whose power controls all things. It is "the LORD who makes the storm clouds," writes the prophet, so why don't you ask him for rain?

This is Zechariah's way of applying the teaching in this oracle, which runs from chapter 9 through chapter 11. In these passages, he ranges over the prophetic horizon, showing the downfall of those who threatened God's people, the triumph of the Jews over the Greeks, and the coming of a true king sent from God. In all this, he depicts a new deliverance on the scale of the exodus. These are all great, if distant, events of salvation. "But what does this mean to us?" the people cried. Here is his answer: "Put your trust in this God for all your needs."

This is always how God's people should respond to news of God's great saving acts, whether they are in the past or the future. After the magnificent miracle of the parting of the Red Sea, Moses had the people gather on the far side and proclaim their faith in God. Exodus 15 tells us of the song he wrote for them: "The LORD is my strength and my song, and he has become my salvation; this is my God, and I will praise him, my father's God, and I will exalt him" (Ex. 15:2). When the next generation prepared to enter the Promised Land, Moses recounted all God's great saving acts, then said to them, "To you it was shown, that you might know that the LORD is God; there is no other besides him" (Deut. 4:35). It was for that same reason that the Jews were shown the great prophecies of Zechariah, and for the same reason that we are told them in the Bible—so that we will trust and revere the Lord as our own God. To the Jews, longing as they were for rain to make the harvest grow, the prophet therefore says: "Ask rain from the LORD in the season of the spring rain, from the LORD who makes the storm clouds" (Zech. 10:1a). He is the Lord of the rain, and furthermore, he is the good and gracious God who answers prayer: "He will give them showers of rain, to everyone the vegetation in the field" (Zech. 10:1b).

PRAYER AND WORK

Verse 1 provides helpful insights on the relationship of prayer to work. The Jews had need for food, year in and year out. Therefore they were right to get to work. They prepared fields, removing trees and debris. They plowed and then planted the seeds they had gathered. It was all hard work and completely necessary. God did not envision their provision apart from their hard and probably backbreaking labor. Life in this world means work, even as God said to Adam after our first father fell into sin and the land was cursed: "By the sweat of your face you shall eat bread" (Gen. 3:19).

Work is necessary, even indispensable. Yet, as verse 1 shows, work alone is not enough to ensure our provision. This is because man finds himself confronting great forces far beyond his control. There is no work man can do to make the rains fall. Despite all their work, the Israelites could not ensure a harvest. Likewise, mankind, despite our vast technological prowess, despite the many things we can do, is still faced with forces far beyond our understanding and control, many of them having to do with the weather and nature. Whenever we grow proud and careless, some new disease seems to rise up, some natural disaster may strike, or some drought may cause our crops to fail and our economy to fall apart. We are not fundamentally different from these ancient Jews; we must work, but we cannot ensure the harvest.

Therefore, we must not only work but we must also pray. We must humbly appeal to the One who is not bound or limited as we are, who is able to ensure all our needs, who is greater than every power in the universe. Prayer is an appeal to God for our needs and a confession of our weakness, our dependence, and our trust in him. Prayer says that he is God, and there is no other.

But how many of us neither think nor act as if we need God's help? We tend to be self-reliant rather than God-reliant, and the evidence of this is uncovered in our lack of prayer. We do not pray for God's Spirit at the beginning of the day, and the reason can only be that we are confident of our own spirituality. We do not ask for wisdom when called upon to make decisions, and this shows pride in our own intellect. We do not pray for God's help in a difficult relationship, because we think we can work it out all on our own.

But, as is bountifully shown in our lives, such self-confidence is badly misplaced. We have a clear need for God's help and therefore for prayer! We desperately need God's Spirit if we are to live in a godly manner; we dearly need wisdom from God to overcome our terrible folly; and we need God's active grace in our own hearts and in the hearts of others if we are to love and enjoy godly harmony. Truly, the apostle James's words are the epitaph emblazoned upon so much of our spiritual and moral deadness: "You do not have, because you do not ask" (James 4:2). The less we rely on ourselves and the greater our sense of God's power and his goodness to those who ask of him in faith, the more we will pray the words our Lord taught us, "Give us today our daily bread" (Matt. 6:11).

FALSE RELIGION OPPOSED

The people in Zechariah's time may not have been praying to the Lord, but they certainly were not spiritually inactive. They needed divine help and they were seeking it—only in the wrong places.

While verse 1 is a call to true religion through faith and prayer, verse 2 exposes and condemns false and idolatrous religion: "For the household gods utter nonsense, and the diviners see lies; they tell false dreams and give empty consolation. Therefore the people wander like sheep; they are afflicted for lack of a shepherd." An idol is anything we trust in the place of God. Zechariah lists two idols prevalent in his time, condemning each in turn. First are the *teraphim,* which were small, portable, household idols, the kind carried by Rachel from her father Laban's house (Gen. 31:19). Offerings were made to them to secure their favor, and they were used to gain revelation about the future. Ezekiel describes the king of Babylon consulting this kind of medium: "For the king of Babylon stands at the parting of the way, at the head of the two ways, to use divination. He shakes the arrows; he consults the teraphim; he looks at the liver" (21:21). The teraphim gave the kind of vague assurance people were looking for to calm their fears, much as today's occult charlatans give assurance of love and riches right around the corner. As is true now, all of this was a great deception and a grave sin against the true God. "The idols," he says, are "utter nonsense" (Zech. 10:2).

Next, we read of *the diviners,* people who claimed to see visions and have revelatory dreams. Balaam, the unsavory figure who appears in the book of Numbers, was one of these. Balaam was impressive in his mystical antics, yet his visions were for hire to the highest bidder, and they made a mockery of those who trusted his so-called powers. People like him tell lies as they think advantageous and speak of dreams they never have had.

223

What is a version of this sin in our own time? Surely it is any approach to religion or spirituality in which we are trying to manipulate divine forces for our own ends. Instead of praying to God and depending on his grace, idolatry seeks to take divine power into its own hands. Idolatry includes things like the occult, New Age mysticism, certain forms of supposedly Christian, but patently godless charismatic experiences. These all claim to offer access to divine power, yet deliver instead only a deceptive and carnal mysticism. Liberal scholars engage in idolatry when they contort the plain teaching of Scripture to serve their god of humanism and culture. Self-righteous religion is another form of idolatry, for it puts our merits in the place of God's grace and tells us that God will be with us because we deserve it. Moreover, evangelicals practice idolatry by demanding that their Christianity serve the interests of a self-absorbed, affluent lifestyle.

How does true religion contrast with these? True religion, the kind Zechariah has been speaking about all through this book, is one that looks to God with a great sense of its own weakness and need. "Ask from the Lord" is its motto, as it stands empty-handed in faith. "Not by might, nor by power, but by my Spirit," says the Lord in chapter 4, verse 6, and true religion is that which looks for salvation by grace alone, through faith in the Savior God has sent. All through Zechariah, the prophet has been pointing to this Savior; true religion asks God for him, and his saving work in our lives. True religion acknowledges our sin and asks God to remove it. It professes our need and seeks his grace, all for the praise of his name. Whereas false religion listens to idols of its own making, true religion hears the voice of God in his revelation, and then believes and obeys that Word.

The verdict on the idols is found in verse 2: "They give empty consolation." There are few things more damaging than false comfort. False comfort tells us we are doing fine, when God says we are sinners in danger of his wrath. False comfort says that God is surely pleased with our worship, when in fact he rejects worship that he has not ordained. False comfort says that since the world applauds, we must be doing great, while in fact the people "like sheep . . . are afflicted for lack of a shepherd" (Zech. 10:2). Instead of true comfort—the comfort that comes from God when he forgives our sins and gives us peace in Jesus Christ—false religion offers mere distractions for foolish hearts, a fleeting comfort that is both unreal and vain. Surely this tells us that it matters greatly what kind of religion we pursue, what kind of divine help we are seeking, and whether or not we are obeying the Word that God has graciously revealed.

OUR HEAVENLY SHEPHERD

Verse 2 ends with God's compassion on the straying sheep, because he knew they were largely victims of fraudulent leaders. This is how Jesus looked upon the crowds in his day. Matthew says, "When he saw the crowds, he had compassion for them, because they were harassed and helpless, like sheep without a shepherd" (9:36).

Therefore, the Lord continues, "My anger is hot against the shepherds, and I will punish the leaders" (Zech. 10:3). Those are sober words for any who seek prominence or power, for God holds the leaders of his people accountable. The word translated as "leaders" in the English Standard Version is the Hebrew word for "he-goats"; the point seems to be that these were illegitimate leaders who had arisen, simply the strongest bullies among the flock and not true shepherds. This reminds us of the Pharisees and other false leaders of Jesus' day. "Woe to you!" Jesus cried against them. "You brood of vipers!" he said. "How are you to escape being sentenced to hell?" (Matt. 23:33). Those are stark words that ought to startle anyone who longs to lead for hypocritical reasons or personal gain.

God goes on to say that he will do more than punish the shepherds, "for the LORD of hosts cares for his flock, the house of Judah" (Zech. 10:3). This is a wonderful promise—that when the leaders turn astray, God himself will care for and guide his true church.

One thing the Bible extensively records is God removing false shepherds and intervening for the sake of his people. Indeed, often this is his first step in blessing the people—providing true leaders in the place of false. A prominent example of this is the case of Saul, Israel's first king. God sent Samuel to take the kingship away from him. "Your kingdom shall not continue," Samuel told him. "The LORD has sought out a man after his own heart, and the LORD has commanded him to be prince over his people, because you have not kept what the LORD commanded you" (1 Sam. 13:14). That man after God's own heart was David, Israel's greatest king, for "with upright heart he shepherded them" (Ps. 78:72). Church history reveals God's same care for the church. The Protestant Reformation provides a stirring example of God providing new leaders to take the people out from the corrupt medieval church and return them to the gospel.

Notice God's motive in providing new shepherds. It is "his flock, the house of Judah," that God will shepherd. Israel then, like the church now, is God's flock and he is responsible for her. Therefore we may always look to God for help, because his own name is bound up with his people, who by his election are called his own. It is God's ownership of the church that gives us confidence of his care. I have heard of one Christian who in trouble or temptation would rightly pray, "Lord, do you see what they are doing to your property?"

How lovely it is to read that God describes himself as the shepherd of his people. This reveals a truth about us, namely, that we are sheep in need of care. Spiritually speaking, we are creatures just as weak and self-destructive as sheep are. Phillip Keller, a pastor who spent years as a shepherd, writes: "It is no accident that God has chosen to call us sheep. The behavior of sheep and human beings is similar in many ways. . . . Our mass mind (or mob instincts), our fears and timidity, our stubbornness and stupidity, our perverse habits are all parallels of profound importance."[1] Those are hard things to hear about ourselves, but they are true. How wonderful, then, that God cares for us, undertaking the difficult project of leading us to heaven. A shepherd's reputation is bound up with the sheep; his success is seen in their health and safety and growth. Thus God is investing himself in us, and with him as our shepherd we can be sure of what Paul wrote in Philippians 1:6: "He who began a good work in you will bring it to completion at the day of Jesus Christ."

A SAVIOR FROM JUDAH

God has taken up the obligation of leading his people, and verse 4 tells us how he will go about it. As earlier in the case of David, he will provide new leadership, which will come from the tribe of Judah (which incidentally was David's tribe and the tribe from which the Messiah was promised): "From him shall come the cornerstone, from him the tent peg, from him the battle bow, from him every ruler—all of them together" (Zech. 10:4). These statements no doubt had a contemporary relevance, in that God would

1. W. Phillip Keller, *A Shepherd Looks at Psalm 23* (Chicago: Moody, 1970), 14.

provide these kinds of leaders for Judah. Indeed, they probably point forward to the Maccabean era, when Israel overthrew the Greeks. But ultimately they point forward to the Messiah, which has been the interpretation of Jewish and Christian commentators alike. The leader to come out from Judah, spoken of so frequently in the Old Testament, was widely understood to be the Christ. This is what Herod's advisors told him when he asked them where the Christ was to be born. " 'In Bethlehem of Judea,' they replied, 'for so it is written by the prophet: 'And you, O Bethlehem, in the land of Judah, are by no means least among the rulers of Judah; for from you shall come a ruler who will shepherd my people Israel' " (Matt. 2:4–6, citing Mic. 5:2).

It is the Messiah, the Christ, who is described in verse 4, and here as elsewhere Zechariah draws together messianic descriptions that have come from earlier prophets. First, he says, "From him [Judah] shall come the cornerstone" (Zech. 10:4). This recalls Isaiah 28:16: "Behold, I am the one who has laid as a foundation in Zion, a stone, a tested stone, a precious cornerstone, of a sure foundation: 'Whoever believes will not be in haste.' " A cornerstone is part of a building's foundation; if it is secure the rest of the structure will hold fast, like a house built upon a rock. In Ephesians 2, Paul speaks similarly of the church, which he says is "built on the foundation of the apostles and prophets, Christ Jesus himself being the cornerstone, in whom the whole structure, being joined together, grows into a holy temple in the Lord" (Eph. 2:20–21).

A cornerstone not only anchors the foundation, but also sets the pattern for the whole structure. In this way, Christ's person and work establish the dimensions for the church; the principles of his life and ministry and saving achievement are the principles for its growth and stability and success. As the church rests and relies upon him, it is sure to be safe, and as it follows his and the apostles' teachings, it is sure to build rightly. In chapter 3 Zechariah wrote of a stone that would be laid, of which God said, "I will remove the iniquity of this land in a single day" (Zech. 3:9). Surely this was the crucified Christ, whose saving work is the cornerstone on which the house of the redeemed is erected.

Next, we read that "from him the tent peg" (Zech. 10:4). The English Standard Version sees this as a stake in the ground that makes a tent secure. But Isaiah 22:23–24 uses this word in the sense of a peg driven into a wall, on which valuables were hung: "I will fasten him like a peg in a secure place, and he will become a throne of honor to his father's house. And they will hang on him the whole honor of his father's house, the offspring and issue, every small vessel, from the cups to all the flagons." Here is one on whom we may rest all our burdens—the guilt of our sin, our cares and needs—and on whom we may securely place all our hopes of glory.

Third and fourth in this list of messianic qualities, we read: "from him the battle bow," and "from him every ruler" (Zech. 10:4). These terms speak of his power to lead the people in victory; these are terms that describe him as the conqueror who comes to smite our every foe. This is what happened in the time of the Maccabees, who violently expelled foreign rulers in the second century before Christ. In the Gospels we see the exceeding violence with which Jesus attacked the devil and his spiritual minions. Indeed, under his leadership the sheep are made to be "like his majestic steed in battle" (Zech. 10:3). Verse 5 speaks of the victory of God's people that will result from his leadership: "They shall be like mighty men in battle, trampling the foe in the mud of the streets."

This reminds us of the spiritual strength Paul writes about when Christians face trouble and hardship, yet triumph through faith in Christ. He writes, "For your sake we are being killed all the day long; we are regarded as sheep to be slaughtered" (Rom. 8:36). This is often true of us as well, but because of Christ's saving presence neither are we vanquished, nor do we have to resort to the world's methods. "No," Paul concludes, "in all these things we are more than conquerors through him who loved us" (Rom. 8:37). As Zechariah 10:5 concludes, "They shall fight because the Lord is with them, and they shall put to shame the riders on horses." What other conclusion ought we to draw from this, than the conviction so well expressed in the words of Psalm 20:7: "Some trust in chariots and some in horses, but we trust in the name of the Lord our God"?

The Good Shepherd

God as shepherd will provide his people with all they need to persevere and triumph. Therefore the image of the shepherd watching over the flock is a precious one to every believer. It is the portrait that our Lord Jesus drew of himself when he said, "I am the good shepherd. The good shepherd lays down his life for the sheep" (John 10:11).

I mentioned Phillip Keller, the pastor who wrote a book about his own experience as a shepherd. To have the Lord as our shepherd, he says, "implies a profound yet practical working relationship between a human being and his Maker. It links a lump of common clay to divine destiny—it means a mere mortal becomes the cherished object of divine diligence."[2] Keller makes four points about Christ as our shepherd.

First, he says, sheep are owned by the shepherd. They are his property, for the simple reason that he paid for them. Likewise, Jesus says that he gave his life for his sheep, for that was the price he paid—the price of his blood—to redeem us from our sins. The apostle Peter writes, "You were ransomed from the futile ways inherited from your forefathers, not with perishable things such as silver or gold, but with the precious blood of Christ, like that of a lamb without blemish or spot" (1 Peter 1:18–19). Similarly, Paul says to us, "You are not your own, for you were bought with a price" (1 Cor. 6:19–20).

Keller tells what it was like when he paid his own hard-earned money for his first little flock of sheep: "Because of this I felt in a special way that they were in very truth a part of me and I a part of them. There was an intimate identity involved which . . . made those thirty ewes exceedingly precious to me."[3] Because he paid for us with his own blood, we are immeasurably more precious in the eyes of Christ.

The second thing a shepherd does, once he has paid for his sheep, is to make them his own. He leads them out of the sheepfold in which they were found. This is what Jesus says: "He calls his own sheep by name and leads them out. . . . He goes before them, and the sheep follow him, for they know his voice" (John 10:3–4). A shepherd places his mark on his sheep, to distinguish them from sheep that belong to others. Keller writes about cutting his mark into the ear of his sheep, the way that shepherds traditionally do. It was painful for him and for the sheep, but afterward they were marked as his own. Jesus places his mark on his sheep, and it too is painful but necessary. His mark is the cross—death to sin and new life to God, sharing his reproach before the world—even as Jesus told his disciples, "If anyone would come after me, let him deny himself and take up his cross daily and follow me" (Luke 9:23).

2. Ibid., 11.
3. Ibid., 13–14.

229

The Good Shepherd buys his sheep, marks them as his own and then, third, he delights in caring for them. It is in this sense, too, that Jesus could say, "The good shepherd lays down his life for the sheep" (John 10:11). "He literally lays Himself out for us continually. He is ever interceding for us; He is ever guiding us by His gracious Spirit; He is ever working on our behalf to ensure that we will benefit from His care."[4] Keller tells how a conscientious shepherd must prepare the grazing lands ahead of the sheep. He goes out and looks over the country, removing poisonous weeds, driving out predators, and plotting out the journey in advance. Psalm 23 speaks of this care in lovely poetic terms: "He makes me lie down in green pastures. He leads me beside still waters. He restores my soul. He leads me in paths of righteousness for his name's sake" (vv. 2–3).

Fourth and finally, the Good Shepherd protects his sheep and brings them safely home. Jesus contrasted the owner of the flock with a mere hired hand, much in the way Zechariah speaks of the false shepherds in his day. The hireling sees the wolf coming and abandons the flock. Jesus said, "He flees because he is a hired hand and cares nothing for the sheep." But, "I am the good shepherd. I know my own and my own know me, just as the Father knows me and I know the Father; and I lay down my life for the sheep" (John 10:13–15). How wonderful and comforting it is to hear Jesus, our Good Shepherd, say of us, "I give them eternal life, and they will never perish, and no one will snatch them out of my hand. My Father, who has given them to me, is greater than all, and no one is able to snatch them out of the Father's hand" (John 10:28–29).

Do you hear his voice? Do you hear the gospel and realize that Jesus Christ, your Good Shepherd, who paid for his sheep with his own precious blood, is calling you? Then follow him. Follow his voice and leave the sheepfold of the world to enter the flock he is gathering from every tribe and nation. Follow him, as Psalm 23 puts it, to lie down in green pastures, to walk beside the quiet waters, to be led in paths of righteousness.

4. Ibid., 14.

20

THE SECOND EXODUS

Zechariah 10:6–12

I will strengthen the house of Judah, and I will save the house of
Joseph. I will bring them back because I have compassion on
them, and they shall be as though I had not rejected them, for I
am the LORD their God and I will answer them. (Zech. 10:6)

Saint Augustine once said that the Old Testament is the gospel in bud, and the New Testament the gospel in bloom. This is something we have been observing all through our studies of Zechariah, which provides some of the clearest prophecies about Jesus Christ—his coming, his ministry, and the salvation he brings.

It is in this continuity between the two testaments—the Old which prepares us historically and conceptually for the New, and the New which fulfills the Old Testament's hope and expectation in Jesus Christ—that the promises we read in the prophets have such relevance for us today. This is why the apostle Paul could write to the Christians at Rome in his day: "Whatever was written in former days was written for our instruction, that through endurance and through the encouragement of the Scriptures we might have hope" (Rom. 15:4).

Our present section of Zechariah, running from chapters 9 to 11, is centered on some of the clearest prophecies of Jesus Christ and his saving reign: "Behold, your king is coming to you; righteous and having salvation is he, humble and mounted on a donkey" (Zech. 9:9). That promise, which the Gospels explicitly tie to Jesus' first coming, links this entire oracle to his messianic work and his gospel of salvation. Now chapter 10 concludes by depicting that salvation in terms of a second exodus for God's people. It sets before us four points: *a description of salvation, a cause for salvation, a method for salvation,* and finally *a model of salvation.*

SALVATION DESCRIBED

Zechariah 10:6–7 associates a number of verbs with the idea of salvation:

I will *strengthen* the house of Judah,
   and I will *save* the house of Joseph.
I will *bring* them back because I have compassion on them,
   and they shall be as though I had not rejected them,
   for I am the LORD their God and I will *answer* them.
Then Ephraim shall become like a mighty warrior,
   and their hearts shall be glad as with wine.

Verse 6 speaks of salvation as strengthening—"I will strengthen the house of Judah"—and as restoration—"I will bring them back." In reading further, salvation is the undoing of rejection—"they shall be as though I had not rejected them"—and God answering or paying heed to their affliction—"I will answer them." Verse 7 adds on the idea of an empowering transformation—they "shall become like a mighty warrior"—and the conveying of joy to the spirit as wine does to the body. Furthermore, this salvation will stretch forward into the future, for "their children shall see it and be glad." These two verses conclude with a wonderful summation of what salvation is all about: "Their hearts shall rejoice in the LORD."

It is hard to imagine a more robust description of salvation. First, it is depicted as *deliverance from affliction and bondage.* At the time of Zechariah's writing, both the house of Judah and the house of Joseph—two tribes that stood for the whole of Israel—were under the oppression of foreign domination. The tribe of Joseph was the royal house of the northern kingdom of Israel, which had been conquered by the Assyrians in 722 BC. These so-called Lost Tribes had been so thoroughly dispersed among the Gentiles as to have disappeared from history altogether. The house of Judah and the southern kingdom had gone into Babylonian captivity in 586 BC, and though Zechariah and his fellow Jews had returned to Jerusalem, the great bulk of their countrymen remained in exile.

Therefore, this statement of salvation has to do with the deliverance of people from the bonds of captivity—the kind of salvation Jesus Christ offers to sinners. God sent Israel into captivity for her iniquities, and in the same way the New Testament sees us held captive and oppressed by the reign of sin into which we have fallen. Saint Augustine described our bondage: "The guilt of sin so dominates in men that it prevents their attainment of that eternal life which is the only true life, and drags them down even to the second death which is penally eternal."[1] Paul speaks of this by simply saying, "The wages of sin is death" (Rom. 6:23). We are held captive by sin's guilt, but also by its power in our lives, so that its influence on all our thoughts and actions is pervasive. Jesus taught, "Everyone who commits a sin is a slave to sin" (John 8:34). Thus Paul wrote of himself, "Wretched man that I am! Who will deliver me from this body of death?" (Rom. 7:24). The answer he gave is Jesus Christ.

Salvation, then, is deliverance from the bondage of sin's guilt and power by the saving work of Christ, just as verse 6 sees the houses of Judah and Joseph restored from their captivity. This is our good news: Christ died to save us from our sins, through faith in his blood. To all who believe in him, God says: "I will be merciful toward their iniquities, and I will remember their sins no more" (Heb. 8:12). John writes, "If we confess our sins, he is faithful and just to forgive us our sins and to cleanse us from all unrighteousness.... Jesus Christ the righteous ... is the propitiation for our sins" (1 John 1:9; 2:1–2).

Today we hear more about dysfunction and felt needs and self-image than about sin. But the salvation we truly need is the one that frees us from our

---

1. Augustine of Hippo, *A Treatise on the Merits and Forgiveness of Sins, and on the Baptism of Infants*, from *A Select Library of the Nicene and Post-Nicene Fathers of the Christian Church*, ed. Philip Schaff, vol. 5, *Saint Augustine: Anti-Pelagian Writings*, 20.

sin—from its guilt before God and its power over our lives. If you have not come to Christ in faith, then you are still in bondage to sin, but God offers to save you through faith in Christ. As the hymnist says:

> He breaks the power of reigning sin,
> he sets the prisoner free;
> his blood can make the foulest clean,
> his blood availed for me.[2]

The most severe effect of sin is that it alienates us from God. This was the worst part of the Jews' exile, that they could no longer worship in his presence, but were cast out from the Lord. But Zechariah describes a remedy, the second description of salvation in this passage: *restoration*. The people were restored not merely to the land, not merely to freedom, but restored to God, to his presence and his wonderful blessing. Verse 6 says, "I will bring them back because I have compassion on them, and they shall be as though I had not rejected them."

Justification is the doctrine that tells us how sinners are restored to God's favor. Sometimes it is said that justification makes me "just as if I'd never sinned." In one sense, that is not true. A justified believer is not one who has never sinned, but one who having sinned is redeemed by the blood of Jesus. Having lost all claims to our own righteousness, we are justified by the righteousness of Christ, which is imputed to us through faith. But there is another sense in which believers are "just as if they had never sinned," and that is with regard to *our restoration to fellowship with God*. When our sins are taken away, we are fully restored so there is no barrier between us and the blessings of God's favor. Harry Ironside writes: "Justification is the sentence of the judge in favor of the prisoner, it is God saying, 'I declare this man not guilty.' . . . Reconciliation goes a step farther; it is not only that our sins are forgiven and that divine justice has nothing against us, but it is that He has received us as His own to His loving heart, and we are reconciled to God."[3]

The apostle Paul writes, "In Christ God was reconciling the world to himself, not counting their trespasses against them, and entrusting to us the

---

2. Charles Wesley, "O for a Thousand Tongues to Sing," 1739.
3. Harry A. Ironside, *II Corinthians* (Neptune, NJ: Loizeaux, 1983), 150.

message of reconciliation. . . . We implore you on behalf of Christ, be reconciled to God" (2 Cor. 5:19–20). This is the gospel message, and it calls out still, inviting sinners to be reconciled to God.

Third, salvation is described in terms of *the joy of the Lord*: "Their hearts shall be glad as with wine. Their children shall see it and be glad; their hearts shall rejoice in the LORD" (Zech. 10:7). Conventional wisdom has it that Christianity is a drag on any joy in life. But our passage assures us that the opposite is true. "In him was life," John writes of Jesus, "and the life was the light of men" (John 1:4). Jesus said, "I came that they may have life and have it abundantly" (John 10:10). What joyous horizons await the man or woman who is reconciled to God, who knows the reality of his favor and his peace within, who sees the smile on his face and his protective hands guiding his beloved child!

The truth is that sin results in misery, but salvation brings us out of misery into true joy, delivering us *from* sin's reign and delivering us *to* the God of all grace, whose light shines in our hearts. Instead of a happiness that comes from carnal pleasures or mere fleeting circumstances, Christians know a joy that is pure, that comes from God, and that like him knows no shadow of turning.

THE CAUSE OF SALVATION

Zechariah's prophecy not only describes salvation, but it also gives the *cause of salvation*, which is the sovereign grace of God.

Israel's situation, to which this passage refers, was so terrible as rightly to be deemed hopeless. God had cast them out because they had broken his law and placed them under the power of mighty nations. In just the same way, every sinner is condemned for breaking God's law. Like the Jews, there is nothing we can do to fix what has been broken, and the power which holds us is too strong for us by far.

This being the case, the Jews were not able to save themselves and neither can we. The reason or cause for our salvation cannot be found in us, so it will have to come from God. This is what Zechariah proclaims, that salvation is based not on something in the sinner, not on something meritorious or lovely in the ones held captive, but on something in God. Verse 6 informs us, "I will bring them back because I have compassion on them . . . for I am the LORD their God and I will answer them."

The prophet proclaims a salvation that is by God's grace alone, a salvation that depends on and derives from God's own compassion and sovereign grace. As Paul wrote to Titus, "He saved us, not because of works done by us in righteousness, but according to his own mercy" (Titus 3:5). First, we must realize that there is nothing in us to which we can appeal to God for salvation. Like Paul we must exclaim, "Wretched man that I am!" (Rom. 7:24). But then God gives us this good news, that there is something *in God* to which we can appeal. There is compassion in God; we can appeal to his mercy. This is the true and only way to salvation, the path of God's compassion that leads to the open door of God's mercy. This is how David came when he realized the guilt of his sin: "Have mercy on me, O God . . . according to your abundant mercy blot out my transgressions" (Ps. 51:1).

Salvation is by God's grace alone, and his grace is sovereign. Why will God bestow his mercy on his people? He tells us in verse 6, "For I am the LORD their God." In other words, he had grace for them because he had chosen them by election; by his sovereign choice he had made himself their God. This is what God said to Israel from the beginning. During the exodus, Moses declared sovereign grace as the reason for their salvation: "It was not because you were more in number than any other people that the LORD set his love on you and chose you, for you were the fewest of all peoples, but it is because the LORD loves you and is keeping the oath that he swore to your fathers" (Deut. 7:7–8).

How do people today know that God's sovereign grace has chosen them? God's election is made known by faith in Jesus Christ, which is his gift to the sinner. Paul explains in Ephesians 2, "For by grace you have been saved through faith. And this is not your own doing; it is the gift of God, not a result of works, so that no one may boast" (vv. 8–9). This means that if you put your trust in Jesus Christ to redeem you from your sins, you can be sure of the grace of God, which reveals itself to you in the very faith by which you are saved.

Some will say, "But you do not know how great a sinner I have been! I am not one of you religious people. I have not served God. I have had no place in the church. I have mocked and denied and hated God. I am not one of those on whom God will have mercy!" What is the Bible's answer to those of us who have great sins? First, we may ask if our sins are greater than those of the tribes of Judah and Joseph. In the Old Testament we find that it would be hard indeed for us to out-sin those rebellious people. Second, we learn from the New Testament that God is glorified in saving the greatest of sinners. The apostle Paul described himself honestly as "the chief of sinners," yet God saved him and used him to preach the gospel. It was Paul who wrote, "Where sin increased, grace abounded all the more" (Rom. 5:20). God's mercy is greater than all our sin, and this is to his great glory. There is a hymn that says, "There's a wideness in God's mercy, like the wideness of the sea." It is not the sea that measures the extent of God's mercy, however, but the outstretched arms of the Lord Jesus Christ, God's own Son, as he died on the cross to take away our sin. This is the length to which God is willing to go to win our salvation; it is a mercy that is greater than anyone's sin.

GOD'S METHOD OF SALVATION

Zechariah 10:6–7 sets forth a description and a cause for salvation. Verses 8–10 speak of *his method of salvation*, depicting God as the shepherd who gathers his people who once were scattered.

Verse 9 tells us that God scattered Israel among the peoples, first the house of Joseph into Assyria and then the house of Judah into Babylonia: "Though I scattered them among the nations, yet in far countries they shall remember me, and with their children they shall live and return." There is an apparent word-play here, dealing with the Hebrew word *zera*, which means both to scatter and to plant. With the same motion with which one scatters, one also distributes seed within a field. This wordplay seems to be in effect here, so that even while God was scattering, he was by grace planting his people for a day to come. Even as he scattered them, God said, "I have *planted* them among the nations."

This is a marvelous example of God redeeming the sin of his people. Though he scattered them in judgment, because of his grace he makes this dispersal a thing of blessing, a planting of his own among the peoples for a far greater salvation. Calvin explains, "For the Jews would dwell everywhere, and be God's seed, and thus be made to produce abundant fruit. . . . Thus the punishment of exile . . . was the means of opening the door for the gospel; and God thus scattered his seed here and there, that it might in due time produce fruit beyond the expectation of all."[4]

4. John Calvin, *The Minor Prophets*, 5 vols. (Edinburgh: Banner of Truth, 1986), 5:296–97.

The age of the apostles offers numerous examples of this. In his second missionary journey, the apostle Paul arrived in Lystra, on the southern coast of Turkey, and what should he find there but a Jewish synagogue. Why? Because in scattering his people, God had planted this seed of the gospel there. There was the reading of the Scriptures, including prophets like Zechariah. Paul, therefore, spoke from the prophets in distant lands, showing how they were fulfilled in the coming of Christ. Furthermore, Paul found there believing women, like Timothy's mother, who were a fulfillment of what Zechariah 10:9 promises: "In far countries they shall remember me, and with their children they shall live and return."

Out of such people, Paul found preachers and pastors for the church. People like these women had remembered the Lord and taught their children the Scriptures, thus waiting for the gospel, which came to bring the seed to life and spread the news of salvation in distant lands. The same thing happened when Paul took the gospel to Europe. The first person he encountered on European soil was a Jew who remembered God, a seed whom God had planted: Lydia the dyer of purple. From Lydia grew a church and from that church sprang the gospel to the nations. What an incredible testimony this is to the goodness of God; even in the chastisement of his people he has a marvelous plan of grace!

First, God planted his seed among the peoples; then he called them to himself. Verse 8 tells us, "I will whistle for them and gather them in." The word "whistle" refers to the whistle or pipe a shepherd used to call his flock. A century ago David Baron wrote of meeting a Bedouin shepherd in the midst of his travels. While they were talking, the man's sheep began to scatter among the rocks and, when he was ready to start out again, he pulled out a pipe they had been trained to recognize. As he played, the sheep all came back, drawing closer and closer to him as the flock was reformed; when they were all together the shepherd started out once more. Watching this, Baron recalled this verse from Zechariah, depicting how God calls his sheep to himself, gathering us to his own fold before leading us forth.[5]

This is just how Jesus described himself as the Good Shepherd. The sheep listen to his voice. In this way, he calls his own sheep out of both the fold of

---

5. David Baron, *The Visions and Prophecies of Zechariah* (Grand Rapids: Kregel, 1972), 363.

Israel and out of all the folds of the world: "I am the good shepherd. I know my own and my own know me. . . . They will listen to my voice. So there will be one flock, one shepherd" (John 10:14, 16).

In what voice does Christ call today? It is through the gospel that he summons his own. "Come to me, all who labor and are heavy laden, and I will give you rest" (Matt. 11:28), he says. And as the gospel goes forth, those who are his own—those who are scattered as seed by God among the peoples and cities and workplaces of this world—hear that call, recognize the voice of the Savior, believe and follow him to salvation. It is not by moving their feet to return to Jerusalem that his people return to the Lord today, but by the moving of their hearts in a response of faith to the gospel as it is heard.

This is God's manner of working salvation throughout history, throughout nations and peoples and places: he plants his own, calls them forth with the gospel, and then makes them spiritually fruitful. Zechariah adds, "I will bring them home from the land of Egypt, and gather them from Assyria, and I will bring them to the land of Gilead and to Lebanon, till there is no room for them" (Zech. 10:10). In this way, the prophet depicts the abundance of God's harvest of redeemed souls, so great a harvest from the seeds he had scattered that the restored land of promise—that is, the church—will literally burst with them.

We remember that this passage is part of the long oracle that focused on Jesus' coming as Savior. Remembering this helps us to see that these figures of Egypt and Assyria stand for all the world into which God has scattered his seed. Gilead and Lebanon point us to the greater promised land that is the New Testament church. Indeed, as we go back in the Bible, we find that it is not just Judah and Joseph that are scattered because of sin. We are reminded here of the book of Genesis, when God divided the people and scattered the nations over all the earth (Gen. 11:8). Even then he had planted the seed among those who would believe and follow and serve the gospel, so that, as he promised through Abraham, "All the families of the earth will be blessed" (Gen. 12:3). Farther back in the Bible we think of the day when God cast Adam and Eve out of the Garden for their sin. In them all humanity was scattered because of God's judgment on their sin. Yet here we see God's plan to gather to himself a people to bear his image, returning them not to the Garden of old but to a spiritual realm of blessing through his gospel, a heavenly city in which Christ dwells in glory.

"I scattered them among the nations," God declared, "yet in far countries they shall remember me, and with their children they shall live and return" (Zech. 10:9). One thing this means is that wherever you go you will find the people God has prepared to receive and believe the gospel, and you will find his kingdom growing within the kingdoms of this world. Paul discovered this when he arrived at the dissolute city of Corinth. "I have many in this city who are my people," our Lord told him (Acts 18:10), and everywhere, even today, God has a people who come forth as the gospel is proclaimed, a church united in faith and in spirit though flung far and wide around the world.

THE EXODUS MODEL OF SALVATION

So far our passage has shown us a *description of salvation*, a *cause for salvation*, and *God's method of salvation* in history and in the world. Verses 10–12 complete this message by referring to *God's model of salvation*, namely, Israel's exodus, which the Bible sees as a pattern for the saving work of Jesus Christ.

Zechariah gives an inkling of this by referring to a return from Egypt, adding to it a return from the second captivity of God's people in Assyria: "I will bring them home from the land of Egypt, and gather them from Assyria" (Zech. 10:10). Both of these were ancient sources of oppression rather than threats current to Zechariah's time, and thus they speak metaphorically of the bondage of sin from which God's people are saved. The prophet then alludes to the great saving works that won Israel's deliverance from Egypt, which he depicts as a prototype for God's greater redemption in the gospel: "He shall pass through the sea of troubles and strike down the waves of the sea, and all the depths of the Nile shall be dried up" (Zech. 10:11). The people will pass through the sea that bars their way as God subdues the waves. The word translated "Nile" may also be used of rivers generally, and here probably refers to the Jordan River instead, since God dried up the Jordan when Israel crossed over into the Promised Land. As Assyria's might was brought down, so was Egypt's power taken away by God's power in the time of Moses. This is the way God will strengthen those he calls to salvation, and as he once led Israel through the exodus, so will they all walk in his name. This plainly refers to the salvation the Messiah will bring, not the return from Babylon, which had already happened, but the second exodus that results from the coming of the Savior-King.

The New Testament frequently employs the exodus as a model for salvation in Jesus Christ. It is for this reason, for instance, that Jesus was sacrificed as the Passover Lamb, connecting his salvation to the exodus of old. Like the ancient Israelites, we are saved and sent forth on our journey to freedom. We are delivered from the house of bondage that is sin, just as Israel was delivered from slavery in Egypt, and like them, we are headed for a promised land, to which we journey as pilgrims in this world. Like Israel then, we now sojourn through the wilderness in a present time of testing. This being the case, this passage points us to what we most need to know, that once we have begun this difficult journey of faith in Christ, God will preserve us through every danger. This is the point: though we pass through the sea of trouble, God will subdue the waves and make level paths before our feet.

Most importantly, the exodus motif of salvation points us to the God of the exodus, and focuses all our hope in him. What matters is not the difficulty of the journey, not the perils along the way, not even our own weakness for the task at hand. What matters is the God who leads us: " 'I will make them strong in the LORD, and they shall walk in his name,' declares the LORD" (Zech. 10:12).

In John 6–8 Jesus made three great statements that identified him as the Savior of the exodus, and thus as the object of our hope. In John 6:35 he compared himself to the manna God sent from heaven: "I am the bread of life; whoever comes to me shall not hunger, and whoever believes in me shall never thirst." What this means is that all those who trust in him will find all the provision they need for the spiritual challenges of this life. Jesus was speaking of the cross when he said, "I am the living bread that came down from heaven. If anyone eats of this bread, he will live forever. And the bread that I will give for the life of the world is my flesh" (John 6:51).

In John 7:37–38 Jesus described himself in terms of the water God made to flow from a rock in the desert: "If anyone thirsts, let him come to me and drink. Whoever believes in me, as the Scripture has said, 'Out of his heart will flow rivers of living water.' " John explains that this refers to God's provision of the Holy Spirit to all who trust in Christ.

In John 8:12 Jesus described himself as the cloud of fire and light that guided Israel through the desert. "I am the light of the world," he cried.

"Whoever follows me will not walk in darkness, but will have the light of life." You see the point. If the life of salvation in this world is analogous to Israel's journey in the exodus, so that this present time is the day of difficulty and trial as we journey to the Promised Land ahead, then just as God was sufficient for all the people's need in that day, our Lord Jesus gives us everything we need as we look to him in faith. He feeds us bread from heaven for eternal life, he sends the Holy Spirit to well up within us as living water, and he guides us, as a shepherd and a shining light before us in the way.

In all those passages Jesus speaks of what he will do. Notice, then, how prominent the expression "I will" is in Zechariah 10:6–12. "I will," says the Lord, over and over, and that is why this is a passage about salvation. Because it is God who says, "I will," we can trust all that he promises here. "I will strengthen," he says to the weak. "I will bring them back," he says of the lost. "I will answer," he says to those afflicted and oppressed. "I will whistle for them and gather them in, for I have redeemed them," he says. In those words is found good news for all who hear, for all who are called by the promise of God, who says, "I will!" It matters not how great the oppression, for his is the power of God. "I will!" he says. It matters not how far you have been scattered, for this is the voice that gathers all who come within its hearing. "I will call you and save you," he says, and so he will.

The passage begins with "I will," but it ends with "they will": "they shall walk in his name, declares the LORD" (Zech. 10:12). The result of God's "I will" is the "they will" of his people. This is the way salvation works: those who are called will walk in the name and strength of the Lord because he wills it that we should. What a glorious salvation this is! Because of the promise of a mighty God, those who trust in Christ may know the power and joy of a new life, a new hope, and a new strength, all to the glory of his name.

21

Two Broken Staffs

Zechariah 11:1–17

So I said, "I will not be your shepherd. What is to die, let it die.
What is to be destroyed, let it be destroyed. And let those who are
left devour the flesh of one another." And I took my staff Favor,
and I broke it, annulling the covenant that I had made with all
the peoples. So it was annulled on that day, and the sheep traders,
who were watching me, knew that it was the word of the Lord.
(Zech. 11:9–11)

Much can happen in a lifetime, as is proved by the life of the prophet Zechariah. Zechariah was born in Babylon to a priestly family, apparently a prominent one, during a time of disgrace. Earlier, the Lord had enacted judgment on his people, allowing their country to be devastated, the nation enslaved and sent into the exile in which Zechariah grew up. It was probably during Zechariah's youth that the first great event of his life took place, the order from the emperor Cyrus in 538 BC to reestablish Jerusalem, the result of which was the initial party that returned to build the temple. Zechariah was part of that group and would have been there for the momentous occasion when the princes Sheshbaz-zar and Zerubbabel laid the cornerstone for the rebuilt house of God.

Zechariah would see the return of prophecy through Haggai, and then would receive his own calling as a prophet, complete with the night of visions that make up the first half of his book. Finally, he was there when the temple was completed and consecrated, signaling the reestablishment of the covenant community before God in Jerusalem.

He had already witnessed a great many exciting and important events, but Zechariah's career was hardly over. The two oracles that conclude his book seem to have come from much later in his life, perhaps even decades after the temple was rebuilt, and they depict a less positive situation. As chapter 11 shows, God called Zechariah to stand up against godless leaders who had taken control of Jerusalem. This was something other prophets had to stand up against, and as Jesus would point out, almost invariably the result was the persecution of God's spokesmen: "O Jerusalem, Jerusalem, the city that kills the prophets and stones those who are sent to it!" (Matt. 23:37). This was, indeed, how Zechariah's long and varied life would come to its end. Jesus identifies him as the last of the prophets so treated, informing us that he was "murdered between the sanctuary and the altar" (Matt. 23:35).

A Lament against False Leaders

Zechariah 11 begins with a poetic lament, three verses which give a clear impression of what lies ahead. They are a precursor to judgment and destruction. Verses 1 and 2 say: "Open your doors, O Lebanon, that the fire may devour your cedars! Wail, O cypress, for the cedar has fallen, for the glorious trees are ruined!"

The picture here is of devastation coming down out of the north, and verse 3 shows that the target audience of this lament is the false shepherds whose ability to exploit the people will be taken away. "The thicket of the Jordan is ruined," says verse 3, broadly speaking of the prosperity they used for their own gain; they were like lions whose feeding grounds have been spoiled. The message is that those placed in leadership over God's people will be held to account and judged.

This chapter is about Zechariah's conflict with the godless leaders of Jerusalem, who are described in verses 4 and 5. First there is a description of the people, "the flock doomed to slaughter." A good shepherd did not slaughter an entire flock, but pastured them with care and wisdom. A far different attitude, however, characterized those ruling in Jerusalem, one that sought personal and short-term gratification: they simply slaughtered the flock. The people of the city were being misused by leaders who exploited them for selfish gain: "Those who buy them slaughter them and go unpunished, and those who sell them say, 'Blessed be the LORD, I have become rich,' and their own shepherds have no pity on them" (Zech. 11:5).

It seems that there were two classes of persons doing the exploitation, the merchants and the political leaders. The scene is that of a sheep market. There we find buyers who slaughter the sheep they have bought, and sellers who gloat over their profits. The latter, it seems, are the merchants who had gained prominence in the city and who nurtured only their own portfolio of riches rather than the greater public good. Additionally, verse 5 speaks of the shepherds who did not spare the flock. These would be the city officials who colluded with the merchants instead of protecting the public welfare.

Passages like this tell us God's standards for leadership. A godly leader has the interests of the followers and of the greater public in mind. It is true that every leader has goals and objectives that must be reached. Yet in the biblical view, "The shepherd is the servant of the sheep; it is their growth and nurture that define his task and set the agenda for his success."[1] A godly leader achieves success by building strong, capable, and motivated followers rather than through ruthless exploitation. This is essential within the church, where leaders are called to be good shepherds. Peter exhorts, "Shepherd the flock of God that is among you, exercising oversight, not under compulsion, but willingly, as God would have you; not for shameful gain, but eagerly; not domineering over those in your charge, but being examples to the flock" (1 Peter 5:2–3).

Verse 5 paints a stark picture of godless leadership in the business arena, presenting a clear challenge to present-day attitudes. It is taken for granted today that the only legitimate purpose for a business enterprise is the accumulation of riches for its owners. Practically anything can be justified if it results in an increase on Wall Street, no matter how fleeting the gain or costly in human terms. "Praise the Lord, I am rich!" is the epitome of spirituality

---

1. Richard D. Phillips, *The Heart of an Executive* (New York: Doubleday, 1999), 7.

for a great many people in business today, including some who call themselves Christians. Yet we see that God condemns those who labor only to line
their own pockets and furnish their own executive homes. Despite demands
for ever-increasing productivity and efficiency, business leaders are warned
against looking on workers as a flock to be used and cast aside. Such an
approach may seem to go unpunished and even prosper, but the message
here is that God will bring false shepherds to account.

Certainly profit-making is legitimate in the biblical view, but the higher
goal is the material and ultimately the spiritual blessing of the community
in general. Anything that falls short of this aspiration is an affront to the Lord.
Then, as now, people foolishly put riches in the place of God as the source
of their security and peace, which is why the apostle Paul specifically described
greed as "idolatry" (Col. 3:5). Certainly, we in the West are living in a time of
vast idolatry, as corporate glory and wealth have ascended the temple of our
lives in the place rightly reserved for God, demanding a commitment and
level of sacrifice that can only be described as religious. Christians must hear
well the words of our Lord: "No one can serve two masters. . . . You cannot
serve God and money" (Matt. 6:24).

When it comes to politics, we want to be careful how we use the Bible. It
is not always obvious which party or which platform is the most consistently
biblical. But one thing our passage makes clear is that God condemns those
placed in authority who abandon the interests of the people who depend on
them and are under their power. "Their own shepherds have no pity on
them," verse 5 laments. This happens when politicians, right and left, align
themselves with corporate groups or special interests, putting aside the public good for the sake of their careers. Verse 17 concludes our chapter by giving God's verdict on the faithless leader: "Woe to my worthless shepherd,
who deserts the flock! May the sword strike his arm and his right eye! Let
his arm be wholly withered, his right eye utterly blinded!"

THE GOOD SHEPHERD PORTRAYED

These are the leaders who came to power in Jerusalem as a result of the
security and prosperity God had given. What follows is one of the great symbolic actions occasionally called for by the prophets. God commanded
Zechariah to engage in a role-play in order to make his point in a very public

way before the people of Jerusalem. Probably the most famous of these prophetic role-plays was staged by the prophet Hosea, whom God told to marry a prostitute to show what it was like for God to be married to Israel. Other prophets received similar instructions, including Isaiah, whom God ordered to go around naked and barefoot for three years to symbolize judgment, and Ezekiel, who lay on his side for over a year to symbolize Israel's sin and represent the siege of Jerusalem. In verse 4 Zechariah is told to engage in one of these symbolic role-plays. God said, "Become shepherd of the flock doomed to slaughter."

What happened next is not entirely clear. Verses 7 and 8 give the prophet's report: "So I became the shepherd of the flock doomed to be slaughtered by the sheep traders. And I took two staffs, one I named Favor, the other I named Union. And I tended the sheep. In one month I destroyed the three shepherds." It seems that Zechariah went before the people bearing these two shepherd staffs as prophetic protest signs, one marked "Favor," which signified God's blessing on the people, and the other marked "Union," signifying the national unity and peace. Thomas McComiskey describes his action as "a prophetic protest against the community's corrupt leaders . . . acted out in public, probably over a period of time."[2] By means that are left undisclosed, he denounced the godless leaders and succeeded in removing "the three shepherds"—probably ringleaders opposed to him. We can imagine the kind of message Zechariah would have pressed forth: a denunciation of greed and exploitation, with a calling for repentance and a change of leadership.

We might think that this kind of protest would result in the prophet being swept up on a tide of public approval. Surely with the people behind him he would be able to clean house and install a new and godly regime. After all, the people were the ones being led to slaughter, the ones exploited by the cruel leaders. But that is not what happened. The prophet continues, "They also detested me" (Zech. 11:8). Not only the false shepherds, but also the flock detested Zechariah! The people did not want a godly regime, despite the benefits to themselves. How revealing this is! The people approved of godless rather than godly leaders. They did not want godly standards because they did not want to give up their own cherished sins. This is what we should

2. Thomas E. McComiskey, *The Minor Prophets: An Exegetical and Expository Commentary*, 3 vols. (Grand Rapids: Baker, 1998), 3:1191.

expect of those who have lost the knowledge of God, even those born into the heritage of God's people. The book of Judges describes an earlier scenario that was apparently repeated in Zechariah's lifetime: "There arose another generation after them who did not know the LORD" (Judg. 2:10). People like that are not going to look favorably on an agenda like Zechariah's, however beneficial it really is.

Many Christians today are dismayed when a godly agenda is detested by the public. There will be an effort to oppose something that is manifestly wicked and harmful, something like abortion-on-demand, for example, or child pornography, or state-sponsored gambling. Christians and others organize to denounce such things, only to find the people against them. They are misrepresented in the press and mocked in the streets. How can this be? The reason is a love of sin that grips the world: "The natural person does not accept the things of the Spirit of God, for they are folly to him, and he is not able to understand them because they are spiritually discerned" (1 Cor. 2:14).

If we want people to think and act in a godly manner, we are first going to have to bring them into a relationship with God through the ministry of Jesus Christ. Godless people will not tend to godliness in their thinking and actions. They will hate God and godly things and godly people. That is why our witness to the world must first and foremost consist of the gospel of grace for sinners, so that people will be reconciled to God and his truth and his love. The dimmer the memory of true religion in any nation, the more the people will detest godliness and godly leaders. How urgent it is, then, for Christian churches not only to stand against worldly sin, but to proclaim the gospel of salvation rather than a merely temporal agenda, however godly. Unless sinners are reconciled to God through the gospel witness of the church, there will never be godliness.

THE FLOCK REJECTED

What happens when a people reject God? Ultimately, after much long-suffering grace, God rejects them. This is what Zechariah describes: "I became impatient with them, and they also detested me. So I said, 'I will not be your shepherd'" (Zech. 11:8–9).

The people were probably relieved to have the prophet gone, but the consequences of their rejection would prove bitter. Zechariah tells us, "And I took my staff Favor, and I broke it, annulling the covenant that I had made with all the peoples. So it was annulled on that day, and the sheep traders, who were watching me, knew that it was the word of the LORD" (Zech. 11:10–11). Without the obligations of a relationship with God they could not enjoy his benefits. Therefore, God's restraint on the nations would now be removed so that they could freely attack the Jews. This is what is meant by his "covenant" with the nations. God had kept the nations at bay, but that restriction would be no more. As verse 11 suggests, it must have been with heavy hearts that the godly in their number watched as the broken halves of the prophet's staff fell to the ground. Verse 14 adds, "Then I broke my second staff Union, annulling the brotherhood between Judah and Israel." Now the integrity of the people as a nation would be lost, because they had despised God, who was and is the only source of true unity for any people.

We need to show care in applying this scenario to our own nation and time, because there are important ways in which Old Testament Israel is different from any secular state today. First, we should apply this situation to Christian churches, many of which turn away from the Bible and over time become either dead or irrelevant or wholly corrupt. Yet we cannot fail to observe how similar this situation is to the one that ours and other Western nations are now facing. Having built our prosperity on a foundation of godly principles and having enjoyed a unity based on values and a shared vision that came from the Bible, we should not be surprised to find our culture threatened by our abandonment of God. We may inscribe "In God We Trust" on our coins, but those are increasingly empty and hypocritical words. In fact, it is the coins themselves we have come to trust. But money and the things it can buy will serve us poorly in the place of the true and living God of the Bible. Like the Jews in Zechariah's time, we will not enjoy the blessings of God without in faith obeying and bending the knee to him as our Lord.

This must have been a very painful episode in Zechariah's life. He had seen so much blessing, but now judgment awaited the people who had turned away from God. Surely it was painful to God as well, yet it was no surprise to him. Indeed, it is clear from this passage that from the start God intended this role-play to symbolize something that had already happened spiritually. Verse 6 explained why he was sending forth the prophet: "For I will no longer have pity on the inhabitants of this land, declares the LORD. Behold, I will cause each of them to fall into the hand of his neighbor, and each into the hand of his king, and they shall crush the land, and I will deliver none from their hand." In verses 15 and 16, God sends Zechariah back to the people to represent the foolish shepherd they chose in his place, "a shepherd who does not care for those being destroyed, or seek the young or heal the maimed or nourish the healthy, but devours the flesh of the fat ones, tearing off even their hoofs." It is always a severe judgment when God gives sinners exactly what they want. People want a life of sin, a permissively debased lifestyle, and God judges them by allowing this lifestyle with its wages of death. As Christian people, in the face of such advancing darkness, we must be ever more eager to stand before our generation with the gospel of grace and truth it so desperately needs.

THE DEPARTED SAVIOR

Verses 12 and 13 complete this prophetic role-play in two ways, first by revealing the contempt of those who rejected God's messenger: "I said to them, 'If it seems good to you, give me my wages; but if not, keep them.' And they weighed out as my wages thirty pieces of silver" (Zech. 11:12). Thirty pieces of silver was the prescribed amount paid for a slave who had been killed. These were slave wages—the most contemptuous salary a person could be given. God therefore told Zechariah, " 'Throw it to the potter'— the lordly price at which I was priced by them. So I took the thirty pieces of silver and threw them into the house of the LORD, to the potter" (Zech. 11:13). This shows that Zechariah rejected the pay; unwilling to give money to the corrupt religious leaders, he cast it instead to the potter, who had his shop in those precincts. What a vivid portrait this is of the world's contempt for true religion, as well as God's rejection of its arrogant offerings.

These two verses complete the passage in another way, linking these events to what would happen over five hundred years later when another good and true shepherd sent by God would be rejected by the people of that very city. This Shepherd was God's own Son, the great and final prophet of Israel. His life was also priced by the religious leaders at thirty pieces of silver, paid to Judas Iscariot for his betrayal. This was, as God said, "the lordly price at which I was priced by them!" (Zech. 11:13). When Judas threw the coins back at the chief priests, they fulfilled what was written in Zechariah by using it to buy the potter's field instead of placing it in the temple treasury. In the Gospel records, this links Zechariah's role-play with the real-life experience of Jesus Christ.

If it was painful for Zechariah to be rejected, how much more so for Jesus, God incarnate, to be rejected by the people he had loved so well. This was the nation to whom God had shown such patient mercy for generations. Jesus had spent his ministry teaching and healing these very people. One of the dramatic scenes of Jesus' last week in Jerusalem took place at the site of that very temple where Zechariah was rejected and later killed. Jesus knew he would be rejected and killed. He knew that a cross awaited him, that the Jews would detest him as the true shepherd Zechariah had foreshown. Jesus lamented not merely his own rejection, but also the salvation these people thereby lost. "O Jerusalem, Jerusalem," he cried, "the city that kills the prophets and stones those who are sent to it! How often would I have gathered your children together as a hen gathers her brood under her wings, and you would not! See, your house is left to you desolate" (Matt. 23:37–38).

The next passage in Matthew's gospel begins by saying, "Jesus left the temple." As Zechariah's role-play had forecast, God's patience had come to an end. The Lord of glory left Jerusalem's temple. All who did not go with him, who did not choose Jesus over the false and wicked shepherds—all except the disciples who followed him in faith—were left behind by him. They were left behind to receive the judgment due their sin, the condemnation for rejecting the Savior God so mercifully had sent. A few days later, as Jesus carried a wooden cross up the hill to Calvary, he turned to some Jewish women who were weeping. "Daughters of Jerusalem," he said, "do not weep for me, but weep for yourselves and for your children" (Luke 23:28). Jesus was going to be raised from the dead, and his disciples were going to receive eternal life, but condemnation awaited all those who rejected him, the true and good shepherd they sinfully crucified in their unwillingness to submit to God.

A Grave Warning

This passage was a sharp warning to the Jews, that rejecting the true and good shepherd would bring disaster on their heads. But Zechariah's prophecy, recalled by Jesus on his way to the cross, would be fulfilled with terrible accuracy. What was foretold in our passage came to life in the form of terrible conquest by the Romans in the aftermath of Jesus' rejection by the Jews.

We have already encountered two very specific prophecies in this section of Zechariah, one about the coming of Alexander the Great (9:1–8) and another about the wars of the Maccabees (9:12–17). Our passage adds a third prophecy that was fulfilled in precise detail. Zechariah 11:1–2 speaks of a terrible invasion coming down from the north, a scorched-earth conquest that left the land desolate. This occurred in the generation after Jesus was rejected by the Jews, the result of God's rejection of them. In A.D. 66 Jewish rebels succeeded in overthrowing the Roman garrison at Jerusalem, and in response the Roman general Vespasian appeared with his legions, trampling across the very northern lands spoken of in our passage. What Zechariah showed by breaking his two staffs became tragically real. God's protecting hand was removed in the aftermath of Jesus' rejection, and without God's presence the unity of the nation dissolved in a time of civil strife and national disorder.

Indeed, Zechariah's prophecy pointedly describes the situation in Jerusalem at the time of its final conquest and destruction in A.D. 70. There were three rival factions in the city when it was surrounded, a situation that hampered negotiations with the Romans and greatly increased the suffering of the people. Zechariah specifically foretold what would happen: "I will not be your shepherd. What is to die, let it die. What is to be destroyed, let it be destroyed. And let those who are left devour the flesh of one another" (Zech. 11:9). This unprecedented horror was realized during the Roman siege as the people were slaughtered in great numbers. As the city starved, some of the people actually resorted to cannibalism. Finally, the city fell to the sword, and as Jesus had prophesied in Matthew 24, not one stone of the temple was left standing. This presents an intense picture with which we have to reckon. On the one hand, the Scripture presents God as eager to forgive and slow to anger, rich in mercy and reluctant to destroy. Yet when his judgment finally comes, how terrible it truly is!

This warning was very specifically fulfilled in Jerusalem, although its lesson remains valid for any nation that rejects Christ as its Lord. But we should also be sure to apply its warning on a personal level. Just as Jesus came to Jerusalem, so he comes to every man and every woman. He offers you salvation—forgiveness by his death for your sins. But he also warns against the consequences of rejecting him as Savior and Lord. Understand that if you reject Jesus, you will cause more than sorrow and sadness in his loving heart. Understand that you will have rejected God. You will have rejected the grace he has offered in love. You, like the Jews of old, will not be able to give the excuse that God withheld his grace from you. He has sent his own Son to be your Savior and Good Shepherd. It is not a harsh God you will have rejected, one who delights in anger and is unworthy of your love. No, it is a God revealed in grace and truth by Jesus Christ. It is the God already revealed in the Old Testament: "The LORD, the LORD, a God merciful and gracious, slow to anger, and abounding in steadfast love and faithfulness, keeping steadfast love for thousands, forgiving iniquity and transgression and sin, but who will by no means clear the guilty" (Ex. 34:6–7).

The warning, then, is this: If you reject the grace and mercy of God, refusing the Savior he has sent, God must then reject you in turn. If you choose sin and its pleasures, you cannot escape sin's judgment. Zechariah reluctantly broke the two staffs that represented God's blessing, and so too will all the godless find themselves without the benefits of God's grace. Jesus spoke of this terrible prospect in his parable of the tenants. Speaking of the people who first rejected God's prophets and finally rejected his Son, crucifying him in their unbelief, Jesus said, "[God] will put those wretches to a miserable death" (Matt. 21:41). Do not, I implore you, be found among that number. Do not enlist for that eternal judgment, of which Jerusalem's horrible fall was but a brief portent, when God so eagerly offers you forgiveness and life eternal through faith in Jesus Christ. And do not think that you can safely wait, for no rejection of God's Son is safe, and no one knows which will be the last chance for him to be saved. "Behold," Paul writes, "now is the day of salvation" (2 Cor. 6:2).

Like the prophet Zechariah, Jesus was rejected and put to death by the enemies of God. For them, and for all who take their place today, the cross is the emblem of their condemnation. But there are others, a multitude beyond counting, who look upon the Good Shepherd with gladness, who hear his voice with delight, who go forth with him into the flock he gathers for eternal life. For these, the cross is the emblem of salvation, because there the Good Shepherd laid down his life for the forgiveness of their sins. "On that day the LORD their God will save them, as the flock of his people," says the prophet (Zech. 9:16). This is the message of the cross of Christ, a warning of the gravest importance. But it is also the message of a God full of compassion, a Savior worthy of our devotion and trust, a salvation freely offered to all who will come in faith, and a call for you to hear and come today so that you may be saved.

22

STRONG IN THE LORD

Zechariah 12:1–9

For the sake of the house of Judah I will keep my eyes open, when
I strike every horse of the peoples with blindness. Then the clans
of Judah shall say to themselves, "The inhabitants of Jerusalem
have strength through the LORD of hosts, their God."
(Zech. 12:4–5)

Chapter 12 begins the final section of Zechariah, beginning the second of two oracles that make up the latter half of this book. It is not certain how these two oracles relate to one another. The first is an oracle focused against the nations opposed to Jerusalem, and now this second oracle is said to be against Israel. Most relevant, perhaps, is the matter of time. In chapters 9–11 we discerned a forward progression in time as its message unfolded. First was a prophecy dealing with the conquests of Alexander the Great, which occurred in the fourth century BC, followed by another concerning the conflict between Jews and Greeks in the wars of the Maccabees in the second century BC. That oracle concluded with a vivid prophecy of the rejection of Christ in Jerusalem, which took place in the early first century AD. It seems that this second oracle picks up at that point, moving forward in history from the cross.

This is good news. The Jews, representing the whole sinful world, rejected the Savior God had sent. But this oracle shows that man's rebellion is not the end of the story. Chapters 12 and 13 form a single unit, and in them we learn how God will employ his people to confound the nations (12:1–4), imbuing his people with a marvelous strength (12:5–9), bringing them to repentance (12:10–14), and ultimately cleansing them from sin (13:1–6). The message is that God himself will make effectual the gospel he has offered. He will preserve, enliven, gather, and purify the church he has ordained to save.

AN ORACLE REGARDING ISRAEL

The first nine verses of Zechariah 12 present the first two of these scenes, namely, God employing his people to confound and destroy the nations arrayed against him, working in them a great strength to prevail. There are, however, a number of matters we should first consider, starting with the title of this section as "a burden of the word of the LORD concerning Israel" (Zech. 12:1).

"Burden" translates the Hebrew word *massa*, which is also put as "oracle." It invariably speaks of a threat of woe in the event of God's coming. This raises a question about the sense in which this title is placed over this section. Since it is a burden against Israel, why do these verses go on to speak of glad tidings for Jerusalem? There are two main approaches to resolving this matter, the first given by H. C. Leupold. Leupold says that this oracle is a burden on Israel not because God will bring woe upon her, but because of the circumstances God's people must endure for their deliverance. In these passages God's city is brought under fierce attack and placed under siege, and though she is delivered, this is a burden to be borne. John Calvin takes a different approach, reminding us that most of the Jewish people had remained in the comfort of their Babylonian exile rather than share the hardships of those who had returned to Jerusalem. He writes, "I therefore consider that the Prophet here reproves those Israelites who had rejected . . . a free return to their own country,"[1] which was their duty according to God's Word.

1. John Calvin, *The Minor Prophets*, 5 vols. (Edinburgh: Banner of Truth, 1986), 5:339.

A second issue has to do with a phrase that is repeated five times in these verses, recurring all through the rest of Zechariah (16 times in these three chapters): "On that day." This is a common phrase in the prophets, in this or in some other form, such as "On the day of the Lord." This expression refers to the coming of God in power to set affairs right upon the earth, both in judgment and in salvation. A close study will reveal that different prophets use this expression to refer to different events. Amos 5:18–20, for instance, uses this term to speak of the conquest of Samaria by the Assyrian Empire. Joel 2:28–31 speaks of the Day of the Lord when God's Spirit will be poured out at Pentecost (Acts 2:16–21). In the New Testament, "the day of the Lord" almost always refers to the second coming of Christ and the final judgment. For this reason, many Christians assume that the expression points to the end even in the Old Testament.

The general statement we can make about "the day of the Lord" is that it refers to the coming of God's judging and saving rule upon the earth. Such a day occurs at various times in redemptive history. The phrase "on that day," therefore, refers not so much to a date marked on the calendar, but to each of the many visitations of God reported in Scripture, always with manifestations of power, holiness, and grace.

Finally, we must deal with the matter of fulfillment. When Zechariah says "on that day," which divine visitation does he have in mind? There are a number of statements in this last oracle that place it in the time after the first coming but before the second coming of Christ. So when will this happen, and who are the people of God who will be saved in the manner spoken of here?

There are two main views. One holds that these passages speak of the Christian church as the true Israel of God in the New Testament age, whereas the other view believes that Zechariah speaks of ethnic and even national Israel. Those who see this chapter as speaking of the church will find its fulfillment taking place all through the current age of grace, while those who hold the latter position generally point to a future and literal attack on Jerusalem that leads to a great deliverance, a general repentance, and the wholesale conversion of the Jews through the gospel. All through Zechariah, we have noted a focus on a spiritual fulfillment in the Christian church, and that is the best way to take this oracle as well. These prophecies refer to the people of God generally, who in Zechariah's day were located in Jerusalem, but who now are found in the Christian church.

John Calvin understood Zechariah's prophecies of Jerusalem as having great importance for what the church was experiencing in Calvin's own day. This oracle speaks of armed forces arrayed against Jerusalem, and it was literally the case that the evangelicals of the Reformation faced military invasion from far stronger powers who sought to suppress the gospel. Calvin wrote:

> We see how Satan raises up great forces, we see how the whole world conspires against the Church, to prevent the increase or progress of the kingdom of Christ . . . [so that] we are ready to faint and to become wholly dejected. Let us remember . . . however boldly may multiplied adversaries resist Christ in the work of building a spiritual temple to God the Father, yet all their efforts will be in vain.[2]

A broad survey of church history, and of the worldwide church in our own day, will show that the church is indeed besieged by the world, and that passages like this in Zechariah very well anticipate both our need and God's faithfulness in upholding his people. It is my view, then, in conformity with the general Reformed view, that this prophecy speaks of God's mighty provision for the salvation of his people in every age, and especially for the church in its stand against a hostile world. Leupold writes, "The claims made for Jerusalem's future find their ultimate fulfillment in the true Zion of God—His church. . . . The whole passage speaks of God's sovereign care and protection of the church of the Old and New Testaments through the ages."[3]

THE NATIONS BROUGHT TO RUIN

Zechariah 12:1–9 breaks into two halves, the first of which speaks of God using the church to overthrow those who rise against him, while the second speaks of God strengthening his people for victory. First, however, is a brief introduction, rehearsing God's own majesty and might. Verse 1 directs our attention to him as "the LORD, who stretched out the heavens and founded

2. Ibid., 5:114.
3. H. C. Leupold, *Exposition of Zechariah* (Grand Rapids: Baker, 1981), 234.

the earth and formed the spirit of man within him." This speaks of God's active sovereignty over the world. This is not the clock-making God of the deists, who winds up history and then lets it run on its own, but the God whose hands arrayed the heavens up above and whose providence rules upon the earth. Since the verses that follow seem incredible to believe, especially in times of weakness and danger for the church, here we are first reminded of what kind of God makes these claims. He is the almighty God of creation and providence.

With that reminder, verses 2–6 depict the world opposing and advancing to destroy God's city. But instead of the church being destroyed, it is her enemies who come to ruin. First, they are confounded. Verse 2 describes Jerusalem as a cup or bowl at which the nations come to drink: "Behold, I am about to make Jerusalem a cup of staggering to all the surrounding peoples. The siege of Jerusalem will also be against Judah." Leupold describes the scene most vividly:

> What a scene: a huge bowl of wine; several men, representatives of Syria, Ammon, Moab, Edom, Philistaea, Phoenicia, crowding around the bowl and setting their lips to it! They are athirst to gulp down Israel. But, strange to say, one after another steps back, reels and staggers as a drunkard, for God has made this to be a bowl of reeling. . . . They are rendered impotent by the wine of the wrath of God and stagger about like drunken fools. The city of God stands undefeated.[4]

Verse 3 then shows the nations injuring themselves in their attempt to dislodge the church: "On that day I will make Jerusalem a heavy stone for all the peoples. All who lift it will surely hurt themselves." The idea is of a farmer who means to plow a field but finds a large stone in the way. Seeking to lift it, he injures himself. Likewise, the world views God's people as an impediment to its sinful program and ambitions. But when the world tries to move the church, God makes her weighty and breaks the back of the ungodly.

Verse 4 sees the armies of the world galloping against the city in all their might. "On that day, declares the LORD, I will strike every horse with panic, and its rider with madness. But for the sake of the house of Judah I will keep

---

4. H. C. Leupold, *An Exposition of Zechariah* (Grand Rapids: Baker, 1971 reprint), 227.

my eyes open, when I strike every horse of the peoples with blindness." We are reminded here of the prophet Elisha, who though surrounded by the horsemen and chariots of Aram was protected by the chariots of fire God had sent to his aid. Elisha prayed and God made the enemy host blind. This seems to be the idea here, that by blinding the enemy and sending their horses into a panic, the Lord overthrows all their vaunted power.

There are two things we should note in these verses. First, there is an increasing intensity as God battles with the hostile world. Initially, God merely confounds and shames them. Next he allows them to be wounded by what they are doing. In verse 4 they are sent into dangerous madness. By the end of this passage we read: "On that day I will seek to destroy all the nations that come against Jerusalem" (Zech. 12:9). There is an increasing intensity, a progressive judgment of those who persist against the Lord; they end up in utter destruction.

Second, we should observe that the harm is brought to these enemies by their own devices. In verse 2 God does not make them drink, but turns their malice into poison. In verse 3 those who apply strength to remove the church have their sources of might injured. What men thought would bring them victory in their rage against the Lord was instead turned against them; he makes the idols they worshiped and trusted a curse and a threat to their lives.

The application of these verses is obvious, that God protectively regards the state of his people and is ready to come to their defense. God says, "For the sake of the house of Judah I will keep my eyes open" (Zech. 12:4). In chapter 2 the angel spoke in similar terms, noting God's close and loving connection to his people: "He who touches you touches the apple of his eye" (Zech. 2:8). Psalm 46 famously says to all the Lord's people in distress: "God is our refuge and strength, an ever-present help in trouble" (v. 1 NIV).

"AFFLAVIT DEUS"

This is something individual Christians find to be true, and it stands as the testimony of the church as a whole. History shows the world trying over and over to stamp out the gospel. The Romans tried to destroy the early church through savage persecution, but the church survived and prospered. Likewise, the Protestant Reformation was gravely threatened by armed invasion.

One memorable example was the Spanish Armada, which sought to invade and crush Protestant England during the reign of Queen Elizabeth. England and Spain were contesting their interests in the New World, but the underlying dispute was over the gospel. Spain was proudly Roman Catholic—its king bore the title "His Most Catholic Majesty"—and England had boldly established its Reformation on the recovery of God's Word.

The Armada launched in 1588 with 130 large and powerful ships, containing 7,000 sailors and 17,000 soldiers. The English had but 90 ships in their entire navy, most of them quite small. The battle raged for days, and the Protestants under Sir Francis Drake fought brilliantly. But all would have been lost were it not for an unexpected storm that churned the waters of the English Channel and drove the Spanish ships into the North Sea, where their fleet was utterly destroyed. It was widely believed by God's people in England, I think rightly, that God had defended his church against the might of the hostile world. Their government commemorated this conviction by minting coins inscribed, *Afflavit Deus*, or "God blew."

Examples like this argue that God's people must not fear the world. Many church leaders and church-growth strategists today present a different picture than the one we find in these verses. They say that the church must accommodate the world, that if we do not make the church conform to worldly styles and expectations—even to a worldly message and agenda—then the world will simply brush us out of the way. But the true Christian church is a weighty thing! She is not so easily moved, since God is in her. The world may not approve of us, and may even hate what we proclaim from God's Word, but the true church as it rests in the power of God will not be moved.

Zechariah spoke these words in God's city with the hope of rousing the Jews from the stupor of their spiritual sloth. Yet we know from the books that follow, particularly from Nehemiah, that within a few years the city of which these promises were made was in a sad spiritual state. J. I. Packer draws a parallel between weak Jerusalem in that time and the weak Christian church in our own time. He says:

Jerusalem is a picture of Christian churches generally in the modern West. Weakness, disillusionment, and the melting away of adherents is the story everywhere.... The secularizing of community life and the faltering of theologians, church leaders, and ordinary clergy has left the majority of congregations in a very low state. . . . Overall the Western church has shriveled and shrunk; it has ceased to count as a community force; the faith of which God made it trustee is largely unknown to the man in the street, and when known it is largely ignored; and the godliness that the church once set forth as true humanness is rated in popular culture as a comic, old-fashioned oddity.[5]

If that is true, it can only be because we have not believed the message of prophets like Zechariah. He tells us that ours is a great God, and since the world will tremble before him, we ought not tremble before the world. Packer points out that a man of faith like Nehemiah could build Jerusalem up again in the power of God. What a worthy cause it is for us to serve the city of God, his church, rebuilding a faith that is worthy of its Savior. If we are to give ourselves to that work, it will begin by recapturing the vision of God's greatness and might, his total and sovereign sufficiency for all our needs, that Zechariah so boldly proclaims.

STRONG IN THE LORD

Verses 1–4 look outside the walls of Jerusalem, but verses 5–9 mainly focus inside—on God's work within the people he loves. This is the second statement in Zechariah's message of salvation, that God blesses his people so that they may prevail over every foe.

Zechariah's oracle speaks of three things God does for his people. First, he makes them strong with his own might. Those entrusted to lead the people rejoice in just this: "Then the clans of Judah shall say to themselves, 'The inhabitants of Jerusalem have strength through the LORD of hosts, their God' " (Zech. 12:5). This is something that faithful pastors always long to see: the whole church strengthened by the presence of the Lord. This also speaks of the confidence we ought to have about all who have truly come in faith: since the Lord Almighty is their God, they shall surely grow in spiritual strength.

But God's people look to their leaders with similar delight. God says, "On that day I will make the clans of Judah like a blazing pot in the midst of wood, like a flaming torch among sheaves. And they shall devour to the right and

5. J. I. Packer, *A Passion for Faithfulness* (Wheaton, IL: Crossway, 1995), 70.

to the left all the surrounding peoples" (Zech. 12:6). The New International Version translates "clans of Judah" as "leaders of Judah," since by "clans" Zechariah seems to mean Judah's chieftains. This is what the church needs, blazing pastors who stand firm against the world in reliance on God, spreading his Word like fire. Indeed, wherever the church stands boldly against the world there are men of God who stand strong in faith, and on the example of such courage the whole of the church greatly depends. This is how Paul exhorted Timothy, a younger pastor he had trained: "Do not be ashamed of the testimony about our Lord, nor of me his prisoner, but share in suffering for the gospel by the power of God. . . . By the Holy Spirit who dwells within us, guard the good deposit entrusted to you" (2 Tim. 1:8, 14).

The prophet speaks of Judah's leaders as a firepot that ignites a woodpile, or a flaming torch among sheaves of dried grain. The point is that their faithful testimony consumed their opposition. But we are reminded here of how many faithful champions of the faith literally went to the flames for the gospel, and by doing so ignited the world.

It was before the threat of that very fate that Martin Luther refused to renounce justification by faith alone at the Council of Worms in 1521. "Here I stand," he replied to their threats, "I can do no other." The English Reformation, too, was a blaze ignited by the flaming deaths of its faithful leaders during the persecution of the Catholic queen, Bloody Mary. Most famous were Nicholas Ridley and Hugh Latimer, courageous preachers whose faith was put to the test in the flames. As they were tied to the stake, Latimer said to his friend: "Be of good cheer, Master Ridley, and play the man. We shall this day light such a candle by God's grace in England as I trust shall never be put out!"[6] This is the strength God calls for and provides in true leaders of his flock, of which there is great need today.

Second, we find here that God makes secure his church and conveys his peace to his people. Zechariah says: "Jerusalem shall again be inhabited in its place, in Jerusalem. And the LORD will give salvation to the tents of Judah first, that the glory of the house of David and the glory of the inhabitants of Jerusalem may not surpass that of Judah. On that day the LORD will protect the inhabitants of Jerusalem" (Zech. 12:6–8). Hugh Martin writes:

6. Marcus Loane, *Masters of the English Reformation* (1954; repr. Edinburgh: Banner of Truth, 2005), 165.

How often, in holy Scripture, do we hear the Lord assuring his people of the perfect, inviolable security of their life, which is hid in him! "No weapon that is formed against thee shall prosper." . . . And how often do we find his people triumphing, with songs of exultation, in the hidden security which with Christ in God they enjoy! "Thou art my hiding place; thou shalt preserve me from trouble; thou shalt compass me about with songs of deliverance." . . . "For thou hast been a shelter for me, and a strong tower from the enemy. I will abide in thy tabernacle for ever: I will trust in the covert of thy wings." "Yea, in the shadow of thy wings will I make my refuge, until these calamites be overpast." Most blessed privilege! To have a spiritual, secret, near asylum, a strong tower, into which the righteous runneth and is safe! . . . Within, the believing soul is altogether safe—safe as Christ is safe, safe with Christ in God.[7]

Finally, these verses show that in his deliverance, God brings unity and concord to his people. We find this in the trust between leader and led. We find it as well in the manner of God's deliverance, for he brings together great and small in the same salvation: "The LORD will give salvation to the tents of Judah first, that the glory of the house of David and the glory of the inhabitants of Jerusalem may not surpass that of Judah" (Zech. 12:7). Christians often think it is only those in illustrious positions who may count on God's help in extraordinary ways. But here the ordinary people of God, and not those who dwell in the shadow of the temple and near to the throne, are told of God's special care for them. Though lowly in the world, they are not forgotten by God. It is one of the glories of Christianity that the weakest may be most sure of the Lord's strengthening hand.

Just as verse 9 sums up the whole passage—God opposing those who threaten his city and his church—verse 8 sums up his work in the lives of his people: "On that day the LORD will protect the inhabitants of Jerusalem, so that the feeblest among them on that day shall be like David, and the house of David shall be like God, like the angel of the LORD, going before them." He speaks of a supernatural empowering for all of God's people, from the least to the greatest. Even the feeblest among his people will able to achieve feats of faith in his name, like those displayed in the life of David, the man after God's own heart. As for the leaders, they

---

7. Hugh Martin, *Christ for Us* (Edinburgh: Banner of Truth, 1998), 199.

shall rise up in the might of God, guiding and inspiring confidence in the church as did the angel of the Lord for the tribes of Israel.

In the time of David, Jerusalem was impregnable, and in the exodus the tribes of Israel marched victorious because the angel of the Lord, manifested in a cloud of smoke and fire, was striding at their head. In due time, the One who was that angel, and who has appeared numerous times in Zechariah as such, came into the world enfleshed in lowly humanity, that he might be our champion and Lord. Jesus Christ conquered our foes—sin and the devil and death—on the cross, and now he reigns as our king forever. When Peter professed the gospel, Jesus proclaimed, "On this rock I will build my church, and the gates of hell shall not prevail against it" (Matt. 16:18). In his might, that church will find strength to endure in days ahead, until the final trumpet sounds and the battle lines are separated by his return in glory. Meanwhile, in all our struggles with fear and temptation and sin, we may look confidently to him for help, seeing his design that "the inhabitants of Jerusalem have strength through the LORD of hosts, their God" (Zech. 12:5).

COURAGE TO STAND

John Calvin argued that this passage was at least in part directed against Jews in Zechariah's day who were afraid to come live in Jerusalem. Its walls were not yet rebuilt, her enemies were many, and her problems obvious. Yet here we find that God would protect and strengthen all who dared to trust in him.

In a similar way, these verses come to each of us. Are you reluctant to be a Christian—to be numbered in the world with the disciples of a crucified Christ? Let this embolden you unto faith, that "the LORD will protect the inhabitants of Jerusalem" (Zech. 12:8). If you are a Christian, are you reluctant to take your stand boldly among the people of God? Are you afraid that people at work or in your family will find out that you have become a disciple of Jesus? It is true that many will reject and oppose you for your faith, but God will watch over you and give you his own strength. Are you slow to strive against your sin, to labor in your own heart, and to stand against the works of the devil and the temptations of sin? Surely God will be your strength, working in you with the power that emboldened his people in other generations, so that God will lead you in victory over all your foes, to the glory of his name.

23

MOURNING FOR THE ONE THEY PIERCED

Zechariah 12:10—14

And I will pour out on the house of David and the inhabitants of Jerusalem a spirit of grace and pleas for mercy, so that, when they look on me, on him whom they have pierced, they shall mourn for him, as one mourns for an only child, and weep bitterly over him, as one weeps over a firstborn. (Zech. 12:10)

In 1955 John Murray published an influential book on theology titled *Redemption Accomplished and Applied.*[1] The title alone is helpful to our thinking about Christian salvation. The first half of the book, and of the title, focuses on the *accomplishment* of salvation—that is, those objective acts performed in history for the salvation of sinners: chiefly the life, death, resurrection, and ascension of the Lord Jesus Christ. The second half deals with the subsequent *application* of salvation. These are God's subjective dealings with individuals to apply the work of Christ so that they will be saved. Among these are effectual calling, regeneration,

1. John Murray, *Redemption Accomplished and Applied* (Grand Rapids: Eerdmans, 1955).

266

faith, and repentance. Just thinking in this way is helpful, that God first *accomplished* our salvation in Christ and then *applies* by the Holy Spirit what is needed for us to receive that salvation.

What brings this to mind here is the sequence displayed in the last oracle of the prophet Zechariah, from chapters 12 to 14. All through this book God has been emphasizing the salvation he will *accomplish* both in Zechariah's time and later through the Messiah. Now, in these chapters, we see that salvation *applied* to his people by the Holy Spirit. Here we encounter the inward strengthening of faith, the gift of repentance, the purification and then perseverance of believers, and finally their glorification in holiness at the very end. This oracle begins with the city weak and besieged, on the brink of conquest and death, an apt description of man in sin. But by the end of chapter 14 we will read that every square inch of this same city has been reclaimed by the Lord and made holy unto him: "On that day there shall be inscribed on the bells of the horses, 'Holy to the Lord.' And the pots in the house of the Lord shall be as the bowls before the altar" (v. 20).

In the previous chapter, we considered verses that speak of God giving his people strength against their enemies. Now, at the end of chapter 12, there is a greater victory set before us, the victory by which our hearts are conquered by God. Indeed, when we think of the many feats that God's empowering Spirit enables in the human heart, none is greater or more significant than the sorrow of true repentance for sin and a turning back to God: "When they look on me, on him whom they have pierced, they shall mourn for him" (Zech. 12:10).

A GREAT PROPHECY

Before we consider this message, there are some observations we should make about it. First, Zechariah 12:10 is an exceptional prophecy of the Lord Jesus Christ, speaking of "him whom they have pierced." For hundreds of years this prophecy lay in waiting, though in full public view. The time came when Jesus Christ lived, was rejected in fulfillment of Zechariah 11, and then was handed over to the Romans to be crucified. After several momentous hours, the Roman soldiers went to Jesus to break his legs, but found him already dead. Instead, one of the soldiers—a Roman who surely had never heard of Zechariah's prophecy—"pierced his side with a spear, and at once there came out blood and water" (John 19:34). The apostle John tells us, "These things took place that the Scripture might be fulfilled: 'Not one of his bones will be broken.' And again another Scripture says, 'They will look on him whom they have pierced'" (John 19:36–37).

Second, Zechariah 12:10 provides a classic instance of the doctrine of the Trinity as it is expressed in the Old Testament, as well as of the deity of Christ. While the full doctrine of the Trinity—the teaching that there is one God in three persons: Father, Son, and Holy Spirit—is explicitly taught only in the New Testament, we have here one of the many Old Testament passages that reflects this reality about the Godhead. Indeed, verse 10 makes no sense apart from the doctrine of the Trinity. "They will look on *me*," says the Lord, "on him whom they have pierced, and they shall mourn for *him*." The one who is pierced is God himself, and yet God then speaks of "him," showing a multiplicity of persons within the Godhead. Only a man can fulfill this prophecy by being pierced, yet we find that the man is himself God.

Third, we need to inquire about the broader fulfillment of this passage, which began with Christ's piercing on the cross. A further fulfillment takes place as he is looked upon in sorrow by the people. Indeed, there are at least four ways in which this can be said to be fulfilled even after the crucifixion. The first was at Pentecost, when God poured out his Spirit in Jerusalem. Just weeks after Jesus' death, Peter directed the Jews to look upon the one they had pierced: "This Jesus, delivered up according to the definite plan and foreknowledge of God, you crucified and killed by the hands of lawless men" (Acts 2:23). On the occasion of that first Christian sermon, we are told that God fulfilled the prophecy of the sending of his Spirit upon the house of David to bring repentance.

Another way in which it seems we should take this prophecy has to do with ethnic Israel. In Romans 11:26, Paul speaks of a future large-scale conversion of the Jews, saying, "All Israel will be saved." This promise will be fulfilled in conjunction with this prophecy, which says of the Jews that they will mourn for the one they pierced.

A third fulfillment is spoken of in Revelation 1:7, when Christ comes again at the end of days: "Behold, he is coming with the clouds, and every eye will see him, even those who pierced him, and all tribes of the earth will wail on account of him." Seeing all of these ways in which the passage is fulfilled, we may see it as a paradigm for all of redemptive history. Thomas McComiskey gives his assessment that this prophecy "establishes a philosophy of history that has its goal in a suffering figure who represents the intrusion of divine redemption into history. . . . Christ is this suffering figure and his presence in human history enlightens the words of this ancient prophet, giving them meaning and life for subsequent generations."[2]

GODLY SORROW AS THE HEART OF TRUE REPENTANCE

There is a fourth way in which this passage is fulfilled, namely, whenever any individual comes to God in repentance to be saved. That is the meaning of this text as it applies to us, who by our sins fully participated in the piercing of God's only Son on the cross. In this regard, Zechariah's prophecy makes four main points, the first of which is that *godly sorrow is the heart of true repentance.*

The book of Zechariah began with a call to repentance: "Return to me, says the LORD of hosts, and I will return to you" (Zech. 1:3). God similarly calls every sinner to repent and turn to him. This is how Jesus Christ began his preaching of the gospel: "Repent, for the kingdom of heaven is at hand" (Matt. 4:17). It is often pointed out that repentance means turning around. It means turning away from sin and turning toward Jesus Christ for new obedience. This describes the *action* of repentance. But, more centrally, what we find here is the *heart* of true repentance, a godly sorrow for our sin: "They shall mourn . . . and weep bitterly" (Zech. 12:10).

God always desires our hearts. "My son," he says in Proverbs 23:26, "give me your heart." Moses declared to Israel, "Circumcise therefore the foreskin of your heart, and be no longer stubborn" (Deut. 10:16). David cried in his psalm of repentance, "For you will not delight in sacrifice, or I would give it; you will not be pleased with a burnt offering. The sacrifices of God are a broken spirit; a broken and contrite heart, O God, you will not despise" (Ps. 51:16–17).

We know an analogy to this focus on the heart in a relationship between a man and woman, especially between a husband and wife. What is it that we most long to discover when anger or sin has broken down the bond of love? Certainly, a conflict in marriage calls for action—for words to be said

2. Thomas E. McComiskey, *The Minor Prophets: An Exegetical and Expository Commentary*, 3 vols. (Grand Rapids: Baker, 1998), 3:1216.

and remedies to be made. But what truly heals the breach and restores what has been damaged in the relationship is sorrow from the heart. How often, when long arguments have failed to reconcile two people, or have even made things worse, genuine tears of remorse quickly restore the union.

So it is in our relationship with God. In this case, it is only we who have sinned. If accusations are made, he is the only one who has a just case. But God's loving heart desires not merely to win the argument but to win our hearts back to himself. Jesus taught this in his parable of the prodigal son, who had taken his portion of his father's inheritance and squandered it in sinful living. Finally, he came to his senses, and resolved to return in remorse to seek his father's grace. He said, "I will arise and go to my father, and I will say to him, 'Father, I have sinned against heaven and before you. I am no longer worthy to be called your son. Treat me as one of your hired servants' " (Luke 15:18–19). The father, seeing him return in sorrow, gladly received him back in love. Jesus described it this way: "While he was still a long way off, his father saw him and felt compassion, and ran and embraced him and kissed him" (Luke 15:20). This is a picture of God's loving heart for us, and the sorrow for sin he desires as the heart of our repentance.

Zechariah offers two pictures of the intensity of the sorrow God envisions. First are parents who mourn the loss of a child: "They shall mourn for him, as one mourns for an only child, and weep bitterly over him, as one weeps over a firstborn" (Zech. 12:10). This is a deep and bitter sorrow, one that is not gotten over quickly or easily, if in fact at all. Charles Spurgeon speaks of such an occasion as perhaps the most painful errand on which a Christian minister can be called. How much more painful when, as our passage says, it is an only child who has died, an only son who would have borne the family name. This was proverbial in Israel for a great magnitude of grief, as Amos 8:10 shows, speaking of the coming of the Lord to judge: "I will make it like the mourning for an only son and the end of it like a bitter day."

Next, the prophet refers to the national mourning in Israel at the death of Josiah, the last of Judah's godly kings, which took place in the plain of Megiddo: "On that day the mourning in Jerusalem will be as great as the mourning for Hadad-rimmon in the plain of Megiddo" (Zech. 12:11). Second Chronicles 35:24–25 tells us of that great lamenting, led by the prophet Jeremiah and commemorated for generations by all the people. Josiah was, as one commentator explains, "the last hope of the declining Jewish kingdom, and in his death the last gleam of the sunset of Judah faded into night."[3]

Verses 12–14 then communicate the universality of this mourning among God's people. It is not just for some in the church, but all will have this sorrow. "The land shall mourn, each family by itself." Zechariah relates the house of David, the head of the kingly line, to the house of Nathan, one of his descendants: "The family of the house of David by itself, and their wives by themselves; the family of the house of Nathan by itself, and their wives by themselves" (Zech. 12:12). He does the same for the priestly line, with the house of Levi and that of his descendant Shimei, thus showing that from the high to the low, young and old, from one generation to the next, God will lead his people back to himself along the trail of tears in sorrow for sin: "The family of the house of Levi by itself, and their wives by themselves; the family of the Shimeites by itself, and their wives by themselves; and all the families that are left, each by itself, and their wives by themselves" (Zech. 12:13–14).

Godly sorrow is at the heart of true repentance, and it leads us on to a full and complete return to God. Paul said in 2 Corinthians 7:10–11: "For godly grief produces a repentance that leads to salvation without regret. . . . See what earnestness this godly grief has produced in you, but also what eagerness to clear yourselves, what indignation, what fear, what longing, what zeal, what punishment!" Godly sorrow is the garden in which all sorts of good fruits are grown, especially the repentance that leads to salvation.

GODLY SORROW AS THE GIFT OF THE SPIRIT

Zechariah makes clear the source of such mourning, stating that *godly sorrow is the gift of the Holy Spirit.* "I will pour out . . . a spirit of grace and pleas for mercy," verse 10 says. Charles Spurgeon explains: "It is always a creation of the Holy Spirit. . . . There never was any real godly sorrow, such as worketh repentance acceptable unto God, except that which was the result of the Holy Spirit's own work within the soul."[4] It is not, Spurgeon adds, the

3. David Baron, *The Visions and Prophecies of Zechariah* (Grand Rapids: Kregel, 1972), 451.
4. Charles Haddon Spurgeon, *Metropolitan Tabernacle Pulpit*, 53 vols. (Pasadena, TX: Pilgrim Publications, 1969), 50:589–90.

product of mere conscience, which though pricked is not able to rise to these spiritual heights. It is not produced by mere terror of judgment, without the quickening of God's Spirit. Instead:

> Genuine mourning for sin comes as a gift of divine grace. . . . Grace comes into the heart, and enlightens the understanding, so that the man understands what his criminality is in the sight of God. Then the grace of God operates upon the conscience so that the man sees the evil and the bitterness of the sin which he has committed against the thrice-holy Jehovah. Then the same grace affects the heart, so that the man beholds the infinite graciousness and eternal love of Christ, and then begins to loathe himself to think that he should ever have treated Christ so ill. So, by a work of grace upon the soul, and not by any other process, does the Spirit of God make men weep for sin so that they hate it, and turn away from it.[5]

This mourning is spiritual, which is why it is called "a spirit of grace and pleas for mercy." This is why it always leads to prayer: "Despairing repentance does not pray. . . . But godly repentance, which the Holy Ghost gives, always sets the sinner praying."[6] Pharaoh grieved for the effects of his sin when God punished him for refusing to let his people go. But, tellingly, he said to Moses, "[You] pray to the LORD" (Ex. 8:8 NIV), showing that his remorse was no work of God's Spirit, which is a spirit of grace and supplication. Judas Iscariot grieved deeply for his sin, but it was the grief of despair, without salvation, because he lacked God's grace for faith and repentance. Matthew tells us he was "seized with remorse." "I have sinned," Judas declared (Matt. 27:3–4 NIV). But then he left the temple and hanged himself, never turning to God in prayer. True mourning, which rises up to be received by God, always grieves for the sin and not just for the situation into which it has brought us.

THE OBJECT OF GODLY SORROW

Third, this prophecy points us to *the object of godly sorrow*, namely, that we look to Jesus Christ, pierced on the cross because of our sins. This is the sight that makes our hearts to mourn: God's perfect Son pierced, crucified because of us.

5. Ibid., 590.
6. Ibid., 591.

What is it about Jesus that causes such sorrow when we see him pierced? First, it is his loveliness, the excellency of him who bore our sins. Here is one utterly pure in heart, one so holy that before him angels veil their faces. In him there never was any sin, and to this his whole life bears testimony. Furthermore, Jesus is a model of humility. Paul tells us that he, "though he was in the form of God, did not count equality with God a thing to be grasped, but made himself nothing, taking the form of a servant . . . he humbled himself" (Phil. 2:6–8). Mark tells us as well that he was "filled with compassion" (1:41 NIV), and thus he placed his healing hand on the sick and dying. Looking to us from the cross with eyes of boundless mercy, he rasps, "Father, forgive them, for they know not what they do" (Luke 23:34).

Why, we ask, looking to him now pierced, is it he who bears our punishment? We perhaps grow callous to suffering, but here is One who truly does not deserve any of what he is receiving. We are the ones who deserve it, and he, as Isaiah said, "was pierced for our transgressions, he was crushed for our iniquities" (Isa. 53:5 NIV). We mourn because of the beauty and the excellency of him who is pierced.

Second, we sorrow to see what suffering he endures. He is rejected and falsely accused. He is mocked and beaten; his face is spat upon; into his scalp is pressed a crown of thorns. His arms are stretched upon a wooden cross, and nails are beaten through his hands and feet; he writhes with pain as the cross is slammed into the earth.

Yet his greatest suffering, we find, is not physical, but spiritual. Hear his cry upon the cross: "My God, my God," he screams, "why have you forsaken me?" (Matt. 27:46). The sky is covered by darkness, torn by the crash of lightning, visibly portraying the terrible wrath of God descending on this man. J. I. Packer writes: "The physical pain, though great . . . was yet only a small part of the story; Jesus' chief sufferings were mental and spiritual, and what was packed into less than four hundred minutes was an eternity of agony— agony such that each minute was an eternity in itself."[7]

In that light we see, to our grief, the gravity of our sin. It is here, upon his body and in his spiritual torment on the cross, that we see just what we have done—what is the work of our hearts and of our hands. It is, says the prophet, our iniquity that God has laid on him (Isa. 53:6); for

7. J. I. Packer: *Knowing God* (Downers Grove, IL: InterVarsity, 1974), 176.

our sins Christ is pierced. If grace and supplication are poured into our hearts by God, then surely we will cry aloud with mournful sorrow:

> My sins, my hateful, cruel sins,
>   his chief tormentors were;
> Each of my crimes became a nail,
>   and unbelief the spear.
> 'Twas you that pulled the vengeance down
>   upon his guiltless head,
> Break, break my heart! O burst mine eyes,
>   and let my sorrows bleed.[8]

This is the sorrowful logic of the mourning heart, seeing the sinfulness of sin, which pierced the loving heart of God and placed the cup of wrath into Jesus' hands. J. C. Ryle observes: "Terribly black must that guilt be for which nothing but the blood of the Son of God could make satisfaction. Heavy must that weight of human sin be which made Jesus groan and sweat drops of blood in agony at Gethsemane and cry at Golgotha, 'My God, My God, why hast Thou forsaken Me?'" (Matt. 27:46).[9]

Sorrow for Christ's suffering is a true sign of spiritual life in the breast of a sinner. It marks the beginning of salvation, a true return to God, and it charts the path of true spirituality all through a Christian's life. "When they look on me, on him whom they have pierced, they shall mourn for him" (Zech. 12:10). This can only be said of the Israel of faith—those on whom God has poured the Spirit of his grace.

LOOKING TO HIM IN FAITH

The fourth thing this passage shows is that *saving repentance results from saving faith in Jesus Christ,* as we find in verse 10: "When they will look on me, on him whom they have pierced, they shall mourn." *Looking to him* is a way of describing faith, as was said in Isaiah: "Turn to me and be saved, all you ends of the earth" (Isa. 45:22 NIV). Indeed, it is looking to the cross in

---

8. Octavius Winslow, "Christ's Finished Work," n.d.

9. J. C. Ryle, *Holiness: Its Nature, Hindrances, Difficulties, and Roots* (Durham, England: Evangelical Press, 1979), 6.

faith that unblocks the springs of true repentance; it is when we see the grace we have offended, and behold the horrors worked by our sin on the cross, that our hearts are broken in mourning.

We may sorrow for the consequences of our sin without mourning for sin itself and without looking to Christ in faith. A woman caught in sexual sin fears she is pregnant and is sorry for her immorality, but when the danger is passed she returns to her ways without a thought. A man is caught in a lie and mourns his deceitful tongue, but when another lie covers his tracks, his anguish is relieved. Mourning for getting caught in sin is a far cry from what our text describes; such sorrow neither changes us nor makes us right with God. Saving repentance is always joined to faith in Jesus Christ.

Jesus made this point in his discussion with Nicodemus, recorded in John 3. There, he linked two great *musts*. First, he said, "You must be born again" (John 3:7), referring to the outpouring of God's Spirit spoken of in Zechariah. But then Jesus added another *must*: "As Moses lifted up the serpent in the wilderness, so must the Son of Man be lifted up, that whoever believes in him may have eternal life" (John 3:14–15). This refers to the time of the exodus, when God punished Israel's unbelief by sending a plague of poisonous snakes, and those who were bitten began to die. Numbers 21:8–9 tells us: "The LORD said to Moses, 'Make a fiery serpent and set it on a pole, and everyone who is bitten, when he sees it, shall live.' So Moses made a bronze serpent and set it on a pole. And if a serpent bit anyone, he would look at the bronze serpent and live.'" Arthur Pink comments:

> There, summed up in a single word, is expressed the *need* of every descendant of Adam—to turn the eye away from the world, off from self, and to look by faith to the Saviour that died for sinners. There is the Divine epitome of the Way of Salvation. Deliverance from the wrath to come, forgiveness of sins, acceptance with God, is obtained not by deed of merit, not by good works, not by religious ordinances; No, salvation comes by Beholding—"Behold *the Lamb of God* which taketh away the sin of the world." Just as the serpent-bitten Israelites in the wilderness were healed by a look, by a look at that which Jehovah had appointed to be the object of their faith, so today, redemption from the guilt and power of sin, emancipation from the curse of the broken law and from the captivity of Satan, is to be found alone by faith in Christ.[10]

10. Arthur W. Pink, *The Seven Sayings of the Saviour on the Cross* (Grand Rapids: Baker, 1958), 60–61.

Faith looking to Jesus is the only kind of repentance that will save. You may beat your breast and tear your clothes, you may resolve to be a better person, but unless you look in faith to him who was pierced, you are not reconciled to God. The devil is delighted with a moral man who will not look to Jesus—who will not come to God in godly sorrow—because repentance without faith leads us away from and not toward the forgiving arms of our loving God.

There is no true mourning for sins that does not come from the cross. It is only there, where we see the testimony of God's redeeming love alongside the evidence of his terrible wrath, that any of us can be honest about ourselves. Looking everywhere else we hold to at least a shred of merit. Only the man or woman who looks with tears and sees a complete salvation as the gift of God through the offering of his Son, can finally remove the tawdry rags of self-vindication. Only at the cross are we instructed to sing as Christians:

> Not the labors of my hands
> can fulfill thy law's demands;
> Could my zeal no respite know,
> could my tears forever flow,
> All for sin could not atone;
> thou must save, and thou alone.[11]

If your heart can sing like that, it can only be because your faith has seen the cross of Christ, finding there a salvation that is of grace alone, that takes away your sin and that gives to you the righteousness of Christ.

"Every Eye Will See Him"

I mentioned that this text is referred to in the New Testament on more than one occasion. John mentions it in his account of Christ's death, and we see it come to pass in Peter's Pentecost sermon. But it also appears at the end of the Bible, in the first chapter of Revelation. There John writes of Christ's return in glory, and he speaks of every eye turned to him, every heart mourning at the return of him who was pierced: "Behold, he is coming with the

---

11. Augustus Toplady, "Rock of Ages," 1776.

clouds, and every eye will see him, even those who pierced him, and all tribes of the earth will wail on account of him. Even so. Amen" (Rev. 1:7).

This is a grave warning, and it tells us that while now only some will look upon Christ to be saved, the day will come when all will see him—every eye—and "all tribes of the earth will wail on account of him." Now Jesus presents himself to you as Savior, but then he will come as Judge. Now God grants the spirit of grace and supplication to all who look upon his Son, but then it will be a spirit of terror and despair when all will see his pierced Son returning in his wrath. Revelation 6:15–17 portrays the anguish of that dread day:

> Then the kings of the earth and the great ones and the generals and the rich and the powerful, and everyone, slave and free, hid themselves in the caves and among the rocks of the mountains, calling to the mountains and rocks, "Fall on us and hide us from the face of him who is seated on the throne, and from the wrath of the Lamb, for the great day of their wrath has come, and who can stand?"

Then they will be sorry for their sin; then they will mourn the pierced Christ, not unto salvation but unto destruction because of their unbelief. This is the legacy of sin in this world: all will sorrow for sin—some now in faith unto salvation, others then through unbelief unto eternal condemnation, in terror when the day of his wrath has come.

What will become of you then? Now Jesus speaks to you a word of his grace, calling for you to look to him, to mourn for the sins that he bore on the cross, and find in him salvation for your soul. As Jesus said, "Blessed are those who mourn, for they shall be comforted" (Matt. 5:4), and "blessed are you who weep now, for you shall laugh" (Luke 6:21).

The English poet John Donne captured the plea that rises to God from every heart in which his Spirit has been poured, and from every eye fixed in hope to the Savior on the cross. His words are a prayer for all who mourn for him they have pierced:

> Now thou art lifted up, draw me to thee,
> And at thy death giving such liberal dole,
> Moist, with one drop of thy blood, my dry soul.[12]

---

12. John Donne, "La Corona," from *The Complete English Poems* (New York: Knopf, 1985), 432.

24

A Fountain for Cleansing

Zechariah 13:1–6

On that day there shall be a fountain opened for the house of
David and the inhabitants of Jerusalem, to cleanse them from sin
and uncleanness. (Zech. 13:1)

hapter 13 of Zechariah follows without a break in thought from
chapter 12, so that we ought to think of their messages together.
This is true both chronologically and thematically. Chronologically, both chapters locate their events "on that day," that is, when God comes
to earth to reign and to save. Thematically, they also are closely linked. Chapter 12 ends with a promise of God's Spirit to produce deep mourning for
sin in light of the One who was pierced. Chapter 13 follows up with another
promise that perfectly answers the need of every mourning sinner: "On that
day there shall be a fountain opened for the house of David and the inhabitants of Jerusalem, to cleanse them from sin and uncleanness" (v. 1). John
Calvin says, "It was the Prophet's object to show, that the repentance of which
he had spoken would not be useless, for there would be . . . provided for them
a cleansing by the blood of his only-begotten Son, so that no filth might pre-
vent them to call on him boldly and in confidence."[1]

---

1. John Calvin, *Minor Prophets*, 5 vols. (Edinburgh: Banner of Truth, 1986), 5:377.

Why Are You Downcast, O My Soul?

When we talk about mourning, as we did in our last study, we need to realize how many people are oppressed with feelings of worthlessness, guilt, and impending doom. Martyn Lloyd-Jones wrote a valuable book on this subject titled *Spiritual Depression: Its Causes and Cure.* Spiritual depression is a phenomenon he encountered all through the Bible, especially in the Psalms, as well as in contemporary society. When it comes to Christians, Lloyd-Jones is especially concerned about spiritual depression, both because it robs believers of the joy that ought to be theirs and because a joyless Christian poorly commends the gospel to the world.

Lloyd-Jones gives a number of reasons why so many people have a mournful outlook on life. First, many people have gone through terrible experiences, whether from ravages of war or as a result of the increasingly inhuman effects of sin as it wreaks havoc in our families and society. Others are spiritually cast down because of some great sin of which they are constantly aware; their past lives of waste or wickedness or folly oppress them in the present. Others suffer from what Paul called in Romans 8:15 "the spirit of slavery," which Lloyd-Jones explains as the depression that arises from the sheer difficulty and humiliation and fatigue of constantly dealing with a sinful human nature. Additionally, some are downcast by looking at the threatening world around them the way Peter looked at the waves while walking on the waters and thus began to sink.

In studying spiritual depression, Lloyd-Jones took as his theme Psalm 42:5, which asks, "Why are you cast down, O my soul, and why are you in turmoil within me? Hope in God; for I shall again praise him, my salvation and my God." Here is a man whose whole countenance, his entire aspect, speaks of a broken spirit. Verse 3 sums up his life: "My tears have been my food day and night, while they say to me continually, 'Where is your God?'" This is a situation many understand from experience, the remedy to which seems most elusive. Lloyd-Jones sees the way out as illustrated by the dialogue of this Psalm, as the believer, as he puts it, "takes himself in hand . . . he talks to himself. This man turns to himself and says, 'Why art thou cast down, O my soul, why art thou disquieted within me?'" Lloyd-Jones summarizes his position:

I suggest that the main trouble in this whole matter of spiritual depression in a sense is this, that we allow our self to talk to us instead of talking to our self. . . . Have you realized that most of your unhappiness in life is due to the fact that you are listening to yourself instead of talking to yourself? . . . You have to take yourself in hand, you have to address yourself, preach to yourself, question yourself. You must say to your soul: "Why art thou cast down"—what business have you to be disquieted? You must turn on yourself, upbraid yourself, condemn yourself, exhort yourself, and say to yourself: "Hope in God"—instead of muttering in this depressed, unhappy way. And then you must go on to remind yourself of God, Who God is, and what God is and what God has done, and what God has pledged to do. Then having done that, end on this great note: defy yourself, and defy other people, and defy the devil and the whole world, and say with [the writer of this psalm]: "I shall yet praise Him for the help of His countenance, who is also the health of my countenance and my God."[2]

A FOUNTAIN FOR CLEANSING

If Lloyd-Jones is right, if the key to overcoming depression is to stop listening to our downcast spirit and start preaching to it instead, then we need a great message to proclaim. This is what Zechariah 13:1 is all about, a promise that God will open a fountain to cleanse us from all sin and impurity. Chapter 12 ended with a promise that God's Spirit would enable sinners to mourn; chapter 13 begins with an accompanying promise of light for darkened souls, and comfort for those who sorrow over sin.

The idea of a fountain for cleansing is not new to Zechariah. In the Levitical code of Israel's priesthood, various cleansings were prescribed dealing with the removal of sin, usually through the sprinkled blood of a sacrifice. To these were added washings of water to make one ritually clean for service to God. An example took place on the day of atonement, when the high priest first offered the blood of an animal sacrifice, and then cleansed himself with water before going forward (Lev. 16:4–5). Since Zechariah was himself a priest, these cleansings could not have been far from his mind.

We have seen, as well, that Zechariah was extremely conversant with the writings of earlier prophets, and there we also find the idea of cleansing. Ezekiel 36:25 especially employs this theme: "I will sprinkle clean water on

2. D. Martyn Lloyd-Jones, *Spiritual Depression* (Grand Rapids: Eerdmans, 1965), 20–21.

you, and you shall be clean from all your uncleannesses, and from all your idols I will cleanse you." Zechariah foresees a whole fountain of such cleansing fluid opening up, not just a sprinkling but an abounding, flooding provision of grace, as the remedy for the great sorrow of those who look on the One whom they pierced. The idea is that of a pent-up spring now let loose, so that waters long confined may now gush forth in abundance.

This is a remarkable promise, because from this fountain comes a cleansing for "sin and uncleanness." It is therefore a particularly apt depiction of Jesus Christ's cleansing blood, shed upon the cross. This cleansing, the prophet says, will be made available to the house of David and the inhabitants of Jerusalem. Given the earlier statement that God's Spirit will make us mourn for the pierced one (Zech. 12:10), it is clearly the blood of the Messiah that comes forth to cleanse.

This idea finds clear expression in the gospel of John. John's account of Jesus' death is remarkably brief, covering John 19:28–30. The evangelist gives more focus to what happened immediately after Jesus' death; this account is twice as long, running from verses 31 to 36. In our last study we saw that John considered the prophecy of Zechariah 12:10, the piercing of the Messiah, to have been fulfilled when the Roman soldier pierced Jesus' side with a spear. But John evidently had Zechariah's accompanying promise in mind as well, that a fountain was opened, because he adds that the piercing brought forth from Jesus "a sudden flow of blood and water" (John 19:34). James Montgomery Boice puts this together:

When [John] saw the surprising issue of blood and water from the side of Christ, he must have remembered . . . that in the Old Testament sacrificial system, blood was the appointed means of cleansing sin, and that in the temple ceremonies, water was used for ceremonial purification from uncleanness. Moreover, he would have known that the passage he was quoting from Zechariah (Zech. 12:10, "They will look on . . . the one they have pierced") is followed four verses later by the text . . . "On that day a fountain will be opened to the house of David and the inhabitants of Jerusalem, to cleanse them from sin and impurity" (13:1). Seeing the flow of blood and water and putting these two bits of information together, John must have concluded that deliverance from sin's penalty and cleansing from its defilement are to be found in the death of Jesus only.[3]

3. James Montgomery Boice, *The Minor Prophets*, 2 vols. (Grand Rapids: Zondervan, 1986), 2:215.

We see, therefore, that the New Testament conceives of the saving effects of Jesus' blood in terms of the Old Testament sacrifices and cleansings. At the same time, however, this verse speaks of something new: it is a fountain that now—"on that day"—is suddenly opened. The writer of Hebrews dwells on the new and better nature of Christ's sacrifice in his ninth and tenth chapters, pointing out the outward and temporary nature of the old sacrifices compared to the inward and permanent effects of Christ's cleansing blood. In Hebrews 9:13–14 he writes, "For if the sprinkling of defiled persons with the blood of goats and bulls and with the ashes of a heifer sanctifies for the purification of the flesh, how much more will the blood of Christ, who through the eternal Spirit offered himself without blemish to God, purify our conscience from dead works to serve the living God." Just as Jesus' suffering was spiritual, so also is his cleansing of an inward and spiritual nature, cleansing not the body but the heart, and thereby giving peace to the weary soul.

The writer of Hebrews emphasizes that the Old Testament sacrifices, which had to be constantly repeated, really served to show forth the need for a new and effective sacrifice. Hebrews 10:3–4 says, "In these sacrifices there is a reminder of sin every year. For it is impossible for the blood of bulls and goats to take away sins." But Christ's saving blood points us to forgiveness, to the permanent removal of our sin; being effectual to cleanse, his blood was shed once for all. Hebrews 10:10–14 sums up the transforming blessing of the precious blood of Christ: "We have been sanctified through the offering of the body of Jesus Christ once for all. . . . By a single offering he has perfected for all time those who are being sanctified."

This cleansing was offered in Jerusalem when Peter preached the Pentecost sermon, when through God's Spirit so many looked to Christ and mourned. By faith in Christ, his fountain of cleansing blood was opened up for them, as Isaiah had foretold: "Though your sins are like scarlet, they shall be as white as snow; though they are red as crimson, they shall become like wool" (Isa. 1:18). If this is how God responded to those who rejected and crucified his only Son, by opening for them a fountain for cleansing by his death, how will he not do the same for you, who have also hated him and by unbelief have crucified his Son? Now, as then, is the day of salvation, and through faith in Christ you too may come, as the hymn explains:

I lay my sins on Jesus,
    the spotless Lamb of God;
he bears them all, and frees us
    from the accursed load:
I bring my guilt to Jesus,
    to wash my crimson stains
white in his blood most precious,
    till not a spot remains.[4]

CLEANSING BY THE BLOOD

When we have considered the topic of sin in Zechariah, we have noted the twofold sense of sin, involving its guilt and its power. The fountain that flows from Jesus cleanses both, his blood simultaneously *propitiating* God's wrath and *expiating* our sin. Zechariah 13:1 tells us that this is our problem, sin that must be propitiated and defilement that must be expiated.

To *propitiate* is to offer a sacrifice to turn aside someone's anger. In this case, it is the wrath of God against our sin that is propitiated by the blood of Christ. John Stott writes, "The wrath of God . . . is his steady, unrelenting, unremitting, uncompromising antagonism to evil in all its forms and manifestations."[5] God's wrath arises from his holy character; being holy, he must hate sin. We see, then, why we desperately need a propitiation to avert God's wrath from us, since our sin is such an offense to his holiness.

What this verse tells us is that God himself provides the sacrifice to accomplish this propitiation. Because God loved us, he sent his only Son to die in our place so that his holy justice might be satisfied in Christ's blood. God's wrath is propitiated by a sacrifice. To trust in Christ, then, is to know that God's anger has been turned from you to the cross and, henceforth, you may look to God without fear of judgment.

The fountain flowing with Jesus' blood also works *expiation*, which speaks of the removal of our sin. If God's wrath is the object of propitiation, sin's defilement is the object of expiation. This is what Zechariah 3 so vividly presented in the vision of the high priest standing in filthy rags before the angel of the Lord. Verse 4 of chapter 3 provides a classic statement of sin removed: "The

4. Horatius Bonar, "I Lay My Sins on Jesus," 1843.
5. John R. W. Stott, *The Cross of Christ* (Downers Grove, IL: InterVarsity, 1986), 173.

angel said to those who were standing before him, 'Remove the filthy garments from him.' And to him he said, 'Behold, I have taken your iniquity away from you, and I will clothe you with pure vestments.'" Calvin explains the expiating work of Christ's blood, writing, "The sacrifice of expiation is that which is intended . . . to wash sins and cleanse them that the sinner, purged of their filth and restored to the purity of righteousness, may return into favor with God."[6]

This is what we have in the cleansing blood of Christ—propitiation toward God so that his wrath against sin is satisfied, and expiation toward us so that sin's defilement is removed.

What a difference this makes to the mournful soul! Here is a message for us to preach to our forlorn hearts, that God has opened a fountain to cleanse us from the penalty and defilement of our sin. Here is good news for those cast down by a sense of guilt and unworthiness—a fountain flowing forth from the wounds of Jesus Christ. John wrote about this in his first epistle, saying, "This is how we set our hearts at rest in his presence whenever our hearts condemn us. For God is greater than our hearts, and he knows everything" (1 John 3:19–20 NIV). When our downcast souls speak to us of misery and dread, this is God's own testimony that is greater, the testimony of a Savior who died in our place to reconcile us to God's love. In 1 John 1:9 we read, "If we confess our sins, he is faithful and just to forgive us our sins and to cleanse us from all unrighteousness."

This is wonderfully dramatized in John Bunyan's *Pilgrim's Progress*. The pilgrim, named Christian, had fled the coming wrath of God, seeking safety in the Celestial City. But his progress was hindered by a burden on his back, representing the weight of sin upon our souls. On the way he was met by Mr. Worldly Wiseman, who gave him worldly counsel on the removal of this burden of guilt, advising Christian to indulge himself in worldly comforts, adding a strong dose of morality, so that he could simply forget the burden. Christian found, however, that neither the pleasures of the world nor the pursuit of moral virtue removed the burden of this guilt of sin. On he journeyed, wearied by his load. Finally, Bunyan writes,

He ran until he came to a peak where a cross stood; a little below, in the bottom was a tomb. When Christian reached the cross, his burden became loose, fell

6. John Calvin, *Institutes of the Christian Religion*, ed. John T. McNeill (Philadelphia: Westminster, 1960), III.xiv.13.

from his back, and tumbled into the tomb. I never saw the burden again. . . . As he stood looking and weeping, three Shining Ones approached and greeted him. "Peace," the first said, "Your sins are forgiven." The second removed his filthy rags and dressed him in rich clothing. The third put a mark on his forehead and gave him a sealed roll. He told Christian . . . to leave it at the celestial gate [to enter the Celestial City].[7]

Christ's cleansing fountain is given to speak peace and joy to mournful hearts. But we must believe this good news to have our burden relieved. Lloyd-Jones comments, "If you do not believe that word, and if you go on dwelling on your sin, I say that you are not accepting the Word of God, you are not taking God at His word, you do not believe what He tells you and that is your real sin."[8]

It is unwillingness to believe God that is the real source of our misery, just as trusting his gospel is the cause of true and lasting joy. It is for the sinner, cleansed by the blood of God's only Son and calling clean what God has made clean, that these words were written:

Jesus, thy blood and righteousness
my beauty are, my glorious dress;
'midst flaming worlds in these arrayed,
with joy shall I lift up my head.

Bold shall I stand in thy great day;
for who aught to my charge shall lay?
Fully absolved through these I am
from sin and fear, from guilt and shame.[9]

WASHED WHITER THAN SNOW

Verses 2–6 show the purification of the land and the people as a result of this cleansing from sin. Sin affects us through its guilt, but also through its power over our lives, and the impurity it works in our hearts. For this the fountain provides cleansing water to purify our hearts for new obedience

---

7. John Bunyan, *Pilgrim's Progress* (Nashville: Thomas Nelson, 1999), 35–36.
8. Lloyd-Jones, *Spiritual Depression*, 72–73.
9. Nikolaus Ludwig von Zinzendorf, "Jesus, Thy Blood and Righteousness," 1739.

and eternal life. Just as John reports that blood and water flowed from Christ's body on the cross (John 19:34), so also do redeeming blood and cleansing water flow from the fountain prophesied by Zechariah 13:1.

It is Ezekiel's prophecy of cleansing and the provision of a clean heart for obedience that Zechariah especially has in mind. Like water cleansing the body, so will the Spirit come to cleanse and renew the inner man, granting power for a new and pure relationship with God:

> I will sprinkle clean water on you, and you shall be clean from all your unclean-nesses, and from all your idols I will cleanse you. And I will give you a new heart, and a new spirit I will put within you. And I will remove the heart of stone from your flesh and give you a heart of flesh. And I will put my Spirit within you, and cause you to walk in my statutes and be careful to obey my rules. You shall dwell in the land that I gave to your fathers, and you shall be my people, and I will be your God. And I will deliver you from all your uncleannesses. And I will summon the grain and make it abundant and lay no famine upon you. (Ezek. 36:25–29)

God always saves us from both the guilt and the power of sin, so we can never be forgiven without being called to a new life of obedience. Verses 2–6 portray this situation, emphasizing repentance from idolatry and the rejection of false prophets. These two evils were the twin banes of Israel's existence before the Babylonian captivity. Now, in the age of restoration, their rejection is especially indicated as a sign of God's cleansing grace.

Verse 2 speaks of idolatry: "And on that day, declares the LORD of hosts, I will cut off the names of the idols from the land, so that they shall be remembered no more." This is a statement of total rejection—the names of the idols cast from the land and from the people's minds. This is truly a sign of God's indwelling and cleansing power, now as much as in the time of Israel. An idol is anything we put in God's place, whether another religious object or things such as our possessions, our jobs, our popularity, our wealth, our leisure—anything that we serve and cherish so that it stands between us and God, between his Word and our readiness to obey, or between his love and our grateful response. In the cleansing fountain of the cross of Christ, our hearts are renewed so that idols are removed and we are drawn to worship

God in spirit and in truth (see John 4:23). Ultimately, as the progressive work of Christian sanctification goes forward, the very names of our idols will be removed and they will not even be remembered anymore.

Verses 2–6 tell of the removal of false prophets, those who spoke in the name of the Lord but led the people into unbelief and sin. False prophecy was always the handmaiden to idolatry, and wherever idolatry was found, so too were the false prophets. Now, as a result of this cleansing fountain, the land will be thoroughly relieved of their presence and "the spirit of uncleanness" that went with them. Verse 2 concludes: "And also I will remove from the land the prophets and the spirit of uncleanness."

Verse 3 depicts a remarkable devotion to the Lord and rejection of the false prophets. According to Deuteronomy 13:6–10, it was the duty of all God's people to oppose false prophets even if they were the closest of family members. So fervent was the rejection of false prophets that the first hand to strike against them was to be that of a father or mother or brother or sister. In verse 3 we read, "And if anyone again prophesies, his father and mother who bore him will say to him, 'You shall not live, for you speak lies in the name of the LORD.' And his father and mother who bore him shall pierce him through when he prophesies." The devotion of those cleansed of sin and impurity will be so intense that love for God and zeal for his Word will overwhelm even the strongest of natural affections. We are reminded by this of the words of Jesus: "Whoever loves father or mother more than me is not worthy of me, and whoever loves son or daughter more than me is not worthy of me. And whoever does not take his cross and follow me is not worthy of me" (Matt. 10:37–38).

Given that kind of fervor, verses 4–6 envision a situation where those who falsely spoke in God's name are now unwilling to be known as prophets anymore: "On that day every prophet will be ashamed of his vision when he prophesies. He will not put on a hairy cloak in order to deceive, but he will say, 'I am no prophet, I am a worker of the soil, for a man sold me in my youth.' And if one asks him, 'What are these wounds on your back?' he will say, 'The wounds I received in the house of my friends.' " These wounds refer to the scars received in ecstatic pagan rites involving self-mutilation. Many commentators think "the house of my friends" refers to a house of sexual and drunken sin, so that the false prophet is more ready to be exposed as a licentious drunk than to be known as one who spoke falsely in the name of the Lord.

Let us not think this has nothing to say to us, as if our time lacks false prophets. A false prophet is anyone who claims to speak with spiritual authority, but then speaks contrary to the Word of God. Such prophets proclaim matters of faith and practice that come from fleshly wisdom and worldly philosophy rather than from God's own revelation in the Bible. Paul warned of this in Colossians 2:8: "See to it that no one takes you captive by philosophy and empty deceit, according to human tradition, according to the elemental spirits of the world, and not according to Christ." In our time, these false prophets include liberal theologians who deny the Bible, heretical teachers who contort the Bible to give a message of worldly prosperity, and church-growth consultants who promise success to all who imbibe from their supposedly foolproof but unbiblical agendas.

According to Zechariah, a sure mark of one cleansed and renewed by the fountain of Christ is that he or she craves the Word of God, rejecting any message not grounded in the authority of God's own truth. The truly spiritual man or woman is like the Bereans of Acts 17, who made Paul prove that what he taught was from Scripture. Of them it was said, "Now these Jews were more noble than those in Thessalonica; they received the word with all eagerness, examining the Scriptures daily to see if these things were so" (Acts 17:11). Perhaps our greatest need in the church today is Christians like that, who can say with David in Psalm 119, "Your word is a lamp to my feet and a light to my path.... I incline my heart to perform your statutes forever, to the end" (vv. 105, 112).

A Fountain Filled with Blood

The name probably best associated with Zechariah 13:1–6 is that of William Cowper, one of England's greatest poets. By all accounts Cowper possessed a sensitive, even fragile, disposition, and his mother's death when he was six years old left him mentally unstable. Frequently battling depression, he sought to protect himself by staying busy and keeping his mind diverted. A crisis came, however, when both his father and stepmother died, and then his closest friend was drowned. The result was a mental and emotional collapse, so that Cowper ended up in an insane asylum. At length, he was entrusted to the care of a Christian man, and it was during that time that Cowper came to grasp the meaning of the gospel and the knowledge that Christ had died for him. He explains: "Immediately I received strength to believe it and the full beams of the Sun of Righteousness shone upon me. I saw the sufficiency of the atonement He had made, my pardon was sealed in His blood. . . . I could only look up to heaven in silent fear, overwhelmed with love and wonder."[10]

Before long Cowper was able to leave the asylum, his heart having been cleansed by the fountain of Christ's blood. Throughout his life his mental struggles would continue and he even attempted suicide at various times, yet it was this gospel that led him through a difficult life with light piercing the darkness of his soul. Many of Cowper's hymns remain popular still, with titles like "God Moves in a Mysterious Way" and "O for a Closer Walk with God." But the hymn for which Cowper is best known comes from Zechariah 13:1, titled, "There Is a Fountain Filled with Blood." There, he gave this testimony to the cleansing grace of Christ, recording his own experience and that of countless others of a burdened heart that was set free "on that day" when the blood of Christ was shed for our sins:

> There is a fountain filled with blood,
>   drawn from Immanuel's veins;
> and sinners, plunged beneath that flood,
>   lose all their guilty stains.
>
> The dying thief rejoiced to see
>   that fountain in his day;
> And there have I, as vile as he,
>   washed all my sins away.
>
> E'er since by faith I saw the stream
>   your flowing wounds supply,
> redeeming love has been my theme,
>   and shall be till I die.
>
> Dear dying Lamb, your precious blood
>   shall never lose its pow'r,
> till all the ransomed church of God
>   be saved to sin no more.

10. Cited from Elsie Houghton, *Christian Hymn-Writers* (Evangelical Press of Wales, 1982), 149.

25

THE SHEPHERD STRUCK

Zechariah 13:7–9

"Awake, O sword, against my shepherd, against the man who stands next to me!" declares the LORD of hosts. "Strike the shepherd, and the sheep will be scattered; I will turn my hand against the little ones. (Zech. 13:7)

In 415 BC, the Athenian general and statesman Alcibiades was commanding his nation's armed forces in their attack against the Sicilian city of Syracuse. Alcibiades was the most brilliant leader of his age, but was regarded by many as a self-serving rogue. In keeping with the standards of Athenian democracy in that time, as soon as Alcibiades set sail his political enemies arranged for him to be tried in absentia, convicted for treason and impiety, and sentenced to death. He received news of this on the deck of his flagship, and instead of returning to Athens to face the verdict, he fled to Sparta, Athens' chief rival. There he provided crucial leadership to the enemy coalition, and this episode was one of several calamities that led to Athens' defeat in the 27-year-long Peloponnesian War. It was a classic instance of a principle Jesus once declared, "A house divided against itself will fall" (Luke 11:17 NIV).

AWAKE, O SWORD!

Zechariah seems to depict a similar kind of situation, only here it is God's own house that is divided. Here we find God warring against his own fellow, a civil war within the very Godhead! This is a very dramatic passage, coming as it does on the heels of some of the greatest promises of the Old Testament. In chapter 11 we saw the true shepherd rejected by the people, but in chapter 12, God said that in the day to come they will look on him and mourn for the one they pierced. Chapter 13 began by predicting that this will open up a fountain for cleansing from sin and impurity. Here are the gospel events prophesied in bold relief!

Now, in response, we have in verses 7–9 an exclamation that bursts from the lips of the Lord himself. It is a theological reflection on what has been presented, and sums up the gospel mystery in three brief verses. The sword of God's justice is awakened and raised, but, as one writer asks, "Upon whom shall it fall? Not upon the wicked and the ungodly, but, mystery of mysteries! upon Him who is not only absolutely innocent and holy, but who stands in the nearest and closest relationship to Jehovah."[1]

It is no surprise to the reader of Zechariah that a sword is drawn against God's true shepherd. But what is so astonishing here is that God himself is heard calling it forth! " 'Awake, O sword, against my shepherd, against the man who stands next to me,' declares the LORD of hosts. 'Strike the shepherd,' " God commands (Zech. 13:7). Far from reluctance or remorse at what we know to be a terrible event, God shows his eagerness for this day to come, this thing to take place, this sword to strike his own Shepherd.

There is little ambiguity in the text regarding the identity of this shepherd. The Hebrew word *amiyti* means "neighbor" or "fellow" and has the connotation of "peer." Old Testament scholar C. F. Keil therefore writes, "He whom God calls His neighbor cannot be a mere man, but can only be one who participates in the divine nature, or is essentially divine."[2] Typologically, this might be thought to refer to Zechariah, as God called

1. David Baron, *The Visions and Prophecies of Zechariah* (Grand Rapids: Kregel, 1972), 475.
2. C. F. Keil and F. Delitzsch, *Commentary on the Old Testament*, 10 vols. (Peabody, MA: Hendrickson, reprint, 1996), 10:617.

him to stand in the place of the false shepherds over Jerusalem. But the language actually used calls for a fulfillment Zechariah himself could not realize, a mystery in which a man is a fellow or peer with the eternal God.

The New Testament explains this by means of the incarnation, God becoming flesh in the person of his Son, Jesus Christ. Indeed, it is from Jesus' own lips that we learn that this spoke directly of him. In Matthew 26:31, Jesus quoted this very verse to predict that his disciples would fall away when he was arrested: "This very night you will all fall away on account of me, for it is written: 'I will strike the shepherd, and the sheep of the flock will be scattered'" (NIV).

This being the case, it might appear that this shows a division within the very Godhead, the house of God divided against itself. "Awake, O sword," cries the Father, pointing to the Son, "against my shepherd, against the man who stands next to me" (Zech. 13:7). This conveys the impression of a heavenly civil war, one that could only undo the purposes of God, just as destruction was brought to Athens.

In fact, the opposite is the outcome of this apparent division: it served to establish rather than to undo God's purpose. This verse shows what the New Testament declares: it was God's will that Christ be slain so that we might be cleansed of our sin. It was for this that Jesus came into the world, in obedience to what theologians call the "covenant of redemption" between the Father and the Son, also known as the "eternal council" by which they arranged our salvation.

Evidence abounds in the Old and New Testaments that Jesus Christ came into this world with a work to do that was agreed upon in advance. Indeed, the picture we have is that God the Father laid upon the Son a charge that he voluntarily accepted, along with promises that would be bestowed upon its success. Thus Jesus prayed shortly before his arrest, "Father . . . I glorified you on earth, having accomplished the work that you gave me to do" (John 17:4). According to the classic view of this covenant of redemption, Christ accepted the following conditions: 1) that he should take up human flesh, being born of a woman and under the law; 2) that he should fulfill the whole law of God on behalf of his elect, achieving for them a full righteousness where Adam had failed; and 3) that he should receive in their place the punishment his people had deserved by their sins. In return, God promised him the salvation of all the elect as his brothers adopted through him, as well as dominion over all things.[3]

Hebrews 10:5–7 refers to Christ's obedience, placing the words of Psalm 40 into Jesus' mouth: "Sacrifices and offerings you have not desired, but a body have you prepared for me. . . . Then I said, 'Behold, I have come to do your will, O God, as it is written of me in the scroll of the book.' " In response, God the Father promised a great salvation through his Son's obedience: "I will also make you a light for the Gentiles, that you may bring my salvation to the ends of the earth . . . to say to the captives, 'Come out,' and to those in darkness, 'Be free!' " (Isa. 49:6–9 NIV). Isaiah also says of the faithful Servant of the Lord, whom Matthew 8:17 identifies as Jesus Christ:

> It was the will of the LORD to crush him; he has put him to grief; when his soul makes an offering for sin, he shall see his offspring; he shall prolong his days; the will of the LORD shall prosper in his hand. Out of the anguish of his soul he shall see and be satisfied; by his knowledge shall the righteous one, my servant, make many to be accounted righteous, and he shall bear their iniquities. (Isa. 53:10–11)

R. L. Dabney reminds us that this is not a contingent covenant between two fallible parties, as if either party doubted the fulfillment of the other. "But," he writes, "it has always been certain from eternity, that the conditions would be performed; and the consequent reward bestowed, because there has always been an ineffable and perfect accord in the persons of the Trinity."[4] Dabney asks, "What motive prompted them to this [arrangement] of amazing love and mercy?" and then replies, "The only consistent answer is their own will, moved by their own intrinsic benevolence, compassion and other attributes."[5]

This is the covenant between Father and Son that stands behind the gospel declared in the pages of the New Testament. It was God the Father who, for love of sinners, sent God the Son on a mission that found fulfillment on the

3. See A. A. Hodge, *The Confession of Faith* (Carlisle, PA: Banner of Truth, 1958), 127; and Herman Witsius, *The Economy of the Covenants between God & Man*, 2 vols. (Phillipsburg, NJ: Presbyterian & Reformed, 1990), 1:171.

4. Robert L. Dabney, *Systematic Theology* (Edinburgh: Banner of Truth, 1985), 431.

5. Ibid., 435.

cross, where the judicial sword of God's own wrath struck him as foretold by the prophet: "Awake, O sword, against my shepherd, against the man who stands next to me" (Zech. 13:7).

This proves that Jesus' death is sure of achieving its promised end, and that God will certainly accept his sacrifice for our reconciliation. It was to this end that the Father sent the Son with a work to be done. God is not reluctant in our salvation; the holy Judge of all the universe is not forced to accept us against his wishes. Rather, in the way most costly to himself, he removed the barrier between us and him.

This cost also shows the enormity of the horror and problem of sin, which we take so lightly. T. V. Moore writes:

> There is in the whole compass of human knowledge, nothing more awfully sublime, than this seeming schism in the Godhead. It is as if sin was so dreadful an evil, that the assumption of its guilt by a sinless Mediator must for a time make a division even in the absolute unity of the Godhead itself. It is the most awful illustration of the repulsive and separating power of sin, that the history of the universe affords.[6]

Yet in foreseeing the putting away of sin and the salvation he would make, the Father's heart leaps with anticipation: "Awake, sword," he cries. "Strike the shepherd," he commands, to effect his work of greatest marvel, the righteous justification of sinners he has loved through the death of his Son Jesus on the cross.

My Shepherd, My Kinsman

Verse 7 sheds a great deal of light on the person and work of Jesus, which itself is the focus of the whole Bible. Zechariah 13:7 describes him as "the man who stands next to me," a mystery unraveled only by the incarnation. But why was this necessary? Why did God the Son have to be born in a manger, take up our humanity, and in that manner become our Savior? One answer, given by the book of Hebrews, is that God the Son joined himself to us in the flesh so that he might join us to himself in the spirit, with the result of our adoption in him as children of God: "he who sanctifies and those who

6. T. V. Moore: *Haggai, Zechariah, & Malachi* (Edinburgh: Banner of Truth, 1979), 292–93.

are sanctified all have one origin. That is why he is not ashamed to call them brothers, saying, . . . 'Behold, I and the children God has given me' " (Heb. 2:11–13).

The second reason that Jesus was both God and man, as foretold in Zechariah 13:7, is so that he might pay the penalty of our sins and do so without himself being overcome by that penalty, namely, death. Hebrews 2:14–17 says:

> Since therefore the children share in flesh and blood, he himself likewise partook of the same things, that through death he might destroy the one who has the power of death, that is, the devil, and deliver all those who through fear of death were subject to lifelong slavery. . . . He had to be made like his brothers in every respect, so that he might become a merciful and faithful high priest in the service of God, to make propitiation for the sins of the people.

The classic theological statement regarding the necessity of Christ's incarnation was given by Anselm of Canterbury in the eleventh century, in his book *Why God Became Man*. Speaking of Christ's atoning death, Anselm wrote:

> It could not have been done unless man paid what was owing to God for sin. But the debt was so great that, while man alone owed it, only God could pay it, so that the same person must be both man and God. Thus it was necessary for God to take manhood into the unity of his person, so that he who in his own nature ought to pay and could not should be in a person who could.[7]

As man, Christ paid to God the debt of men; as God, he had the means with which to pay it. Thus we see that the One who was struck needed to be both man and God, as verse 7 indicates: "the man who stands next to me." Indeed, only one who possessed such qualifications could represent God as this shepherd over his people. Jesus made it clear that this prophecy refers to himself in his famous Good Shepherd discourse, which makes direct application of

---

7. Anselm of Canterbury, *Why God Became Man*, in Eugene R. Fairweather, *A Scholastic Miscellany: Anselm to Ockham* (Philadelphia: Westminster Press, 1961), 176.

the shepherd prophecy of Zechariah: "I am the good shepherd. I know my own and my own know me, just as the Father knows me and I know the Father; and I lay down my life for the sheep. . . . I lay down my life that I may take it up again. No one takes it from me, but I lay it down of my own accord. I have authority to lay it down, and I have authority to take it up again. This charge I have received from my Father" (John 10:14–18).

Finally, Zechariah 13:7 shows that Jesus' death was judicial in character. T. V. Moore writes:

> The sword is the symbol of judicial power. . . . Hence the great doctrine here set forth is, that the death of Christ was a judicial act, in which he endured the penalty of that law whose penal power was symbolized by this sword of divine wrath. The sheep had deserved the blow, but the shepherd bares his own bosom to the sword, and is wounded for the sins of his people, and bears those sins in his own body on the tree. The vicarious nature of the atonement is therefore distinctly involved in this passage.[8]

"Awake, O sword, against my shepherd, against the man who stands next to me" (Zech. 13:7). This is how God looked forward to the redeeming act made possible by the incarnation of Christ, when he applied his justice against the only one who could bear it, as agreed in the eternal counsel of their love. We look back in a wonder of praise perhaps best set forth in the hymn by Charles Wesley: " 'Tis myst'ry all! Th'Immortal dies: who can explore his strange design? . . . 'Tis mercy all! Let earth adore, let angel minds inquire no more. Amazing love! How can it be? That thou, my God, shouldst die for me?"[9]

THE SHEEP SCATTERED

Jesus applied Zechariah's prophecy to himself, but the point he was making had as much to do with his disciples. They had gone out to the Mount of Olives, having just received in the upper room the first communion supper signifying his death for them. "Then Jesus said to them, 'You will all fall away because of me this night. For it is written, 'I will strike the shepherd,

---

8. Moore, *Zechariah*, 294.
9. Charles Wesley, "And Can It Be That I Should Gain," 1738.

and the sheep of the flock will be scattered'" (Matt. 26:31). In the case of the disciples, this meant that they would go into hiding to save their own lives, Simon Peter even denying him in the process.

It seems from our passage that this principle also applies to the Jewish people, who would be terribly affected by their rejection of the true shepherd: "Strike the shepherd, and the sheep will be scattered; I will turn my hand against the little ones. In the whole land, declares the LORD, two thirds shall be cut off and perish, and one third shall be left alive" (Zech. 13:7–8).

As we have seen before, this prophecy seems to have been fulfilled in the aftermath of the Jews' rejection of Jesus. Verse 8 does not give a numerical percentage of those destroyed, but says, literally, that "two portions" will be struck down. In the Roman destruction of Jerusalem in AD 70, and its aftermath, it is probable that at least two-thirds of the Jews living in Palestine did perish. Since then, the Jews have been scattered and have experienced the most intense purges and persecutions, in keeping with Zechariah's prophecy.

If this prophetic word does apply to the ethnic Jews, the point is not just that they would be scattered and scourged for rejecting the Messiah, but also that God would preserve a remnant that ultimately would return to him in faith: "They will call upon my name, and I will answer them" (Zech. 13:9). God reaches out his hand once again to shepherd them in their need. In any case, it is clear that a sizable remnant will remain; God is not yet done with his people Israel.

The apostle Paul teaches in Romans 11 about the eventual coming of the Jews to faith in Christ: "All Israel will be saved. . . . As regards the gospel, they are enemies of God for your sake. But as regards election, they are beloved for the sake of their forefathers. For the gifts and the calling of God are irrevocable" (Rom. 11:26–29). Some regard this as being fulfilled in the ongoing witness of the church to the Jews, as to others, and that may well be true. But I think Paul's prophecy more reasonably speaks of a general repentance as seen in Zechariah 12:10 and again in 13:9, so that a widespread return of the Jews resounds to the glory of God.

A number of years ago I was an assistant professor at the United States Military Academy at West Point. The corps of cadets regularly put on parades, and large crowds of tourists often came to watch. In particular, it was not unusual for a large number of buses to pull up, disgorging masses of Hasidic Jews from nearby New York City. *Hesed* is the Hebrew word for "faithful," and these Hasidic Jews are devoted to make every attempt to put the Old Testament codes into practice. This includes the food restrictions, the clothing they wear, the unshaven locks of all the men's hair, and abstention from forms of entertainment that are popular with others today.

Often I stood in awe gazing upon hundreds of these Jews—men and women and children, living specimens of the past. I marveled with praise to God to see them, reflecting that there is no place where you can find a Babylonian from old, or an ancient Egyptian, or a Philistine or an Amorite or a Hittite—yet there before my eyes were multitudes of the very people God had promised to preserve, the little and weak and oft-persecuted people, the Jews. "What did God have in store for them? Why are they still here? For what great thing are they being preserved?" I asked. Surely the answer is the one given here, that God might gather them back, that he might turn his hand toward them in their weakness and bring them back to his heart.

King Frederick the Great once accosted his court chaplain, demanding that he give plain proof of the Bible. "I can prove the Bible in a single word," the chaplain calmly replied. To Frederick's astonished doubt, he then explained, "That word is this: Israel." His point was that the Jews' presence in this world is a living proof of the Bible and its prophecy. Verse 9 tells us that God will bring them into and through the fire, refining them and removing by trials the dross of their unbelief, until the day will come that they will call on his name and he will answer: "I will say, 'They are my people,' and they will say, 'The LORD is my God' " (Zech. 13:9). According to Paul, God's unbounding patience and faithfulness to the word he swore to their fathers, resulting in the eventual widespread salvation of the Jews, teach us to trust his promise for our own salvation. Suggests one Jewish writer:

> Is it only the Jew who is incapable of seeing and hearing all that others see and hear? Are the Jews stricken with blindness and deafness as regards Messiah Jesus, so that to them alone he has nothing to say? . . . Understand, then, what we shall do: We shall bring him back to us. Messiah Jesus is not dead for us—for us he has not yet lived: and he will not slay us, he will make us alive again. His profound and holy words, and all that is true and heart-appealing in the New Testament, must from now on be heard in our synagogues and taught to our children, in order that the wrong we had

committed may be made good, the curse turned into a blessing, and that he at last may find us who has always been seeking after us.[10]

This was written by a Jew who had not yet trusted Jesus as his own Savior from sin, and it does not say that the Jews are on the verge of turning to Christ. But it does show that there are some Jews who are reading and listening, and Lord willing, the day will soon come when many of God's ancient people will be his people of faith again.

A LOVE WORTH SEEKING

In the shadow of the cross, it was to his own disciples that Jesus applied these verses. Having told them they would be scattered after his arrest, Jesus added, "But after I have risen, I will go ahead of you into Galilee." Even as his own were scattered, the Good Shepherd would go out to find and lead them. Ultimately, their scattering served to spread the gospel all through the world.

Verse 9 tells us three things about God's dealings with his people that are applicable to us. First, starting at the end, we see that God is interested not just in quantity but in quality. The goal of this costly saving work is nothing less than true fellowship with our hearts: "They will call upon my name, and I will answer them. I will say, 'They are my people'; and they will say, 'The LORD is my God' " (v. 9). This is the ancient formula of covenant union, the marriage vow of the loving God and the bride he has won. Costly as it was to overcome the barrier of our sin and redeem us from his own judgment, God is willing to employ extreme measures to win our hearts fully to himself. He demands the most fervent devotion, and labors in our hearts until our greatest joy is to bask in the knowledge that God has cherished us to himself. The end result that God seeks and will achieve is set forth in 1 Peter 2:9: "You are a chosen race, a royal priesthood, a holy nation, a people for his own possession, that you may proclaim the excellencies of him who called you out of darkness into his marvelous light."

To this end, we are shown, secondly, that despite these wonderful promises of grace, very heavy trials await us in this life. Paul and Barnabas told

10. Constantine Brunner, *Der Judenhass und die Juden* (Berlin: Oesterheld, 1918), 34.

the early disciples, "Through many tribulations we must enter the kingdom of God" (Acts 14:22). The reason is given by this metaphor of verse 9, which speaks of God's people being purified from sin and made into a truly holy nation of God: "I will put this third into the fire, and refine them as one refines silver, and test them as gold is tested" (Zech. 7:9). A goldsmith heats the metal into a glowing red ore, then bathes it in cold water, scraping away the impurities, known as dross. The process is repeated over and over, with more and more dross separated and scraped away, until the goldsmith knows he is done because he looks at the now-refined metal and sees his own reflection. This is God's process for making us his true people; his goal in all our trials is to test and purify our faith, separating us from sins and the world, until finally he gazes on us and sees his own image and we have attained the spiritual excellence he has ordained, the beauty for which our salvation is designed.

Third, these verses present to us a love of God that is worthy of our most devoted love in return. "They will call upon my name, and I will answer them" (Zech. 13:9), he says, as the final object of his own heart's desire.

The whole of this great prophecy of Zechariah proclaims to us a great God of love who is the most fitting of all objects and persons and things for our highest devotion and love. Here is a love worth seeking! Isn't this what verse 7 shows us, that when God calls forth the sword he is striking with a lover's fervor to rescue his own from the house of their destruction, willing to assume the most costly of all imaginable sacrifices—God the Father striking God the Son—to spare the sword from us! Donald Grey Barnhouse speaks eloquently of the costly, and patient, and gracious love of God that shines through the darkness of the cross:

> He will give man the trees of the forest and the iron in the ground. Then He will give to man the brains to make an axe from the iron to cut down a tree and fashion it into a cross. He will give man the ability to make a hammer and nails, and when man has the cross and the hammer and the nails, the Lord will allow man to take hold of Him and bring Him to that cross; He will stretch out His hands to that cross, and in so doing will take the sins of man upon Himself and make it possible for those who have despised and rejected Him to come unto Him and know the joy of sins removed and forgiven, to know the assurance of pardon and eternal

life, and to enter into the prospect of the hope of glory with Him forever. This is even our God, and there is none like unto Him.[11]

God is pursuing us with his love, working through circumstances, trying us through tears, that in the desert of our trials we would call on him for salvation. When prosperity and success have torn our hearts from him, God sends us into trials that we would call on his name. When we, like Christ's disciples, have fled from his cross, he awaits us in resurrection power in the places to which we have fled.

Here is the love our hearts have been seeking, a love that calls us now through Jesus Christ. We will never find a love more fervent than that which overcame the guilt of our sin. We will never receive a love more determined than his, which works all through our lives to hear the words of our devotion to himself. "God is love," says the Bible (1 John 4:8). Although we often shy away from thinking of him as a swooning romantic, yet in the highest and most noble sense, God is a romantic—the first and last of the red-hot lovers. All of his greatest work, his most costly gift, is aimed at this romantic end, to which he draws us even now: "I will say, 'They are my people,' and they will say, 'The LORD is my God' " (Zech. 13:9). In those few words, all of history—the great aim of God before there was even time—achieves its true fulfillment and realization, the exchange of true love between God and his people, through Jesus Christ our Savior and Lord.

11. Donald Grey Barnhouse, cited in James M. Boice, *The Minor Prophets*, 2 vols. (Grand Rapids: Baker, 1983, reprint, 2003), 1:25.

26

THE LORD WILL BE KING

Zechariah 14:1–11

*The LORD will be king over all the earth. On that day the LORD
will be one, and his name one.* (Zech. 14:9)

One of the main words that depicts salvation is "peace." We speak of peace with God and peace with other people. Paul writes of a "peace which surpasses all understanding" (Phil. 4:7). Peace is the end of strife and danger, the coming of true security and blessing. No wonder the traditional Jewish greeting is *Shalom,* that is, "Peace." Jerusalem, Israel's capital city, means "City of Peace," and it was to such a place that Zechariah had come along with the others who returned from exile to restore God's city. In 538 BC the Persian emperor Cyrus made provision for their return, and in 515, prodded by the prophets Haggai and Zechariah, the temple was finally rebuilt and consecrated to the Lord. Yet, their great hope was still for peace.

These exiles had returned to God's city with great promises and expectations, yet the city was vulnerable and exposed. It would be at least another generation after Zechariah's death before Nehemiah would come to rebuild Jerusalem's broken walls and provide physical security. In Zechariah's day the prospect of another conquest seemed quite real and peace seemed elusive. It is against this backdrop that the final chapter of Zechariah's prophecy both confirms the people's fears and affirms their fondest hope.

QUESTIONS ABOUT FULFILLMENT

Martin Luther's commentary on the fourteenth chapter of Zechariah begins with words that are less than encouraging. "Here, in this chapter, I give up," he writes. "For I am not sure what the prophet is talking about."[1] It is a difficult chapter and there are a number of different views regarding its interpretation.

Zechariah 14 speaks of a great battle when all the nations will gather against Jerusalem, plundering it with great violence. After this, the Lord will come with all his holy ones, and with great cosmic disturbances, to establish his reign of peace. The main question has to do with the sense in which we should understand this prophecy being fulfilled.

There are three main views. The first looks upon this chapter as a figurative description of the church age, instead of literal events that will take place at a specific place and time. Adherents of this view point out that this is apocalyptic literature, that is, a form of writing that employs dramatic scenery and vivid events to reveal spiritual realities that are normally hidden to the eye. The kind of statements made in this chapter, they point out, are used generally in prophetic literature to speak of God's coming to judge or save his people (see Joel 3:16; Amos 1:2; Micah 1:3–4). These dramatic representations of cataclysmic activity are, says Thomas McComiskey, "anthropomorphic representations of Yahweh's entry into the arena of human history . . . and we need not understand them literally." They constitute, he says, "a vivid pictorial representation of the activity of the invisible God in history."[2]

This view, generally associated with postmillennial eschatology, argues that Israel and Jerusalem in the Old Testament correspond to the Christian church in the New Testament, a point that I have often made in these studies of Zechariah. Paul speaks of Christians as "the Israel of God" (Gal. 6:16). Hebrews 12:22–24 says that Christians have spiritually come to the

---

1. Martin Luther, *Luther's Works* (St. Louis: Concordia, 1973), 20:337.
2. Thomas E. McComiskey, *The Minor Prophets: An Exegetical and Expository Commentary*, 3 vols. (Grand Rapids: Baker, 1998), 3:1230.

heavenly Jerusalem, the city of the living God where the church gathers in assembly. All that Jerusalem was is now found in the church. In Zechariah, many of the prophecies concerning Jerusalem seem best fulfilled in the church (see 1:16–17; 2:4–5; 8:1–8). H. C. Leupold summarizes this view: "Our verses do not, therefore, apply to any one situation. They do not describe a siege, capture, and captivity which actually occurred. By means of a figure they describe a situation which obtains continually through New Testament times."[3]

There are some good reasons to object to this approach, as the second view of Zechariah 14 does. First, there is a concern that these quite specific prophecies would be "spiritualized" into vague principles. Second, many writers point out an inconsistency. We take other prophecies literally, they note, as I have done with many prophecies in these final chapters of Zechariah. I have argued that Zechariah 9:1–8 was literally fulfilled by the conquests of Alexander the Great. The New Testament shows Zechariah 9:9 literally fulfilled when Jesus entered Jerusalem on a donkey. The verses prior to our passage, 13:7–9, are said by Jesus himself to be fulfilled in his death: "Strike the shepherd, and the sheep will be scattered" (Zech. 13:7). On what grounds, then, will we now declare these subsequent prophecies to be merely figurative?

According to this second view, associated with premillennial eschatology, Zechariah 14 predicts a physical attack on the city of Jerusalem in the future, in which it is conquered and ravaged. The Lord Jesus Christ will then literally return to the Mount of Olives, from which Acts 1:11 tells us that he ascended. His coming will cause a physical split of that barrier to the east of Jerusalem so that the people escape, after which the Lord will establish his rule on the earth from a throne in that city.

What can we discern about these two views? The first view is right to urge caution in taking apocalyptic presentations as literal depictions of events. This is simply not how that literature functions, as the book of Revelation most vividly demonstrates. Furthermore, throughout Zechariah we have interpreted his prophecies about Jerusalem as pertaining ultimately to the New Testament church, not to some future restoration of God's ancient city. This is consistent with the New Testament's own view of its relationship to the Old. All that Jerusalem stood for in the Old Testament—the city of God—

---

3. H. C. Leupold, *Exposition of Zechariah* (Grand Rapids: Baker, 1981), 259.

now is found in the New Testament church, and so, after Christ's transformational first coming, prophecies about Jerusalem are fulfilled in the life and experience of the church. The New Testament Jerusalem is not a city in Palestine, but the church throughout the world.

The premillennial view is surely right, however, in insisting that this chapter points to actual events that will happen in the future, however figurative the depiction may be. Zechariah 14 conforms, for instance, to Paul's statements in 1 and 2 Thessalonians, and especially to the picture of the book of Revelation. Verses 6 and 7 indicate a cataclysmic transformation of the order of nature, which Revelation 21 also describes. Verses 8–11 speak of blessings for God's city that are repeated in Revelation 22. Therefore, the premillennial view is right to demand some literal fulfillment of these prophecies, even though it errs by not recognizing Jerusalem as a type for the New Testament church.

This leads to a third view that strikes a balance between the first two, a view associated with amillennial eschatology. This view observes that Zechariah 14 completes the historical progression we have followed all through these final oracles that began in chapter 9. They start with the centuries to come shortly after the restoration of Jerusalem, including the conquests of Alexander (9:1–8) and the Maccabean wars of the Jews (9:13). The great bulk of these prophecies then focus on the coming of the true king (9:9), his rejection by the people, and God's subsequent judgment on Jerusalem (11:1–14), but then the cleansing of many who look on the One they had pierced and are saved (12:10–13), which takes place in our present gospel age. As we follow the progression of redemptive history, the next great event, after the first coming of Christ and the spreading of the gospel, is his second coming to vindicate his beleaguered people, judge the earth, and bring his eternal reign of blessing and peace. That is what chapter 14 brings to our view, not just broad principles about life in this world, and not the beginning of a thousand-year political reign of Christ centered on the earthly city of Jerusalem, but the end of all things in the consummation of God's eternal city in purity and peace. T. V. Moore summarizes this chapter by saying, "It seems to point to the last great struggle of the powers of evil with the Church, which is to be ended by the coming of Christ in great power, and the complete establishment of his kingdom of glory."[4]

4. T. V. Moore, *Haggai, Zechariah, & Malachi* (Edinburgh: Banner of Truth, 1979), 293.

THE RANSACKED CITY

Zechariah 14:1–11 presents a threefold progression. First, there is a successful attack of the nations against God's city (Zech. 14:1–2). Second is the Lord's appearance to fight for and defend his people (Zech. 14:3–5). Third, verses 6–11 show the result of this in the end-times cataclysm that brings in the eternal reign of God.

Verse 1 makes a general statement that is developed in verse 2: "Behold, a day is coming for the Lord, when the spoil taken from you will be divided in your midst. For I will gather all the nations against Jerusalem to battle, and the city shall be taken and the houses plundered and the women raped. Half of the city shall go out into exile, but the rest of the people shall not be cut off from the city."

It is important for us to note the link between this and the previous verse, Zechariah 13:9, in which God says of his people, "I will put this third into the fire, and refine them as one refines silver, and test them as gold is tested." This is how God brings about the true devotion with which that verse ends, by purifying his people in severe hardship and removing the worldliness from our hearts. The picture of the first two verses is terrible, but the fact is that God offers spiritual blessings that sometimes come through great worldly trials. What Paul taught the early Christians in Acts 14:22 was true for the Jews before and is true for us as well: "Through many tribulations we must enter the kingdom of God." "You have been grieved by various trials," Peter also explained, "so that the tested genuineness of your faith . . . may be found to result in praise and glory and honor at the revelation of Jesus Christ" (1 Peter 1:6–7).

It is surely the case that the majority of Christians underestimate the cost of following Christ in this world. We expect a little social awkwardness, or perhaps some problems at work or in our families, but we hardly imagine what these verses show: God himself gathering the nations to tear his city apart. But this has happened many times in church history, such as during the persecutions of the Roman Empire and the great persecutions that accompanied the Protestant Reformation. In every case, intense persecution glorified Christ before the world through the suffering faithfulness of his people, and prefaced a new victory for his kingdom of grace. Persecution also served to test and purify Christ's people. Philip Schaff writes of the persecutions against the early church: "As war brings out the heroic qualities of men, so did the persecutions develop the patience, the gentleness, the endurance of the Christians, and prove the world-conquering power of faith."[5]

This should prompt us to ask if we are willing to endure intense affliction as Christians. Are we, men and women alike, willing to accept pain and humiliation for Jesus? Would we renounce the faith before suffering the fate described by Zechariah?

If we are not willing to suffer in these ways for our faith, then the fact is that we cannot be Christians. Not all believers will suffer intense forms of persecution, but we must all be ready and willing in such an event. The book of Hebrews records the steadfast suffering of God's people under trial: they "were tortured and refused to be released, so that they might gain a better resurrection. Some faced jeers and flogging, while still others were chained and put in prison. They were stoned; they were sawed in two; they were put to death by the sword. They went about in sheepskins and goatskins, destitute, persecuted and mistreated—the world was not worthy of them" (11:35–38 NIV). These things have happened to Christians all through the ages, are happening even now in places like the Sudan and Indonesia, and could happen in the West all too easily. Should God bring upon us a true persecution, our numbers would no doubt dwindle, but his purpose of purifying the church would surely succeed.

Zechariah specifically depicts a heightened persecution of God's people that will come just before the end. The day of the Lord "will not come, unless the rebellion comes first, and the man of lawlessness is revealed, the son of destruction, who opposes and exalts himself against every so-called god or object of worship, so that he takes his seat in the temple of God, proclaiming himself to be God" (2 Thess. 2:3–4). Passages like Daniel 9:24–27 speak in similar terms, telling of a savage attack on God's city. Ezekiel 38 and 39 also prophesy such an attack. Revelation, with its several recapitulations of church history, likewise shows a time of heightened tribulation which the church must endure before salvation in the end. Therefore, Christians should take Zechariah 14:1–2 quite seriously, as a terrible and vicious assault that will come upon the church, God's Jerusalem, before the end of this present age.

5. Philip Schaff, *History of the Chrisitan Church,* 8 vols. (Peabody, MA: Hendrickson, 1858, reprint 2002), 2:33.

THE LORD WILL COME

The emphasis here, however, is not on the suffering of God's people but rather on the great deliverance that follows. God does not allow his people to perish but enters the scene in time to save his city: "Then the LORD will go out and fight against those nations as when he fights on a day of battle" (Zech. 14:3).

Again, we have a general statement that is filled in by the verses that follow. "As when he fights on a day of battle," refers us to previous times when God had appeared in history to defend his people. The Old Testament provides a great number of examples. Think of Joshua and his conquest of Jericho; by God's supernatural power that mighty city was laid low. Think of Gideon, who went forth with a tiny force to fight the host of Midian, whom the Lord caused to fight among themselves and flee. Later on, Jehoshaphat was faced with a vast army from Moab and Ammon. "Stand firm," he was told, "and see the salvation of the LORD on your behalf" (2 Chron. 20:17). While God's people sang hymns of praise and thanks, the Scripture tells us, "the LORD set an ambush against the men of Ammon, Moab, and Mount Seir, who had come against Judah, so that they were routed" (v. 22). In the days of Isaiah, the Lord struck down 185,000 men under Sennacherib who were besieging Jerusalem, when King Hezekiah prayed for deliverance. The king sought the help of the Lord in tearful prayer, and "that night the angel of the LORD went out and struck down 185,000 in the camp of the Assyrians" (2 Kings 19:35). In a similar manner, the Lord now promises to come to fight for his people.

One of the greatest examples of God's deliverance was the parting of the Red Sea during the exodus. Moses and the Israelites were trapped against that body of water, but God drove back the waves and made a passage for their escape, destroying Pharaoh and his chariots when they tried to follow. In like manner, now the Lord will part the Mount of Olives to provide an escape toward the east:

> On that day his feet shall stand on the Mount of Olives that lies before Jerusalem on the east, and the Mount of Olives shall be split in two from east to west by a very wide valley, so that one half of the Mount shall move northward, and the other half southward. And you shall flee to the valley of my

mountains, for the valley of the mountains shall reach to Azal. And you shall flee as you fled from the earthquake in the days of Uzziah king of Judah. (Zech. 14:4–5)

Apparently Azal was a village just to the east beyond the Mount of Olives. Through this suddenly opened pathway, the people will flee away as they had done from devastating earthquakes in earlier times.

This fits the pattern by which God often rescues his people. Christians are beset by dangers and many fall away in fear. But those who hold fast to the Lord find a way of deliverance they could not have imagined, as the Lord suddenly comes to their aid. Paul says this about the temptations we experience even now. He writes, "No temptation has overtaken you that is not common to man. God is faithful, and he will not let you be tempted beyond your ability, but with the temptation he will also provide the way of escape, that you may be able to endure it" (1 Cor. 10:13). This is what Christians are called to do against sin and in trials. Moses said to the tribes of Israel with their backs to the Red Sea, "Fear not, stand firm, and see the salvation of the Lord, which he will work for you today" (Ex. 14:13). We need to remember this when times are dark and hope is dim, how God has wonderfully delivered his people before and will again, and therefore to be strengthened in our faith.

Zechariah foresees the Lord coming to stand upon the Mount of Olives, that is, the hill to the east of Jerusalem that provides the best vantage point, creating in his presence a refuge for all who look to him in faith. Psalm 46:1 says, "God is our refuge and strength, a very present help in trouble." This is true for us now, but it will especially be true in the great tribulation at the end. "Then the Lord my God will come," says the prophet, "and all the holy ones with him" (Zech. 14:5).

This prophecy refers to the return to the earth of our Lord Jesus in power and glory, as foretold in Acts 1:11: "This Jesus, who was taken up from you into heaven, will come in the same way as you saw him go into heaven." In Mark 8:38 Jesus spoke of the Son of Man returning "in the glory of his Father with the holy angels." These are "the holy ones" verse 5 speaks of. Paul adds in 1 Thessalonians 4:14, "We believe that . . . God will bring with him those who have fallen asleep." Furthermore, Paul indicates that those who flee the devastation by the path God has made will join up with this host and enter with them in his triumph: "The Lord himself will descend from heaven with a cry of command, with the voice of an archangel, and with the sound of the trumpet of God. And the dead in Christ will rise first. Then we who are alive, who are left, will be caught up together with them in the clouds to meet the Lord in the air" (1 Thess. 4:16–17). The symbolism varies somewhat between Paul and Zechariah, which is another reason to understand Zechariah's prophecy as presenting a pattern rather than a literal picture of Christ's return. But in both Zechariah and Paul it seems clear that included among the holy ones who enter in the Lord's train of victory are those who are delivered from destruction and have fled to his presence. In all these things, our Lord is glorified by saving his people and overthrowing his enemies.

The Lord Will Be King

This deliverance leads us to a great description of the eternal kingdom that the Lord will bring at the end of history. First, we are told of a cataclysmic change in the order of nature: "On that day there shall be no light, cold, or frost. And there shall be a unique day, which is known to the Lord, neither day nor night, but at evening time there shall be light" (Zech. 14:6–7). There is a translation difficulty with the second half of verse 6; what the English Standard puts as lacking "cold or frost" is rendered by the majority of commentators as the loss of light from the "stars or planets," a translation that better fits the overall flow. Zechariah describes a unique or singular day—a day like no other. It is a new day, an entry into the eternal realm where day and night, with their respective lights, are gone. As Revelation 21:23 says, "The city does not need the sun or the moon to shine on it, for the glory of God gives it light, and the Lamb is its lamp" (NIV). Here is the day "known to the Lord," to which all history is moving.

The verses that follow provide four descriptions of what will happen at the consummation of our final salvation. Verse 10 tells of the exaltation of Jerusalem, which is situated among larger hills in uneven country: "The whole land shall be turned into a plain from Geba to Rimmon south of Jerusalem. But Jerusalem shall remain aloft on its site from the Gate of Benjamin to the place of the former gate, to the Corner Gate, and from the Tower of Hananel to the king's winepresses." Jerusalem's surrounding terrain is flattened out;

the territory of Judah, bounded by Geba and Rimmon, becomes like the Arabah, which is the plain region through which the Jordan River flows. The hills are made level to form a plateau wall, while Jerusalem is raised up to be seen all around. Verse 10 gives the dimensions of the city in its greatest days; the whole city will be made secure and will rise up exalted. This is the scene Ezekiel described in similar terms in his vision of the exalted kingdom, with the glorified temple in its midst (Ezek. 40–48).

The point here is theological rather than topographical; it is the prophetic ideal achieved in the glorification of God's mountain and city. Isaiah foretold: "It shall come to pass in the latter days that the mountain of the house of the LORD shall be established as the highest of the mountains, and shall be lifted up above the hills; and all the nations shall flow to it" (Isa. 2:2).

Jerusalem was a small and insignificant city in the eyes of the world. Babylon, Susa, Memphis—these were the exalted cities, the centers of action and the first in importance. But in the end will be revealed what has always been true: it is God's city—his church, his people—which really is foremost in significance. It is always the case that, unnoticed by the world, what really matters is what God is doing through his people. It is the simple act of service born of faith in Christ, the caring witness to the gospel, the worship arising from a humble heart—things about which the world does not care, and which will never bring praise from men—that God values most and which he will exalt on that day. Revelation 21:10–11 speaks of God's city raised up in glory and shining with the holy works of his people: "He carried me away in the Spirit to a great, high mountain, and showed me the holy city Jerusalem coming down out of heaven from God, having the glory of God, its radiance like a most rare jewel, like a jasper, clear as crystal."

Second, we are told of a river that flows perpetually from this city: "On that day living waters shall flow out from Jerusalem, half of them to the eastern sea and half of them to the western sea. It shall continue in summer as in winter" (Zech. 14:8). This is a great symbol of the blessings of salvation. The Garden of Eden was watered with the flowing waters of four rivers (Gen. 2:10). Ezekiel's vision spoke of a river flowing out from under the threshold of the temple. The farther off it flowed the deeper it became, cleansing and purifying all before it, bringing life. "When the water flows into the sea," he wrote, "the water will become fresh. And wherever the river goes, every living creature that swarms will live.... On the banks, on both sides of the river, there will grow all kinds of trees for food. Their leaves will not wither, nor their fruit fail . . . because the water for them flows from the sanctuary. Their fruit will be for food, and their leaves for healing" (Ezek. 47:8–12).

We might think of this as the river of the gospel or of the Holy Spirit who brings life through faith in Christ. We remember that the earthly Jerusalem does not have a river; all its water comes from underground springs. Yet a river does flow in God's city, from which the faithful long have drunk! Despite its topography, Psalm 46:4 says of God's city, "There is a river whose streams make glad the city of God." This speaks of the waters we drink through faith in Jesus Christ; Zechariah sees the church in the end as a glorified city, with this river flowing within. How dramatic it was, then, when Jesus stood at the temple in the midst of the Jerusalem Zechariah and his generation rebuilt, crying out, "If anyone thirsts, let him come to me and drink. Whoever believes in me, as the Scripture has said, 'Out of his heart will flow rivers of living water' " (John 7:37–38). John explained in the next verse, "Now this he said about the Spirit, whom those who believed in him were to receive" (John 17:39). Just as water flowed from Jesus' side when he was pierced on the cross, so also does the Holy Spirit flow through his saving ministry, fulfilling all that the psalmists and prophets had always foreseen of the refreshing river of God's grace.

Third, and at the center of this great statement of the coming day, is the coming of the Lord as king: "The LORD will be king over all the earth. On that day the LORD will be one and his name one" (Zech. 14:9). Here is the true consummation of all history, the crowning of the Lord Jesus Christ as king over all. This is what Paul described as the end of all God's redemptive work. Jesus was obedient to the Father in bearing our flesh and dying on the cross: "Therefore God has highly exalted him and bestowed on him the name that is above every name, so that at the name of Jesus every knee should bow, in heaven and on earth and under the earth, and every tongue confess that Jesus Christ is Lord, to the glory of God the Father" (Phil. 2:9–11). Thus the voices of heaven cry, "The kingdom of the world has become the kingdom of our Lord and of his Christ, and he shall reign forever and ever" (Rev. 11:15).

The Lord who has been king *de jure* is now king *de facto*; here, he takes up in fact the authority that all along he has possessed by right. All his rivals are put beneath his feet; in all the world there will be but one Lord and one name to which all will look for salvation. H. C. Leupold writes, "The fact that He is King over all has always been true. He shall now really be regarded as what He actually is, for men will have come to a true knowledge of Him."[6]

So glorious is this scene of kingly triumph that to depict it we do better to turn to the bards than to the scholars. One epic depiction comes from the pen of J. R. R. Tolkien, who analogizes the coming of Christ to his city in his famous novel, *The Return of the King*. What he writes of his hero, Aragorn, rising with his head newly crowned, truly applies to the unveiling of Jesus Christ as king before the assembled cosmos: "All that beheld him gazed in silence, for it seemed to them that he was revealed to them now for the first time. Tall . . . he stood above all that were near; ancient of days he seemed and yet in the flower of manhood; and wisdom sat upon his brow, and strength and healing were in his hands, and a light was about him." Then up went the cry, "Behold the King!"[7] So shall it be, in the epic history yet to unfold upon the mount of the city of God.

Fourth, and finally, we see the effects of the blessed rule of this glorious king. Zechariah has shown God's city, the church, exalted among the nations, a river of grace flowing forth, and as the centerpiece, the crowning of Jesus Christ as Lord over all. Now he says of this well-blessed city: "And it shall be inhabited, for there shall never again be a decree of utter destruction. Jerusalem shall dwell in security" (Zech. 14:11).

Every believer looks forward to this coronation at the end of the history in which we now find ourselves, with all of its dangers and threats. James Boice writes, "The outward changes in the land are symbolic of what will also be spiritually true. Evil will be eliminated from the city. God will be with His people, and salvation will flow like a stream from Zion."[8] Probably the greatest pictorial expression tying all these themes together is found in Revelation 22:1–5, which seems deliberately to look back upon Zechariah's prophecy:

> Then the angel showed me the river of the water of life, bright as crystal, flowing from the throne of God and of the Lamb through the middle of the street of the city; also, on either side of the river, the tree of life with its twelve kinds

6. Leupold, *Zechariah*, 267.
7. J. R. R. Tolkien, *Return of the King* (Boston: Houghton Mifflin, 1955), 947.
8. James Montgomery Boice, *The Minor Prophets*, 2 vols. (Grand Rapids: Zondervan, 1986), 2:224.

of fruit, yielding its fruit each month. The leaves of the tree were for the healing of the nations. No longer will there be anything accursed, but the throne of God and of the Lamb will be in it, and his servants will worship him. They will see his face, and his name will be on their foreheads. And night will be no more. They will need no light of lamp or sun, for the Lord God will be their light, and they will reign forever and ever.

CHRIST'S REIGN OF PEACE

This is how the Bible ends, just as history will end, and with it comes an invitation to enter into the blessings that are to come. "Blessed are those who wash their robes," says Jesus, "so that they may have the right to the tree of life and that they may enter the city by the gates" (Rev. 22:14). "Come!" he says, "And let the one who hears say, 'Come.' And let the one who is thirsty come," Jesus says. "Let the one who desires take the water of life without price" (Rev. 22:17). The salvation which awaits all God's people—living and dead—at the end of history, comes only through faith in Jesus Christ. He invites us all to wash our robes in the blood that he shed by believing on his name and, being cleansed, to find eternal life in him.

But what about now? Some may say, "I'm glad to know that sometime ahead I will enter into heaven if I can hold fast to Jesus. But how am I to overcome the foes that afflict me now: temptations, sin's power, and the difficulties and hazards of this life?" If you want peace now, you are like the people of Zechariah's day, dwelling in Jerusalem in all its weakness, seeking security and blessing in their difficult situation.

But this message is not just about a distant future. It tells us that where Jesus Christ comes to reign, there is peace. This is true now, just as it will be throughout the earth on that great day to come. Zechariah prophesies Christ's return to his city with a mighty salvation. If you through faith will crown Jesus king of your life, then he will come to you now with the same power, to remove your sin, cleanse your walls, and strengthen you to join him in triumph. And as king, he will be your Lord and protector, leading you through life until "on that day" he has finished your salvation, and you, like his city, dwell in security and peace forever.

27

HOLY TO THE LORD

Zechariah 14:12–21

And on that day there shall be inscribed on the bells of the horses,
"Holy to the LORD." And the pots in the house of the LORD shall be
as the bowls before the altar. And every pot in Jerusalem and
Judah shall be holy to the LORD of hosts, so that all who sacrifice
may come and take of them and boil the meat of the sacrifice in
them. And there shall no longer be a trader in the house of the
LORD of hosts on that day. (Zech. 14:20–21)

n the opening chapter of the book of Revelation, the apostle John shows us a vision of the exalted Lord Jesus Christ. Among the striking features he describes, like gleaming hair, blazing eyes, and a face shining like the sun, is this: "From his mouth came a sharp two-edged sword" (Rev. 1:16). Commentators are generally agreed that this depicts the two-edged nature of the gospel, which means salvation for those who believe and judgment for those who do not.

There is a close relationship between Zechariah 14 and the book of Revelation, both of which feature striking visions of what is yet to come. This two-sided nature of the gospel is another point of similarity. Zechariah's final prophecy begins with a vision of Christ's second coming to bring salvation to his own (Zech. 14:1–11). But now this chapter adds the stark reality of judgment for the enemies of God.

JUDGMENT ON THE NATIONS

Zechariah 14:1–5 showed the attack of the nations on God's city, which was initially successful but confounded by the coming of the Lord. Verses 6–11 went on to speak of the salvation brought to his people by the Lord's coming. Now, verses 12–15 tell the opposite side of that story, the opposite edge of that sword. The prophet writes, "This shall be the plague with which the LORD will strike all the peoples that wage war against Jerusalem" (Zech. 14:12). He then describes God's terrible judgment with three graphic scenes. In verses 12–15, Zechariah uses terms that are native to his Old Testament setting to communicate the horrible reality of the judgment of God, employing what seems to be a collage of Old Testament examples and concepts. C. F. Keil writes, "To express the idea of their utter destruction, all the different kinds of plagues and strokes by which nations can be destroyed are grouped together."[1]

The first of these judgments involves the rotting away of flesh from those who are still living: "their flesh will rot while they are still standing on their feet" (Zech. 14:12). This seems to be the kind of plague described in Deuteronomy 28:22, and may be a reference to Numbers 14:37, where this same word for plague is used of the Israelite spies who brought back a false report and were struck down before the Lord. Similarly, Sennacherib's invading army was wiped out by a plague outside the walls of Jerusalem (2 Kings 19:35). Special notice here is made of the eyes which had looked upon God's city in lust—"their eyes will rot in their sockets." Also, the tongues with which they had blasphemed the Lord "will rot in their mouths" (Zech. 14:12).

The second scene of judgment is one that has numerous precedents in the history of Israel: "And on that day a great panic from the LORD shall fall on them, so that each will seize the hand of another, and the hand of the one will be raised against the hand of the other" (Zech. 14:13). This is how God

---

1. C. F. Keil and F. Delitzsch, *Commentary on the Old Testament*, 10 vols. (Peabody, MA: Hendrickson, reprint, 1996), 10:624.

overthrew the hosts of Midian through Gideon, and how Jonathan overcame the Philistines (see Judg. 7 and 1 Sam. 14). Perhaps most prominent is the great victory observed by the godly king Jehoshaphat while he and the people sang hymns of praise to God: "The men of Ammon and Moab rose against the inhabitants of Mount Seir, devoting them to destruction, and when they had made an end of the inhabitants of Seir, they all helped to destroy one another" (2 Chron. 20:23). Thomas V. Moore observes that this picture of the ungodly striking one another is an apt depiction of hell. "Hell shall be hate," he says, "in its fiercest and hatefullest forms. Sin is now the cause of all the quarrels on earth; it shall be the cause of endless quarrels in hell. . . . This is but sin left to itself."[2]

The point of these verses is not merely the reality of God's final judgment, but the terror of it for those who are condemned and sentenced to eternity in hell. Today we hear a good deal about hell not being so bad; it often seems to be precisely the kind of place sinners would like to be sent. It is true that God's judgment involves giving sinners what they have asked for, but it is sin worked out to its ultimate and final conclusion, a place of torment and bitter strife. "Hell is simply the absence of God's presence," many say. Yes, God's grace and mercy are absent, but as these images show, God's condemning power and holy justice are hardly gone. The book of Revelation uses images different from these; it speaks of a "lake of fire and sulfur where . . . they will be tormented day and night forever and ever" (20:10). Different books use different images, so perhaps we should take these pictures in Zechariah figuratively. But they are figurative of something that is quite real and, if anything, far worse than mere words can describe.

The third picture of God's judgment seems mild until we reflect on it. Like much of Zechariah 14, this picture involves a translation difficulty. The English Standard Version translates it as "Even Judah will fight against Jerusalem." But given that the context describes the deliverance and blessing of God's people, the New International Version probably puts it better: "Judah too will fight at Jerusalem" (Zech. 14:14). This speaks not of discord but of a unity among God's people. Zechariah has frequently expressed himself this way, with the people of the towns joining with the city-dwellers as one, describing the cohesion of God's people.

2. T. V. Moore, *Haggai, Zechariah, & Malachi* (Edinburgh: Banner of Truth, 1979), 310.

But the real terror for the ungodly is found in the adjoining statement: "And the wealth of all the surrounding nations shall be collected, gold, silver, and garments in great abundance" (Zech. 14:14). This occurred a number of times in the Old Testament. To the enemies of God it means that all they have trusted, all they have loved, all they have set their hearts upon in his world will be taken from them in the judgment. They will be bereft of all the worldly comforts and joys with which they dulled their spiritual awareness in this life. The terrible irony for them is that it is the church, which has not even sought such treasure, that receives the riches they have loved. H. C. Leupold rightly says, "The general principle of all history is: the nations strive but have not the ultimate profit of their endeavors; the church comes into the acquired inheritance."[3]

The judgment concludes with God destroying even the transport used by his enemies: "And a plague like this plague shall fall on the horses, the mules, the camels, the donkeys, and whatever beasts may be in those camps" (Zech. 14:15). This probably alludes to the principles of Old Testament holy war, in which God commands the total destruction of everything associated with his enemies, including their livestock.

Before passing beyond these stark descriptions, we should note the expressions here of a universal judgment. Verse 12 says this plague will strike "all the peoples" that opposed God's church. Verse 13 says that "each man" will be caught in mutual destruction, and verse 14 says that the "wealth of all the surrounding nations" will be seized to recompense God's people. The point is one that we should note, namely, that no one who opposes God, no one who in the end has rejected his authority and spurned his gospel, will escape final judgment. Those who hate and refuse God now will all be brought to his account. This is intended to comfort the people of God, now afflicted in the world, that God will bring all her oppressors to a terrible account. We may safely, then, leave all vengeance to him, thankful for our own salvation and busy in the work of the gospel.

CHRIST'S SOVEREIGN REIGN

What follows are perhaps the most difficult verses to interpret in this very difficult chapter. Again, the prophet seems to be employing Old Testament

3. H. C. Leupold, *Exposition of Zechariah* (Grand Rapids: Baker, 1981), 272.

images to represent to his readers a great and future reality. That reality here is the sovereign reign of the Lord when he comes to judge the earth.

It is hard to imagine anyone surviving the kind of divine judgment depicted already, but verse 16 says, "the survivors from all the nations that have attacked Jerusalem will go up year after year to worship the King, the Lord Almighty." This is a figurative depiction of Christ's reign at the end, in the city into which have been gathered even many from the nations of his enemies.

Verses 16 and 19 make specific mention of the feast of tabernacles in the worship of the Lord. The commentators offer two main explanations. First, this feast celebrated God's deliverance of his people in the exodus. Now, in the true and final Promised Land of heaven, the Lord Jesus receives praise for shepherding his people to the ultimate land of promise. Second, the feast of tabernacles (or booths) celebrates "the gathering of the nations to the Lord and especially His tabernacling among them."[4] This feast alone possessed an eighth day, which many believe pointed to the eternal state beyond the resurrection, of which Revelation 21:3 says, "Behold, the dwelling place [tabernacle] of God is with man. He will dwell [tabernacle] with them."

These verses show the sovereignty of Christ's reign as king as he receives universal homage. Again, Zechariah employs figures from Old Testament history to depict the absoluteness of this rule. Verse 17 says, "And if any of the families of the earth do not go up to Jerusalem to worship the King, the Lord of hosts, there will be no rain on them." This recalls God's judgment on the rebellious nation in the days of Elijah (Deut. 28:23–24). For three years, no rain fell because of their apostasy, yet it did not bring about repentance and a renewal of faith. Now, this reign fully succeeds in bringing submission. Verse 18 notes that a denial of rain would have little effect on Egypt, which gets its water from the Nile River, so the Lord will enforce his will on them by means of the plagues: "And if the family of Egypt does not go up and present themselves, then on them there shall be no rain; there shall be the plague."

This threat has special poignancy for the land of Pharaoh, whose resistance was broken once before by the plagues of God (Ex. 7–11). In these ways, as verse 19 sums up, all the nations will be punished that "do not go

4. Charles Feinberg, *Zechariah: God Remembers* (Portland, OR: Multnomah, 1965), 203.

up to keep the Feast of Booths." These verses see fulfilled what was prophe-sied of God's Son in Psalm 2:8–9: "I will make the nations your heritage, and the ends of the earth your possession. You shall break them with a rod of iron and dash them in pieces like a potter's vessel."

For those committed to a dispensational view of a millennial age, these verses are a classic and literal presentation of what will occur after the return of Jesus Christ. Having returned to the city of Jerusalem, which is physically besieged by the nations of the earth, Christ defeats them and sets up his earthly throne from that city. For a thousand years he oversees what amounts to a worldwide establishment of Old Testament religion, literally employ-ing supernatural droughts and plagues to enforce his rule. Only after a thou-sand years of this earthly reign of Christ does the final battle commence, fol-lowed by the judgment day and the eternal state of glory.

While I admire an effort to take the text of the Bible at its plain word, I am yet restrained from this particular view for several reasons. First, and mainly, it envisions the Lord Jesus Christ returning at the end of the gospel age to establish the law of Moses, which is an unthinkable regression in redemptive history. The book of Hebrews makes plain that the law was a shadow that passed away with the coming of the reality in Christ (Heb. 10:1). It is impossible to imagine Jesus, having shed his own blood once for all, coming back to have bulls and goats and sheep shed once more for the remis-sion of sin. Hebrews 9:28 says, "Christ, having been offered once to bear the sins of many, will appear a second time, not to deal with sin but to save those who are eagerly waiting for him." This is the fatal flaw in the thinking of those who look forward to a rebuilding of the temple in Jerusalem and the reestablishment of Old Testament religion as some advance in God's redemp-tive program.

Second, as we saw in the previous chapter, there is ample reason to link Zechariah 14 to the final and eternal state of heaven described at the end of the book of Revelation. Verses 6 and 7 spoke of a change in the order of nature, a new day that closely matches the scenes of Revelation 21 and 22. Speaking there of Jerusalem, the apostle John plainly refers to the church and not to an earthly city: "I saw the holy city, new Jerusalem, coming down out of heaven from God, prepared as a bride adorned for her husband. And I heard a loud voice from the throne saying, 'Behold, the dwelling place of God is with man'" (Rev. 21:2–3). This chapter describes, therefore, not a millennial hiatus in earthly Jerusalem, but the end in glory, the "city that has foundations, whose designer and builder is God" (Heb. 11:10).

Third, while we admire the devotion to the text of Scripture, this kind of literalism poorly grasps the message conveyed by this genre of biblical literature. The prophet employs the descriptions of verses 16–19 not to provide details of the day to come, but to convey the absoluteness of the reign of Christ and the worship he receives.

But there is something else at work in this depiction. Malachi, the last of the Old Testament books, ends by looking forward to the coming of John the Baptist, who would go before the Lord, and thus the whole Old Testament ends looking forward to Christ. The next-to-last book is Zechariah, and in many ways it reaches backward, summing up the entire prophetic era. Zechariah consistently uses the expressions and symbols of earlier prophets. He was the last of the prophets before Christ to be killed by the people of Jerusalem; Jesus tells us he was "murdered between the sanctuary and the altar" (Matt. 23:35). With him the Old Testament prophetic line finds its summary as it looks forward to the day of the Lord.

Now, at the end of his writings, Zechariah looks back to Elijah and says, "You stopped the rain for three years and yet the people would not repent, but the day is coming when your hope will be fulfilled and the Lord's reign will succeed." To Moses, whose plagues broke Pharaoh's grip but never broke his idolatrous will, he says, "The time comes when every knee shall bow and every tongue confess that the Lord is king." *How long!* was the lament of all the prophets, as they surveyed a rebel world opposed to God, and they recoiled at the monstrosity of unbelief. To all his prophetic brothers, Zechariah, at the end of their era, proclaims, "The day of the Lord comes, and then the Lord will be worshiped and obeyed in his almighty power!"

Zechariah tells us that the hope of all the prophets is fulfilled in the coming and the reign of our Lord Jesus Christ. We began these studies in Zechariah observing that this is one of the most Christ-centered of all the Old Testament books. It is always our goal to preach Christ from the Scriptures, but Zechariah especially must be interpreted in terms of its focus on Christ. In every chapter we have encountered him. In chapter 1, he appeared among the myrtle trees mounted on a red horse, proclaiming the Lord's care for his beleaguered people. In chapter 2, he came with a measuring line as architect of God's restoration work. Chapter 3 presents one of the great Old

Testament pictures of Christ, removing the soiled clothes from the dirty high priest. "Behold," he said then as he says now, "I have taken your iniquity away from you" (Zech. 3:4). Chapter 4 presented the two olive trees, speaking of a union of the priestly and the kingly line, which in chapter 6 is portrayed with the high priest enthroned. Chapters 7 and 8 proclaim his day of feasting that puts an end to fasts. In chapter 9, he comes as the gentle king, "righteous and having salvation is he, humble and mounted on a donkey" (Zech. 9:9). In chapter 10 he is the cornerstone and the peg from which hang the hopes of Judah. Chapter 11 sets forth the Good Shepherd, rejected by the flock. In chapter 12 he is the pierced one, to whom his people look and mourn for sin. Chapter 13 tells of the fountain that springs forth from him, to cleanse those who mourn from sin and impurity. Now, at the end of Christ's work, so fully chronicled by this great prophet who sums up all the rest—at the end of a history that is centered on Christ and finds its end in his glory— our Savior is established without question, without denial, without opposition, as Lord of all. He is the reigning king who is not only worthy but who actually receives the homage of the entire subdued creation. This is the message of the whole Bible, and it finds fulfillment in Christ's glorious reign.

HOLY TO THE LORD

Every king needs a consort, and, as the book of Esther shows, only the most beautiful bride will do. Therefore, the achievement of all God's desire in history is crowned not only with the eternal reign of Christ as Lord, but also in the presentation of a perfect and holy bride for God's Son. Paul tells us in Ephesians that Christ conquered in this world not merely to establish his throne—that he might have done without dying for sin—but also that "he might present the church to himself in splendor, without spot or wrinkle or any such thing, that she might be holy and without blemish" (Eph. 5:27). According to Ephesians 1:4, this fulfills the intention of God's plan from the beginning: "He chose us in him before the foundation of the world, that we should be holy and blameless before him" (1:4). God's great purpose is an entire holy creation, washed of guilt by Christ's blood and renewed by the Spirit. How wonderful to read, then, as the conclusion to the entire book of Zechariah, a depiction of this very accomplishment in a comprehensive and ultimate form. Zechariah has been concerned throughout for the glory of God's redeemed city, and to this hope his eyes return at the end: "On that day," writes the prophet, "there shall be inscribed on the bells of the horses, 'Holy to the LORD.' And the pots in the house of the LORD shall be as the bowls before the altar" (Zech. 14:20).

This statement runs parallel to many others in Scripture that present the eternal reign of Christ in glory. Isaiah concludes with the purified city in a new creation. Ezekiel concludes his final vision of the heavenly city, saying "the name of the city from that time on shall be, The LORD is there" (48:35). The book of Revelation presents the most developed form of this prophecy, saying of the city, "Nothing unclean will ever enter it, nor anyone who does what is detestable or false, but only those who are written in the Lamb's book of life" (21:27).

The final verses of the prophet Zechariah present the same triumphant end—the complete holiness of God's city in the new creation. First, he refers to the inscription that in the Old Testament was worn on the headdress of the high priest, *Holy to the Lord*, only now he says that it will be so common that it "will be inscribed on the bells of the horses" (Zech. 14:20). Thomas McComiskey explains, "So pervasive will be the rule of righteousness in the new order that even the most common objects will be holy to God. Nothing will belong to the sphere of the common or profane. Even the trappings on the horses will be holy to God."[5] With all sin removed, everything in God's city will be sanctified and consecrated to him to the degree once achieved only by the high priest's turban.

Second, "the pots in the house of the LORD shall be as the bowls before the altar" (Zech. 14:20). The bowls that poured the sacrificial blood were especially sacred, but now the cooking pots in the temple will be no less consecrated. Everything in God's house will be equally and perfectly holy. Third, we read, "Every pot in Jerusalem and Judah shall be holy to the LORD of hosts, so that all who sacrifice may come and take of them and boil the meat of the sacrifice in them" (Zech. 14:21). The highest degree of holiness will permeate every home, and even the most common of vessels will attain the highest measure of sanctification.

Finally, verse 21 concludes, "And there shall no longer be a trader in the house of the LORD of hosts on that day." The Hebrew text literally says there

5. Thomas E. McComiskey, *The Minor Prophets: An Exegetical and Expository Commentary*, 3 vols. (Grand Rapids: Baker, 1998), 3:1244.

will no longer be "a Canaanite" in God's house. This term refers to the ungodly people God judged and destroyed when Israel entered the Promised Land. In Zechariah's day the term commonly referred to all ungodly people but especially to dishonest merchants. Among those who wear God's colors, in that day there will be none who are Canaanites at heart. The picture is that of total and complete holiness: in the sphere of public life, pictured by the bells on the horses in the streets; in religious life, shown by the pots in the Lord's house; and finally in private and domestic life, which will be fully hallowed unto God, down to the most menial pots and pans.[6]

Zechariah is saying that heaven will be completely holy. God's entire redemptive purpose and plan, reaching back into eternity and spinning out through the ages, has as its goal a perfectly holy people in a perfectly holy city. This is what the reign of Christ achieves: holiness issuing forth in praise to God and blessings for his people.

This is the greatest encouragement to all of God's people, but also our highest challenge. The flow of these last chapters of Zechariah tells us why this is such an encouragement. This final chapter is part of a great oracle that began in chapter 12. Remember how it began: with Jerusalem weak and besieged, surrounded by armies intent on its destruction. God could not have painted a bleaker beginning, nor one more appropriate to our own condition in this life—weak, crumbling, tempted, corrupt. But look how this story ends, all because of the cleansing blood of Christ and through his reign of grace! Every last square inch of that same city is now inscribed HOLY TO THE LORD!

One day God will win the same victory in our lives, however weak and defeated we may be at the start. "He who began a good work in you," writes Paul, "will bring it to completion at the day of Jesus Christ" (Phil. 1:6). In Romans 8:30, he states, "Those whom he predestined he also called, and those whom he called he also justified, and those whom he justified he also glorified." Martyn Lloyd-Jones writes eloquently on the assurance of our sanctification if we are in Christ:

> We are not chosen with the possibility of holiness, but to the realization of holiness. God has not chosen us before the foundation of the world in order

---

6. See David Baron, *The Visions and Prophecies of Zechariah* (Grand Rapids: Kregel, 1972), 531.

to create for us the possibility of holiness; He has chosen us to holiness. It is what He has purposed for us; not possibility, but realization. . . . God will make you holy because He has chosen you unto holiness.[7]

What better news could there be than a holy future in perfect glory! But this is also our highest calling and duty in this life. As Paul states in 1 Thessalonians 4:3, "For this is the will of God, your sanctification."

Sanctification is progressive in this life. It is a process, and one that is never complete before our deaths. Paul said about himself, "Not that I have already obtained this or am already perfect, but I press on to make it my own, because Christ Jesus has made me his own. . . . One thing I do: forgetting what lies behind and straining forward to what lies ahead, I press on toward the goal for the prize of the upward call of God in Christ Jesus" (Phil. 3:12–14).

The apostle John writes in his first epistle about the marvel of knowing that if we have trusted in Christ we are destined for holiness. "Beloved," he writes, "we are God's children now, and what we will be has not yet appeared; but we know that when he appears we will be like him, because we shall see him as he is" (1 John 3:2). John shows how that confidence produces a determination to work toward that very end in this life. He adds, "Everyone who thus hopes in him purifies himself as he is pure" (1 John 3:3). Being confident of perfect holiness in eternity is inseparable from a pursuit of holiness in life. Jonathan Edwards was right to say, "The beginnings of future things are in this world. The seed must be sown here; the foundation must be laid in this world. . . . If it is not begun here, it never will be begun. . . . The light must dawn in this world or the sun will never rise in the next."[8] Therefore, all who hope for heaven must seek a heavenly life here on earth.

ON EARTH AS IT IS IN HEAVEN

Let me conclude, then, with an observation and a question. The observation is the necessity of holiness. "Blessed are the pure in heart," Jesus said, "for they shall see God" (Matt. 5:8). The writer of Hebrews speaks similarly when he exhorts: "Strive for peace with everyone, and for the holiness without which

7. D. Martyn Lloyd-Jones, *An Exposition of Ephesians*, 8 vols. (Grand Rapids: Baker, 1978), 1:103–4.
8. Jonathan Edwards: *Altogether Lovely* (Morgan, PA: Soli Deo Gloria, 1999), 225–26.

no one will see the Lord" (12:14). These are plain and direct statements, saying that unless we are made holy we may not draw near to God. It is true that our holiness is God's work in and for us, through Christ's cleansing blood and by the indwelling Holy Spirit. But in contrast to justification, which we receive empty-handed by faith alone, sanctification is a work to which God calls us as his fellow-worker. This is what Paul meant when he wrote, "Work out your own salvation with fear and trembling, for it is God who works in you, both to will and to work for his good pleasure" (Phil. 2:12–13).

This prompts my question: "What do you think you will like about heaven if you do not love holiness now?" Heaven, we find, is altogether holy. The angels there are holy. The worship there is endlessly holy. The thrice holy God reigns there, giving holy light to his city. Therefore, if you find it hard to come to church, to sit through a service, to hear about God and give praise to him, what do you think heaven will be like? It will be no place for you, unless at least the seed of holiness is sown and growing in you now. The point is that holiness is necessary to the Christian, and without it we will never gaze upon the Lord in heaven. Robert Traille rightly concludes:

> O, sirs, do not deceive your own souls; holiness is of absolute necessity.... It is not absolutely necessary that you should be great or rich in the world, but it is absolutely necessary that you should be holy; it is not absolutely necessary that you should enjoy health, strength, friends, liberty, life, but it is absolutely necessary that you should be holy. A man may see the Lord without worldly prosperity, but he can never see the Lord except he be holy.[9]

How do we become holy? By the renewing of our minds and hearts through God's Word and in the power of the Holy Spirit. That is what this great closing chapter of Zechariah is for. The greatest possible incentive to holiness is what these final verses set before our eyes of faith: the glory of God in the holiness of his people by the saving reign of the Lord Jesus Christ. If this is the band to which you belong—if this is the Lord whom you love and serve—then you cannot but gaze upon this scene without longing for more of that holiness now that someday will be perfectly yours, without striving after holiness in the practical spheres of your life, and without crying

---

9. Robert Traille, cited in J. C. Ryle, *Holiness: Its Nature, Hindrances, Difficulties, and Roots* (Durham, England: Evangelical Press, 1979), 322–23.

out to God, "Lord, make me holy, to the glory of your name and for the sake of Jesus Christ!" If you look upon this your city, on the bells and the pots, on the most common and lowly of objects, all of them inscribed HOLY TO THE LORD, you can be sure that God will answer that prayer as you trust in him. And on the great day to come, you will be there. The God who grants you entry into this city by faith in Christ alone will fit you to live there with him forever. He will bring you to perfect holiness in manifest glory. To him be glory, both now and forever.

INDEX OF SCRIPTURE

Index of Subjects and Names

Lloyd-Jones, Martyn, 59, 160, 189, 279–80, 285, 324–25
Long, Burke, 17
"Lord of hosts," 21–22, 31, 36
Lord's Supper, the, 185
love, 14, 34, 39, 113, 130, 139, 158, 161, 175
  covenant, 160
  of God, 168, 301
Luke, gospel of
  genealogies of Jesus in, 113–14
Luther, Martin, 64, 69, 161, 263, 303

Maccabeus, Judas, 214
Macedonia, 202
Machen, J. Gresham, 114
Maclaren, Alexander, 145, 149
Martin, Hugh, 263–64
martyrs, 36
Mary (mother of Jesus), 114
Mary I (queen), 263
materialism, 204
Matthew, gospel of
  genealogies of Jesus in, 113–14
McComiskey, Thomas E., 10n, 53, 67, 184, 201n5, 209, 268, 303, 323
measuring line, 42, 43
Mede, Joseph, 196
Medo-Persian empire, 8, 10, 21, 113, 137, 198
  defeated by Greeks, 199, 213
  judgment of, 199
Megiddo, 270
Melanchthon, Philipp, 69
Melchizedek, 145
menorah, 87, 89
  See also lampstand
mercantile sins, 122
mercy, 30, 39, 160, 161, 236
  pursuit of, 166
  seat, 112
  See also under God
Mesopotamia, 137

Messiah, 6, 78–79, 82, 107, 108, 114, 114, 144, 147, 151, 179, 186, 220, 227–28, 267
  coming of, 196
  expectations for, 79
  longing for, 181
  as king, 145
  as priest, 145
  represented by lampstand, 97
  See also Christ; Jesus of Nazareth (Christ)
might, 91
millennium, 44, 305, 321. *See also* dispensationalism; eschatology; premillennialism
Miller, C. John (Jack), 102
missionary, 187
  work, 58
Moore, Thomas V., 12, 48, 81, 89, 138, 146–47, 186–87, 204, 294, 296, 305, 317
morality, 123–24, 144
  renewal of, 169
Moriah, 133
Moses, 150, 272
Mount of Olives, 133, 304, 308
Mount Zion, 8, 9, 21, 29, 32, 40, 58, 63, 91
mountain(s)
  of brass, 140
  to bronze, 132–33
Murray, John, 266
mutseqet, 88
myrtle trees, 18

Napoleon, 19
Nathan, 271
nations, 180, 185–88, 190, 191, 196, 209, 306
  destruction of, 260
  gathered against Israel, 307
  God's judgment on, 200, 315
Nazareth, 94